HELL FROM THE HEAVENS

HELL FROM THE HEAVENS

THE EPIC STORY OF THE USS *LAFFEY* AND
WORLD WAR II'S GREATEST KAMIKAZE ATTACK

JOHN F. WUKOVITS

DA CAPO PRESS
A Member of the Perseus Books Group

Designed by Trish Wilkinson
Set in 11 point Adobe Garamond Pro

Library of Congress Cataloging-in-Publication Data

Wukovits, John F., 1944–
    Hell from the heavens : the epic story of the USS Laffey and World War II's greatest kamikaze attack / John F. Wukovits.
        pages   cm
Includes bibliographical references and index.
    ISBN 978-0-306-82324-4 (hardcover) — ISBN 978-0-306-82325-1 (e-book) 1. Laffey (Ship) 2. World War, 1939–1945—Naval operations, American. 3. World War, 1939–1945—Campaigns—Pacific Area. 4. World War, 1939–1945—Aerial operations, Japanese. 5. Japan. Kaigun. Kamikaze Tokubetsu Kogekitai. 6. Kamikaze pilots—Japan. I. Title.

D774.L3W85 2015
940.54'252294—dc23

2014042127

First Da Capo Press edition 2015

Published by Da Capo Press
A Member of the Perseus Books Group
www.dacapopress.com

Da Capo Press books are available at special discounts for bulk purchases in the U.S. by corporations, institutions, and other organizations. For more information, please contact the Special Markets Department at the Perseus Books Group, 2300 Chestnut Street, Suite 200, Philadelphia, PA 19103, or call (800) 810-4145, ext. 5000, or e-mail special.markets@perseusbooks.com.

10 9 8 7 6 5 4 3 2 1

To my granddaughter,
Megan Grace Dickerman,
whose cheerful spirit lights up any room she enters.

CONTENTS

Contents

MAPS

PREFACE

After writing *For Crew and Country: The Inspirational True Story of Bravery and Sacrifice Aboard the USS Samuel B. Roberts*, my editor asked if there were another World War II ship that piqued my interest. He felt it might be an apt companion to the story of the destroyer escort. Of a handful of options, one shone above the rest: the exploits of the USS *Laffey* (DD-724). I was convinced that readers would be moved by the crew's stirring April 16, 1945, performance against twenty-two kamikazes off Okinawa.

I soon found that the destroyer had amassed quite a record before that penultimate act. After experiencing her initial combat during the Normandy invasion, where *Laffey* supported the ground forces from the June 6, 1944, landings through the end of the month, she participated in three Philippine assaults and the landings at Iwo Jima, and screened for a carrier task group as it charged north to attack the Japanese Home Islands. My interest heightened when I learned that the ship still exists as a floating museum in South Carolina, meaning that I could walk the decks and gain a feeling for the crew stationed inside the five-inch mounts and on deck among the 40mm and 20mm antiaircraft guns.

I was delighted to learn that the veterans of the destroyer formed an active survivor's group. The USS *Laffey* (DD-724) Association hosts reunions bringing together not only the veterans from World War II but also the men who served aboard the ship during the Korean conflict and after. The Association's website holds a wealth of information and provided me with my initial material about the destroyer, and the current president, Sonny Walker, compiled a list of the World War II survivors that I might contact.

Interviews and other research led to the present volume. In arriving at this point, many people helped along the way. Atop that list are the men who served aboard *Laffey* during World War II, who kindly offered their time for interviews, as well as their letters, photographs, and other memorabilia. Ari Phoutrides, who had already posted riveting material on the Association's website, was available for in-depth interviews or for those times when I needed a quick answer to a question. He also took me on a tour of his destroyer when I visited the ship on the sixty-ninth anniversary of the April 1945 encounter. In addition to our many interviews, Robert Johnson kindly offered the large collection of letters he wrote during the war and shared photographs with me during an early 2014 visit to his Richmond, Virginia, home. Daniel Zack of Massachusetts offered meticulous insight into the ship's operations during many interviews, and the family of the late Wilbert Gauding gave me access to his World War II diary. Joel Youngquist provided a compelling account of his time on the aft guns during the April 1945 action, and he, Lloyd Hull, and Jay Bahme opened up the world of an officer aboard a wartime destroyer. Robert Dockery, Dr. Andrew Martinis, Joseph Dixon, Fred Gemmell, and Lee Hunt helped me better understand the ship's operations from the enlisted viewpoint. Marguerite Fern, whose love for her late husband and crew member, Tom, shines to this day, opened her impressive collection of articles, photographs, and wartime letters when I visited her Massachusetts home in 2013.

A special thanks goes to my gifted agent, Jim Hornfischer. I could not have asked for a more professional person to help steer me in the right direction, and his attributes—as an agent, a fellow World War II author, and friend—have been one of the true blessings of my writing career.

A team of editors at Da Capo Press, led by Bob Pigeon offered comments that improved the manuscript.

As always, I cannot forget the advice and friendship of two men. The words of Dr. Bernard Norling, my history advisor at the University of Notre Dame and my consultant through the years, and Tom Buell, my writing mentor and the author of acclaimed biographies, influence me each day, even though, sadly, both are no longer with us. Their memories prod me to produce the best possible manuscript I can deliver.

I have been fortunate to enjoy the amazing support of family. My three daughters, Amy, Julie, and Karen, and my older brother, Tom, a naval aviator and Vietnam War veteran, freely exhibit their pride with my work and with me. The grandfather in me loves that my four grandchildren, Matthew, Megan, Emma, and Kaitlyn, think it is cool that I write books, and the past two decades would not have been as fulfilling without the companionship of

Terri Faitel, an extraordinary mathematics teacher/coordinator who meticulously scours my manuscripts with the same fervor with which she attacks the Pythagorean theorem.

Finally, three family members who are no longer with me provide impetus to exert my utmost. My parents, Tom and Grace Wukovits, gave unquestioned love throughout their lives and were proud that I reached my dream of writing history books. My younger brother, Fred, would also have shown his pride, most likely through a humorous remark or a wry smile.

Two final notes. I have used two sources in determining the ranks and ratings of the crew—the list of survivors included in the Appendix to F. Julian Becton's *The Ship That Would Not Die*, and the *Laffey* muster rolls for March 31, 1945. In the interest of uniformity, I used those designations throughout the book, even if earlier in the war a crew may have held a different rank or rating.

Also, the two poems I have referenced throughout, "An Ode to the USS *Laffey* (DD-724)" by Gunner's Mate 3/c Owen G. Radder and "Invicta," by Lieutenant (jg) Matthew C. Darnell Jr., can be found respectively at http://www.laffey.org/glenrodetolaffey.htm and at *Laffey News*, April–June 1990.

John F. Wukovits
Trenton, Michigan
June 30, 2014

CHRONOLOGY

FEBRUARY 8, 1944
The USS *Laffey* (DD-724) is commissioned in Boston.

MARCH 2–31, 1944
Shakedown cruise in Bermuda.

JUNE 6, 1944
Laffey participates in the Normandy invasion.

JUNE 25, 1944
Laffey duels with Battery Hamburg at Cherbourg.

AUGUST 26, 1944
Laffey begins her voyage to the Pacific.

SEPTEMBER 18, 1944
Laffey enters Pearl Harbor.

OCTOBER 23, 1944
Laffey proceeds to Eniwetok, Marshall Islands.

OCTOBER 25, 1944
At Leyte Gulf in the Philippines, Japan unleashes her first organized kamikaze assault of the war.

NOVEMBER 11–19, 1944
Laffey participates in four carrier air strikes against the Japanese in the Philippines.

DECEMBER 6–7, 1944

Laffey participates in the Ormoc landings in the Philippines.

DECEMBER 12–16, 1944

Laffey participates in the Mindoro landings in the Philippines.

JANUARY 6–21, 1945

Laffey participates in the Lingayen Gulf landings in the Philippines.

FEBRUARY 16–17, 1945

Laffey participates in air strikes against the Japanese Home Islands.

FEBRUARY 18–23, 1945

Laffey participates in the Iwo Jima landings.

FEBRUARY 24–26, 1945

Laffey participates in a second round of air strikes against the Japanese Home Islands.

MARCH 26–29, 1945

Laffey participates in the seizure of Kerama Retto southwest of Okinawa.

APRIL 1–2, 1945

Laffey participates in the landings on Okinawa.

APRIL 3–12, 1945

Laffey operates off the coast of Okinawa.

APRIL 13, 1945

Laffey receives orders posting her to Picket Station No. 1.

APRIL 14–15, 1945

Laffey operates at Picket Station No. 1.

APRIL 16, 1945

Twenty-two kamikaze aircraft attack *Laffey* at Picket Station No. 1.

APRIL 17–21, 1945

Repair crews work on *Laffey* at Hagushi.

APRIL 27, 1945

Laffey anchors in Saipan.

MAY 12, 1945

Laffey enters Pearl Harbor.

MAY 24, 1945

Laffey moors in Seattle.

MAY 25–30, 1945

The Navy opens *Laffey* to public inspection in Seattle.

JUNE 26, 1945

Becton steps down as commander of *Laffey.*

JULY 1946

Laffey participates in the Bikini Atoll nuclear weapons tests.

1981

Patriots Point Naval and Maritime Museum in Charleston, South Carolina, accepts *Laffey* from the Navy as a floating museum.

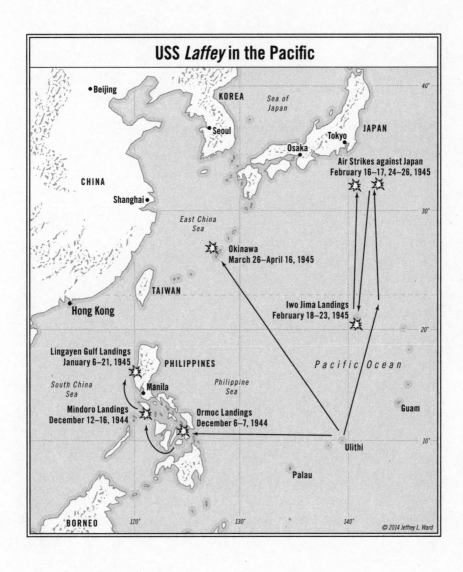

PROLOGUE

In his most terrifying nightmare Seaman 1/c Jack H. Ondracek could never have imagined the sight that confronted him that April 16, 1945, morning. As he leapt into the straps of the 20mm antiaircraft gun aboard the destroyer, USS *Laffey* (DD-724), a Japanese aircraft raced directly toward him.

Ondracek took this attack personally, for the human being piloting the aircraft did so with the lethal intent of killing Ondracek and mortally damaging his ship. It hearkened to those days that pitted single warrior against single warrior, the path hostilities had taken for centuries past. But one-on-one encounters were for Caesar's swordsmen or medieval knights, not for a sailor on a World War II destroyer, where combat usually pitted five-inch guns and torpedoes against enemy plating.

As the lone aircraft bore down on him, Ondracek's gun beat a steady rhythm that matched the pounding of his heart. His 20mm gun was effective up to one thousand yards. He brushed aside the sobering thought that although his opponent had closed to within the range of his gun, he now had fewer than fifteen seconds to destroy the hurtling plane before it smashed into the ship. His best defense—his only defense—was to kill the pilot before the pilot killed him. "You either kill them or get killed," said Gunner's Mate 2/c Lawrence H. Delewski. "You were playing for keeps and it was a very deadly game."[1]

As the aircraft eluded Ondracek's bullets and narrowed the gap, the seaman knew it would be only moments before either he or the kamikaze pilot, or both, perished in a deafening explosion.

Nothing in his tour of duty had prepared Ondracek for this moment. He experienced his first taste of combat off the Normandy coast in the June 6, 1944, D-Day invasion, when the *Laffey*'s five-inch guns lambasted German gun emplacements as Allied troops rushed ashore. He had participated in four prior assaults of enemy positions in the Pacific—at Ormoc, Mindoro, and Lingayen Gulf in the Philippines, and at Iwo Jima—where their guns again blasted land targets while Marines and infantry battled across the terrain. He had seen kamikazes purposely crash into other destroyers and cruisers and had witnessed firsthand the bloody results of those crazed tactics, but until now he had avoided being the target of such suicidal actions.

His good fortune appeared over. As Ondracek glanced skyward, it seemed that the entire Japanese air force had assembled directly above. At one point the *Laffey*'s radar plotted fifty enemy aircraft converging on the ship, their dots all but obliterating the radar screen.

On that April 1945 day off the Pacific island of Okinawa, Ondracek and the rest of the crew contended with one of the war's most terrifying weapons. First appearing in late 1944, kamikazes caused American skippers and sailors untold heartache and misery. "Few missiles or weapons have ever spread such flaming terror, such scorching burns, such searing death, as did the kamikaze in his self-destroying onslaughts on the radar picket ships [at Okinawa]," wrote the eminent naval historian, Samuel Eliot Morison. "And naval history has few parallels to the sustained courage, resourcefulness and fighting spirit that the crews of these vessels displayed day after day after day in the battle for Okinawa."[2]

Prominent among those picket ships was the crew of the USS *Laffey*.

PART I
THE NORMANDY TRAINING GROUND

CHAPTER 1

THE FORMATION OF A CREW

Born in Bath Maine
With an already famous name
The crew got her in shape
For her destiny with fate.
    —"An Ode to the USS *Laffey* (DD-724),"
    Gunner's Mate Owen Radder

"An Officer Is Supposed to Worry about His Men First"

The men who battled so gallantly in April 1945 took their cue from their skipper, Commander F. Julian Becton. A man of considerable combat experience, Becton was born in Des Arc, Arkansas, on May 15, 1908. He became interested in the Navy in 1925 while in high school, when an aunt mailed photographs of the Naval Academy to the family. Becton, who had already been attracted by billboards touting "Join the Navy and see the world," marked Annapolis as his destination.

After graduating in 1931, Becton quickly rose through the ranks. He served aboard two battleships and two destroyers, absorbing valuable knowledge in the ships' engineering departments. In 1935 he journeyed to China, where he served as engineering officer aboard first a gunboat and then a destroyer.

Along the way he started what became a lifelong habit of writing down words of famous individuals he found meaningful. One of his favorites came from an 1897 speech Civil War General John M. Schofield delivered at West Point, in which he reminded the cadets how important it was to treat the men under their command with respect, for "the differences among men are far less than they generally seem." General Schofield added, "the road to military honor will be guarded all the way by the hearts of those who may be your subordinates. You cannot travel that road unless you command those hearts."[1]

A two-year stint at the Naval Academy to teach marine engineering interrupted his Pacific duty. In 1940 Becton returned to those waters as engineering officer on the USS *Gleaves* (DD-423), followed by a posting to the destroyer USS *Aaron Ward* (DD-483) as executive officer.

Following the outbreak of war, the *Aaron Ward* steamed to the South Pacific as part of the United States's August 1942 effort to seize the Solomon Islands northeast of Australia. A series of dramatic naval clashes unfolded in the waters about Guadalcanal, including the November 13 nighttime encounter known as the Naval Battle of Guadalcanal. In that action the *Aaron Ward* joined five cruisers and six destroyers under the command of Admiral Daniel J. Callaghan to prevent a stronger Japanese force from bombarding American forces on Guadalcanal.

A widespread melée erupted. Japanese and American vessels darted through the darkened waters, rapidly firing at enemy targets while just as quickly trying to evade incoming shells. "It was disorganized. It was individual [action], with every ship for herself,"[2] recalled Becton later.

Though the American forces sustained heavy damage—nine shells struck Becton's *Aaron Ward*, killing fifteen and wounding fifty-seven—they turned back the Japanese and safeguarded for the moment the troops and aircraft ashore. Becton did not fail to notice that an aggressive commander like Callaghan, even though he lost his life in the encounter, could defy the odds and snatch victory from a more potent foe.

Becton learned another lesson that night. One mile astern from the *Aaron Ward* the destroyer USS *Laffey* (DD-459) went down after a stout fight in which the gun crews maintained fire until their shipmates could abandon ship. Becton never forgot the heroism exhibited by the *Laffey* and made a silent promise that, if he ever commanded a ship, he would try to perform as valiantly.

"Later on in World War II," wrote Becton, "when it came time for me to take *Laffey*'s successor into battle, I could never forget the example she set for all of us in those brief final minutes of her life. Thus the story of the first *Laffey*'s last fight is an inseparable part of the tale I have to tell."[3]

With Becton aboard, the damaged *Aaron Ward* was towed to safety, repaired at Pearl Harbor, and in late March 1943 returned to the South Pacific with a new commander—Becton. Three weeks later, on April 7, 1943, while the *Aaron Ward* escorted an LST (Landing Ship, Tank) near Savo Island in the Solomons, two waves of Japanese aircraft attacked the destroyer. One delay action bomb punctured an eighteen-inch hole in the after engine room before exploding inside, which, according to Becton's action report, "raised the deck above the after engine room about ten inches and riddled it with shrapnel holes." Four near misses hit within five yards of the damaged destroyer, "rocking it violently and seeming to practically lift it out of the water."[4] The attack left twenty men dead and seven others wounded.

The crew exerted every effort to save the *Aaron Ward.* Becton's communications officer, Lieutenant (jg) David W. Riesmeyer, recalled that "we worked below, stuffing mattresses, pillows, towels and anything we could get into the holes and shored them up with timbers, but it was a hopeless task."[5] The ship had absorbed too much damage to remain afloat.

Becton safely extricated the survivors, but the loss of his shipmates and of his first ship haunted him. "Long after it happened I continued to feel I could have done more to prevent it," he wrote. He added that "her loss depressed me and my memories of it were painful."[6]

In his action report Becton cited his "gallant crew and officers" as being "splendid in their conduct during the action and in their later efforts to save the ship." He remarked that the crew was "particularly desirous of staying together and of getting back on a fighting ship to soon avenge the deaths of their heroic shipmates."[7] Becton, who shared the same aggressive spirit as his crew, longed for a second shot as skipper of a ship, where he could both prove his worth as a commander and inflict retribution on the Japanese for what they had done to his first crew.

Though Becton had to wait six months before receiving another command, he was far from deskbound. His first posting, as operations officer on the staff of the commander of Destroyer Squadron Twenty-One, placed him in the middle of three surface actions in the Solomons—the July 6, 1943, Battle of Kula Gulf, the July 13 action off Kolombangara, and the August 17–18 fighting off Vella Lavella.

For those actions, Becton received the Silver Star. According to the citation, Becton helped coordinate "the attacks of the vanguard destroyers of a cruiser-destroyer force in which several enemy ships were sunk and many damaged." He then orchestrated a successful destroyer charge against attacking Japanese ships, which "caused the destruction of two destroyers, severe damage to a third and the annihilation of a number of landing barges."[8]

As a participant in some of the fiercest destroyer actions in the South Pacific, and earlier as skipper of a destroyer, Becton gained indispensable experience in ship navigation and learned how to manage a crew. "An officer is supposed to worry about his men first, then think about himself,"[9] Becton said. The harsh experiences of 1942–1943 fashioned Becton into the officer he became in 1944.

In November orders returned Becton to the United States. When he arrived at the Bureau of Naval Personnel in Washington, DC, superiors greeted him with the news that he would be the skipper for a vessel still under construction at Bath, Maine—the USS *Laffey* (DD-724). Honored at commanding the namesake of the ship he saw battle so admirably in 1942, and intent on living up to the honor bestowed by the Silver Star, Becton vowed to maintain that proud heritage and to ensure the second *Laffey* did not suffer the same fate as her predecessor or the *Aaron Ward*.

"It was going to take some doing to live up to her record," he wrote. "I wanted her to match *Laffey*'s record of accomplishment in battle. But I also wanted her to do that with as few or fewer casualties as we had had when *Aaron Ward* was lost. I vowed that I would do everything in my power to make this possible. Odds or no odds, we were going to both win *and* survive."[10]

Becton's interlude in the United States was not all business. He spent his off-duty hours in the company of an attractive singer/actress from his Arkansas hometown. During high school Imogen Carpenter had lived a few blocks from Becton's family home. During a visit to New York City he saw a poster announcing her appearance at the Cotillion Room at the Hotel Pierre. He contacted her and the two began dating. Carpenter often took him to watch her rehearse her small role in a new Broadway show, *High Kickers*, starring Sophie Tucker and George Jessel.

Becton left the Broadway rehearsals with profound respect for the dedication and hard work the director, actors, and actresses applied to perfecting their craft. Like those stage personnel, he intended to seek perfection in his crew. "In both cases," wrote Becton, "the drills had to be endlessly practiced until every participant could respond perfectly when the curtain went up. Theater rehearsals and Navy exercises both required discipline, dedication, and concentration."[11] He planned to do everything he could to prepare his men for whatever lay ahead.

Becton continued his relationship throughout the war with Carpenter, whose cheery letters bolstered his morale and whose photograph, clipped from movie magazines, adorned at least one bulkhead posted by crew, who were simultaneously jealous and proud of their handsome skipper.

"She Presented a Beautiful Picture"

Becton traveled to Bath, Maine, confident that he had a capable ship waiting for him. Revered among shipbuilding firms since the days of wooden vessels, and enjoying close ties with the Navy, for whom they had constructed ships since 1890, the Bath Iron Works operated with the motto, "Bath Built Is Best Built."[12] Using mass production techniques and standardized parts that enabled crews to work simultaneously on multiple hulls, the Bath Iron Works laboring force—which had soared to 12,042 in December 1943 from its prewar numbers of 1,850—handed the Navy a new destroyer every seventeen days. Their World War II output of eighty-three destroyers alone almost equaled the destroyer productivity of all Japanese shipyards.

Rather than toiling on a single vessel, teams of workers, each assigned a different standard task, swarmed waiting hulls, completed their work, and rushed to the next hull to accomplish the same task. Among the ships they constructed were twenty of the new Allen M. Sumner Class destroyers, including Becton's ship. The keel for the USS *Laffey* was laid on June 28, 1943, at which time shipyard workers descended to transform the unfinished chunk of metal into a sleek warship within a year. Named after a Civil War recipient of the Medal of Honor, Seaman Bartlett Laffey, who battled hand-to-hand with Confederate opponents on March 5, 1864, *Laffey* joined the Navy as part of the initial five Sumner Class destroyers delivered by Bath workers between December 30, 1943 and March 14, 1944. For much of the conflict *Laffey* served with the four other original destroyers—the USS *Barton* (DD-722), USS *Walke* (DD-723), USS *O'Brien* (DD-725), and USS *Meredith* (DD-726)—as Destroyer Division 119, a unit that gained the reputation for being "where the action is."[13]

As Becton meandered through a maze of material and ship sections that waited on the yard for assembly that January day, he heard the common shipyard sounds of steel against steel indicating that workers were at their tasks. Anxious for a look at his new ship, Becton spotted the *Laffey*, then still an unfinished hull. Though resting in the water, the *Laffey* was connected to land by hundreds of cables, hoses, and lines, reminding the officer of umbilical cords from a mother pumping life into a yet unborn child.

Like those shipyard workers who meticulously fashioned a seaworthy vessel from raw materials, Becton, too, would have to create a top-caliber crew from the raw seamen then pouring out of the Navy's training camps. The task would be challenging, but as long as he enjoyed a core of veteran officers and chiefs, he could mold the young sailors into an efficient fighting force.

The early nucleus of the crew offered a solution. A small group of *Laffey* officers and enlisted had gathered at Maine to study the new ship as the shipyard workers pieced her together. In doing so they could learn the intricacies of the destroyer and in turn train the rest of the crew that would join them later in Boston. The skilled veterans, including Chief Gunner's Mate Norman Fitzgerald, Gunner's Mate Warren Walker, Fire Controlman Ralph Peterson, and Chief Electrician's Mate Albert Csiszar, eased Becton's concerns. Combined with a handful of other veteran officers and enlisted then gathering in Boston, they would provide the foundation upon which he could build an effective crew.

"I joined the *Laffey* on December 16, 1943, while the ship was still in the yard at Bath, Maine," said Albert Csiszar. The veteran had already seen action in the Solomon Islands, where he survived the June 1943 sinking off Rendova Island of the transport, USS *McCawley* (APA-4), Rear Admiral Richmond Kelly Turner's flagship. "I was the CEM (Chief Electrician's Mate), with a bunch of new, young electricians I had to train. I had about 20 men, and the ship had 400 to 500 electric motors. I was so busy that I slept on the workshop bench for at least three months. I couldn't get to my bunk. It was a bunch of new fellows and a new ship."[14]

The seagoing saga of the USS *Laffey* commenced in early February. Becton and the nucleus crew, joined by shipyard inspectors from different departments, boarded the ship to take her from Maine to Boston. They cast off at dawn in a mild snowstorm, and for the first time *Laffey* was underway under her own power.

Once clearing the mouth of the river and reaching the open sea, Becton ordered full power and set course toward Boston. The *Laffey* carried a small amount of ammunition and some depth charges for defense in the unlikely event a German U-boat crossed their path, but an uneventful outing brought the *Laffey* to the Boston Navy Yard, where the rest of the ship's officers and enlisted stood in formation on Pier 1. Becton quickly surveyed the waiting collection and, as he expected, concluded that it comprised mainly young, inexperienced sailors.

One of the men standing at attention on Pier 1 was seventeen-year-old Quartermaster 2/c Aristides S. "Ari" Phoutrides from Portland, Oregon. A freshman at the Massachusetts Institute of Technology when he enlisted in May 1943, Phoutrides longed to join the Marines but needed his parents' permission. "I wanted to do something for the war effort. I was underage and wanted to go into the Marines, but my mother remembered what had happened to the Marines at Guadalcanal [Marines waged a bloody campaign with the Japanese in late 1942] and said no way, so I went into the Navy."[15]

One look at the new ship convinced Phoutrides that his mother had been correct. "She presented a beautiful picture as she lay alongside Pier #1. Her main decks were covered with snow, and icicles hung from the 5" guns and the yardarms. This was a striking contrast to her deep blue paint job. As I noted her then, lifeless so to speak, and with no activity on board, it was difficult to conceive that she would someday be hurtling tons of destruction toward the enemy. The thought that she would someday be fighting for her very existence never crossed my mind."[16] Phoutrides liked that Becton already had war experience. That would come in handy, he believed, should they land in a tight spot.

The sailors boarded ship, changed into clean blues, and began readying the *Laffey* for the commissioning ceremony, at which time the Navy would officially take possession of the destroyer from Bath Iron Works. They chipped ice from the railings and made certain that everything shined; their first effort as a crew impressed Becton that though the men might be raw recruits, they worked well together. The men "tried to look like sailors," wrote Lieutenant (jg) Jerome B. Sheets, "even though about 80 per cent were reserves, civilians at heart, and for the vast majority this was their first ship."[17]

"This Is the Day I Start Out to Be a Real Sailor"

"The U.S.S. *Laffey* was placed in commission on 8 February 1944 at the Boston Navy Yard, Charleston, Massachusetts, with Commander F. J. Becton U.S. Navy assuming command."[18] So stated the initial entry of the War Diary that would recount *Laffey*'s actions for the remainder of the war.

A typically wintry Massachusetts afternoon greeted Navy officials and guests for the commissioning ceremony. With the temperature hovering around fifteen degrees, the crew lined up at divisional formation on the pier while guests, including Imogen Carpenter and families who could make the journey to the shipyard, occupied seats on stands facing the new destroyer.

As Commander Becton and the Captain of the Yard approached the gangway, the crew snapped to attention and the officers were piped over the side. After a reading of the orders, sailors hoisted the commissioning pennant to the gaff, and Becton assumed command of the *Laffey*. Becton spoke of the ship's Civil War namesake and of the valiant fight her courageous predecessor, the USS *Laffey* (DD-459), had waged in the Solomons. He promised the families assembled before him that under his command, this new *Laffey* would honor the tradition that had been begun by Bartlett Laffey in 1864 and was continued by the first destroyer in 1942. The ceremony ended with a Navy band playing the National Anthem.

At that moment the wartime experiences aboard the USS *Laffey* commenced. "This is the day I start out to be a real sailor," Seaman 1/c Thomas B. Fern of Massachusetts wrote his mother after the ceremony. "The ship was commissioned today."[19] Fern, who had committed to memory the story of two Fern relatives who had been awarded medals, Corporal Patrick H. Fern during the Civil War and Corporal Henry M. Fern during World War I, often asked himself if he had what it took to live up to their standards. That thought drove him to do well in training and to be attentive on watches, for the last thing Fern wanted to do was bring dishonor to his family. He hoped this would be the start of an honorable career at sea that matched his ancestors' exploits on land.

Another member of the crew was not as much nervous as he was pensive about the future. "To the mind of each mother and father and every member of the crew must have flashed the thought, 'What does fate have in store for this ship—where will the tides of war take her?'" wrote twenty-three-year-old Lieutenant Sheets at the time. He added that "this mass of steel, machinery and guns was to be their home and country, their only protection against the forces of nature and war." Sheets, a 1943 graduate of the University of Michigan and a member of the first NROTC class produced by that institution, gazed at his new home for the indeterminate future, proud to be part of such a worthy warship. "She would disintegrate with age, she would be beaten and broken by the forces of God and man. She would take America's young manhood away from all that they held dear," wrote Sheets, but he was certain that the new captain and crew would meet whatever emergencies of war they faced. "Time will dictate the future of this man-made woman of the seas."[20]

Fern and the other crew "went aboard to a madhouse. Everybody had seabags and hammocks all over—guys trying to get their gear into deck (foot) lockers. I had to get rid of a lot of extra junk to make room for my stuff & a

little extra room in my locker. I finally got settled about 2030 (8:30 p.m.)."
The young sailor did nothing to calm his mother's nerves by mentioning, "I
bunk after the fantail just under the stern 5" guns with explosives all around
us," but added of the ship that "the boys like it here!!!" After settling in, he
continued, "we'll be here about two more weeks before we go out on a short
shake down. We're going to have to work to morrow & the next few days
loading ammo & supplys."[21]

At this moment future events meant little to Fern and his shipmates.
They had just boarded a new ship, and like most young people, their visions
stretched no farther than the coming few days. "Very simply then," recalled
Quartermaster 2/c Phoutrides, "her life began. Little did we know that in the
next 18 months she was to attain one of the most outstanding battle records
of WWII."[22]

The next morning Becton assembled his seventeen officers (he would
eventually command twenty-five) in the wardroom, where he outlined the
principles of command he expected every officer to follow. He emphasized
that as they now supervised an inexperienced crew, their first order of business was to show the men their fire stations and where the fireplugs, hoses,
and fire-fighting equipment were stored in case a fire erupted. Becton explained that the only way the men could be prepared for this and any other
emergency, including combat, was with constant training and with each officer exhibiting his own thorough preparation and skill at his tasks. If his
seventeen officers followed these few steps, Becton added, confidence among
the crew in their officers and their ship would develop, and the *Laffey* would
be better equipped to engage the enemy. Becton insisted that his officers
refrain from using foul language, which in his opinion indicated a serious
loss of self-control. He explained that the men encountered enough salty talk
elsewhere throughout the day, and that few would be impressed by hearing
their officer swear.

Becton ended by emphasizing that precision, cohesiveness, and performance of duty had more impact on a ship's fate than luck. He had earlier
heard a man remark that he had a feeling the ship would be a lucky one, a
topic of concern for sailors plagued with aquatic superstitions. Becton disagreed. "I've always been one who believed that what a crew *could* do, and
what they *did* do, was what made a ship lucky."[23] He told his officers he
would do everything in his power to make certain the crew would perform
to the best of their capabilities.

With this meeting Becton established the foundation of his command and the tone he wanted to permeate the ship. He believed it was the initial step in transforming those young men into a crew that could operate efficiently in the heat of combat.

Over the next few weeks Becton progressively increased the tempo of training. He started with simple exercises, such as manning stations as if the ship was getting underway and taking the ship for brief excursions out of the harbor. As the men gained confidence, he intensified the difficulty and duration of his drills, dropping depth charges one day and executing sharp turns on another.

When an officer asked him about the graduated pace, Becton compared their tasks to that of a parent. "Getting a brand-new ship and a brand-new crew on a completely operational footing is much like raising a child. You do it by degrees."[24]

"One of Those Greyhounds of the Fleet"

The crew quickly settled into their new surroundings. During World War I, destroyers had often served primarily for torpedo attacks, but the newest destroyers now joined the fleet as multitasked warships designed to provide a variety of services. As such, the *Laffey* could utilize her speed and guns not only to protect a battle line, but also to engage enemy warships, drop depth charges as part of the antisubmarine warfare, and man antiaircraft guns to protect themselves and other ships from air attacks. As Lieutenant Jerome Sheets wrote, she was "one of those greyhounds of the fleet, a fighting ship, bristling with 5-inch, 40-mm, and 20-mm guns, torpedoes, and depth charges, a ship built for a multitude of jobs."[25]

The Navy had ordered the construction of sixty-nine Sumner Class destroyers on August 7, 1942, the same day American Marines began their assault on the Solomon Islands in the South Pacific. They emphasized the need for a larger destroyer that could better execute the variety of tasks demanded by the heightened naval combat in Pacific waters, where the ships would be subjected to the triple threat of attack from surface ships, from submarines, and from air attacks. Becton and the crew liked the thought of serving aboard a ship as well equipped as the *Laffey*, which offered enhanced design features, including twin-gun turrets and dual rudders for improved maneuverability.

Sheets's observation that "in her 376 feet were packed all the instruments of war"[26] was not a wild exaggeration. Spouting a beam eighteen inches wider than that of her predecessor, the Fletcher Class destroyers, *Laffey* enjoyed increased stability while losing only one knot in speed from the Fletcher Class ships. The extra stability allowed designers to pack her superstructure with extra guns.

Besides a main battery of six five-inch, thirty-eight caliber guns, *Laffey* could bring to a fight twelve 40mm antiaircraft guns spread along her length, eleven smaller tub-mounted 20mm antiaircraft guns, ten torpedo tubes in two five-tube mounts, Y-gun depth-charge throwers port and starboard, and two long depth-charge racks near the fantail. The guns could fire independently, or be synchronized and controlled to fire as a unit by the ship's gunnery officer.

The six five-inch guns rested in three twin mounts, with two mounts located forward and the third placed fifty feet from the stern. All six stood atop rotating pedestals that enabled them to fire in an arc from port to starboard, and each tossed a seventy-five-pound projectile nine miles out and six miles up. The guns could fire at enemy warships on the surface, enemy positions on shore, or aircraft approaching from above.

The *Laffey*'s twelve 40mm antiaircraft guns, two more than featured on the Fletcher Class destroyers, could make enemy aircraft pay dearly for their assaults. Gaining acclaim in navies throughout the world for their potency and developed in Sweden by the Bofors Company after World War I, the guns rested along *Laffey*'s length in open, twin-gun tub mounts and in one quadruple-gun mount farther aft. Gun crews loved the capabilities of the automatic guns, which could rapidly propel high-explosive antiaircraft shells at attacking planes or armor-piercing rounds against enemy warships. Unlike the larger five-inch guns, which fired 15 rounds per minute, the 40mm guns could throw 160 rounds in sixty seconds at airplanes or ships.

The smaller Swiss-built Oerlikon tub-mounted 20mm guns sprinkled about the deck were rarely used for anything but antiaircraft fire. Those eleven guns could each pump 480 rounds per minute at ranges up to one thousand yards.

Though the five-inch gun mounts were enclosed in turret-like steel boxes, the thin armor for both the 40mm and the 20mm guns, no more than a quarter-inch thick, would do little to protect those gun crews from enemy shrapnel, let alone from direct hits. The curved steel sheeting, which rose only waist high, existed more to prevent sailors from falling off the platforms and to give minimal shelter from rougher seas. Heavier defensive plating took second place to enhanced offensive capabilities.

Ten torpedo tubes stood in two five-tube mounts, one amidships and one forward. Each could launch at an enemy warship a twenty-foot torpedo, twenty-one inches in diameter and weighing 1.5 tons. Seventy depth charges, more than any other antisubmarine vessel then in use, handed Becton a powerful tool with which to engage enemy submarines. Two Y-gun depth-charge throwers stood port and starboard on the main deck forward of the aft five-inch mount, each capable of tossing three-hundred-pound charges from either side in a semicircle 270 yards forward of the ship. Two long depth charge racks placed on either side of the stern 20mm gun tub dropped six-hundred-pound charges over the stern.

The *Laffey* offered features belowdecks as well. Twin rudders enhanced *Laffey*'s maneuverability and reduced her turning radius, which handed her an edge in evading approaching enemy aircraft or eluding enemy shells. Berthing spaces placed half the officers and enlisted forward and half aft, so that an explosion in any one location would not kill a majority of the experienced men. An enclosed ship-length interior passageway, newly introduced on the Sumner Class destroyers, protected the crew from heavy seas.

Like earlier destroyers, the *Laffey* was powered by two sets of boilers and two engines, arranged in pairs. A fireroom with two boilers stood forward of the forward engine room, while the aft fireroom with two boilers preceded the aft engine room. These units could either work in tandem or be independently operated as a split plant. This preserved for Becton the ability to maneuver even if he lost one of his boiler-engine room units. "That could mean the difference between life or death," wrote Becton. "A destroyer dead in the water is a sitting duck for enemy bombs, shells, or torpedoes, and at the mercy of heavy seas." He added, "a ship that could move was a ship that could survive and fight on,"[27] a factor which was important to Becton.

The ship had a few flaws. Due to the extra 250 tons of weight added to the same-length hull as the Fletcher Class destroyers, the *Laffey* was one knot slower and less fuel efficient. In rougher seas the ship sometimes tended to roll heavily because of her narrower beam-to-length ratio and the extra weight topside from the enhanced weaponry, Becton feared the *Laffey* might be difficult to handle. Becton found that the overhead to the pilothouse was too low in the Sumner Class destroyers, making him and others vulnerable to cracking their heads during the excitement of combat action or drills.

Finally, the ship lacked a captain's sea cabin and head, a place adjoining the bridge for the skipper to catch a quick break from the demands of the bridge, but close enough that he could quickly return if summoned to an emergency. Becton placed his concerns in a report to Navy officials, who answered that while they could not rearrange the low overhead due to architectural concerns, they would add a sea cabin as soon as possible.

Otherwise, Becton was delighted with his new home. So, too, was the crew. After observing Becton and inspecting the ship, teenager Phoutrides was filled with awe, "not only of the ship, but also of its young and dashing commanding officer." How many ship crews could brag that their skipper was not only a cited war hero, but also a good-looking man who whisked about town with a gorgeous starlet on his arm? Phoutrides, whose station on the bridge placed him near Becton, wrote his sister that the captain's "steady girl is a Powers model in New York. I literally fly down to his stateroom when I'm told just to get a look at her picture,"[28] which rested on Becton's desk.

Mature for his tender years, Phoutrides postponed his final conclusions about Becton until he observed the man in combat. Phoutrides respected his father, a Greek Orthodox priest, and measured other men by how they compared with him. He liked what he saw so far, and hoped Becton would measure up, but only time and battle action would provide the definitive answer.

"Quite a Job Facing Us"

Becton had concerns when it came to the crew. As many as eighty-five percent of the 325 enlisted were naval reserves, rushed into the Navy to man the hundreds of warships being constructed in Maine and other shipyards. Not only the enlisted ranks, but even a few of his officers, seemed barely out of high school. Although a minority had gone to college for a year or two, about as many had enlisted at age sixteen or seventeen. Most had at least graduated from high school, but with only five weeks of Navy training preparing these naval neophytes, Becton and his officers faced a stern test. Some estimated that it might take six months of training before the crew was whipped into shape.

Lieutenant Sheets observed that the crew came from every corner of the nation and from every ethnic group. "The multitude of men (to be sure they were all classified as men, although some as yet had not bristle to shave off) literally poured aboard, representing the America of 'U.S.A.,' boys from the farm, men from Dixie, toughies from Brooklyn, volunteers, draftees, fathers, sons, brothers, boots and veterans—boys away from home for the first time, old men who saw the previous war. Yes, these men and boys were the America of World War II."[29] Becton wished he could command the cream of the Navy, but like every skipper of a new destroyer, he had to be content with taking into battle a representative sampling of the nation.

He had Quartermaster Phoutrides, who had attended the prestigious Massachusetts Institute of Technology, and the religious Boatswain's Mate 2/c Calvin Wesley Cloer, who with his first and middle names seemed destined to be the preacher he was in civilian life. He had men without high school diplomas, men who had landed in trouble with the law, and men who came from caring families. He had men like Gunner's Mate 3/c Robert I. Karr of West Virginia, who trapped skunks, possum, and muskrat, and Gunner's Mate 2/c Lawrence H. Delewski of Pottstown, Pennsylvania, renowned for his football prowess at Redding High School.

Becton also relied on a diverse group of officers. While Becton could be affable and compassionate his communications officer, Lieutenant Theodore W. Runk, was gruff and brusque with the men. Few doubted Runk's expertise, but most wondered about the humanity of the officer who went by the book in all matters. Runk's iron-fisted methods and oft-repeated command, "I don't give a good Goddamn. Do it!"[30] earned him the nickname "Ivan the Terrible" from the crew.

On the other hand Lieutenant (jg) Matthew C. Darnell Jr., the ship's doctor, volunteered for the Naval Reserve after completing an internship at a prestigious Boston hospital. Darnell loved a good party and always seemed to have a smile on his face, while the more lenient Lieutenant (jg) Joel C. Youngquist, nicknamed "Pay" because he handled the ship's payroll, seemed to have the crew's best interests at heart, at times giving to a man in need of funds an advance on his pay. Becton knew from experience, though, that whether the men loved or hated an officer meant little in combat. Heroes often came from the least likely of places.

Becton and two other Naval Academy graduates, executive officer Lieutenant Charles Holovak and the assistant gunnery officer, Lieutenant Paul Smith, brought the most knowledge to the *Laffey*. Becton had great confidence in Holovak, who as executive officer managed the ship under the skipper's guidance, ensured Becton's orders were followed, and assumed command should Becton be incapacitated. During combat Holovak would also run the Combat Information Center (CIC), the brain of the ship that supplied the crucial information upon which Becton formed his decisions.

Becton warmed to his fellow Academy graduate at once and figured he could rely on the officer to come through in tough circumstances.

Not counting Becton, only three officers—assistant engineers Lieutenant (jg) James Fravel and Lieutenant (jg) William H. Shaw, and torpedo officer Lieutenant (jg) G. A. G. "Gag" Parolini—had seen any action. Most were like Lieutenant (jg) J. Bahme, a twenty-two-year-old graduate of Baylor University in Texas with little knowledge of the military behind him, or Lieutenant Youngquist, who had gone straight from Harvard Business School to the Navy. With the need for officers and enlisted to man their warships, the Navy streamlined its training to rush them to the fleet.

To be an effective warship, Becton needed the ability to maneuver and to shoot. Fortunately, he could rely on his capable engineering and gunnery officer, Lieutenant E. A. Henke. From Illinois Tech, Henke looked like a college professor, but his knowledge of how to produce the maximum horsepower from the ship's boilers, condensers, and turbines, combined with his ability to lead men, made him invaluable to Becton. In charge of the black gang, the nickname for the crew that operated the machinery belowdecks, Henke commanded almost one-third of the crew.

Gunnery Officer Lieutenant Harry Burns was an introspective man with an air of confidence who had learned gunnery aboard a cruiser in Atlantic waters. Aided by assistant gunnery officer, Lieutenant Paul Smith, Burns controlled the ship's guns, including the five-inch, 40mm, and 20mm guns.

Becton leaned heavily on his supply officer, Lieutenant Youngquist. The affable officer from Burlington, Iowa, seemed to have contacts everywhere the ship went, and if Becton needed something unusual, Youngquist somehow produced it from out of nowhere. Before the commissioning, Becton asked if he could locate something every ship's crew desired—an ice-cream maker. Figuring it would be great for morale, Becton sent Youngquist ahead to Boston. Following the commissioning ceremony, Youngquist inched next to Becton and whispered that the machine would be aboard the next day.

"He Is Known for Fighting Any and Everything"

Meningitis bug aboard.
Pill to crew, and push on forward.
Shakedown testing high she scored.

—"Invicta," Lieutenant Matthew C. Darnell

From February 8 to February 26, the ship remained at the Boston Navy Yard while undergoing the fitting-out process. Workers installed a fixed sound dome to the hull, calibrated the ship's degaussing (anti-mine) equipment and magnetic compasses, and performed other last-minute alterations to prepare the *Laffey* for action.

Becton made use of every available moment to prepare his men for action, for at that stage of the war, the Navy moved vessels from shipyard to combat with amazing rapidity. He had the crew man stations while the ship remained docked so they became familiar with their responsibilities, then took the ship out of the harbor, where they dropped depth charges, fired guns, and executed turns. On February 23, for instance, they expended in practice 27 five-inch rounds, 96 40mm shells, 330 20mm shells, and dropped 11 depth charges. "We drilled a lot," said Lieutenant Youngquist, "so we'd be ready for action. We had some drill to do every day."[31]

Becton warned his officers that they and the crew had best become accustomed to daily training, for there would be no room for mishap in combat. "We would all need to practice, practice, and practice again," said Becton, "so that when our time came, we could face the enemy with more than just courage to help us win." He insisted upon a clean ship, as filthy ones bred disease and disrupted morale for men living in such close proximity with each other for lengthy periods of time. Becton also believed that a man who took pride in maintaining his ship would step up when called for. "Men who cared enough about their ship to keep her spotless were men who would fight to defend her when things got rough."[32]

At 6:35 a.m. on February 27, Becton took the ship out of the Boston Navy Yard and set course for Washington, DC, where an inspection awaited. As this was their first overnight voyage, Becton noticed that some of his officers appeared anxious about standing watch on their own. He reassured the young ensigns and lieutenants that he had complete confidence in them, and should they be the officer of the deck—the man in charge while Becton was off the bridge—they should never hesitate to contact him, even if he was asleep. Although this eased their concerns, only actual experience at sea would bring the self-assurance he hoped his officers would eventually possess.

Little danger remained that a German U-boat might attack, but Becton placed everyone on Condition III watch, which called for a third of the armament to be manned and the crew to operate on a four-hour on, eight-hour off schedule. The step gave every man the opportunity to stand at least one watch during the overnight cruise to the nation's capital.

At 5:45 p.m. the next day, the *Laffey* pulled up to Pier 2 West at the Washington, DC, Navy Yard. Until March 2 the ship remained moored for inspection and for final preparations to depart on the shakedown cruise. After successfully passing inspection, at 8:02 a.m. March 2, the *Laffey*, now a part of Destroyer Squadron 60 of the Atlantic Fleet, got underway for Bermuda.

Mostly known as a vacation playground, during the war luxuriant Bermuda offered the stage for the United States Navy to break in its newest warships and train crews about to embark for combat. Destroyers such as the *Laffey* left homefront shipyards, steamed to Bermuda, and before receiving an assignment overseas, spent more than three weeks in and around the island practicing every imaginable drill and firing every gun. Becton and his officers noted deficiencies in performance that required further work or defective parts that needed repair.

The training off Bermuda was as realistic as possible, with the *Laffey* sometimes working solo while at other times operating in conjunction with other ships. Often with naval observers taking notes on their performance, Becton conducted visit-and-search drills, towing exercises, and smoke laying. He scheduled nighttime maneuvers in which the crew fired star shells for illumination while the *Laffey* screened other ships. Gruff chiefs barked commands as seamen dropped depth charges over the side, launched and recovered dummy torpedoes, or fired their antiaircraft guns at target sleds pulled by aircraft.

The Bermuda shakedown provided all gun crews with valuable training, but it especially helped the five-inch crews, who would need to be sharp in the coming months when they targeted German land batteries and units in providing gun support for American infantry in troubled situations. As many as fourteen men and one gun captain operated each of the three duo-barreled mounts. Communications connected each mount with the bridge, which selected the target. If it were a land target, the bridge fed the distance to the mounts. If the target were an aircraft, men on the bridge punched into the computer-like apparatus the target's speed and direction, the wind speed, and the ship's speed and direction, which produced the proper fuse setting that determined when the projectile would explode.

Teamwork was vital in the enclosed mounts. In the lower handling rooms below each mount, men operated the powder and shell hoists that lifted the explosives to the loaders above. The loaders placed the powder cans and shells into the barrels, which by then had been trained at the target. The gun captain usually stood toward the back, near a door leading to the outside.

Seaman 1/c Robert W. Dockery and Gunner's Mate 3/c Owen G. "Glen" Radder in Mount 52, the second five-inch gun forward, and Gunner's Mate 2/c Delewski, the aft gun captain of Mount 53, which his men affectionately labeled Ole Betsy, were drenched in sweat as the crews labored in the Bermuda sun to develop a rhythm in which shell and powder could be brought from below, lifted to the barrel, and fired every three seconds. At first the enlisted men in the gun crews moved too slowly, taking double the amount of time Delewski and the other captains demanded. Guided by a handful of experienced crew—including Boatswain's Mate Cloer and his buddy, Coxswain James M. La Pointe, veterans who earlier in the war had ships shot out from under them—the young sailors molded teams that whittled down the times.

Delewski, a hulk of a man who starred on the high school football field, was not much older than the men he supervised, but he earned everyone's respect with his confident airs and booming voice. "Ski," as his crew called him, recognized that the ship would soon be in a battle, most probably in the expected Allied invasion of Europe, and pushed his crew to be ready.

As the days passed, the crew became more proficient in their tasks, but tempered their pride with reality—they might perform splendidly in drills, but wondered how they would react when enemy guns and aircraft replaced the shakedown's practice targets. They received a partial answer on March 10, when at 7:00 a.m. their Talk Between Ships (TBS) crackled with orders for Becton to hasten to the rescue of survivors from a Navy PBY-5A patrol plane, piloted by Lieutenant A. H. Cowart, that had been forced into the ocean by engine trouble. Becton left his shakedown partner, the USS *Walke* (DD-723), and raced sixty miles northwest to the location, where lookouts spotted nineteen survivors huddling in three rubber life rafts. Becton moved the ship near the rafts so his crew could help the nineteen aboard.

A grateful Lieutenant Cowart later wrote to Becton, "maybe it wasn't your ship's first real operation, but for me, it was certainly her best." Becton was delighted that his crew had saved fellow Americans, but was equally satisfied that the men had responded so well to the crisis that they received official praise. "I believe that incident did more to teach us all to work together smoothly than any training exercise during our shakedown,"[33] Becton later wrote.

Officers and enlisted began to develop confidence in their skipper. "Becton was fair to everyone, and the officers and crew all respected him," said Lieutenant Bahme. "He was a very strict captain, liberal but strict," said Seaman 1/c Joseph E. Dixon, first loader on one of the 40mm guns. "Everybody liked him. He let you go ashore when he had the chance. He ran a tight ship, but knew when to back off."[34]

Although he was not as positive about some of the officers, Quartermaster Phoutrides liked what he observed of Becton off Bermuda. He still planned to delay his final evaluation of Becton until the ship had been in combat, but he thought Becton would be a valued commander. "I'm glad for one thing— that we have a good Captain," he wrote his parents on March 14. "He's young and understands his crew. Many a time I've been discouraged because of one thing or another. Just about that time he does or says something that makes us all forget our troubles. He's a fine man and holds the respect of his whole crew."[35]

In a subsequent letter to his sister, Aspasia, Phoutrides added, "gee, Spa, he's one of the finest men I've met in a long time." He explained that some of the men did not get along with a handful of the officers, and only avoided handing in a request for a transfer because of their affection for Becton. As an example, Phoutrides relayed an incident that occurred during the ship's speed trials at Bermuda. Becton raced the destroyer at full speed in rough seas, with water splashing over the bridge and the ship rolling 30° to each side. "Our morale was definitely low. So what does he do? He broke out one of his restricted publications and started to read us Japanese propaganda. Within 2 minutes he had us laughing our heads off and made us forget all our troubles." Phoutrides added that Becton had already been honored for his bravery in the Pacific. The captain "is known for fighting any and everything he runs into," the young quartermaster wrote. "As long as he stays aboard this ship, the whole bridge gang stays."[36]

After nearly a month of training, in mid-afternoon on March 31 the *Laffey* departed Bermuda's sunny environs en route to Boston, where they arrived on April 2. During their time in Boston, Becton asked Youngquist to pick up two bottles of alcohol because he was hosting a dinner for Imogen Carpenter and an officer from the *Walke*, Hollywood actor Robert Montgomery.

Until May 5 she remained in drydock while new sonar gear and other items were installed, then left for the Naval Operating Base in Norfolk, Virginia, for additional training. Three days at Norfolk ended May 9, when the *Laffey* got underway for New London, Connecticut, for antisubmarine warfare exercises with submarines.

Their stay in Connecticut was cut short on May 11, when Becton received orders to take the *Laffey* to New York. There she would join the other four original Sumner Class destroyers built at Bath, take on supplies, and accompany a fast convoy for the voyage across Atlantic waters to Europe. Becton guessed that the *Laffey* and her sister ships, the most heavily gunned destroyers in the fleet, were not needed solely to escort other ships when destroyer escorts could do the job. It had to mean one thing—*Laffey* was to be a part of the long-awaited invasion of Europe.

"Was I eager for combat? Yes!" said Quartermaster Phoutrides. "When you're young, that's how you feel."[37]

For Phoutrides and his shipmates, combat was at hand.

CHAPTER 2

OFF NORMANDY'S SHORES

Chasing foe on Dixie Line
Dodging shell and bomb and mine,
Pill-box blasting, hunting's fine.
　　—"Invicta," Lieutenant Matthew Darnell

On a serene Sunday afternoon on May 14 the USS *Laffey* headed to war. Becton guided the sparkling warship past New York's famed skyline and the Statue of Liberty on her way to the Atlantic Ocean's broader waters. It was a fitting start to the voyage, for although the crew lacked specific knowledge of their destination, the warship would soon be battling to liberate France and free the people whose graciousness in 1886 had made the statue a reality.

The crew responded crisply, partly because of their training but also because they sensed the significance of the moment. What could be more impressive than steaming by the Statue of Liberty, going to war to defend your country, in the best destroyer that the United States Navy had then produced? War's sordid sides awaited the crew in both Atlantic and Pacific waters, but for now all was glorious and grand.

Accompanied by three other ships from Destroyer Division 119—*Meredith* would join and complete the unit in four days—and two other destroyers, *Laffey* took her station in a screen escorting convoy, TCU 24B, a collection of ships carrying ammunition, gasoline, and oil. For the next thirteen days she shepherded the tanker, USS *Aucilla* (AO-56), and thirteen merchant vessels—"all carrying valuable, strategic cargoes,"[1] according to the *Walke*'s War Diary—across the Atlantic at fifteen knots. Operating on the flanks of the formation, *Laffey* and her companion destroyers probed the waters ahead and below with their radar and sonar, intent on safely conducting the convoy to its European destination.

"I didn't realize we would be going over so soon," said Seaman 2/c Robert C. Johnson, whose duties standing watch happily interrupted the chipping and painting that occupied most of his day. "I joined the ship in April, and in May we were on our way to Europe. Boy, we're going to see some action soon, I thought."[2] He never expected it to occur this quickly, though.

"We Felt Very Comfortable with Him"

"Well I'm really going places now," wrote Seaman Fern to his mother on May 15. He assumed that with the war in Europe heating up, it would not be long before he saw some action. "When I get back this time I'll most likely be wearing one or two more ribbons."[3]

To have his ship and his crew ready for any contingency, from the beginning Becton established his pattern by scheduling drills as frequently as he could. In addition to fire, collision, and damage control drills, Becton conducted gunnery exercises on four of the first six days at sea. Remembering all too clearly what had occurred in the South Pacific, when Japanese air power so effectively attacked his destroyer, Becton emphasized air recognition training and antiaircraft firing exercises. He gave the crew little time off, for each mile the ship traveled from US shores placed them a mile closer to combat.

"We had a pretty fair trip on the way over," wrote Seaman Fern to his mother in May, but added that Becton and the officers extended few breaks to the raw crew. "Today was Sunday. I never realized it because we worked like slaves. Every time you stopped or finished some Bos'n or Cox'n had more work."[4]

Despite the rigorous days and nights, the crew gained an appreciation for Becton's command skills. The men sensed that he knew what he was doing and that he had their best interests at heart. As novices to war, they were more than happy to serve under Becton, who had already been involved in multiple Pacific combat actions, rather than under an officer fresh from the Academy. "My immediate impression was that he fit the role of captain real well," said Seaman Johnson. "He was tall and good looking. I had heard good things about him and was impressed. He was very knowledgeable about naval matters and was doing a great job. He had experience in the Pacific, so we felt very comfortable with him, and as time went on I felt real confident with him."[5]

More than once Youngquist observed Becton dealing with other officers. Rather than micromanage every detail, Becton described what he wanted done, and then trusted the man to accomplish it. "'Now go ahead and do it,' Becton would say," according to Youngquist. "'I assume you can do it. Let me know if you have any trouble, but otherwise it's yours.' He put his trust in us."[6] Youngquist believed he and the other young officers responded to that trust and gained confidence that when the action started, they would capably respond.

The crew did not have to wait long to learn how they reacted to alerts. Within the first five days either the *Laffey* or one of the other ships picked up contacts on radar and scrambled their crews to general quarters, with depth charges at the ready. Each time, a destroyer split from the screen to investigate, but returned after losing the contact or determining it was either a friendly vessel or one of the merchant ships off station. "A school of black fish were sighted in the near vicinity,"[7] the *Walke* described in her War Diary for May 16. Even though the contacts proved false, *Laffey's* crew could not relax, for they never knew if one might turn out to be an enemy U-boat and require them to take action.

On May 20, two-thirds of the way across the Atlantic, the convoy ended its eastward course and veered northeast for its final run into the British Isles. Because these waters had once been fertile hunting grounds for German U-boats, Becton cautioned his crew to be particularly vigilant. He asked Pay Youngquist, whose nighttime station was in the decoding room, to decode and relay to him not just the messages coming in to the *Laffey*, but also all those earmarked for other destroyers. Becton wanted to be informed of everything going on in the convoy.

"We Were Part of the Invasion"

On May 24 convoy ships began peeling away from the unit to embark on the final leg into their ports of destination. Six transports proceeded to Loch Ewe, Scotland, during the morning, while that afternoon *Laffey* and the rest of Destroyer Division 119 detached, formed a column on the *O'Brien*, and headed to Greenock, Scotland, twenty-five miles west of Glasgow. Shortly before midnight *Laffey* moored in Greenock's harbor in the River Clyde to refuel.

Early the next day, with the *Laffey* stationed 1,500 yards on the starboard beam of *O'Brien*, the five ships descended the Firth of Clyde and steamed through the North Channel into the Irish Sea on their way to ports in southern England. No one yet knew what lay in store for the ship and crew, but most guessed that combat would soon replace their duties escorting convoys.

On May 26, one day out from their English port, the *O'Brien* picked up a sonar contact. *Laffey* joined *O'Brien* to check the report, but resumed her station fourteen minutes later when the contact proved negative. Eighty-six minutes later *Laffey* radar detected another contact 1,100 yards distant, sending everyone scurrying to stations. "This was it, at last," wrote Becton, who ordered general quarters. "We weren't drilling anymore. This was the real thing."

The *Laffey* crew dropped eleven depth charges on the contact, which soon disappeared from their radar. Becton later concluded that the contact was most likely a whale or a rock pinnacle, but the episode nonetheless handed the crew its first taste of action. Becton wrote that, "we had dropped depth charges as if we had been in action. Whale, pinnacle, or U-boat, we had finally been playing for keeps."[8]

The next afternoon, the five ships formed a column with *O'Brien* in the lead and entered the channel leading to Portland Harbor, Plymouth, England, the same port from which the determined Puritans had departed in 1620 for the New World to seek freedom from religious intolerance. Now, 324 years later, Becton and crew returned to participate in an invasion that would free occupied Europe from Nazi tyranny.

Atrocious weather made navigating the harbor treacherous. "Fog had set in, reducing visibility to zero,"[9] described the *Laffey*'s War Diary for that day. The fact that hundreds of other vessels lay at anchor in the confined waters heightened the tension, for few, if any, could be seen until the ships were perilously close. *O'Brien* cautiously led the collection forward until 6:07 a.m., when a radar malfunction forced her to hand the lead duties to Becton and *Laffey*. Becton moved the ship to the head of the column, taking station 1,000 yards ahead of the second ship in line.

For half an hour Becton guided the column through the congested waters. He relayed information from *Laffey*'s radar via voice radio to the other ships, informing them of the subtle course changes they had to make to avoid anchored vessels. Often, Becton relayed one course change only to have to send another within moments. "We could hardly see," said Lieutenant Youngquist, "and that was very scary."[10]

The onset of daylight and the lifting of the fog revealed hundreds of warships of all sizes bobbing quietly at anchor, making the five arrivals seem mere appendages to an immense operation. Becton took one glance at the accumulated might and concluded that an invasion against Hitler's Europe was imminent. Quartermaster Phoutrides scanned the horizon and thought that he had never seen more ships. "It was filled with every type of ship," he recalled. "We knew then that we were part of the invasion of Europe."[11] In less than four months the crew had gone from boarding a ship still bearing signs of shipyard work to the eve of the largest invasion of the war.

At 10:05 Becton moored *Laffey* to the *O'Brien* and three British destroyers in Plymouth Sound, Plymouth, England and settled in to await further developments. It would not be long, Becton knew, before orders and events rearranged the lives of his young crew and placed his ship in harm's way.

The ships that moored in Plymouth, one of the many British ports bulging with cruisers, destroyers, and landing craft, dwarfed the *Laffey*. The destroyer that had departed New York only days ago was a tiny piece of the thousands that United States President Franklin D. Roosevelt, British Prime Minister Winston Churchill, Supreme Allied Commander General Dwight D. Eisenhower, and other top officials had assembled for the vast operation soon to unfold.

Ever since German leader Adolf Hitler had started World War II by invading Poland in 1939, Roosevelt and Churchill had longed for the time they could assault Hitler's Fortress Europe, liberate the occupied countries, and defeat Hitler. Their hopes were about to materialize in May 1944 as Becton and his crew arrived in crowded Plymouth.

On May 29 Becton joined other naval commanders, captains, and communications officers in an old theater in Plymouth, where they at long last learned what they had suspected—that they were about to invade Europe. Superiors informed Becton and his fellow commanders that on June 5, only seven days hence, more than 4,000 ships, divided into the British-dominated Eastern Naval Task Force and an American-dominated Western Naval Task Force, would land thousands of American, British, and Canadian troops along a fifty-mile section of France's northern coast and begin the long-awaited march across Europe into Germany. The American effort focused on the western half, where troops would drive inland before veering west and seizing the important port of Cherbourg.

Five task forces would transport, land, and support the troops set to hit five beaches—three British/Canadian and two American. The Western Task Force contained two US units: Task Force "O" to support operations at Omaha

Beach, and Task Force "U" under Rear Admirals D. P. Moon and M. L. Deyo to support the infantry landing at Utah Beach. Part of the unit commanded by Admiral Deyo, *Laffey* would join the 931 vessels of Task Force "U" assigned to the operations at the westernmost beach.

"As they always had been," wrote Becton, "destroyers were to be the work-horses of the naval forces."[12] In addition to shepherding the landing craft on the way across the English Channel, *Laffey* and other destroyers would screen the battleships and cruisers as they bombarded German gun positions ashore, engage the German navy should it approach the landing area, and use their guns as artillery to destroy German pillboxes, casemated guns, and mobile artillery until the Army could land their own artillery units. *Laffey* and her trio of five-inch guns could concentrate an impressive volume of shells on German positions, and with the target coordinates relayed from a Shore Fire Control Party (SFCP), *Laffey* could fire with more accuracy than the erratic aerial bombing.

Allied strategists did not expect the German navy to be a significant factor, as earlier naval clashes had greatly reduced Hitler's fleet. However, U-boats and the smaller E-boats, which were similar to the American PT boats that operated in the South Pacific, were threats. Becton's main concern was that the speedy E-boats stationed at the Cherbourg Peninsula on his right flank would advance at night along the coast and execute a high-speed run against vulnerable American landing craft and resupply vessels. He intended to keep his men sharp, as even a surprise appearance by a handful of enemy ships could inflict considerable damage.

"The Prospect Was a Bit Exciting"

Becton returned to the *Laffey* but, as ordered, divulged none of the invasion details until June 2. Periodic enemy air raids reminded the crew that danger was never far away. Forty minutes after midnight on May 30, for instance, air raid sirens blared in the Plymouth area after a handful of German aircraft were spotted. Later that day Becton announced that the crew of the *Laffey*, like the crews of every other ship, would be confined to their vessels. The order sparked rumors about when they would leave and what their destination would be.

Quartermaster Phoutrides knew with certainty that the *Laffey* would be a part of the imminent invasion when a whaleboat pulled alongside the ship and a sailor handed him an envelope to take to Becton on the bridge. Becton stared at the sealed envelope for a moment and then told Phoutrides to take it to his safe. "Walking down," explained Phoutrides, "I glanced at the envelope and it had written across it, 'OPEN UPON RECEIPT OF CERTAIN RADIO SIGNAL.' I thought, 'I'm holding the invasion plans in my hands!'"[13]

On June 2 Becton gathered his officers in the wardroom for the final pre-invasion meeting. Becton informed Pay Youngquist, Jay Bahme, and the others that the ship would leave Plymouth June 3, and that the infantry would land on the coast of Normandy June 5. He checked to make certain each department had what it needed to operate efficiently, and queried each officer whether he fully understood his duties. He ended by telling the officers that they could now inform the crew. Within minutes of the meeting everyone aboard ship knew the news. A quiet, almost relaxed air encompassed the destroyer, because now men could at least deal with the known rather than fret about the unknown.

Becton addressed the coming assault in a memo to the crew issued shortly after he informed the officers. "We are getting into the war zone where the chips are down and the game is played for keeps!" cautioned the skipper, who moved directly into an item that bothered him. "General Quarters stations are still manned much too slowly." He remarked that some men must be stopping for showers during morning alerts "judging from the time it takes to get to their stations." He added that "if you don't sleep in your clothes, don't wait to button your shirt and trousers and lace your shoes before manning your station. Grab your clothes and your helmet and life jacket and <u>GET GOING!</u> [emphasis Becton's]. You can put on the finishing touches after reaching your station." Becton had seen improvement since the Bermuda shakedown, but with combat coming in the next few days, he wanted his men at peak efficiency.

He emphasized that every man's job was important, and that the crew was to keep a sharp lookout, especially for low-flying planes that radar might miss. He told his 40mm and 20mm gunners that they had his permission to open fire immediately on any aircraft that dived toward the ship. "If they're our own planes, they shouldn't be diving at us." He reminded them that while firing at balloons in practice, they mistakenly aimed too low and failed to lead the target sufficiently, and cautioned them, "Don't fire at planes going away!" Such gunfire endangered nearby ships and Allied fighters, but he warned against the tactic mostly because it took the gunners' attention from "the real enemy—the plane approaching the ship that <u>HASN'T DROPPED HIS EGG AS YET. HE'S</u> the baby we want to get!!"[14]

"The prospect of the invasion was a bit exciting and a bit frightening," said then-eighteen-year-old Seaman 1/c Robert W. Dockery. Sonarman 3/c Daniel Zack, like most of the young crew, looked forward to his first battle. "When you're young you don't think about the dangers or know that they are a part of what you are about to face. We were immortal." Although hardly surprised to learn of the destination, Seaman Johnson liked the certainty of knowing his destination. "It took some of the anxiety away. Now we knew we were heading for France."[15]

From Felixstowe on England's eastern shore to Milford Haven in Wales, Great Britain's southern ports bulged with vessels of all sizes in preparation for the invasion of France. The ports would soon empty of their warships and troop transports, leaving behind in Great Britain and elsewhere an apprehension over whether the invasion would succeed or fail. Great Britain's citizens had become accustomed to hard times, holding on gamely throughout the bombing blitz that ravaged much of London in 1940 and 1941, but if Germany rebuffed this effort, the war would take a drastic turn for the worse.

At least Seaman Fern felt better. He wrote his mother that for the first time in a long while, he was able to attend Catholic Mass when a service was arranged aboard the *Laffey*. The ceremony calmed the young sailor in the hours before heading into combat.

During the overcast afternoon of June 3, *Laffey* steamed to Point Able, where she rendezvoused with *Barton* and the other escorting ships tasked with protecting the 136 vessels composing convoy U-2A2. The escorts then proceeded to Point Dog, the assembly area in the English Channel south of the Isle of Wight, where that evening they met two groups of LCTs (Landing Craft, Tank) coming from Dartmouth and Brixham. Within two hours the LCTs had formed in two sections of three columns each and, with *Laffey* screening 1,000 yards off the port flank of the second section, turned in the heavy seas and rough weather and started the five-knot journey toward Normandy.

Even at that moderate pace, sailors moved about cautiously to avoid being knocked off their feet by the wind and waves. "The wind was stronger, the sky overcast, visibility low, and an intermittent rain fell throughout the day," described the *Barton*'s War Diary for that day. The ships dared not proceed above five knots lest the convoys lose their cohesion in the challenging conditions. The troops aboard transports suffered in the uncomfortable craft, as unrelenting waves carried hulls up and down and wind buffeted them from side to side. "During that first trip," said Sonarman Zack, "I felt sorry for the guys in the landing craft. The waves were coming over them. We felt the rocking in our destroyer, but it was rougher for them."[16]

General Eisenhower was concerned, too. When he met with his top commanders to discuss canceling or postponing the operation due to the weather, his air commanders informed him that aircraft could not take off and his naval commanders cautioned that the Channel waters would make life miserable for smaller ships. After great deliberation, Eisenhower postponed the invasion for twenty-four hours and recalled the force. By late afternoon on June 4 the order had been sent, and four hours later Becton reversed course and took *Laffey* and the convoy back to England.

Quartermaster Phoutrides was at his post on the bridge when the recall order came. He saw no visible reaction among his shipmates, but "when you head out for the invasion, you are all ready to go, so it was a letdown of sorts." Seaman Dockery said the feeling was uniform throughout the ship. "We were disappointed when we had to turn back. Once you started, you wanted to go do it. We also worried that the Germans might find out about the invasion."[17] Sonarman Zack saw it more as a temporary inconvenience than anything, because logic dictated that within a few days their ship would again set out for the French coast.

According to her War Diary, during the return trip *Laffey* "rode herd" on the port flank, assisting LCTs that had "engine trouble, breakdowns, leaks, etc."[18] One craft, LCT 2489, slowed, then stopped dead in the water from mechanical failures. Receiving her signal for help, Becton carefully moved *Laffey* to one side to serve as a buffer from the wind and lessen the roll until another vessel took the LCT in tow.

One LCT capsized while being towed to port, while another had her ramp ripped off south of Portland. Others lost power, had plates loosened, and took on water. After a long day shepherding the craft back to England, the *Laffey* arrived at Weymouth on June 5, carrying a weary but safe crew.

The men had barely had time to relax with a meal and cup of coffee when three and a half hours later Becton received the order to return to the Channel and again escort the landing craft to Normandy. The invasion, delayed for twenty-four hours, was on once again. With an overcast sky, occasional rain, and fifteen-knot winds (seventeen miles per hour), *Laffey* left at daybreak.

For almost three hours Becton rounded up the landing craft and gathered them into formation for the trip across the channel. The *Barton* escorted the lead group of LCTs, while *Laffey* remained behind to accompany a second group.

Laffey and *Barton* escorted 136 LCTs and LCIs (Landing Craft Infantry) from Weymouth to the staging area off Utah Beach, a three-mile strip of shore between Pouppeville and La Madeleine, France. The two groups left England from Point Z, the ten-mile-wide assembly area thirteen miles south of the Isle of Wight through which every ship in the vast invasion force steamed before turning toward Normandy.

Once beyond the assembly area, nicknamed Piccadilly Circus, ships navigated into one of five swept lanes, one for each beach. Now in his assigned lane at the westernmost end, Becton believed that there was no turning back this time.

Only a handful of hours separated the untested crew from its first taste of combat.

"*Laffey* Was Always on the Move"

Halfway across the Channel each of the five lanes split into two, one for the speedier vessels and a second for the slower troop transports and landing craft. Planners added two safeguards to help ships maintain their proper course. Vessels showing identification flags in daylight and flashing an identifying letter in the dark stood at every spot calling for a course change, and minesweepers dropped lighted buoys one mile apart along the channels.

Becton kept *Laffey* on her station along the port flank of the second group, ready to assist vessels in trouble as the landing craft slowly churned across the Channel in rectangular fashion. At times Becton stationed the destroyer at the formation's head, then veered to the sides to make certain every landing craft maintained position. He communicated with the landing craft by semaphore or by lights rather than electronic means, which the Germans might have intercepted, and the landing craft featured red lights aft so the LCIs behind could follow and remain in station. "*Laffey* was always on the move, checking on ships," said Sonarman Zack. "Sometimes a landing craft would sustain damage from the seas and call us. We'd signal to another landing craft to help them. We were like a shepherd."[19]

Laffey's group made steady progress throughout the evening of June 5 and into the early morning hours of June 6. Suddenly, the thundering roar of aircraft drowned out other noise as planes sped toward Normandy to deliver the paratroopers behind lines. Though no one aboard *Laffey* could see the aircraft in the darkness, men knew from the sounds of multiple engines that the sky had to be packed with transports on their way to deliver the first punch against Hitler's defenses. The moment surprised the crew, who had not been told of the paratroopers, but it assured them that by the time they arrived off the French coast, the Germans would already have been in a fight.

For an hour or so after the last plane flew by, silence again covered *Laffey*'s group. Then more noise, louder than before, indicated that a fleet of bombers was winging its way to lambast the French coast.

In mid-afternoon lookouts spotted a floating mine two and one-half feet in diameter five hundred yards to starboard. Becton ordered seaman with rifles to detonate it, but when their bullets failed to explode the multipronged device, Becton's 20mm guns dispatched the threat. Two hours later the minesweeper, USS *Osprey* (AM-56), emitted smoke when she either ran into a mine or was struck by a torpedo. While *Laffey* circled to provide protection, a second minesweeper moved alongside and removed the entire complement shortly before the vessel capsized and sank.

Other than those few difficulties, Becton shepherded his group across the Channel and delivered his ships to the embarkation point for the assault. With every man at battle stations, Becton prepared to execute the remainder of his tasks assigned for D-Day.

Rear Admiral Alan G. Kirk, Naval Commander for the Western Task Force of which *Laffey* was a part, had issued a message emphasizing the importance of their assignments and the challenges they would face. "In two ways the coming battle differs from any that we have undertaken before," Kirk wrote. "It demands more seamanship, and more fighting." The English Channel would require Becton and every commander to operate in strong currents and twenty-foot tides, after which "we must destroy an enemy defensive system which has been four years in the making, and our mission is one against which the enemy will throw his whole remaining strength." In addition, they would face "prepared positions, held by Germans who have learned from their past failures. They have coastal batteries and minefields; they have bombers and E-boats and submarines. They will try to use them all. We are getting into a fight." Kirk reminded his men that they had "one task only—to land and support and supply and reinforce the finest Army ever sent to battle by the United States. In that task we shall not fail. I await with confidence the further proof, in this the greatest battle of them all, that American sailors are seamen and fighting men second to none."[20]

D-Day: June 6, 1944

"A Once in a Lifetime Experience"

Men quieted as their ship, accompanied by hundreds of other warships and landing craft, drew closer to assigned stations off the Normandy coast. Gunner's Mate Delewski had experienced nerves on the football field, where an errant tackle or miscue could mean the difference between a win and a loss, but those times now shrank to insignificance. Heightened senses overwhelmed Sonarman Zack, Seaman Fern, and the other initiates to combat. Hearts beat faster, palms turned clammier, and perspiration dampened shirts.

Naval intelligence estimated that twenty-eight German batteries containing 110 guns, ranging from the smaller 75mm artillery to the mammoth 170mm batteries, defended Utah Beach alone. The battleships and cruisers were to silence those batteries while destroyers escorted the landing craft to the beaches. When the first boat wave was moments from reaching shore, the commander was to fire a smoke rocket to indicate they had touched land, at which time the bombardment would lift from the beaches to selected targets inland.

"I didn't realize how large the invasion was," said Seaman Johnson. "It was huge, but when you're sitting in one spot, you don't think about that. You're more focused on what's in your line of vision. As we neared the coast, we worried about mines. They were a larger worry than aircraft, as we had such air superiority that we didn't worry about attack from the air."[21]

As *Laffey* arrived in the Baie de la Seine area with the landing craft, German E-boats concerned Becton. The German navy, still licking its wounds from naval losses in the Atlantic and the Mediterranean, could call on a collection of destroyers and minesweepers, as well as sixty E-boats, scattered along the French coastline. Though hardly imposing, these smaller, speedy craft could draw close to or even penetrate the screen and wreak havoc with their torpedoes.

"D-Day was here," recalled Gunner's Mate Delewski, stationed in the aft five-inch gun. "The skies were gray and the waters choppy. As one sat on the ship in the Channel, one had to be impressed with the tremendous number of planes overhead. Allied air superiority was very evident."[22]

In the predawn darkness on June 6, each battleship and cruiser had anchored at its assigned spot and prepared for the bombardment. As dawn broke a German shore battery broke the stillness by firing at two destroyers. Thirty-one minutes later a thundering American barrage announced to Normandy and to the world that the long-awaited assault against Hitler's Fortress Europe had at last begun.

Each time one of the mighty battleships unleashed a salvo, the gun recoil forced the battleship downward and emitted a shock wave that rocked *Laffey* and other nearby vessels. At each of the five Normandy beaches, as the first glimmers of dawn cracked through the darkness, arcs of shells streamed from battleships and cruisers toward shore targets.

A deafening noise enveloped *Laffey*. Crew on *Laffey's* deck observed the impressive opening with a combination of admiration and thanks that they were not on the receiving end. At his designated time, Becton gave the order to his five-inch mounts, which commenced with a ship-rattling salvo that sent *Laffey's* first shots of the war racing toward the enemy. Their fire blended with that of the battleships, cruisers, and other destroyers, some of which were stationed closer to the beaches than *Laffey* and fired point-blank at the enemy.

"At that time of the morning you can actually see the shells," said Sonarman Zack. "They are red hot. I wondered how the Germans could live through it, and I thought that it sure would open the beaches for the infantry. It made me glad I was where we were instead of on land."[23]

One hour later aircraft dropped a protective smoke screen between the troops about to head into Utah Beach and the shore. Seaman Dockery caught a quick glimpse of the landing craft before settling into his station inside a five-inch gun mount. "It was impressive seeing all those landing craft heading to shore, a once in a lifetime experience."[24]

As part of his duties as Quartermaster of the Watch, Phoutrides recorded the times and events as they occurred. He worked in the pilothouse along with Quartermaster 1/c John "Jack" Doran, a recent transfer from the battleship, *Texas*, who was the helmsman, the person who handles the wheel and steers the ship. Phoutrides also worked alongside the annunciator, the sailor who passed instructions from Becton to the engine room. Should either of the other two men became incapacitated during the battle, Phoutrides was to assume their tasks.

"I didn't feel scared," said Phoutrides, who gained a panoramic view of the day's events from the flying bridge and a partial view from the portholes in the pilot house. "I was a young man anxious to see action. Everywhere we looked, there were ships, some with antiaircraft balloons above. Everywhere we looked skyward, there were U.S. aircraft. All you saw were ships and planes. It was an awesome sight!" The spectacle bolstered Phoutrides's confidence, but he still postponed forming a conclusion on Becton, who sometimes stood inside the pilot house with them and at other times outside on the flying bridge where he might have a better view. "I had partial confidence in the skipper, but I had to see how he handled himself in combat. Every enlisted man wants to see how his officer will react under fire."[25]

Laffey and other destroyers darted about the landing craft, simultaneously firing their five-inch guns toward German fortifications while ensuring that the vessels maintained their proper course toward shore. The bombardment lifted as the landing craft neared the beaches, and at 6:31 a.m., only one minute behind schedule, the first ramps lowered at Utah Beach and troops of the Army's 4th Infantry Division swarmed ashore. While German machine gun fire at Omaha Beach cut down swaths of American infantry before they could gather on the beach, men at Utah Beach landed against light opposition, in part because currents had swept them slightly off course into a landing area that was lightly defended and partly because battleship fire had knocked out three ten-inch German batteries guarding that stretch of sand.

Now fully involved in their first combat action as a crew, the *Laffey* men jumped to action. Men inserted plugs or cotton in their ears to mask the whistling and screeching of the shells and other noises of the bombardment. At his 40mm mount on the starboard side near the No. 1 stack, Seaman Johnson passed racks of four shells to the loaders above.

Eighteen-year-old Seaman 1/c Donald E. "Doc" Brown watched from the torpedo deck as *Laffey* and nine other destroyers opened fire at German targets ashore. Spaced about half-mile apart, the ships moved in an oval, firing when their ship traversed the shoreward arc. *Laffey*'s two twin-mounted forward guns and one twin-mounted aft gun fired in succession, with a minute's pause between each. Combined with the firepower of the other ships, a steady stream of five-inch shells coursed shoreward.

When Brown saw flashes inside a church steeple, indicating enemy gunfire from that location, he radioed the bridge and asked Becton for permission to fire. Becton checked with his superiors about targeting a church, and gave Brown the go-ahead when he received an affirmative. "Next time we came past," said Brown, "we demolished it. We started with the steeple and leveled it right down to the ground. It was a pretty good-sized church, too."[26]

As the infantry moved inland and broadened the beachhead, larger land-ing ships brought in tanks, trucks, and more supplies. *Laffey* stood offshore prepared to lend fire support, but a lack of targets kept her guns silent.

With matters near the beach unfolding smoothly, shortly after 10:00 a.m. Becton moved *Laffey* to her station in a defensive screen around the bom-bardment ships. *Laffey*, accompanied by the *Walke*, her sister ship from De-stroyer Division 119, operated four miles offshore. Although outside the range of most German guns, *Laffey* maneuvered within striking distance of the larger ones, some of whose shells splashed less than twenty feet from the destroyer.

Becton figured that the shallow waters off Utah Beach precluded German U-boats from prowling about, but he could not dismiss the possibility that German fighter planes could sweep down the coast or E-boats from Cher-bourg might dash to an attack. To counter the E-boat threat against the two American beaches, *Laffey* and other destroyers patrolled three to five miles off Normandy along what was called the Dixie Line.

By nightfall of June 6, more than 23,000 troops had landed at Utah Beach and established a six-mile beachhead. Troops had begun advancing inland to join with American paratroopers in starting what would become hundreds of assaults against German pillboxes and strongholds. Three thou-sand men perished at the bloodier Omaha Beach area to the east, while fewer than two hundred died from the lighter resistance at Utah Beach.

The naval support offered by the battleships, cruisers, and destroyers such as *Laffey* helped reduce German resistance at Utah and paved the way for the oncoming troops. SFCPs on land called in coordinates to the ships, which quickly directed their guns on the target. "Never before has it been attempted to silence with naval gunfire so extensive and elaborate a system of coast defenses as found here," summed Commander Cruiser Division Seven's War Diary for June 6. "The surprising thing is that more losses were not sustained by our force in this stage of the operation."[27]

Laffey's crew had been initiated into the war. "Well your big boy has had his baptism of fire a short while ago," Seaman Fern wrote to his mother in June. "No one on my ship was hurt, but others near us weren't so lucky."[28]

The German navy had yet to harass the American fleet, but Becton re-mained skeptical that it had been neutralized. Sooner or later, he was certain, they would make an appearance. Hanson Baldwin, the *New York Times*'s re-spected military correspondent, wrote about the subject in an article headlined,

"Where Is German Navy?" He concluded that most of Hitler's seagoing assets were unavailable or sunk. "However, a number of E-boats were based at Cherbourg and Le Havre and there were destroyers, torpedo boats, E-boats and submarines at Brittany ports, and in the Bay of Biscay enough of all of them to seem to offer a sizable threat."[29]

When or where might they suddenly strike?

June 8–9: Shore Bombardment

"We Were Doing Something Useful"

> The "D" Day invasion
> Was right down her alley
> She blasted the Krauts
> So the ground troops could rally.
> —"An Ode to the USS *Laffey* (DD-724),"
> Gunner's Mate Owen Radder

For the next eighteen days Becton faced four main tasks. Besides providing supporting fire for the infantry ashore in the early stages of the invasion, *Laffey* protected Allied shipping off Utah Beach from German air attacks, countered German mine-laying efforts, and guarded against incursions from German E-boats and submarines. Officers and enlisted alike learned they had to be flexible, one hour collaborating with battleships and cruisers and the next battling toe-to-toe with German land batteries. They had to search the skies for enemy aircraft and scour the sea for mines, and juggle these exacting responsibilities while learning on the job. The tasks demanded much of a young crew that had first gathered only four months earlier, yet Becton, other ships' crews, the infantry ashore, and officers reaching into Eisenhower's headquarters counted on them to do their jobs.

Having already witnessed in the Pacific the destructiveness of sudden air attacks, Becton kept his men on alert lest the ship be caught off guard. "The first two days we were at GQ 24 hours a day,"[30] said Quartermaster Phoutrides. Becton had told the men that, when possible, they should grab a few moments of sleep at their station, but to let the men near them know what they were doing.

German aircraft rarely appeared during the day, but at night they either planted mines in the water or attacked after dropping flares that so brightly illuminated the area that the crew swore they could read by them. Once the flares revealed a vessel, the German pilot would dive in for an assault.

"At night a small number of German planes did manage to get through," Gunner's Mate Delewski wrote after the war, "and then one had to be impressed with the comparative brilliance of the German flares. They lit up the area like Main Street on a Saturday night."[31] Allied air superiority provided a tight blanket over the ships, but Delewski and his shipmates never knew when an enemy aircraft might burst through the curtain.

While *Laffey* patrolled one night, flares suddenly brightened a three-hundred-yard area around the ship. "We sped up because a bomber would be coming after us," said Zack, who was so certain that a bomb would follow that in the interval he was unable to mutter a sound. "The waiting, after the flare, was scary," he said. "We were going to get it now." The German pilot dropped his bomb, but it exploded harmlessly off *Laffey*'s fantail.

During another nighttime patrol, lookouts spotted a German plane approaching as if to drop mines or a torpedo. However, at the last minute the German pilot, who had apparently not picked up the destroyer, veered rapidly to the right to avoid colliding with *Laffey*. In the attempt his wing hit the water and the aircraft flipped over and exploded, but the *Laffey* was safe. "Had he not turned he would have hit us," said Sonarman Zack. "He was as surprised as us and turned at the last moment."[32]

Until the infantry had advanced far enough inland to be out of range of *Laffey*'s guns, the ship's five-inch gun crews zeroed in on German mobile 88s and enemy gun emplacements on the ridges that fringed the beaches. Standing a few miles offshore, *Laffey* opened fire whenever the SFCP radioed in coordinates for a target. With the information in hand, Lieutenant (jg) Lloyd Hull in the CIC plotted the target on the grid, and sent the range and bearing to the gunnery officer, Harry Burns, in the fire-control director. Men observed where onshore the dust and smoke arose, then adjusted the firing to bring the shells directly onto the target.

A busy two days started June 8 when SFCP called on Becton eleven times to help destroy enemy emplacements blocking the advance of the 4th Infantry Division toward Montebourg, France. From an average range of ten thousand yards the five-inch crews fired 610 rounds of shells in seven hours, eliminating German howitzers, machine gun and rocket gun emplacements, and enemy troop concentrations.

Gunnery was not a simple operation to conduct from a ship at sea, swaying in the waves and in constant motion. "Hitting what you aimed at was no easy task with the swells that kept the ships rolling," said Gunner's Mate Delewski. "Because the area was crowded with ships, we could not make the necessary speed to keep *Laffey* steady."[33] Delewski credited the training instilled in the gun crews as making the difference between success and failure.

That afternoon the ship fired one salvo when the SFCP frantically radioed for help from gunfire that had pinned down the unit. "We're lying on our stomachs in a ditch under enemy fire," they radioed. Hating to direct five-inch shells onto fellow Americans, Burns gave the order to fire, then anxiously waited for eleven minutes, when the radio crackled to life with the announcement, "Right on target! You did it!" The relieved shore party added, "Whoever was shooting at us has stopped so you must have done all right."[34]

Their June 8 fire proved so beneficial that the SFCP radioed back its congratulations. The message stated "that every mission given the ship so far had been successfully completed, that there were dead Germans everywhere, and that he would call us back when he had more missions."[35]

In bloodying the enemy for the first time since their February commissioning, the crew had completed an action that assisted their brethren infantry battling for every yard ashore. "Yes, we were proud of that," said Quartermaster Phoutrides. "We were doing something useful."[36]

Unlike the infantry, though, theirs was an impersonal fight, waged with invisible enemies and completed with hidden bloodshed and death. Speedy, surgical, and one-sided, their initial foray into battle gave the false impression that naval combat was clean. The handful of combat veterans, like Becton and Csiszar, could tell them otherwise, but their words would not sink in until Phoutrides, Fern, and the other newcomers to war witnessed a more sordid side in the Pacific.

More of the same occurred the next day, when the SFCP called on *Laffey* twelve times to target concrete pillboxes and fortifications. In a busy seven-hour span, the five-inch crews fired 375 rounds, taxing a group of officers and men who had completed their first bombardment fewer than twenty-four hours earlier. Crammed inside the sweltering five-inch gun mounts, Seaman Dockery and others labored in the June heat, taxing muscles and producing perspiration. Though they could not see the results of their labors, they were proud that whereas many of the other ships fired 100–200 rounds during these days, *Laffey* all but emptied her magazines against different targets.

Most of the day's action consisted of eight or ten rounds against machine gun positions or troop concentrations, but during one eighty-minute barrage, the gun crews fired 275 rounds shoreward. Afterwards the SFCP reported, "Excellent shooting. Targets were 88mm guns and machine guns that had been giving our troops a lot of trouble. You made direct hits on two enemy pillboxes containing 88mm guns, and inflicted great damage. Will call you again when we have another opportunity to plaster them."[37]

In Becton's opinion, the crew functioned smoothly in their first combat action, crisply following orders and efficiently maintaining a flow of five-inch shells from handling room to gun and from gun to shore. He concluded in his action report that on both June 8 and June 9 "communications with shore fire control parties were very good and the bombardment was carried out with little difficulty."[38]

The First Week: Menace of the Mines

"You Never Knew If You Were Safe"

Even with Allied air superiority clamping a tight blanket over the shipping, *Laffey* gun crews had to watch for possible air attacks. An occasional German plane slipped through, such as the Heinkel bomber that drew within 1,000 yards of *Laffey* before other ships' guns splashed it. Late in the evening on June 9 the ship's starboard 20mm and 40mm antiaircraft guns opened fire at two aircraft that dived out of the clouds. Fire from twenty other ships joined in, but ceased when the planes were identified as friendly. Fortunately, neither plane was damaged, but Becton castigated the officer in charge first for allowing such an impulsive reaction and then for the gun crews' poor shooting performance. "Planes' maneuvers fortunately were much superior to the machine gunners' marksmanship," Becton sardonically wrote in his report, "and neither was shot down nor apparently hurt judging from their maneuverability and speed in clearing the area."[39]

Laffey spotters also had to keep watch for German mines that infested the waters off Utah Beach. Nearly every night three groups of enemy aircraft flew over. While one group dropped flares to illuminate the area and another executed runs against the beach to draw antiaircraft fire, the third sneaked in and dropped mines that, shielded by the darkness and the waves, floated among the ships. Because the currents along Utah Beach ran parallel to shore, a mine dropped at one end of the area drifted among the ships by morning.

The *New York Times* military analyst, Hanson W. Baldwin, described the sea action off Normandy. "The struggle between the minesweepers and the minelayers," he wrote, "is continuous; the Germans lay mines each night from planes and from E-boats or other surface ships, and each day the sweepers steam back and forth across the Bay of the Seine and the English Channel, undoing the work of the enemy." He added that "the Germans are indefatigable at this type of sea guerrilla warfare."[40]

Mines hampered *Laffey* not only at night, but prevented them from reaching the next day's station until minesweepers had cleared a path. One day Becton followed the minesweepers into a channel. At one spot the channel swerved around a ship that had been previously sunk, and just as *Laffey* navigated the turn a destroyer escort behind her exploded. The ship's back end lifted out of the water, and the destroyer escort split in half and sank within minutes. *Laffey* had escaped harm because the Germans had planted a pressure mine that was set to permit the first vessel to pass by unharmed while detonating with the approach of a second ship. "After this you never knew if you were safe, even if the path had been cleared," said Sonarman Zack. "Mines were a huge concern because every night German planes dropped more."[41]

The weapons exacted a bloody toll at Utah Beach. On June 6 the USS *Corry* (DD-463) struck a mine and sank, taking twenty-two men to their deaths. The next day a second mine ripped a huge hole in the minesweeper, USS *Tide* (AM-125) and lifted her out of the water as she cleared lanes for fire support ships, killing her commanding officer. The troopship USS *Susan B. Anthony* (AP-72), sustained forty-five wounded when she struck a mine and sank. On June 8 the destroyer USS *Glennon* (DD-620) lost twenty-five dead and thirty-eight wounded to a mine, then three other mines ripped off the stern of the USS *Rich* (DE-695) as she maneuvered alongside to assist the sinking *Glennon*, killing almost one hundred crew.

The loss of the *Meredith*—their sister ship, one of the original five destroyers comprising Destroyer Division 119, and the sixth ship to be lost off Utah Beach to mines in three days—most affected the *Laffey* crew, however. *Meredith* struck a mine on June 7 while screening other vessels, losing seven dead and more than fifty wounded. She remained afloat for two days, when a German plane planted a bomb that broke the destroyer in two. The loss of a ship that had been constructed at Bath, Maine, and carried the same identifying features as *Laffey*, was not easily forgotten, and forced Fern and the others to realize how slim was the gap between living and dying in combat.

The other threat, E-boats, often left their anchorage at Cherbourg for nighttime forays against Allied shipping and to lay additional mines. Usually operating in groups of five to seventeen boats, the Germans followed a failed raid the night of June 8–9 with a second on June 11 in which with a single torpedo they sank the fleet tug, USS *Partridge* (AM-16), killing thirty-two men.

Becton was proud of his crew's first week in combat. By June 9 they had provided so much fire support for the troops ashore that the ammunition rooms were almost empty. That afternoon, when Becton informed the Commander Task Group 125.8 that his ship had expended eighty percent of her shells, the commander ordered *Laffey*, after firing a few farewell salvos, to leave the line and return to England for replenishment. Within hours her relief ship, the USS *Shubrick* (DD-639), drew close aboard so the *Laffey* could pass along any information about mines and shore batteries, and *Laffey* was on her way back to England.

"The last week I've been sleeping at my Battle Station," Seaman Fern wrote his mother about his first week off Normandy. "We've seen a little action but nothing important or unusual. Some of the boys are speculating already on when we'll get back."[42]

Becton did not share Fern's optimism about steaming to the United States. When *Laffey* left at dawn on June 10 for her return trip to England, the captain knew that the respite from combat would last only as long as it took to replenish her ammunition and fuel supply for continued action off Normandy. It was simpler to send a destroyer back to England for supplies than to transport those materials to Normandy, and the four and one-half hour trip across the Channel only briefly took a ship out of the action.

Later that Saturday afternoon Becton steered the ship into Plymouth, where the crew spent the rest of the day refueling and loading ammunition. Sailors formed a long line from the ship to shell storage facilities near the shore. "Guys were handing shells from man to man," said Seaman Dockery, "passing shells to the ship."[43] When they remained in Plymouth overnight to avoid making a night voyage back to Normandy, Becton rewarded his crew for what he considered their outstanding performance the previous four days. Instead of the usual fare, he ordered steak for everyone. The unexpected feast, plus resting for the moment on the calmer side of the Channel, gave everyone in the crew the chance to enjoy a breather from the war.

After a welcome respite, on Sunday morning *Laffey* again set course for France. When she arrived off Normandy later that day, Becton positioned the destroyer at her screening station and ordered everyone to battle stations. E-boat warnings had been posted for the Western Task Force area. That night he observed 40mm gunfire and star shells to the north and east, and concluded that those E-boat alerts might draw the ship into action.

Laffey's first experience with combat was over. Round two was about to begin.

CHAPTER 3

TO THE PACIFIC

A call came from Cherbourg
That said "How about a hand?
We need a diversion from their 88s."
So we sailed right into their harbor
And opened the gates.
  —"An Ode to the USS *Laffey* (DD-724),"
  Gunner's Mate Owen Radder

June 13–24: E-Boats and Patrols

"As Yet Nothing Has Happened to Me"

The chaos and violence of the June 6 landings had receded, enabling Phoutrides and others to enjoy the quiet offered by the night of June 11–12. Becton had placed the ship in position on the Dixie Line near the intersection of Omaha and Utah Beaches. One mile to the northwest, the destroyer USS *Nelson* (DD-623) prowled the waters, while the USS *Somers* (DD-381) guarded the east. Becton and the other skippers told their crews to be alert for E-boats, but nothing as yet had disturbed the stillness.

A contact five miles out at shortly after midnight interrupted the calm. The radar crew at first thought that a small cloud created the image on their screen, but as the image drew nearer, it split into five or six smaller blips. Becton immediately turned *Laffey* toward the contact and alerted his gun crews to stand by to illuminate the area with star shells.

Fifteen minutes later Becton ordered his forward mounts to fire the star shells. When the *Nelson* started shelling the contacts, now positively identified as E-boats, the German craft launched their torpedoes, reversed course, and increased speed. One minute later *Nelson* reported over voice radio that a torpedo had blown off her fantail and that she needed a tow to Portsmouth for repairs.

Becton jumped to the chase. *Laffey* sliced through choppy waters at thirty-two knots, with Becton altering the heading so that *Laffey* offered "as small a torpedo target as possible." Even though he gave what he termed "repeated orders to control to open fire"[1] over phones and loudspeaker, for some reason Lieutenant Burns's guns remained silent. When Becton brusquely asked him to explain the delay, Burns replied that he had not been given the proper bearing and range on the targets. Becton ordered his CIC to supply the gun crews with the needed information and finally, eight minutes after the pursuit began, the forward guns responded. Gun 51 illuminated the area with star shells while Gun 52, the other forward five-inch gun, pumped high-explosive rounds at the enemy. They fired for nine minutes, until the enemy craft veered so close to a friendly southbound convoy that Becton reluctantly ceased fire rather than risk hitting Allied shipping.

Though Becton lost contact with the E-boats, he crisscrossed the area for seventy-five minutes in hopes of locating the elusive foe. After an unsuccessful search, the screen commander ordered Becton to halt the pursuit and return *Laffey* to her screening station.

Laffey's two forward guns had fired forty-five star shells and seventy-five five-inch rounds in the action. Though disappointed with the tardy reaction from his forward mounts, Becton concluded that the ship's five-inch shells broke up their formation and probably caused some damage because "the single strong radar pip at which we were firing broke into two very weak pips and the targets slowed considerably."[2]

When Becton investigated the delay in opening fire, he found that during the heated action the flow of transmissions, both from within the ship and from other ships, multiplied, thus slowing the men who relayed those messages to the bridge and gun mounts. Consequently, the gunnery officer failed to receive Becton's message about being ready with star shells. When he finally learned the skipper's wishes, the gun crew had to hurriedly unload the hoists, bring up star shells, and properly reload the forward mount, all while an impatient Becton waited.

To remedy the mishap, Becton stated that in the future he would send messages to the gunnery and engineering officers over the captain's command circuit and would require acknowledgement from them in return. Henceforward, one forward mount was to be ready with star shells while the other stood prepared with AA common ammunition, and each day before dark the gunnery officer was to deliver a precise account of the number and type of ammunition at each mount.

The crew settled into a routine during the week of June 13–19. Each day *Laffey* screened for the battleships and cruisers that provided gun support for the forces ashore, and each night they kept watch for E-boats. "I am feeling fine and as yet nothing has happened to me," wrote Seaman Fern to his parents on June 19. "Every night for the last two weeks I've had to sleep on the deck outside my G.Q. [general quarters] station." He joked that in the moments off duty, he and his buddies listened to German radio. "Every night about 8 o'clock we've been listening to a propaganda program. Ow— is it corny—inane songs and ditties and such 'cracks' they make about us. They make a big play on the homesick angle."[3]

On one occasion Becton rushed to the aid of a fellow ship under heavy fire from an accurate German battery. Becton maneuvered *Laffey* near the destroyer to draw fire from the distressed ship, which impressed his men. "He saw something that he could do to help, and he did it," said Sonarman Zack. "The crew talked about it and complimented him when they said that he put us in harm's way to help someone else, something we'd want from another ship if we were in that spot."[4]

The worst storm in four decades lashed Normandy on June 19. Northeast winds gusting to thirty-two knots combined with torrential rains to halt the unloading of crucial supplies for the next three days. When the storm finally abated on June 22, supply crates and wrecked landing craft littered the beaches.

With the storm diminishing, during the evening of June 21 Becton left for England to again replenish his fuel and ammunition supply. He anchored *Laffey* in Portland the next morning, at which time part of the crew rigged fuel lines while others filled the ship's magazines with ammunition.

Those who hoped for time ashore were disappointed, as the ship was again needed off Normandy. Infantry advancing toward Cherbourg had encountered stiff opposition from German artillery batteries and forty thousand defenders. To eliminate the resistance, the Army turned to the Navy's big guns. *Laffey*, fuel tanks and ammunition magazines full, left England for another round of combat off France.

June 25: Action off Cherbourg

"You Never Know When You Are the Target"

The tardy progress against Cherbourg alarmed the Supreme Allied Commander, General Dwight D. Eisenhower. He needed the deepwater port of Cherbourg and its complex of docks, piers, and railroads to maintain his fragile hold in Normandy and to prepare for a major breakout into the heart of France. The June storm made it more imperative for him to possess ports in France.

When the United States infantry reached Cherbourg's perimeter, they ran into stalwart enemy defenses that ringed the city. Infantry now paid for the advance, measured in yards rather than miles, with their limbs and lives, and by the night of June 24 they faced a protracted struggle to break into the city.

On June 25 *Laffey*, escorting the battleships USS *Texas* (BB-35) and USS *Arkansas* (BB-33) and accompanied by four other destroyers, steamed toward Cherbourg as part of Bombardment Group 2 under Rear Admiral C. F. Bryant. Near noon *Laffey*'s unit, as well as the eleven ships of Bombardment Group 1, arrived fifteen miles off Cherbourg and prepared for a ninety-minute bombardment of the twenty coastal batteries protecting the port city. Bombardment Group 1 targeted the batteries west of Cherbourg as *Laffey* and Bombardment Group 2 faced Battery Hamburg, a formidable array of guns six miles east of the city comprising the most powerful artillery in the Cotentin Peninsula. Steel shields similar to naval gun turrets, reinforced by concrete casemates, protected four massive eleven-inch guns. On their flanks, antiaircraft guns were poised to add to their firepower. To execute their mission, *Laffey* and other destroyers had to place themselves within range of those powerful batteries, an unsettling thought for the crews as their ships entered the harbor.

The battleships opened fire thirty minutes past noon. As enemy shells splashed nearby, *Laffey* and her companions maneuvered in plain view of the French coast, their guns pouring salvo after salvo at land targets. The German batteries responded by firing first on the destroyers closer to shore, and then switching to the larger ships. Battery Hamburg churned the waters about

Laffey, causing Lieutenant Youngquist and others to wonder if the next shell would crash into the ship. "The Germans had the harbor gridded," said Lieutenant Youngquist, "and shells were splashing all around us. It was scary."[5]

"We were between the battleships and the shore," added Seaman Johnson. "We felt pretty vulnerable. The Germans opened up on us, and you saw the water sprouts and the shells overhead. We were just waiting to see if they would get us."[6]

Four ships near *Laffey*, including *Texas*, sustained hits. A salvo of shells struck *Barton*, stationed just ahead of *Laffey*. Becton maneuvered to avoid the oncoming shells, and, two minutes later, successfully evaded another salvo that struck dangerously close to the bow. "It was quite a feeling to look toward the shoreline and see that black spot coming toward you," said Gunner's Mate Delewski. Even if they hit short, "the shells frequently skipped like stones thrown across the pond"[7] directly toward *Laffey*.

A few moments later a shell splashed off the port bow, drowning the deck with water and rocking the ship, "just as if a giant's hand had smacked the water."[8] In the commotion of what everyone assumed was a near miss, no one noticed that the shell ricocheted into the side of the destroyer above the waterline just forward of the anchor and punctured the hull. Fortunately, it failed to detonate before coming to rest in the tight confines of the boatswain's locker belowdecks.

Becton had his hands full trying to evade the oncoming missiles. Watching from his post near the skipper, Phoutrides assumed Becton would turn the ship seaward, but instead the quartermaster held his breath as Becton adopted a course shoreward toward the battery. "I thought Becton was crazy and was going to get us all killed," he recalled. "I wanted to be headed in the opposite direction, out to sea." Phoutrides expected a rain of shells to slam down on the inbound destroyer, but instead the next German salvo cracked over their heads and splashed "right where the ship would have been where I wanted, going out to sea. *That* [emphasis Phoutrides's] was the moment I had full confidence in the skipper." When Phoutrides later asked Becton about his maneuvering, the skipper explained that he figured the German battery would expect Becton to retreat seaward and would send their next salvo farther out. Instead, he did the opposite. "He had probably thought all this out beforehand," said Phoutrides of his captain. "He didn't brag about it to me, just mentioned it. He was a very modest man."[9]

When spotters aboard *Laffey* observed flashes from the beach, Becton ordered his five-inch guns to take out the positions. For the next twelve minutes *Laffey* and other destroyers engaged in a spirited duel with the German batteries, their shells stitching a crisscross pattern in the sky.

Inside Mount 52, the second forward five-inch gun, Seaman Dockery watched the dials that regulated gun elevation and estimated the distance from the ship to the target. Fellow crew grabbed powder and shells from storage directly below and hoisted them to men inside with Dockery, who loaded them into the guns. When the pointer and trainer had properly positioned the gun, a gunner's mate opened fire. After the first few shells, the mount crew developed a steady rhythm, blocking out the sounds of battle and the fears that come with war as they pumped shells toward shore. Operating in a closed mount, they could see neither the damage their shells caused nor any incoming German shells, but they were too focused on their tasks to think much about it. Besides, if a German battery had their number, there was little they could do about it anyway.

During the action a German salvo crashed into *O'Brien*'s bridge, damaging the CIC and causing thirty-three casualties. "I wasn't so nonchalant," said then-eighteen-year-old Seaman "Doc" Brown of witnessing *Laffey*'s sister ship sustain damage. "I started thinking, 'This is real.'"[10]

After a heated exchange with Battery Hamburg, *Laffey* ceased firing to assist the battleships. While *Laffey* and the destroyers distracted the German batteries, the damaged *Texas* and the *Arkansas* retreated to the northeast and began the short trip back to England. After securing the safety of the battleships, *Laffey* pulled away from France and enjoyed her first calm moments of the morning.

Laffey and the other ships of Group 2 fired 816 shells at Battery Hamburg, knocking out one of the four main guns. Their performance weakened German resistance and enabled American infantry to register significant gains that helped them take Cherbourg two days later.

Rear Admiral Bryant in the battleship *Texas* sent a congratulatory message to *Laffey* and the other destroyers. "Your conduct today has been exemplary. Were it not for your prompt assistance in covering us at crucial moments we would have been severely damaged. The batteries firing at us were particularly accurate and powerful. Yet not one of you flinched. In fact you were willing to press home the attack. Well done to you all."[11]

In his action report Captain William L. Freseman, Commander of DesRon 60, concluded that *Laffey* "in a most courageous manner interposed herself between our task group and the enemy shore batteries and continued firing on the shore batteries in spite of their superior fire power, until the minesweepers and battleships, screened by the *Hobson* and *Plunkett*, had drawn out of range." Freseman added that *Laffey* covered the retirement of the battleships by purposely remaining close to shore and diverting the German battery's attention from the battleships, "despite the heavy and accurate fire which was then being delivered against our task group."[12]

"For Christ's Sake, Get It Out!"

Cherbourg's shell between the eyes
Didn't cut her down to size.
Intact shell tossed oversides.
   —"Invicta," Lieutenant Matthew Darnell

From his time with the *Ward* in the Pacific, Becton remembered vividly the damage that near misses could cause. As *Laffey* left Cherbourg behind, Becton ordered damage control parties to inspect the ship thoroughly. No one yet knew of the unexploded shell that had lodged itself in the cramped boatswain's locker in the bow, but he was concerned that one of the many near misses might have damaged the ship and allowed seawater to gush through a yet-undiscovered hole below the waterline.

Electrician's Mate 3/c Leonard B. Miller Jr. remembered that during one near miss, a meter checking the degaussing cable had suddenly plunged to zero. The cable, which ran lengthwise inside the hull, was supposed to reduce the magnetic force of the destroyer so that it would not trigger German magnetic mines. Miller informed Chief Electrician's Mate Albert Csiszar, who started aft and worked his way forward, carefully checking the cable for damage. When he came to the boatswain's locker, which was almost even with the ship's waterline, Csiszar climbed down, opened the door to the small room, and was promptly hit with a wall of water. "I opened the door to a little locker, a closet, and got a bath," recalled Csiszar. "There was a big shell in there."[13]

Csiszar stared as Channel water gushed through a hole in the port bulkhead. Resting on its nose amidst the water was a 240mm shell, three feet long, 9.6 inches in diameter, and weighing more than four hundred pounds. The shell had opened a four-foot hole in the port side, a smaller hole on the starboard side, and cracked the main deck above the locker. Csiszar, who knew the shell could slice off the ship's bow if it exploded and ignited some of

Laffey's five-inch ammunition, relayed the information to Becton. When he learned of the dud, Becton hurriedly replied, "for Christ's sake, get it out!"[14]

Csiszar and one other man inched inside the confined locker and nudged the shell to where others could lend a hand. He and Lieutenant Samuel Humphries, the damage control officer, rigged hoisting gear to carefully lift the shell through the hatches to the main deck, where they would toss the shell overboard. While they worked, Becton reduced *Laffey*'s speed and avoided unnecessary course changes to eliminate sudden movements that could strain the hoisting gear or ignite the bomb. "One little slip, one little jar could have set the thing off," wrote Becton, "and no one dared breathe until that monster finally stood on the main deck."[15]

The men brought the shell up and stood it on the main deck. Csiszar and Humphries, joined by Lieutenant E. J. Samp Jr., Electrician's Mate 1/c Claude E. Scott, and Chief Boatswain's Mate H. Lewis, gently dropped the shell over the side, praying that the impact against the water would not set it off, and watched the shell disappear beneath the surface. The repair party placed canvas over the hole to temporarily prevent additional water from entering the ship until *Laffey* returned to England for more extensive work.

"A Conspicuous Display of Courage"

The German garrison at Cherbourg surrendered on June 27. Allied units quickly invested the city and its port facilities, and by July 16 the first freight docked. From that point on an uninterrupted flow of supplies coursed from Great Britain, though Cherbourg, and on to Allied armies sweeping across France. By autumn Cherbourg was second only to Marseilles in southern France as a logistics port for US land forces in Europe.

For the Navy, the success had been gained at the cost of fourteen dead and thirty-five wounded, most sustained aboard the *O'Brien*. More than half the ships, including *Laffey*, had been hit or showered by shell fragments, but only three vessels were badly damaged.

Army commanders credited the naval force with giving the Army an opportunity to advance into the city. Lieutenant Colonel Fred P. Campbell, liaison officer from VII Corps, said every officer believed the bombardment broke the back of the German defense of Cherbourg. "I took a look for myself," he wrote to Rear Admiral Morton Deyo, "and am convinced that you did tremendous damage to those batteries. Some were never active after the bombardment, and still pointed out to sea when the city fell, even though they could have been turned." General Eisenhower concluded, "the final assault was materially assisted by heavy and accurate naval gunfire."[16]

Soviet dictator Joseph Stalin congratulated President Roosevelt on liberating Cherbourg. *New York Times* military correspondent Hanson Baldwin called June 25 a red-letter day for the Navy and labeled the operation "as gallant as it was risky." He claimed, "the fall of Cherbourg last week was a great strategical victory for the Allies" because it guaranteed an avenue of supplies for the infantry, forced the Germans to abandon the peninsula, and ensured that the Normandy foothold begun June 6 would endure. Baldwin said the seizure negated Germany's strategy, "which for the last year and a half has been devoted to one end and one end only—thorough and final repulse of the Allied invasion of western Europe."[17]

German leaders came to similar conclusions, about Cherbourg as well as the overall naval contribution to Allied success at Normandy. A German military publication commented shortly after the Normandy combat, "the fire support provided by the guns of the Navy so far proved to be one of the best trump cards of the Anglo-United States invasion Armies. It may be that the part played by the Fleet was more decisive than that of the air forces because its fire was better aimed and unlike the bomber formations it had not to confine itself to short 'Bursts of Fire.'" The publication continued that, even though the invading Allied troops had little artillery on the ground at their disposal, the fleet easily handled the deficiency by bringing overwhelming fire support. Additionally, their mobility at sea allowed them to concentrate that firepower at almost any location desired. "It would be utterly wrong to underestimate the fire power of warships even of smaller vessels,"[18] continued the German publication, explaining that even destroyers, such as the *Laffey*, possessed a punch equivalent to a battery of artillery.

Laffey's gun crews fired 121 rounds of five-inch shells at Battery Hamburg, second only to *O'Brien*'s 192 shells of the seven Group 2 ships. After a shaky performance on June 12 against the E-boats, the communications issues that plagued the ship off Normandy had been resolved, and Becton and his officers encountered no further problems sending and receiving messages to the gun crews and elsewhere throughout the ship.

Captain Freseman wrote that *Laffey*'s fire support "indicates an outstanding performance while subjected to enemy gunfire, and while underway in waters heavily mined." Admiral Deyo wrote that he "cannot praise too highly the outstanding performance of the *Laffey* during this [Cherbourg] action," and added that he was more impressed with *Laffey* and the other ships of

DesDiv 119 because those vessels "had very recently finished their shake-down period and their performance is considered most creditable."[19]

Freseman singled out Becton for additional praise, citing Becton's calm leadership and bravery as instrumental in the ship's success. "In spite of one dud hit, many straddles, and near misses, the *Laffey* gave a conspicuous display of courage and intrepidity in face of superior enemy batteries."[20] Ignoring the inherent risks, Becton placed his ship between Battery Hamburg and the American bombardment force to divert fire, and remained close to shore engaging the enemy until the minesweepers and battleships could retire. Becton received a Gold Star in lieu of a second Silver Star for his actions off France.

After the war Becton attended a meeting of officers. He was pleasantly surprised when an Army officer stepped over to him, gave him a warm hug, and thanked Becton for the support *Laffey* had given to his troops as they slugged their way through rigorous German defenses. The officer stated that *Laffey*'s work had made theirs easier.

Becton was more proud of the tributes that came from his men. Facing combat for the first time, as was the case for most of *Laffey*'s crew, magnifies fears and self-doubts. During the month of June 1944, first off Normandy's beaches and then off Cherbourg, Becton's calm demeanor, courage, and poise breathed confidence throughout the crew. Any doubts that a sailor or an officer harbored about Becton were eradicated by his actions off France. "Our complete faith in him was established firmly at the bombardment of Cherbourg a few days after the Invasion of France," wrote Quartermaster Phoutrides, who now had the proof he wanted about Becton. "He was one of the few officers I truly respected."[21] Phoutrides's respect grew with each ensuing action involving the destroyer.

That faith and confidence transformed *Laffey* from a loose collection of inexperienced individuals to a unified crew. By performing capably in their initial combat, the crew concluded that they could trust the man making those wrenching decisions that meant the difference between returning to loved ones or perishing on distant waters. He, in turn, could trust them.

"Everything seemed to run smoothly," said Seaman Johnson. "Everyone stepped up and did what needed to be done. I assume most of the crew, as this was their first encounter with the enemy, was proud of what they did and what the ship did." Johnson also discovered that in the thick of the fight, he could control his emotions and carry out his responsibilities. "You never know when you're a target, but you block it out and do your tasks, do what you needed to do. That helped me later in the Pacific."[22]

Normandy handed the crew the experience it needed to face the future. Each time they took a German battery under fire or screened for a cruiser, they gained added confidence and expertise. "The more you do something," said Seaman Dockery, "the better you are." Johnson, part of a starboard 40mm gun crew, believed the *Laffey* was commissioned at the perfect time. Before racing to the Pacific they were able to participate in the Normandy landings and off Cherbourg, where they gained valuable knowledge that they later utilized in the bitter Pacific fighting. "It was an opportunity to get training and experience that helped us later in the Pacific. An inexperienced crew benefited from Normandy. It learned the ropes."[23]

"From what I saw, I had more confidence in Becton, the officers, and the crew," said Lieutenant Youngquist. "Thus, I knew I didn't have to worry. They knew what they were doing. That's a good frame of mind for someone going to the Pacific."[24] That assurance, in themselves and in Becton, would pay dividends in subsequent actions. The officers and enlisted emerged from Normandy a better crew than the one that entered combat. Service off France sowed dividends that would be reaped in the Pacific.

Besides, *Laffey* was developing the reputation for enjoying a charmed life. Two ships in their division had been damaged, with one sunk, yet the only shell that hit *Laffey* failed to explode. Furthermore, the ship had suffered no casualties during the Normandy operation. Crew began to think that they were blessed by serving aboard a lucky ship. "It made you feel good that all went well," said Sonarman Zack, whose battle station was switched after Normandy to Mount 52, the second five-inch gun forward. "We had good luck with the dud and with the plane barely missing us. That helped us in the Pacific."[25]

As they later discovered, they would need that help.

"To Panama & Points West"

> *After taking a trip*
> *Through the Panama Canal*
> *We headed west*
> *To give Tojo hell.*
> —"An Ode to the USS *Laffey* (DD-724),"
> Gunner's Mate Owen Radder

Laffey remained in Portland from June 25 to June 29, at which time she and the other ships of DesDiv 119, accompanied by two battleships and two cruisers, departed for Belfast, Ireland. As that port was the embarkation point for ships returning to the United States, the crew hoped it meant a lengthy sojourn with family before leaving on their next assignment.

During the morning of July 3, the four ships of DesDiv 119—*Laffey*, *Barton*, *O'Brien*, and *Walke*—formed a column and moved north away from Ireland. As soon as the Emerald Isle receded, Becton announced over the ship's PA system their destination: Boston. Crew cheered the news, which meant they could rejoin family and friends and enjoy a welcome respite from the war. Fireman 1/c Wilbert C. Gauding, who kept a diary—against Navy regulations—scribbled simply, "Homeward bound."[26]

The jubilation was not surprising. Only days before, they had successfully completed a transformative month of combat against Hitler's Atlantic Wall. The inexperienced officers and enlisted who had left the United States returned home as combat veterans brimming with confidence.

The Normandy training ground, intense as it was, foreshadowed the rigors of Pacific combat. The men would not be as cavalier if they knew of a meeting occurring at almost the same hour on the other side of the world. On the day *Laffey* left European waters and Becton announced to his crew that they were going home, Japan set in motion the development of a terrifying instrument of war that would within ten months turn its full fury on Becton, Lieutenant Youngquist, Seaman Fern, and the rest of the crew.

"You Cannot Hope for Survival"

On Iwo Jima, a part of the Volcano Islands chain eight hundred miles south of Tokyo, Commander Tadashi Nakajima addressed the officers of the Yokosuka Air Wing. Sub-Lieutenant Saburo Sakai, who would become Japan's leading ace, noticed that Nakajima seemed upset. He had reason to be. American bombers had unceasingly pounded Japanese air installations on Iwo Jima, and Hellcat fighters had shot down their aircraft in record numbers until all that remained of a once powerful air arm were nine fighters and eight bombers.

Nakajima told the assembled group that he and the staff officers had argued through the night about what action to take against the numerically superior Americans. One faction pled for more aggressive moves, such as a strike against an American task force 450 miles south-southeast of Iwo Jima. A second group doubted that any action with seventeen aircraft would prove effective.

The Iwo Wing Commander, Captain Kanzo Miura, settled the argument. No matter how outnumbered they were, the time for timidity was over. He planned to lead a strike against the Americans later in the day, believing that an attack on what would then be July 4, Independence Day, in the United States, would be an appropriate way to deliver a "holiday greeting." The group agreed, even though they realized it meant almost certain death for the pilots in those seventeen aircraft.

Nakajima told Sakai and the others, "I realize what we are sending you out to do. There is no use in my saying otherwise; you will be flying to almost certain death. But, the decision has already been made. You will go." He then recited the names of those selected, including that of the revered Sakai, who would lead the formation of nine Zeros.

Captain Miura told the pilots that the time had come to supplant passive tactics. "You will strike back at the enemy. From now on our defensive battles are over." He added, "you cannot, I repeat, you cannot hope for survival. Your minds must be on the word attack!" He explained that "you must dive against the enemy carriers together! Dive—along with your torpedoes and your lives and your souls."

As an astonished Sakai listened, Miura said, "I know that what I tell you to do is difficult. It may even seem impossible. But I trust that you can do it, that you will do it. That every man among you will plunge directly into an enemy carrier and sink the vessel."

The gifted Sakai had flown many missions and was on his way to shooting down sixty-four Allied aircraft, but he had never been given such explicit orders. "We had been sent out before this on missions where our chances of survival seemed hopelessly remote. But at least we had the chance to fight for our lives! This was the first time a Japanese pilot had actually been *ordered* to make a suicide attack." It had been an unwritten code in the Japanese navy that once a plane was crippled and the pilot had no hope of returning to his base, he would attempt to dive on an enemy warship rather than simply disappear at sea. "But no Japanese air commander had ever told his men, 'Go out and die!'"

Despite his misgivings, Sakai noticed that Miura's words moved the pilots. "Now that they *knew* they would never return, the men took on an air of determination. Their lives were no longer to be wasted. The sacrifice of their small number would be more than compensated for by the loss of one or more huge enemy ships, possibly causing the death of thousands of Americans."[27]

When the nine fighter pilots, including their commander, Sakai, paced toward the airfield, they looked at their parachutes, glanced at each other, and in unison tossed the packs onto the volcanic ash beside the runway. As the pilots prepared for takeoff, mechanics and support staff stood at attention on both sides of the runway, then waved handkerchiefs as the aircraft gained speed and lifted off.

The first purposely planned kamikaze mission of the war failed. Before the Japanese spotted a US warship, sixty American Hellcat fighters jumped on the group and sent twelve aircraft in flames to the ocean. Sakai continued to search for the American carriers, but unable to locate the fleet before darkness approached, turned back to Iwo Jima.

The raid, which was conducted without the knowledge of superior officers, was not reported to the Japanese high command. Since neither the American Hellcats nor their carriers knew that the planes had been dispatched as suicide aircraft, no special mention was recorded in American records at the time. As far as they were concerned, they had merely deflected another enemy attack.

The raid was more than another routine mission, though. It represented a shift toward desperate tactics as the war soured for the Japanese. Six months of triumphs followed the December 7, 1941, strike against United States ships and installations at Pearl Harbor as the Japanese seized Wake Island, Guam, Singapore, Hong Kong, the Philippines, and other Pacific locations. However, at Midway in June 1942, a crushing naval reverse against the Americans commenced a downward spiral for the Japanese that continued even as the *Laffey* fought at Normandy. A bitter defeat at Guadalcanal in the Solomon Islands northeast of Australia started a Japanese retreat in the South Pacific, while American advances against the Gilbert and Marshall Islands opened a path through the Central Pacific toward Tokyo. Nine days after *Laffey* and the other Allied units opened the June 6 assault against Hitler, US forces swarmed ashore at Saipan in the Marianas. Four days later the US Navy delivered another crushing defeat of the Imperial Japanese Navy, and especially her air arm, in the Battle of the Philippine Sea. The far-flung Japanese Empire fashioned with speedy triumphs rapidly crumbled against the numerically superior United States military, which benefited from the vast resources then gushing out of American factories.

In May 1944 Japan's Supreme War Guidance Council, cognizant of the costly losses, decided that drastic measures had to be taken if they were to halt the US military then churning through the Pacific toward Japan. Though it did not mention suicide aircraft by name, the council's willingness to consider revolutionary notions created an atmosphere of acceptance for any and every idea. On June 25, the same day the *Laffey* opened fire against Battery Hamburg at Cherbourg, the Japanese emperor lent his approval to extreme steps when his spokesperson, Prince Fushima, urged military leaders to think creatively. Without mentioning suicidal measures by name, Fushima said that "both the army and navy must think up some special weapons and conduct the war with them. This is urgent. Now that the war situation has reached this difficult stage, special aircraft, warships, and small vessels need to be deployed and quickly used."[28]

The military turned to an array of devices, including bomb-laden balloons that drifted to the American West Coast and explosive-packed small boats that crashed into enemy ships. In late June 1944 Captain Eiichiro Jyo, the commander of the light carrier, *Chiyoda*, upped the ante by urging the creation of special units employing crash-diving techniques. In his opinion, normal air and land tactics had lost their relevance in light of the defeats absorbed on all fronts. Lacking the industrial capacity to match the outpouring of ammunition, aircraft, and ships that came from US factories, Japan had to make every weapon count. "No longer can we hope to sink the numerically superior enemy aircraft carriers through ordinary attack methods. I urge the immediate organization of special attack units to carry out crash-dive tactics, and I ask to be placed in command of them."[29]

Jyo's military record—his courage was legendary among the men in his air units—gave prestige to the notion of utilizing suicide tactics. Japan's high command was willing to examine different proposals, but more calamitous events, such as the loss of the Philippines, would have to occur before they turned to organized suicide units as part of their scheme.

"Proceeding Singly Enroute to Pearl Harbor"

While developments intensified in the Pacific, back in the Atlantic, after a month filled with combat, the *Laffey* crew enjoyed the more leisurely pace of the six-day trip home. Becton celebrated July 4, the day Captain Miura organized the unsuccessful suicide attack, by conducting gunnery practice, with five-inch and 40mm shells more than adequately substituting for fireworks.

On July 6 Becton conducted an awards ceremony at which he handed out letters of commendation to those officers and crew who performed with distinction off Normandy. In addition to the five who removed the unexploded shell, Becton singled out his executive officer, Lieutenant Charles Holovak, Chief Gunner's Mate Norman Fitzgerald, Chief Engineer Al Henke, and Steward's Mate 2/c Henry Teague.

The seas turned nasty the next day with *Laffey* nearing Newfoundland. Waves buffeted the sides and wind snapped the pennants flying on the yard-arm, giving the helmsman all he could handle to keep the ship on course. Men who had yet to become seasick now joined their brethren who already had, and sailors inside Mount 52 bailed out water three feet deep by the bucketful. "The waves made us think the ship was a toy," said Sonarman Zack. "We had never been tossed around like this."[30]

On July 9 the unit entered the Boston Navy Yard at Charleston, Massachusetts, where the ship was scheduled to undergo a month of repairs and alterations to the bridge and superstructure, including cleaning and painting the bottom, and installing improved sonar gear and fire control radar. During that time Becton divided the crew into two groups, retaining one aboard *Laffey* while the other enjoyed a ten-day leave.

Becton kept one man behind. The same day that *Laffey* pulled into Massachusetts, Lieutenant Holovak reported a sailor for being disrespectful toward a superior officer and for disobeying orders. As the man had already amassed a troublesome record—Becton had twice placed him on bread and water for prior infractions—Becton turned to a more severe penalty. He ordered Lieutenant Holovak to convene a summary court martial, at which three court officers found him guilty. They assessed a fine, gave him a bad-conduct discharge, and sent the man to the Navy Yard brig pending completion of his papers.

Becton considered the fine appropriate, but feared that the discharge, which would go on his record and follow the man for the rest of his life, was too harsh. Becton summoned the sailor to his cabin, and when the remorseful sailor promised to improve, Becton trusted his instincts and allowed him to remain. He cautioned, however, that he had used up his final chance. Becton retained the fine, but remitted the discharge pending good behavior for one year. To Becton's pleasure, the man became one of the most valued members of the crew.

After dealing with these matters Becton traveled to New York City to see Imogen Carpenter, who in his absence had performed at war bond shows in New York City with Louis Prima and the Mills Brothers. He returned by August 8, when *Laffey* began seventeen days of sea trials to test the alterations. On August 24 *Laffey* was underway for Norfolk, where the next day she moored at the naval base to prepare for departure for the Panama Canal and Pacific combat.

Seaman Fern, facing a lengthy sojourn at sea, wrote his mother and asked that she send the Sunday cartoon strips, humorous books, writing paper, envelopes, and boxes of Band-Aids. "You may wonder why I ask for this but I think when we leave the states again it will be for quite a while."[31]

"We're going to move today about 3:00 this afternoon—going to Panama & points west,"[32] Seaman Fern wrote his mother on August 26, announcing that *Laffey* was on her way to the Pacific. At 3:56, less than an hour from Fern's guess, *Laffey* weighed anchor and left Norfolk as part of Task Unit 20.17.7, consisting of *Laffey* and the dock landing ship, USS *Shadwell* (LSD-15). As senior officer, Becton was designated the commander of the task unit.

For the next five days the two vessels steamed south toward the Canal Zone. Each day Becton conducted antiaircraft firing exercises to sharpen his gun crews, for they now steamed to a theater of war where, unlike France, they were certain to encounter air attacks. "We had training exercises all the time," said Quartermaster Phoutrides. "That should be a part of what every skipper does, but not all do. Becton focused on it."[33]

In the sweltering afternoon heat on September 1, the *Laffey* entered Limon Bay, the harbor at the Canal Zone's Atlantic terminus, and proceeded on the short journey through the famous canal. Most of the crew had never seen the engineering wonder, and men eagerly flocked to the deck to marvel at the locks that raised and lowered the ship and to see the tropical jungles that enclosed much of the route. At 9:15 p.m. *Laffey* reached the Pacific end and anchored at Balboa, Canal Zone, where Becton granted liberty to any man who wanted it.

During the morning of September 2 the ship refueled while Lieutenant Youngquist supervised the loading of stores and ammunition, and then shortly before evening departed with two other destroyers for San Diego, California, her final stop before turning west toward Hawaii. Becton again ordered antiaircraft drills for his gun crews, but also scheduled carrier screening exercises at least one hour each day for a crew that had never operated with aircraft carriers in a combat zone. In mid-morning of September 10 *Laffey* passed through the antisubmarine net gates into San Diego Harbor for two days of replenishment and preparation for departure.

"At 1405 [2:05 p.m.] on September 12, *Laffey* got underway, proceeding singly enroute to Pearl Harbor,"[34] described the ship's War Diary. *Laffey* steamed to Pacific combat alone, one ship leaving the United States to do what she could to help win the war. She took the first steps west toward an epic duel with Japanese pilots willing to sacrifice their lives to sink *Laffey*.

"We Had to Have Teamwork"

The six-day trip to Hawaii offered more of the same for the crew—watches and drills followed by drills and watches. "We had not heard a lot," Seaman Johnson said of Pacific combat. "Maybe about some of the sea battles, and that Japan had a tremendous navy. But we knew the Pacific would have more naval fighting than Europe."[35]

Laffey completed an uneventful trip when, midday on September 18, she passed through the antisubmarine net gates and moored in Pearl Harbor. The crew on deck witnessed a sobering sight as the ship inched by the sunken remnants of the December 7, 1941, attack, including the battleship USS *Arizona* (BB-39). In the vast ocean stretch between California and Hawaii, the war had recessed, but one look at the devastation brought the conflict front and center in stunning fashion.

The ship remained in Pearl Harbor until September 22 while the crew made repairs. For more than three weeks the ship drilled off Hawaii with other destroyers of DesDiv 119 to prepare for combat with an enemy that had in recent months intensified its aerial onslaught against American ships. The 20mm and 40mm crews had not faced enemy air attacks off France, but in the Pacific those crews would be severely tested. Becton scheduled as many exercises for those gun crews as time allowed.

In three different periods of time, interrupted by breaks in which the crew could enjoy Hawaii, *Laffey* operated with other destroyers in a series of drills. From September 22 to September 26, *Laffey* conducted torpedo firing and tracking exercises, spotting practice, night firing exercises, antisubmarine and radar exercises, and firing at targets in the water. Unlike previous exercises, where gun crews rarely expended more than fifty shells, the numbers now soared in direct proportion to the dangers they would soon face. On September 25, for instance, gun crews fired 771 shells, a number that rocketed to 3,437 shells on September 29, including 485 in night firing exercises.

"We stressed aerial gunnery and antiaircraft practice to get prepared for the Pacific," said Seaman Johnson. "Becton focused on this. We trained almost every day." The increased pace was not lost on the men, who assumed that danger would become a constant. "I'm sure it made me think about things," said Johnson. "When we got to the Philippines we knew why we needed them."[36]

Sonarman Zack's work at his new station at Mount 52 greatly differed from his duties in the sound room. In the gun mount, teamwork was constantly emphasized, for the failure of the crew here at any gun station about the ship to function smoothly would open a corridor in the ship's defenses through which the enemy could bring death and destruction.

"We were doing everything as if we were in battle, passing up the powder and ammunition," said Zack. "A plane was pulling a [target] sleeve, and the gunnery officer would call out which mount to fire." He and Gunner's Mate Owen "Glen" Radder had to maintain a constant stream of powder cans and shells if the crews in the mount above fired every three seconds. "The drills helped the men work as a team," said Zack. "We had to have teamwork. Like eating, you just do it without thinking, automatically. The more you do something, the better you get."[37]

Sweat covered Zack in the confined handling room below the mount, but at least he was not stationed on one of those 40mm or 20mm guns on deck. If the enemy did attack, those men were in the open, completely exposed to the Japanese bullets and shrapnel that Zack's mount would deflect.

On the forward 40mm starboard gun, Seaman Johnson and the other eight men attempted to duplicate with their smaller shells the same rhythm Delewski's Mount 52 team achieved with their five-inch shells. Ammunition passers handed the four-shell clips to loaders, who inserted them into the barrels. Two gunners, one on each side, pumped the rounds at targets as fast as the shells were shoved in.

"We had a lot of antiaircraft gunnery and shore bombardment," said Seaman Johnson. Becton had a purpose for everything, and back in his familiar Pacific haunts, he seemed driven to give his men every edge he could. "Becton knew from his previous trip that there would be a lot of air combat, so he gave extensive training to prepare for that. There wasn't as much air combat in Europe, but now we were facing a stronger air arm with the Japanese."[38]

Now aware of the looming threat from the air, the four men operating each 20mm machine gun welcomed the extra training. They stood as the last line of defense for *Laffey*, and if they failed to knock down an intruder, the plane was almost certain to crash into the destroyer.

By the time training ended October 18, Becton's gun crews regularly scored among the highest in their division, whether it was against sleeves pulled by aircraft or against surface targets. The gunners sometimes so thoroughly shredded the towed sleeves that the gun crews of other ships had to wait for new sleeves to be brought in, and Becton's gunners were designated the best in DesDiv 119. "Perhaps we would take some hits," Becton wrote. "But the Japs were going to pay very dearly to score them."[39] Although he would conduct drills as the ship journeyed west toward combat, he concluded that his men, especially his 20mm and 40mm antiaircraft guns, would perform capably when called on.

As usual, the religious Tom Fern kept his parents informed of his activities, at least as much as the censor would permit. He told them that, since they left Boston, he hadn't "been able to get off the ship for some time to go to Mass or to Confession. I wasn't able to get off today either because I couldn't get away from work." Understanding that he would soon leave Pearl Harbor for the Western Pacific, Fern ended with his usual best wishes before adding, "this may be the last letter for quite awhile. I've a hunch that we're going to leave soon so I'm going to close."[40]

Their days in Hawaii ended, however, as developments in the Pacific demanded their quick entry to war. Becton and his crew were about to join their naval brethren already fighting the Japanese in the Philippines, for on October 20 American forces landed on Leyte Island to commence the reconquest of the Philippines. Bitter combat, on land and at sea, would fill the coming months, and new weapons of warfare would make spectacular debuts.

"I Ask of You This Sacrifice"

Vice Admiral Takijiro Onishi, the Chief of the General Affairs Bureau of the Aviation Department in the Ministry of Munitions, would have much to say about *Laffey*'s fate. Unpopular with some senior officers because he so stubbornly advocated his views, Onishi cared little for personal glory. A naval aviator who started his career as an officer aboard a World War I sea-plane tender, Onishi wanted his navy to abandon reliance on battleships and cruisers and place its main effort in aircraft. He discounted as idiots those in the naval hierarchy who disagreed with him. "Replace the anchor mark of the navy with propellers," he said. "Turn the navy into an air force."[41]

Familiar with every type of aircraft in the navy, he knew more about planes and engines than most of his contemporaries. "He was fearless and undaunted, aggressive and full of fighting spirit," said Captain Rikihei Ino-guchi, a senior staff officer to Onishi. His subordinates loved Onishi because he cared for them and "led by example as well as by command."[42]

Onishi helped conceive the plans for the Pearl Harbor attack, and as Chief of Staff in the Eleventh Air Fleet had approved the air strikes against American bases in the Philippines on the war's opening day. Now, in late 1944, with the conflict spinning madly against Japanese fortunes, Onishi was given command of the First Air Fleet in the Philippines and tasked with blunting American assaults in the region.

Onishi arrived in the Philippines on October 17, while Becton and *Laffey* conducted shore bombardment exercises off Hawaii. From his work in the Ministry of Munitions he understood that Japan could never match the American industrial output in aircraft, and he realized that his nation's pool of aviators had shrunk to an alarming low, meaning that few reinforcements would come his way. Devastating American air strikes against Japanese air-fields in the next few days, combined with the already critical shortage of aircraft and aviators, convinced Onishi that only a drastic step—kamikaze aircraft—would slow the enemy's attacks. Rather than sending a surface force of multiple ships and hundreds of men to engage the enemy, one man in one plane, willing to smash into an enemy aircraft carrier or battleship would, by his death, achieve maximum results with minimum use of re-sources. The pilot's sacrifice would, at the same time, stir his nation to in-creased effort. "The gods will provide us with victory only when all Japanese are devoted to the spirit of special attacks," said Onishi. "Death is not the objective, but each person must be resigned to death and try to destroy as many of the enemy as possible."[43]

Guided by that philosophy, Onishi assembled a special unit of pilots to counter American moves in the Philippines. It would eventually grow into a force that would spread fear throughout the Pacific in late 1944 and into 1945, and some day send twenty-two kamikaze aircraft against a solitary American destroyer—the USS *Laffey*.

To purposely send young men to their deaths illustrated the desperation Japan faced in late 1944. From their vantage the war had dramatically worsened as American forces swept through Central Pacific islands and landed units in the Philippines. If they could not prevent the enemy from drawing closer to the Home Islands, the Japanese faced the unacceptable specter of surrender. The first step was to prevent an American conquest of the Philippines, lest the enemy sever the crucial supply lines channeling sorely needed natural resources from the Philippines and Japan's other possessions in Southeast Asia.

"Time is against us," Vice Admiral Kimpei Teraoka, Onishi's predecessor in the Philippines, wrote in his diary for October 18. "Available airplanes are limited in number. We are forced to take the most effective method to fight in this operation. The time has arrived for consideration of Admiral Ohnishi's proposal to employ crash-dive tactics."[44]

With sentiment in favor of employing suicide aircraft growing, Onishi took action. On the night of October 19 he arrived at Clark Field on Luzon Island fifty miles northwest of Manila. He explained the gravity of the situation to Inoguchi, the senior staff officer of the First Air Fleet, discussed recent developments with Commander Asaichi Tamai, the executive officer of the 201st Air Group, and said that the fate of the Empire depended upon their successfully halting the enemy, which had already appeared off the mouth of Leyte Gulf. "In my opinion," said Onishi, "there is only one way of assuring that our meager strength will be effective to a maximum degree. That is to organize suicide attack units composed of Zero fighters armed with 250-kilogram bombs, with each plane to crash-dive into an enemy carrier."

Commander Tamai asked to be excused. The respected officer spoke to the twenty-three noncommissioned pilots of his air group, veterans of much Pacific combat, explained what they and their nation faced, and asked if any would be willing to pilot a suicide plane into an enemy warship. To Tamai's delight, the arms of every man rose.

Tamai told Onishi, "I shall never forget the firm resolution in their faces. Their eyes shone feverishly in the dimly lit room. Each must have been thinking of this as a chance to avenge comrades who had fallen recently in the fierce Marianas fighting, and at Palau and Yap." In a firm voice, Tamai announced that the 201st would execute Onishi's plan. "I well remember Admiral Ohnishi's expression as he nodded acquiescence," Inoguchi wrote afterward. "His face bore a look of relief coupled with a shadow of sorrow."

The trio next discussed a name for the new unit. Inoguchi suggested the word, *kamikaze*, meaning "divine wind," a reference to the typhoon that in 1281 wrecked Kublai Khan's Mongol fleet as it carried a hundred thousand warriors intent on invading Japan. The three, who hoped to create another divine wind that would save Japan, agreed.

The next day Onishi addressed the pilots about to conduct the first organized kamikaze attack. He explained that on October 25 the unit would fly against enemy carriers operating in Leyte Gulf, destroying carrier decks and aircraft with their own planes and, by their sacrifice, helping to protect their nation. "Japan is in grave danger. The salvation of our country is now beyond the power of the ministers of state, the general staff, and lowly commanders like myself. It can come only from spirited young men such as you. Thus, on behalf of your hundred million countrymen, I ask of you this sacrifice, and pray for your success."[45]

With these words Onishi initiated his nation's suicide squadrons.

As Commander Becton, Quartermaster Phoutrides, and Seaman Johnson drilled in Hawaii during these October days, they had no idea of the storm clouds forming that would in a few months engulf their destroyer.

PART II
INTO PACIFIC COMBAT

CHAPTER 4

KAMIKAZES STAGE A TERRIFYING INTRODUCTION

[Ulithi's] fun and games and beer
Only partly quelled the fear
Of Kamikazes lurking near.
    —"Invicta," Lieutenant Matthew Darnell

As much as they might have wished to remain, the crew's sojourn in the Hawaiian Islands wound down. After weeks of gunnery exercises and aircraft recognition drills, Becton began priming the ship for combat. Sailors topped the fuel tanks, brought aboard the stores and ammunition they would need to venture west into the Pacific, and finished last minute preparations to enter the forward area and action against the Japanese.

Although at Normandy they had already been participants in the war's largest assault, they had yet to engage an enemy fighter plane approaching from above. They had faced German land batteries, mines, and E-boats, but defending themselves against an attack from the air remained a mystery. Japanese aircraft based in the Philippines were certain to challenge the *Laffey*. What would that be like and how would the crew respond?

A trying five-week stretch would begin answering those questions. From early December through the middle of January 1945, the crew participated in four operations involving hostile aircraft as they leapfrogged up the Philippine west coast. The period taxed every man aboard *Laffey*, and by the time they completed the January Lingayen Gulf landings, they had witnessed the horrors of the kamikaze.

The young sailors who had so recently come together in Boston were soon to be sobered by the grim realities of Pacific combat.

"The Psychology Behind It Was Too Alien"

Under warm skies on October 23, Becton guided the *Laffey*, now sporting black-and-white camouflage paint, from her Hawaiian anchorage. He turned toward the open sea and joined five other destroyers, including *Barton* and *Walke*, in escorting the battleship, USS *North Carolina* (BB-55), twenty-eight hundred miles southwest to Eniwetok, Marshall Islands. With the combat zone drawing nearer every day, Becton stepped up the pace of his drills. The next day his gun crews fired 454 rounds of 40mm ammunition and 1,046 rounds of 20mm ammunition at sleeves towed by aircraft from the *North Carolina* in aircraft tracking exercises. "Some men wondered why we had all the training," said Lieutenant Youngquist, who realized what the skipper was doing. "Becton wanted us prepared. He kept us on our toes."[1]

Becton's concerns that their future experiences would be worse than Normandy were not ill founded. On their second full day at sea in their seven-day voyage, forty-seven hundred miles to the west, US and Japanese naval forces met in the far-flung Battle of Leyte Gulf in the Philippines. In four separate encounters comprising the largest naval clash in history, ships, submarines, and aircraft battled for supremacy in the islands to which in early 1942 General Douglas MacArthur had sworn to return.

The monumental battle introduced the first organized kamikaze assault of the war. They came suddenly, with lethal intent and without warning. Their October 25 attack heightened fear for those engaged in a war that had already gained a reputation for barbarity.

That morning a group of aircraft from the Shikishima Unit, led by Lieutenant Yukio Seki, lifted from the runway at Mabalacat on the island of Mindanao in the southern Philippines and turned north toward the American carriers that had assembled off Leyte Gulf to provide support for MacArthur's infantry ashore. They came in low, hugging the water's surface to avoid American radar, rapidly climbed to six thousand feet, then dived at the ships. They appeared so unexpectedly that American fighter aircraft providing air cover lacked enough time to intercept them. Unsuspecting carrier crews in the process of recovering their own aircraft from the morning's engagement halted operations and rushed to their guns. One Japanese fighter crashed into the port catwalk of the escort carrier, USS *Kitkun Bay* (CVE-71). A second punctured the flight deck of the USS *St. Lo* (CVE-63), burst into flames, and sparked eruptions that tossed men and aircraft hundreds of feet into the air as the ship entered her death throes. Other kamikaze aircraft slammed into the USS *Kalinin Bay* (CVE-68), damaged the USS *White Plains* (CVE-66), and struck the USS *Fanshaw Bay* (CVE-70).

Radio Tokyo trumpeted Seki's unit as national heroes, while Imperial General Headquarters communiqués warned that a wave of kamikaze pilots would save Japan. Sub-lieutenant Saburo Sakai, who had initial misgivings about a suicide unit, changed his tune. Sakai wrote that "now there was no denying the tremendous blow which had been struck at the American fleet off the Philippines. Even I had to acknowledge the fact that the suicide dives appeared to be our only means of striking back at the American warships." Sakai added, "The *Kamikazes* gave us tremendous new strength."[2]

Vice Admiral Matome Ugaki of the navy's general staff gushed about the bravery exhibited by the kamikaze pilots. "Oh, what a noble spirit this is!" he wrote in his diary. "We are not afraid of a million enemies or a thousand carriers because our whole force shares the same spirit."[3]

American sailors reacted with revulsion. Captain Raymond Tarbuck, a senior naval officer on MacArthur's staff, wrote in his journal the night of October 25 that "an innovation of this battle is the suicide dive. If he has a hundred planes, which will be shot down tomorrow, he might as well 'suidive' them today and burn out a hundred ships. A countermeasure must be found soon."[4]

The carnage continued four days later when another kamikaze plunged into the aircraft carrier USS *Intrepid* (CV-11). Concern among top Navy officials heightened the next day when kamikazes badly damaged the carriers USS *Franklin* (CV-13) and USS *Belleau Wood* (CVL-24), killing 148 and destroying 45 US aircraft. Suicide planes swarmed the USS *Enterprise* (CV-6), whose gunners in thirty minutes defended their ship against eight attacking planes in "one of the most vicious enemy attacks she had ever encountered," according to the *Enterprise* action report. The report suggested that "this day's action should leave no doubt of the determined manner in which the enemy intends to defend his ill-gotten Philippines. Suicide tactics will no doubt be continually employed as we approach his homeland."[5]

Lieutenant Carl Solberg, an officer who worked on Admiral William Halsey's bridge, noticed the desperation among his fellow officers as the various kamikaze attack reports poured in to Halsey's flagship. They reacted silently, as if confronting a problem for which they could offer no solution, and took their cue from Halsey, who seemed repulsed by his enemy's apparent willingness to surrender their lives. "The psychology behind it was too alien to us; Americans, who fight to live, find it hard to realize that another people will fight to die. We could not believe that even the Japanese, for all their hara kiri traditions, could muster enough recruits to make such a corps really effective."[6]

The news of the kamikazes stunned the American home front. In its November 3 issue, the *New York Times* first used the term *kamikaze* in describing the Pacific carnage. According to the article, Tokyo employed suicide planes, which the Japanese called "a V-1 with a pilot," against MacArthur's ships. "The planes were described as practically flying bombs," continued the article, "carrying just enough fuel to reach their targets and named Kamikaze for the Japanese god of the winds."[7]

In the oppressive ninety-degree heat of October 30, *Laffey* arrived at Eniwetok Atoll, Marshall Islands. Becton and his men had little time to pause, however, as the Navy, in light of the losses suffered in the Battle of Leyte Gulf, needed every available ship in the Philippines. They left the next day, bound first for Ulithi in the Caroline Islands.

Normally a recreation spot where weary crews enjoyed a break from the war, Ulithi offered no respite, as *Laffey* remained only long enough to replenish before exiting for the combat zone. Ten hours after entering Ulithi, *Laffey* formed with the other twenty-two ships of Task Group 38.4 under the command of Rear Admiral R. E. Davison in the *Enterprise*. In a formation that Phoutrides and the rest of the crew had not observed in the Atlantic, three carriers were equally spaced on an inner 2,500-yard circle, protected as if in a cocoon by two outer rings of cruisers and destroyers. One battleship, the *North Carolina*, and four cruisers steamed on a 4,000-yard inner circle, while *Laffey* and fourteen other destroyers sliced a circular path 2,000 yards farther out. The combined firepower of the twenty-two ships, which cut through Pacific waters like an armored behemoth, was designed to shield the carriers from enemy aircraft.

"Now we were heading to the serious stuff as the Japanese were on the move," said Sonarman Zack. "Everyone had to be on his toes. Something big was going on, and we had to get to the Philippines. For eighteen and nineteen-year-olds, it was exciting to go into action."[8]

Seaman 1/c Andrew J. Martinis and Quartermaster Phoutrides one day discussed their prospects for combat. Both had seen action off Normandy.

Now, Phoutrides wanted nothing to do with Japan's newest weapon, but Martinis expressed a desire to at least catch a glimpse of the kamikazes, but only from afar, he assured the quartermaster.

The exhilaration grew on November 2 when *Laffey*'s radar registered a Japanese plane. "Spotted our first Japanese plane,"[9] Fireman Gauding wrote in his diary for that day. However, the aircraft remained safely out of range of the destroyer's guns and departed without attacking. Still, the incident emphasized that *Laffey* would soon be in Pacific combat.

"You Had to Be on the Ball"

The Navy's need to rush *Laffey* to the Philippines did not surprise Becton. Heavy rains had altered Philippine airfields into muddy quagmires, denying MacArthur the Army air support he needed for his infantry. The Navy's carriers had to fill the void, and *Laffey* would join other destroyers to provide protection for those carriers.

The assignment placed *Laffey* in dangerous seas. Eager to avenge their defeat at Leyte Gulf, the Japanese were likely to pounce on those carriers and any other ship in Philippine waters. The appearance of the first kamikazes eleven days earlier proved that the enemy would overlook no tactic to retain their hold on the crucial islands.

Becton cautioned his officers that "this was a much more complex ball game as far as *Laffey* was concerned" than Normandy. The naval thrashing absorbed at Leyte Gulf enraged the Japanese, and Becton assumed they would hold nothing back to gain vengeance. As he later wrote, recent events had made the Japanese "more desperate, their resolve more fanatical. For us, the worst was still ahead."[10]

The crew did not have to wait long for its first Pacific action. With *Laffey* and other destroyers watching for enemy planes under tropical skies on November 11, aircraft lifted from the decks of four carriers bound for Ormoc Bay west of Leyte Gulf. Over the next four hours carrier crews launched and recovered aircraft on their way to and from bombing attacks and strafing runs against Japanese shipping.

The carriers and their accompanying battleships, cruisers, and destroyers made an impressive spectacle. As planes alighted in the distance, *Laffey* steamed back and forth, providing the first line of defense for the carriers nestled in the middle. To avoid colliding with a vessel that could handily snuff *Laffey* out of existence, Becton carefully watched the carriers in case the mammoth warships swerved into an emergency turn. "The carrier is always right, and you better be able to alter your course to fit theirs," explained Sonarman Zack. "You had to be on the ball, or you could lose your ship."[11]

Laffey was a spectator to the morning air strikes, but matters intensified in the afternoon. As *Laffey* took on fuel from the cruiser, USS *Minneapolis* (CA-36), Becton sounded general quarters when radar spotted unidentified aircraft twenty-three miles out. The crew hurriedly cast off fuel hoses and lines while Becton increased speed to twenty-five knots, but the aircraft proved to be friendly. Several other reports filtered in throughout the afternoon, but in each case the battle group's combat air patrols (CAP) either classified them as friendly or chased away and shot down the intruders.

Action arrived later that afternoon when another report indicated that a large number of enemy aircraft were approaching from the west. Becton again sounded general quarters as radar scoured the skies. "Suddenly," recalled Becton, "we heard a strained voice on our TBS [Talk Between Ships] from one of our picket destroyers on station far out from the main body. 'Three Jap planes diving at me . . . got one . . . out!'" At the same moment "the sky over us was filled with others. Every gun in the task group opened up."[12]

The men tensed at the prospect of attack. Unlike Normandy, where the encounters occurred at a distance, this was up close and personal. The Japanese, recently bolstered by the inclusion of kamikaze aircraft, were coming to them. Crew manning 40mm and 20mm antiaircraft guns scrutinized the sky, eager to catch a glimpse of their first Pacific target but at the same time apprehensive over the damage the planes might inflict.

A symphony of noise shattered the heavens as *Laffey*'s guns joined those of nearby ships. The whump-whump-whump of Seaman Fern's 40mm guns blended with the guttural boom of Delewski's and Zack's five-inch guns, while the sharper, speedier retort of the 20mm machine guns pumped steady streams of bullets and tracers skyward. Puffs of smoke so dotted the sky that it appeared as if a painter had whipped his brush at a canvas. Fortunately, the thick antiaircraft curtain either knocked down or turned away every invader. Johnson and Fern, who followed the action from their posts on deck, breathed easier at surviving their first Pacific onslaught, but their racing heartbeats belied their outward calm.

The raid ended suddenly, but one minute later lookouts spotted a parachute to the southwest. Becton searched for the downed pilot for more than an hour before lookouts located the enemy aviator in a life jacket floating a thousand yards away. Chief Boatswain's Mate William Keyes tossed a line to the Japanese, who held on while Lieutenant Samuel Humphries and a seaman climbed down to aid the injured aviator onto the ship. The frightened pilot, who appeared ready to collapse, cringed from a bullet hole in his right hand and a broken arm. Crew stripped and searched the man before the ship's doctor, Lieutenant Matthew Darnell, administered first aid.

"He was pretty banged up," said Quartermaster Phoutrides. "We treated him nicely, although I'm sure some guys probably wanted to toss him overboard." Phoutrides was surprised to see a tall, well-built adversary, who contradicted the typical images disseminated by wartime propaganda. "I expected to see a skinny, bow-legged guy wearing glasses, but he was anything but that. He was well-built and tall."[13]

The ship's interrogator, Lieutenant Frank A. Manson, learned that the prisoner, Yushio, had flown from a carrier until his ship was sunk during the Battle of the Philippine Sea. The next day they transferred Yushio, along with a Japanese chart and the man's identification badge, by boatswain's chair to a tanker, which transported him to the *Enterprise* and further interrogation.

"These Kamikaze Fellows Were Beginning to Worry Me"

Three subsequent days of American air strikes encountered few problems. On November 13 the carriers launched a dawn air strike against Manila area airfields, and continued sending planes over the Philippines until late afternoon. They added their third and fourth rounds of strikes against shipping and airfields in the Manila, Cavite, and Lingayen Gulf areas on November 14 and 19. Although numerous enemy aircraft approached the formation, as Becton's action report stated, "few reached lethal range" and *Laffey*'s gunners were silent as CAP splashed "one plane after another."[14]

Kamikazes dominated the action reports filed by Becton and other destroyer skippers. They observed that the Japanese aircraft often hugged the water's surface, making early detection and interception more difficult, and agreed with Becton's comments about enemy pilots who purposely crashed their planes into American ships. "The men who piloted those diving planes seemed determined to commit deliberate, preplanned self-murder," Becton wrote. "How could any sane human being, no matter how patriotic, ride a burning fireball of a plane all the way in until it hit a ship?"[15]

Following the fourth air strike, the formation turned southeastward for Ulithi, which they entered on November 22. While his crew brought aboard ammunition and supplies, Becton met with other officers at headquarters, where the commanders again concentrated on one topic: how to defend against the kamikazes. Few offered any clear answers to the recent phenomenon. Unless CAP splashed every intruder, which was unlikely, the ships' gun crews, the last bastion against the suicide craft, would have to defend their destroyers.

Becton hoped that his frequent training and drills since their February commissioning would pay off in the western reaches of the Pacific. However, it was one thing to shoot at enemy bombers as they flew overhead, but quite a different matter when those aircraft turned into piloted guided missiles. As Becton wrote, "it had slowly begun to dawn on me that we were up against something entirely new. We had taken the measure of the skilled Japanese professionals and knew how to handle them. But these Kamikaze fellows were fanatics, religious fanatics, and that was beginning to worry me."[16]

In the early morning hours on November 27 *Laffey*, accompanied by her three sister destroyers of DesDiv 119 and two other destroyers, was again underway for the Philippines. Her destination was San Pedro Bay along the northwest corner of Leyte Gulf. There they were to be part of MacArthur's three-pronged advance up the western side of the Philippines to clear the islands of Japanese and gain airfields and staging areas for larger assaults on the way to Tokyo. While MacArthur's land troops pried Japanese infantry out of their defensive positions, the Navy would first transport and land Army units at Ormoc Bay on Leyte's northwest side. They would use the airfields and facilities seized at Ormoc to organize and support landings 500 miles farther north at Mindoro off Luzon's southwest coast, and then employ facilities at Mindoro to support the third and largest assault at Lingayen Gulf, 120 miles above Manila.

The tasks for *Laffey* at all three assaults were the same: she would provide protection for the bombardment ships by screening for enemy submarines and aircraft, and provide gunfire support for the troops ashore. Given that retaining control of the Philippines was vital to the Japanese, who relied on the flow of natural resources and other products from the islands and from Southeast Asia to fuel their military, Becton concluded the fighting would intensify as *Laffey* moved northward during each of the three phases of the advance up the western Philippines. What most alarmed him, however, was that the operations not only placed him within range of enemy airfields but also required *Laffey* to operate at times in restricted waters, where he would enjoy less room to maneuver and avoid kamikazes. Becton concluded that he was about to steam into the lion's den and poke the beast, which was certain to react fiercely to defend what he believed was his. The coming weeks would test Becton's command skills and his crew's preparedness for battle.

One event foreshadowed the hazards that the crew and ship would face. After receiving reports of a Japanese attempt to land reinforcements and supplies through Ormoc Bay off Leyte's west coast, on December 2 three destroyers from *Laffey's* DesDiv 119—the USS *Moale* (DD-693), the USS *Sumner* (DD-692), and the USS *Cooper* (DD-695)—received orders to leave Leyte Gulf and veer north to engage a reported five enemy ships heading toward Ormoc.

Shortly after midnight on December 3 the trio met the enemy in a fiercely contested skirmish that included surface attacks throughout the night and aerial assaults shortly after dawn. *Sumner* and *Moale* extricated themselves and returned safely to San Pedro Bay, but early in the engagement a torpedo ripped into the *Cooper*, sinking the ship in less than one minute and taking 191 of the crew to their deaths.

The *Cooper* served as a cautionary tale to what might happen to ships that operated in proximity to the enemy airfields that heavily dotted the Philippine western side. Her loss profoundly impacted the crew of the *Laffey*. The mental image of *Cooper* survivors struggling in the waters off Ormoc, subject to Japanese air attacks, sharks, or capture, rattled the men, and if one torpedo could inflict this much damage, they wondered what a kamikaze might do.

"The news of the *Cooper's* sinking had a strange effect on our crew," said Quartermaster Phoutrides. "Although she was another ship, she was part of our squadron [Destroyer Squadron 60] and one of us. Many of our friends went down with her." Phoutrides added, "The atmosphere was haunting. No one spoke out of turn. What was said was said quietly and briefly. Now, more than ever before, the war seemed fearfully close to us."[17]

Philippine Assault No. 1: Ormoc

"Caught the Enemy Flat-Footed"

The war drew closer yet as MacArthur's drive up the western side of the Philippines gained steam. He scheduled three landings—at Ormoc, Mindoro Island, and Lingayen Gulf—in the next month. As at Normandy, each landing required *Laffey* to screen for larger ships and provide supporting fire for the infantry, but each operation also placed the destroyer in unique circumstances. As *Laffey* jumped from one to the other, Becton asked his men to meet added challenges, from sprinting through a gauntlet of enemy airfields at Ormoc and Mindoro Island to witnessing the rapidly mounting violence administered by kamikazes on sister ships and crews.

On Leyte Island, MacArthur's Sixth Army cut off the Japanese retreat on three sides, but an open corridor remained at the city of Ormoc on the island's northwest side, through which the Japanese pushed in reinforcements and supplies. An American landing at Ormoc would seal that corridor, hand the Navy a forward base in the Philippines, and trap Japanese forces fighting on the island.

Japanese airfields in the region granted the enemy air superiority in those Philippine inner waters, which disturbed Rear Admiral A. D. Struble, commander of the ships designated to land American troops at Ormoc. The enemy's advantage could cause unacceptable losses to his ships operating in the restricted waters, or even prevent them from reaching Ormoc.

MacArthur's headquarters dismissed Struble's misgivings, and the assault went forward. Late in the morning of December 6, *Laffey* lifted anchor and steamed south as part of Struble's Task Group 78.3. "Underway at 11:30 AM for Ormoc Bay," Fireman Gauding wrote. "Attempts to take this port have so far been unsuccessful."[18] *Laffey* and the accompanying destroyers were to land the Army's 77th Division five miles south of Ormoc, prevent Japanese reinforcements from reaching the area, and provide fire support to the infantry ashore.

The trip to Ormoc proved surprisingly uneventful. Before dawn on December 7, Becton sounded general quarters, and fifteen minutes later *Laffey* and *O'Brien* moved out to cover the minesweepers tasked with clearing mines inside Ormoc Bay. With daylight breaking over the horizon, Becton took *Laffey* to her station in the northern half of the fire support area, and opened fire at preselected targets situated along a five-hundred-yard stretch of beach just north of the Baod River, three miles southeast of Ormoc City. Spotters aboard *Laffey* directed the fire against known enemy positions to a depth of three hundred yards.

"Shelled the beach," wrote Fireman Gauding. "We hit a amunition [sic] dump. Wow."[19] Scanning the beach through his binoculars, Quartermaster Phoutrides followed a Japanese soldier running out of a bunker toward a hill. He paused at his first sighting of a foe, for in all his time off France, he had never seen his adversary.

Laffey continued the bombardment until 7:05 a.m., at which time rocket boats took over the barrage. Five minutes later, with *Laffey* in position to lend fire support, the first infantry hit the beaches. When shells from a Japanese shore battery splashed several hundred yards short of the ship, *Laffey*'s five-inch guns returned fire and silenced the battery. One hour later *Laffey*'s guns zeroed in on a group of Japanese soldiers running up a hillside, and as Becton wrote in his action report, "it is believed the last salvo fired at those troops accounted for a considerable number of them." He described his ship's bombardment that day as "very effective"[20] in blowing up an ammunition dump, silencing a shore battery, and clearing a road of enemy troops. Becton continued maneuvering the ship in her fire support area, prepared to lend a hand if called on, but the operation ashore unfolded so smoothly that at 8:39 the SFCP radioed they had run out of targets and were moving inland.

It had been a good few hours for *Laffey*, for the other ships in the force, and for the troops rushing inland. Aboard Admiral Struble's flagship, *New York Times* war correspondent Spencer Davis observed that the Japanese had no reason to celebrate the third anniversary of Pearl Harbor, "for on this day American warships sailed boldly into Ormoc Bay to land a large Sixth Army force—the Seventy-seventh Division—at the very gates of the enemy's strongest garrison on western Leyte." He reported that the United States had achieved "complete tactical surprise" at Ormoc and that "the landing phase of the operation caught the enemy flat-footed."[21]

That would all change in little more than an hour.

"They Were Like Hornets Whose Nest We Had Invaded"

In anticipation of Japanese kamikaze strikes, Admiral Struble had the transports unloaded in two hours so he could begin pulling out into broader waters, but the Japanese hit just as the ships began leaving. *Laffey* was stationed at the northern end of Ormoc Bay when the kamikazes struck. Becton, left little room to maneuver in the restricted waters, was forced to adopt a circular path in his assigned area, allow the kamikazes to come to him, and hope that his training enabled *Laffey*'s gunners to mount a successful defense. "We had to stay put until we got orders to do otherwise; it was one of the most difficult things I have ever had to do,"[22] he wrote afterward of the passive stance.

For nine hours kamikaze pilots from the Kesshu Special Attack Unit, commanded by Captain Fumio Sakai, the Gokoku Special Attack Unit, commanded by 1st Lieutenant Shigeru Endo, and the Kinno Special Attack Unit, commanded by 1st Lieutenant Takumi Yamamoto, swooped down on the formation, sinking two destroyers, damaging others, and killing or wounding hundreds of men. Little respite ensued between the attacks, forcing Becton and the other ship commanders to keep their men at general quarters throughout the long ordeal and giving his crew little time to rest. "They were like hornets whose nest we had invaded,"[23] wrote Becton of the kamikaze aircraft. Their sting left Struble's ships hounded, harassed, and burning, and handed Phoutrides, Fern, and the others their first eyewitness view of the incredible mutilation kamikazes could inflict.

New York Times correspondents aboard different vessels described a hotbed of activity as "naval guns filled the air with their thundering, rattling tracers." For nine hours "there was scarcely a lull in the incessant dogfights, bombing raids and roar of ack-ack [antiaircraft] batteries."[24]

The kamikazes struck fast. In mid-morning nine Japanese aircraft approached from the west. American P-38 fighters intercepted the group, but four minutes later four twin-engine bombers broke through and executed suicide dives on the USS *Ward* (APD-16), then only four miles from *Laffey*. Three failed to battle through, but one crashed into the destroyer's hull amidships, igniting uncontrollable fires.

O'Brien rushed to the aid of the *Ward*, the ship that at Pearl Harbor three years earlier had fired the first American shots of the war in attacking a midget submarine. After an hour of unsuccessfully battling the fires, however, *Ward*'s skipper ordered his crew to abandon ship. *O'Brien* gunfire sent the ship to her grave.

The turn of the USS *Mahan* (DD-364) came just ten minutes later, when nine kamikaze aircraft approached the destroyer. American fighters shot down three, but a fourth evaded the opposition and smacked into the *Mahan* between the waterline and the forecastle deck. Moments later another kamikaze hit abaft of the bridge, and an ensuing plane crashed directly at the waterline. A seventh Japanese aircraft strafed *Mahan* as it flew by, and the eighth and ninth crashed short of the damaged destroyer. The four-minute attack left *Mahan* a blazing shambles, forcing the commander of the task unit to order *Walke* and *Lamson* (DD-367) to sink the unsalvageable vessel. The *Mahan* lost ten killed or missing and thirty-two wounded in the attack.

The loss of the two destroyers from Destroyer Squadron 60, of which *Laffey*'s DesDiv 119 was a part, thrust the reality of the Pacific war front and center for men aboard *Laffey*. Might the same be in store for them, they wondered? If the Japanese struck with such ferocity now, how terrible might it be when *Laffey* drew closer to the Japanese Home Islands? The excitement of going to war that some of the crew experienced earlier in 1944 diminished each time they observed or learned of an event such of this. Sailors not yet out of their teenage years who once considered failing school grades and lost football contests as catastrophic began to realize that those had been trivial concerns compared to the critical situations in which the war now enmeshed them.

Their work was not finished. Over the remainder of the next nine hours *Laffey* and her companion ships battled fifteen additional kamikaze assaults as they ran a gauntlet of enemy airfields back to San Pedro Bay. Johnson and Fern on their 40mm guns, and crew manning the smaller machine guns, had no respite from the Japanese planes that swarmed about the vessels throughout the day. They remained at their posts despite racing heartbeats. They unconsciously shuffled their feet and glanced nervously around, straining to catch a glimpse of the enemy and direct their fire at him before the pilot gained the upper hand.

"We were under constant air attack from sunrise until dark,"[25] wrote Gauding. One kamikaze dived at a destroyer but overshot and splashed into the water. Another plunged into the bridge of the USS *Liddle* (APD-60), destroying the ship's CIC and killing thirty-six men, including the *Liddle's* captain. A third kamikaze approached, but fell to *Barton's* gunners. At 2:37 p.m. *Laffey's* 20mm and 40mm gun crews helped splash an enemy plane diving toward a destroyer a short distance to their west before it reached its target. Army P-38 fighters lifted from Philippine airfields to engage the Japanese in dogfights, which *Laffey* gunners welcomed, but their appearance also made their chore more difficult as they struggled to distinguish friend from foe.

Additional attacks appeared for the next two and one-half hours. One successful kamikaze ignited raging fires aboard the USS *Lamson* (DD-367), burning twenty-one men to death. The USS *Edwards* (DD-619) shot down three Japanese aircraft, but another crashed into the ship's fantail. When yet another kamikaze raced toward the USS *Flusser* (DD-368), *Laffey* and other ships opened fire, trying to prevent the kind of damage to their destroyers that had befallen the *Lamson* and *Edwards*. American P-39 Airacobra fighters eventually pursued and splashed the plane, giving the gun crews a brief break before the next onslaught began.

A group of kamikazes approached *Laffey* in mid-afternoon. With an effective range of three thousand yards, the 40mm gun crews opened fire first.

In the ammunition room below one of the starboard guns, Seaman Johnson handed clips of shells to the first loader, Seaman Joseph Dixon, standing next to the gun. Dixon placed the clips of ammunition into the weapon, where a trainer trained the gun and an operator fired it. "As first loader I was right next to the gun barrels," said Dixon, who used earplugs to reduce the noise and wore a life jacket in case he had to abandon ship. "They fired so fast and loud—BOOM! BOOM! BOOM!"[26]

When the kamikazes drew within one thousand yards the 20mm guns added their firepower. Unlike the 40mm operators, who sat in seats, gunners at the smaller 20mm stood, strapped to their weapons by harnesses. At the sound of the 20mm's PUMP! PUMP! PUMP! men at other stations knew it was time to hit the deck, for the enemy had drawn uncomfortably close. "When the 20mm guns opened fire," said Seaman Johnson, "you knew it was getting risky!"[27] If a kamikaze had drawn within range of their 20mm guns, the crews had fewer than fifteen seconds to destroy it before the plane crashed into the destroyer. *Laffey*'s port 20mm and 40mm guns, including Tom Fern's, opened fire on a Japanese Judy dive bomber as it dived on the port side of the formation. Tracers from *Laffey* machine guns ripped into the plane, which emitted a trail of smoke as it crashed into water ahead of *Barton*.

Men stifled their exhilaration at downing the kamikaze the next minute when another kamikaze, pursued by P-38 fighters, crossed astern of the formation and splashed near the *Edwards*. Thirty-five minutes later three Japanese planes attacked the rear of the formation, with one smashing into and damaging an LST. The hectic afternoon continued when *Laffey*'s five-inch guns directed eighty rounds at four kamikazes before American fighters chased them away. Three minutes later, a fifth aircraft dropped bombs that landed two hundred yards on *Laffey*'s port beam.

Becton held his men at stations for another ninety minutes as daylight approached. When no aircraft appeared in that span, he secured from general quarters. After nine arduous hours, the crew could finally enjoy a hot cup of coffee and a bite of food. "I breathed a sigh of relief as everything outside the pilothouse disappeared in the blackness," recalled Becton. "It had been a long, tough day."[28]

Sonarman 2/c Charles W. Bell, Becton's bridge telephone talker, removed his earphones after passing along Becton's order to secure from general quarters. He glanced at Becton and then said, "Captain, I've never seen anything like what we've had today in my life, except in a war movie. I hope we don't have to go through that again."[29]

Becton agreed that he had never experienced anything like running this watery gauntlet, but doubted Bell's hope would materialize. The skipper expected rougher days to follow.

Men on the antiaircraft guns congratulated each other, though. For the first time in either theater, they had splashed an enemy aircraft—and two of them at that. Other ships and crews had not been as fortunate, but once again *Laffey* had evaded harm. While other crews tended to the wounded and started initial repairs to damaged bulkheads, *Laffey* men could slowly let their guard down and even step below for a quick mug of coffee, content that with their two kills they had made their mark in the Pacific war.

Even as the *Laffey* accompanied her damaged companions while they limped back to Leyte Gulf, a Japanese radio broadcast hailed the twenty-four kamikaze pilots as heroes who sacrificed their lives to inflict grievous damage to the American force. The pilots sank two destroyers, damaged several more, and killed at least sixty-seven men.

"In serving on the seas, be a corpse saturated with water," the radio broadcast quoted from the squadrons' slogans. "In serving on land, be a corpse covered with weeds. In serving in the sky, be a corpse that challenges the clouds. Let's all die close by the side of our sovereign."[30]

Laffey's crew had witnessed a frightening display of the enemy's determination. This war was not at all like Normandy, where the ship's five-inch guns inflicted the damage at long ranges and no one saw their enemy. This theater featured combat at close quarters, with the Japanese racing in to bring the fight directly to *Laffey*'s decks.

"They Damn Near Got Us"

Laffey anchored in San Pedro Bay in mid-morning on December 8, where Becton met with the commander of Destroyer Squadron 60, Captain William Freseman. "Julie," said Freseman, using Becton's nickname, "they damn near got us yesterday. Julie, those Japs are crazy, absolutely crazy."[31]

References to kamikaze aircraft peppered Becton's Ormoc action report. "This was the first time the Commanding Officer had seen suicide pilots with apparently undamaged planes deliberately dive into ships," he wrote after the encounter. The kamikazes came suddenly, and would often "dive on his victim before he could be taken under effective fire. In other cases they took advantage of the prevailing cloud cover before commencing their dive. Many times they would be in the area when there had been little or no indication on the radar screen of their presence."

Becton believed the kamikaze phenomenon would not be short lived, and concluded that "how to combat them is a problem of considerable magnitude." He wrote that erecting a ring of antiaircraft fire and "pouring steel into them until they disintegrate" would help, but if several kamikazes attacked one ship from various directions, "it is practically an impossibility to prevent their damaging the ship."

Becton advised that because "suicide dives were apparently always aimed at the bridge," removal of flammable material from that area was vital. Radical maneuvering at high speed to avoid a single kamikaze could work, "but to have all of a group of three or four suicides miss even a high speed maneuvering target appears highly unlikely." In his opinion, the best defense would be "a large number of fighters stacked at various altitudes to intercept the bogies before reaching the rim of the formation."

He could see no way to avoid hitting friendly aircraft engaged in dogfights with the kamikazes. "The only solution appears to be to open up with every gun possible on the bandits, and, providing the suicides also miss their mark, standby to rescue such of our pilots as may be shot down during the attack."[32]

Becton disclosed that in the Ormoc landings, *Laffey*'s gun crews fired 426 rounds of five-inch shells, 32 rounds of 40mm ammunition, and 160 rounds of 20mm ammunition. He labeled his men's performance as excellent, and singled out the gun crews for their accurate fire.

General Douglas MacArthur lauded the operation. He claimed that with the Ormoc landings, "we have seized the center of the Yamashita Line from the rear and have split the enemy's forces in two, isolating those in the valley to the north from those along the coast to the south. Both segments are now caught between our columns which are pressing in from all fronts."[33]

Newspaper accounts claimed the landings trapped the Japanese on Leyte, severed their supply lines, and handed the United States a vital deep-water port on Leyte's west coast for use in larger operations to come. *New York Times* reporter Frank Kluckhohn wrote, "this was amphibious war—land, sea and air—at its toughest," but the United States had pulled out a victory. "The end run had produced a touchdown," declared *Time* magazine. "The battle for Leyte was not yet over, but it was decided."[34]

Becton received a second Gold Star in lieu of Silver Star for his actions at Ormoc.

Although the day started well, any of the crew who assumed they were safe from kamikazes now that they had returned to Leyte Gulf received a rude reminder on December 10. While patrolling in the late afternoon, *Laffey*'s gunners splashed an enemy bomber that made a run at the formation. "Jap suicide plane came in and was shot down,"[35] wrote Fireman Gauding in his diary. However, matters quickly soured when a second kamikaze crashed into the destroyer, USS *Hughes* (DD-410). Becton rushed to help the stricken ship and take her in tow until a tug could arrive.

The scene when *Laffey* pulled alongside *Hughes* that evening shocked the men on deck to silence. Becton ordered the floodlights turned on in the darkness, and the illumination revealed the twisted metal and squashed gun mounts that rested where *Hughes*'s mid-section used to be. *Hughes* crew scurried about topside, assisting the wounded or removing debris. Seaman Fern, who occupied a similar gun mount on *Laffey*, mutely stood in place as he surveyed the wreckage of what had once been other 40mm guns and their crews who, like him and his shipmates aboard *Laffey*, never expected to be so savagely attacked. A solitary pilot had, in a violent split-second, inflicted massive destruction and death on a destroyer and her crew.

"The only time kamikazes bothered me was when we helped the *Hughes*," said Sonarman Zack. "It was at night, and the lights were on, and we saw a big hole amidships. That hit us as we could see what one plane could do."[36]

Some *Laffey* men stifled gasps when they helped *Hughes* wounded, most horribly scalded from explosions, aboard ship. At Normandy damage and death happened at a distance and might be more easily dismissed. No similar relief greeted them now, though, as stretcher after stretcher bearing *Hughes* wounded and dying streamed by. Those men personalized the war for Phoutrides, Fern, Johnson, and the rest of the crew, who stared at mirror images of themselves and realized that this, too, could be their fate. "They were brought aboard the *Laffey* to die,"[37] wrote Lieutenant Manson.

"It really hit home when we picked up casualties from *Hughes*," said Seaman Johnson. "We got that close and saw the damage. It was kind of frightening to think of what we were about to face. Nobody had anticipated this kind of thing developing. We heard about planes dropping bombs and strafing, and that was normal, but to see these guys dive right into a ship was something nobody anticipated." Torpedoman's Mate 2/c Fred M. Gemmell looked at the bodies lined up on deck, awaiting transfer to another ship, and conjured a future he had hoped to avoid. "The *Hughes* bodies were lined up on deck to be transferred to another ship. I couldn't believe the kamikaze attacks were really happening. We'd heard about it, but to have it happen so close to home, to this ship, made it real. It was hard to imagine there were pilots who wanted to crash into our ships."[38]

Even the most hardened veteran had difficulty checking his emotions, but all shared one sentiment. Becton noticed that the men were "just plain mad. One, who fainted twice, kept coming back, swearing quietly until the job was done. No longer were the Japs just someone we were fighting. Now they were the enemy, to be hated."[39]

Throughout the ship, groups of men concluded that the disfiguring burns had been caused, in part, because the bushy beards on some of the *Hughes* scalded men had ignited. Becton had always permitted trimmed beards, but after the *Hughes* tragedy, even that restriction no longer needed to be enforced. "A beard or a mustache might look 'salty,' but *Laffey's* crew learned to be clean-shaven in a hurry," recalled Gunner's Mate Delewski. "There was really no need for the Captain's orders stating that while beards were not against Navy regulations, it would be necessary to have said beard trimmed daily by the ship's barber at $1 trim. End of beards."[40]

Laffey remained with the stricken destroyer until the tug *Quapaw* (ATR-110) arrived two hours later, at which time Becton set course for San Pedro Bay.

Philippine Assault No. 2: Mindoro Island

"The 'Tigers of the Deep'"

"I'm well and still in one piece," Tom Fern wrote his mother on December 13. "Still can stand on my two feet, but what I've seen in the past week makes a fellow wonder—am I next? I've never felt the need for prayers as much as I have in the past weeks. A couple of times I felt my prayers were answered when nothing happened to us,"[41] but after experiencing the Ormoc landings, multiple air alerts, the devastation of the *Hughes*, and the appearance of kamikazes, he wondered how much longer his luck could hold.

Becton and crew could not long commiserate before departing on the second step of MacArthur's threefold Philippine assault, a landing against Japanese forces on Mindoro Island off Luzon's southwest coast. Nimitz and MacArthur wanted Mindoro so they could establish airfields and staging areas closer to Luzon, which would be the capstone of MacArthur's Philippine campaign. Mindoro would also place US forces on the flank of Japan's lifeline to the oil, tin, and rubber of the Netherlands East Indies and Malaya, and threaten Japanese dominance in the South China Sea.

The operation would again require *Laffey* and the other ships to steam within range of enemy airfields along much of the route, especially in the Sulu Sea west of Leyte. Hanson Baldwin of the *New York Times* warned his readers that, "we may have to accept large ship losses. For the first time we have sent our shipping into the narrow waters west of the Philippines, waters that are the 'happy hunting grounds' of Japanese submarines and torpedo craft, and into areas where Japanese planes can converge upon us from many directions."[42]

Rear Admiral Struble led an imposing force into battle. Flying his flag on the cruiser USS *Nashville* (CL-43), Struble commanded 73 landing craft, 17 minesweepers, 8 destroyer transports, and 12 destroyers, including *Laffey*. On December 12, less than one day after returning from escorting the damaged *Hughes*, *Laffey* joined the other ships and departed San Pedro Bay on the six-hundred-mile journey to Mindoro. The force feinted to the east as if it were bound for Pacific waters, then reversed to the west an hour after sunset to enter Surigao Strait. After traversing the Mindanao Sea, the ships steamed into the Sulu Sea, where enemy aircraft quickly spotted them and sent alerts to every air unit in the region.

Once picked up by the enemy, Becton expected to be attacked before *Laffey* reached Mindoro. The next afternoon, shortly after *Laffey* entered the Sulu Sea, a kamikaze materialized out of the nearby land formation, hugged the water's surface to stay under the radar, banked steeply, and smashed into Struble's flagship, disintegrating just aft of the bridge on the port side as the *Nashville* steamed five hundred yards to starboard of *Laffey*. The kamikaze appeared so suddenly that no ship had time to open fire before the plane crashed. "*Laffey* personnel did not see [the] plane until it was close aboard *Nashville* on her starboard quarter," Becton wrote in his action report, "and had no time to warn her or open fire on plane before it crashed into her superstructure."[43] The kamikaze killed 133 men, including Admiral Struble's chief of staff, and wounded another 190 men, providing a further example of the damage a single kamikaze could inflict.

Laffey gunners were ready for the second kamikaze. The plane came in on their starboard through a sky filled with black bursts and white puffs from the ship's five-inch guns. Men on the 40mm and 20mm guns were ready to join in, but the aircraft veered away before they had the opportunity. After successfully fending off the kamikaze, Becton steered *Laffey* toward the cruiser, but fires aboard *Nashville* touched off a flurry of exploding five-inch shells that hampered Becton's relief attempt.

Two hours later kamikazes damaged the destroyer USS *Haraden* (DD-585), killing fourteen and wounding twenty-four. "Going to Mindoro a number of ships were attacked," said Sonarman Zack. "I was below and didn't see any of it, but I always wondered if we would get hit. They usually went after larger ships, but you never know."[44]

The force arrived off Mindoro two days later. After firing a few shells over the heads of cheering Filipino citizens unwisely standing on the beach to greet the Americans, on December 15 the ships commenced an early morning preliminary bombardment, as *Laffey* and four destroyers screened for two cruisers. Thirty minutes later the assault waves of 16,500 infantry landed uncontested. Within ninety minutes they had advanced one mile inland, causing veteran soldiers to wonder if the Japanese were drawing them into a trap. However, with only two hundred soldiers to defend the area, the Japanese had abandoned the beaches. A group of twenty kamikazes sank two LSTs, but antiaircraft fire drove the rest away.

While the other ships remained to provide support for the infantry and to unload supplies, in mid-morning *Laffey* and two other destroyers escorted eight high-speed transports and forty-three landing craft back to San Pedro Bay. With bad weather grounding Army fighters based on Leyte, for the next twenty-four hours the unit had to rely on the antiaircraft gun crews from *Laffey* and the other destroyers for defense. Fortunately, few aircraft threatened the slow-moving force as it made its way south to the Surigao Strait and east into Leyte Gulf. *Laffey*'s five-inch guns successfully turned away one plane at ten thousand yards, but otherwise the unit encountered little opposition. On December 17, *Laffey* guided the ships into San Pedro Bay.

The operation had taken *Laffey* and the other ships through the Sulu Sea to Mindoro despite the scarcity of land-based air cover. The Japanese called the American success at Mindoro "an important move by the enemy to turn the tide of the Philippine battle." Frank Kluckhohn labeled it "a brilliant feat."[45]

Laffey's Pacific endeavors made headlines in Bath, Maine, where the company's newspaper used the ship to emphasize to shipyard workers the importance of their labors. The article included a photograph showing *Laffey* firing off Mindoro, and explained the image of one of their ships in action should be proof of the importance of their work. "For there can be no question but what the super-destroyers, in which our firm specializes, are the real 'Tigers of the Deep' insofar as World War II is concerned." The article added that Admiral Nimitz needed many more of "these fierce, fighting ships," which was "why none of us can afford to let down for a single minute in our home front trust—the Battle of Production."[46] Although none of the crew realized it, what they accomplished in the Pacific made an impact on people back home.

Within six days Seabees had constructed an operable airfield on Mindoro, which freed Halsey's aircraft carriers to conduct missions closer to Japan itself. "It would be no surprise to hear some day soon," wrote the *New York Times*, "that planes of the Pacific Fleet were actually over Tokyo."[47]

Other than sporadic air alerts, including one on December 18 in which *Laffey* gunners assisted in downing an enemy plane, over the next two weeks the crew enjoyed a break from the war. Some, like Fireman Gauding, relaxed on a beach for the first time since they left Pearl Harbor. Others caught up on their letter writing to friends and family who were eager for news from the war zone, or scanned letters already worn from earlier readings. Becton celebrated Christmas by arranging a turkey dinner for the crew, who spent the remainder of their days preparing the ship for her next mission.

On December 30 four chief petty officers—Chief Radioman Jack Najork, Chief Machinist's Mate Carl H. Dubbs, Chief Water Tender Roy Wood, and Chief Commissary Steward Clarence B. McIntyre—met with Becton to express the crew's concerns over the kamikazes. The frightening phenomenon unsettled everyone, and the chiefs related that some doubted they would survive what looked to be months, if not years, facing such fanatic opposition.

Becton realized that if four of his most trusted veterans voiced these concerns, his young crew had to be even more apprehensive about the future. He struggled to find the right words, knowing that the quartet would relay his message to the seamen on deck and the firemen below.

Becton answered that the war must be going badly for the Japanese if they resorted to such desperate tactics, and assured them that once the initial waves of fanatical pilots had been expended, the tactic would dissipate.

Becton smoothed the waters for the time being, but he knew his words would last only until the next suicide attack against his ship. He hoped the Navy could devise methods to eliminate this threat before it finished Becton and his anxious crew.

"*Laffey* personnel saw the New Year in from their general quarters' station," the ship's War Diary mentioned on December 31, "but without benefit of fireworks."[48] Those who hoped to be home by Christmas would have to wait another year.

Well wishes for the New Year clogged *Laffey*'s communications center. Admiral Nimitz wrote that although the crew was far from home and loved ones, "there is comfort in the knowledge that the extent of our distance from home is a measure of our success in beating back the aggressor Japan and that through our joint efforts all danger to our homes and families has been removed." Nimitz promised that 1945 "will see new and more powerful blows dealt the enemy" that would bring yet closer the peace that is "the priceless gift you are earning for your loved ones and all future generations."[49]

Captain Freseman, Comdesron 60, added his New Year's Eve wishes to *Laffey* and the other ships of Desron 60. "Comdesron Sixty extends to all hands best wishes for a much better New Year with plenty of luck and a safe return after we knock more hell out of the Japanese apes."[50]

Hanson Baldwin's words offered little comfort. The military reporter wrote that although the United States had waged bitter warfare against the Japanese for three years, "the battles of ultimate decision still lie ahead." He added of the struggles to come that "their difficulty, their costliness and their bitterness can scarcely be exaggerated" and that "the fourth year of American participation in the war, now opening, will be—must be—a year of 'blood and sweat and tears,' lightened only by the sure knowledge of approaching victory."[51]

CHAPTER 5

NORTH FROM THE PHILIPPINES

After several landings on Philippine shores
We helped MacArthur complete his chore.
At Iwo Jima we blasted
As much as we could
To let the Japs know we were there for good.
　　—"An Ode to the USS *Laffey* (DD-724),"
　　Gunner's Mate Owen Radder

Philippine Assault No. 3: Lingayen Gulf

"There Is No Turning Back"

Laffey's orders for the Lingayen Gulf invasion were carbon copies of those for the previous operations: screen for ships and provide fire support for the forces ashore during and after the landings. Becton would have preferred a different route to Lingayen Gulf—one hundred miles northwest of Manila, which took *Laffey* through narrow channels and close to Japanese airfields on Luzon, Formosa, and Okinawa—but it appeared no alternative existed.

He had company in his misgivings. Vice Admiral J. B. Oldendorf, commander of the naval forces involved, wrote a memorandum expressing concerns that his ships might be steaming into a nest of kamikazes along the way to Lingayen Gulf. His superior, Vice Admiral Thomas C. Kinkaid, brusquely ignored his worries. "Once we get underway for Lingayen, we keep going," he chastised Oldendorf. "There is no turning back."[1]

General MacArthur understood what he asked of *Laffey* and the naval units. "The enemy's strength on Luzon was known to be heavy; his suicidal fanaticism, the last ditch of the defeated, was fully comprehended."[2]

On January 2 *Laffey* and the 164 ships of the Bombardment and Fire Support Group operating under Admiral Oldendorf's task group left San Pedro Bay for Lingayen Gulf, eleven hundred miles distant. Six escort carriers steamed on an inner circle two miles from the formation's center, while three battleships, three cruisers, and six destroyers comprised a second ring one and one-half miles farther out. *Laffey* and sixteen other destroyers steamed on the edges, seven miles from center, eyes and radar scouring the seas and skies for flying Japanese aircraft, surfaced submarines, PT boats, and other surface craft.

The armada exited Leyte Gulf and entered Surigao Strait before navigating the Mindanao Sea, where the ships spread out in a formation that stretched to the horizon. Oldendorf expected that enemy aircraft would soon uncover their presence, especially when they entered the Sulu Sea and turned north toward Lingayen Gulf.

"Japanese forces in the Philippines are indeed eagerly awaiting opportunity to annihilate the invader," boasted a Japanese broadcast. The announcer promised "the hottest reception ever recorded in the annals of war on the oncoming enemy convoys."[3] An editorial in one of Japan's leading newspapers claimed that while the United States might be thinking of unleashing a second Normandy assault, they would instead face a second Dunkirk.

The Japanese lay in wait as the task force neared the northern end of the Sulu Sea, presenting plum targets for the 240 aircraft operating from airfields near Manila and elsewhere on Luzon. The attack began in the humid evening hours on January 3, when a kamikaze dived toward the Australian cruiser, *Shropshire*, but crashed into the water one hundred yards ahead of the ship. The kamikaze's appearance meant that the enemy had spotted the force before the ships had reached even the halfway mark. *Laffey* faced the unappetizing prospect of advancing six hundred miles through waters ringed by kamikaze-laden airfields.

"While enroute to and at the objective area prior to S-Day [Landing Day], the Bombardment and Fire Support Group in company with the Escort Carrier Group, or detached task units of the former, were repeatedly attacked by enemy planes, most of them of the suicide variety," described Captain

Freseman, the Commander of Destroyer Squadron 60. "Many of our ships were hit by these planes."[4]

Two suicide planes appeared on January 4. Fifteen minutes after midnight, a kamikaze evaded the CAP and dived on the escort carrier, USS *Lunga Point* (CVE-94), but antiaircraft fire splashed him before he could strike his objective. Later that day, within view of Becton, Phoutrides, and others on the bridge, a kamikaze crashed into the escort carrier, USS *Ommaney Bay* (CVE-79), before her guns could respond. Ninety minutes later the carrier, enveloped in flames, sank, taking ninety-three men with her and leaving another sixty-five wounded.

January 5 proved no better. Now two-thirds of the way to Lingayen Gulf, during the night the force steamed by Mindoro Island, the scene of *Laffey*'s earlier assault, and entered the South China Sea. Before dawn *Laffey* and *O'Brien* fired on an aircraft closing on *Laffey* from five miles west, and halted one minute later when the kamikaze disappeared in a burst of smoke, giving the ship's gunners credit for another plane. A lapse lasted until late afternoon, when in forty minutes one kamikaze exploded into the heavy cruiser, HMAS *Australia*, a second crashed into the destroyer escort USS *Stafford* (DE-411), a third and a fourth kamikaze demolished the flight deck of the escort carrier, USS *Manila Bay* (CVE-61), and a fifth struck the cruiser, USS *Louisville* (CA-28) on the bridge.

"We expected aerial resistance," said Quartermaster Phoutrides. "The *Louisville* was half mile ahead of us. I was on the bridge and watched this Jap plane hugging the ground, coming at us. Our guns hadn't fired because he came so quickly. There wasn't much we could do. We thought we were going to get hit."[5] Crew waited for the kamikaze to crash into the ship, but at the last moment the pilot changed his mind and headed toward the more tempting *Louisville*. Kamikazes inflicted 50 dead and another 157 wounded in the day's grisly attacks.

"The Japanese Had Some Kind of Special Grudge"

"If January 5 was bad," wrote Becton, "it was only a foretaste of what was to come on the sixth." In an eight-hour period, kamikazes swarmed the American ships from a multitude of directions and altitudes, leading Becton to explain "the worst kinds of things began to happen, things that would etch January 6, 1945, in the memory of thousands as one of the worst days of the Pacific war."[6]

While the escort carriers operated northwest of Lingayen Gulf, during the morning of January 6 the Bombardment and Fire Support Groups moved inside the gulf to begin the first of three days of pre-invasion bombardment of the San Fernando area. "We were coming down the gulf, and I could look out from my gun mount," said Sonarman Zack. "All the ships were in line, all coming down the gulf, and all firing. It was a beautiful battle line."[7]

As the tropical sun heated the morning military display, nerves already shaken by the previous day's encounters caused the gunner on Johnson's Mount 41, a starboard 40mm gun, to open fire without orders. He missed the aircraft, which happened to be an American fighter, and when questioned claimed that someone shouted that a Japanese aircraft was flying across the formation. Aware of the tensions that existed, Becton let the man off with a reprimand and ordered additional instructions in aircraft recognition.

Four hours later action involved every gun aboard *Laffey*, from the five-inch mounts to the 20mm antiaircraft machine guns. Two groups, Kongo Unit No. 22 under Sub-lieutenant Teruhiko Miyake and No. 23 under Sub-lieutenant Shigeru Omori, lifted from Clark Field near Manila, while a third, Unit No. 20 under Sub-lieutenant Kunitame Nakano, took off from Mabalacat to the north. The pilots hugged Luzon's hills and valleys to avoid radar and simultaneously stage attacks from several directions and altitudes.

According to Becton's action report, near noon *Walke*, the *Laffey's* companion since commissioning, was "crashed by suicide plane."[8] *Walke* gunners downed three of Sub-lieutenant Nakano's attackers, but a fourth smashed into the bridge, destroying *Walke's* communications, radars, and electrical circuits and enveloping crew in a gasoline fire. Though horribly burned, the ship's skipper, Commander George P. Davis, refused to be taken to the wardroom for treatment. He instead directed firefighting efforts until his executive officer arrived. A few hours later Davis died from his injuries and, along with eleven other casualties, was buried at sea. He was subsequently awarded a posthumous Medal of Honor for his gallantry.

Meanwhile, other kamikazes concentrated on the battleship USS *New Mexico* (BB-40), producing an explosion on the bridge that wounded eighty-seven men and killed another twenty-eight. Included among the casualties were Winston Churchill's personal liaison officer with MacArthur's headquarters, Lieutenant General Herbert Lumsden, the ship's commanding officer, Captain Robert W. Fleming, and *Time* magazine correspondent William Chickering. Becton received orders to screen the cruiser while she maneuvered clear of the other heavy ships.

Within minutes other kamikazes struck the destroyer, USS *Allen M. Sumner* (DD-692), killing fourteen and wounding twenty-nine; rammed the destroyer USS *Long* (DD-209), killing or wounding thirty-six; and damaged the destroyer transport USS *Brooks* (APD-10), killing three and wounding eleven. "I began to think that maybe the Japanese had some kind of special grudge against Destroyer Squadron Sixty,"[9] Becton wrote of the punishment his unit took.

A brief lull ended in midafternoon when a kamikaze struck the light cruiser, USS *Columbia* (CL-56), killing or wounding fifty-seven. *Laffey*'s 20mm gunners and forward five-inch gun opened fire when a bandit crossed directly ahead of the ship on the way to another target, while other kamikazes came out of the smoke and clouds and damaged *Laffey*'s sister ships, *Barton* and *O'Brien*. *O'Brien*'s gunners did not even have time to bring their weapons to bear on the intruder, who materialized from the haze and crashed into her port fantail. A second kamikaze ran at the *Barton* and, according to the ship's War Diary, "passed near port wing of bridge, brushed the starboard edge of forecastle and struck the water about ten feet from ship's side, where it disintegrated and showered the ship with gasoline, water, fragments of plane and parts of the pilot's body."[10]

The attack on their companion destroyers from DesDiv 119 was not lost on the crew. "When you saw the *Walke* and *O'Brien* damaged," said Sonarman Zack, "you have opposite thoughts. You felt you were a lucky ship, but also that sooner or later we might get hit."[11]

A third onslaught in late afternoon added to the devastation when in the span of fourteen minutes kamikazes crashed into the battleship USS *California* (BB-44), the cruiser HMAS *Australia*, the cruiser *Louisville* (CA-28), and the destroyer USS *Southard* (DD-207), killing or wounding 330 men. The brutal day ended shortly after six o'clock when the USS *Belnap* (APD-34) "reported mines attached to descending parachutes."[12]

The carnage inflicted by the twenty-eight kamikazes was, according to acclaimed naval historian, Samuel Eliot Morison, "the worst blow to the United States Navy since the Battle of Tassafaronga on 30 November 1942. It was the more difficult to bear because the recent naval victory at Leyte Gulf had made men believe that Japan was licked." Only *Laffey* of DesDiv 119's four ships had been spared damage. Seaman Martinis by now had seen more than his fill of kamikazes, and Fireman Gauding wrote in his diary that day, "*Walke, Sumner, & O'Brien* hit by suicide planes. Also some of the larger ships got hit with suicide planes. What a day."[13]

The ordeal prodded Admiral Oldendorf to request air support from Admiral Kinkaid. Oldendorf claimed that "Japanese suicide dive bombers seem able [to] attack without much interference owing [to] radar difficulties affecting all ships in Lingayen Gulf area. Airborne radar rarely makes contact with planes."[14] He added that if the transports landing the troops on January 9 received the same reception as this day, the troops might be slaughtered before they reached shore. He asked that Halsey's carrier aircraft and Army fighters continuously bomb enemy airfields on Luzon. Kinkaid responded by moving Halsey's Third Fleet west of Luzon to provide support, which made the ensuing bombardment and landings easier.

The fantail crew noticed something about tactics. Kamikazes invariably tried to hit a ship's most crucial spot, the bridge and communications center in the middle of the vessel. Consequently, in maneuvering out of the way the ship commanders often swung the fantail in the path of the oncoming plane, inadvertently turning the fantail crew into a bull's-eye. The men posted there accepted the risks and harbored no ill toward their skippers, for that is what service people do in wartime, but the prospect was still unsettling.

"The Enemy's Two Big Innings"

Shifting Halsey's aircraft and mammoth batteries appeared to work. Although kamikazes sank one destroyer on January 7, surprisingly minor opposition greeted the three-day bombardment that started that day. Becton positioned Laffey to lend supporting fire for the Underwater Demolition Teams scheduled to remove obstacles before the landings, then joined the shore bombardment to hit assigned beach targets of their own. On January 8 Laffey's guns fired at a Japanese aircraft that dived on a cruiser, obliterated a Japanese shore battery, and bombarded the beaches, the town of San Fabian, and the San Fabian-Damortis Road.

The Laffey crew was now involved in its third successive landing, and while the men would never contend that their duties in screening and gunfire support matched the ferocity of combat faced by the infantry ashore, the task nonetheless offered exhausting challenges. Fern, Johnson, and the other men on antiaircraft duties had to maintain a constant vigilance of the skies, as any lapse could create an opening to the ship for an unwelcome intruder. An SFCP could call on Laffey at any moment, requiring Zack, Dockery, and their mates to be ready around the clock to rain shells on an enemy location that was killing their infantry comrades ashore. Becton had to coordinate his movements with those of other ships and ensure that his officers and men carried out their duties as expected. Phoutrides on the bridge, Lieutenant Lloyd Hull in CIC, and men stationed elsewhere had to crisply execute their tasks if the destroyer was to be as effective as Becton demanded.

Oldendorf's invasion fleet painted a majestic portrait on January 10 as it approached the beaches in two groups, fourteen miles apart, with the Lingayen Attack Force landing on the west and the San Fabian Attack Force, which included *Laffey*, designated to hit the eastern beaches. After a preliminary bombardment, in mid-morning small craft began landing the sixty-five thousand troops that would be on Luzon by nightfall. *Laffey* remained at her post in the fire support area to lend aid to any units moving up the beaches, but spent a calm day as the Japanese had withdrawn and offered little opposition. Although the Japanese had promised a hot reaction that would turn the gulf into an inferno for the US Fleet, only three ships sustained damage during the day's events, all from artillery fire emplaced on ridges about the beaches.

On January 10 *Laffey* and other ships of the Bombardment and Fire Support Group took station northwest of the gulf, where in tandem with the Escort Carrier Group they stood guard against enemy surface attacks. Becton mainly worried about the flotilla of Japanese boats, plywood craft 18.5 feet long, each manned by three soldiers bearing depth charges and hand grenades. The tiny vessels, which sank one landing craft and damaged eight others, under cover of darkness surreptitiously approached their targets from astern, from where soldiers dropped depth charges or grenades over the stern. Security watches on all ships also looked for floating contact mines, Japanese swimmers laden with explosives, and midget submarines.

That morning *Laffey* investigated three objects off her port bow moving in the direction of the cruiser *Minneapolis*. Becton suspected the trio were Japanese soldiers with explosives strapped to their backs. He ordered sailors with M-1 rifles to eliminate the targets and the swimmers soon disappeared from sight.

Even though no enemy aircraft appeared over the next five days, the time wore on nerves. "This watchful waiting is getting everybody," Seaman Fern wrote on January 14, "short tempers and even a couple of tiffs—but even so we get along pretty good. This confinement (by necessity) to a certain spot on the ship is what's bothering us most." He added that he "sure would like to get to a place that has docking facilities or a good anchorage where you can go on the beach for a while," but admitted that even though it was difficult where he was, "still in all I'd rather be afloat than ashore slogging around like those Gi [sic] Joes & Leathernecks."[15]

Fern told his mother on January 18 that he was fine, although he had jammed his hand on a hoist while lowering shells to the magazine and "slit the skin around my knuckles open." Wartime censorship banned Fern from informing his mother of his whereabouts, but he did express his wish for a lengthy break from action. "I hope we won't have any combat duty for a good while—we've been on the go ever since we left Hawaii. Plenty of picket duty & 3 invasions."[16]

On January 22 Fern's wish materialized when *Laffey* left Philippine waters for a well-deserved break at Ulithi. They had just screened and lent gunfire support in three major landings within a month, they had battled kamikazes assaulting the task forces singly and in groups, and they had scrutinized at close hand the deadly aftermath of kamikaze attacks on other destroyers. They conducted this with minimal break, operating at sea for long periods on a ship measuring less than four hundred feet in length and jammed with more than three hundred other men also anxious for a break. Day after day they devoured the same food and swilled the same coffee, and although the food was nourishing, they would have traded a week of meals for a T-bone steak and a bottle of beer. Ulithi did not offer everything, but it at least gave the men a chance to regroup from the past month, share laughs at the beach or ballgames on the fields, and recharge batteries that were certain to be tested sooner than the men wanted.

The ship arrived five days later, at which time the crew began a two-week hiatus from the war while they enjoyed Mog Mog's sand, sun, beer and, as Gauding happily confided in his diary, "Lots of mail."[17] They did, however, intersperse work with their fun as Becton took the ship into a floating dry-dock, where all hands went over the side to chip, clean, and paint the destroyer's hull.

During the respite, Becton filed his action report. He called the crew's performance excellent, lauded his gun crews for firing 3,121 shells at enemy aircraft and land positions, and concluded that the officers and men held their own opposing the "aerial hara-kiri" during "the enemy's two big innings" of January 5–6.[18]

Other summations agreed. Admiral Oldendorf claimed that due to the unrelenting air attacks that greeted his ships, especially those of January 5–6, the Lingayen operation was worse than the bloody affair at Saipan. Frank

Kluckhohn praised *Laffey* and the other ships for making "a daring passage via the Surigao Straits, the Mindanao and Sulu Seas and the Mindoro Strait into the China Sea straight past Manila." Hanson Baldwin explained that the landing "changes the strategic picture in the Pacific"[19] by bringing the Japanese Home Islands within range of bombers based on Luzon, by hampering the flow of Japanese shipping in the South China Sea, and by giving the United States airfields, supply areas, maintenance depots, and staging areas for the inevitable invasion of Japan itself.

Ari Phoutrides, Tom Fern, and the others could take pride in their efforts. They had contributed a small part in driving the Japanese out of the Philippines and knocking them back to defensive positions at Iwo Jima and elsewhere. They were helping to remove a few more bricks in the Japanese defensive line shielding the Home Islands, bringing the war's end a bit closer.

"That was an interesting month," said Quartermaster Phoutrides of the three Philippine landings. "I thought we were lucky not to be hit by kamikazes."[20] The officers and crew learned a great deal about Japanese air tactics and kamikazes, which would aid them later, and the ship emerged unscathed.

Becton received a third Gold Star in lieu of a Silver Star for his actions off Lingayen Gulf, but Phoutrides noticed the toll the past month took on his skipper. Everyone aboard ship faced duties that had to be properly conducted, but only Becton shouldered the complete responsibility of seeing that the *Laffey* functioned smoothly. His executive officer and the other officers could carry some of the weight, but the main onus fell to him as captain of the ship. Every order he issued, every maneuver he took, affected the lives and welfare of every man aboard the destroyer. The officer who in 1943 made the nearly conflicting vows of living up to the record posted by the first *Laffey* by aggressively pursuing the enemy, while simultaneously bringing as many men back alive, contributed increased pressure to an already stressful situation. "I watched Becton's hair go from totally black to partially grey. He was under enormous pressure."[21]

"I Have Been Given A Splendid Opportunity to Die"

The Lingayen operation concluded *Laffey*'s actions in the Philippines. When the break at Ulithi ended, *Laffey* was certain to move closer to Japan, where concerns over kamikaze aircraft would intensify. If the attacks had been so punishing in the Philippines, more than twelve hundred miles from the southernmost part of Japan, they had to be more frightening when *Laffey* operated near the Home Islands. The level of determination and zeal with which a populace fights escalates dramatically as an enemy nears its home shores. Instead of their soldiers and sailors contesting battles in far-flung lands and seas, men and women now fought for their homes, villages, and families. *Laffey* crew would face the sharp end of this collected ardor.

"The menace of enemy suicide crash planes should not be under-estimated," Becton's friend, Captain William Freseman, concluded in his Lingayen Gulf action report, "and we should not delude ourselves into be-lieving that it is a temporary expedient of the enemy that will disappear at a later date. The closer we approach to Japan, and the more desperate the plight of the Japs, the greater will be the number of suicide planes encountered."[22]

Laffey crew struggled with the concept. They could not grasp the men-tality of a Japanese airman flying hundreds of miles with the sole intent of dying once he reached his objective. In a way, kamikazes personalized naval warfare, as it had been in John Paul Jones's time, when naval action featured hand-to-hand combat. The kamikaze pilot flew one plane against one ship, making each man on that ship feel that the kamikaze pilot aimed directly at him. "We were living twenty-four hours a day on a floating target," said Sea-man 2/c William Rowe, who served aboard an aircraft carrier that endured numerous kamikaze attacks. "We constantly thought of being an open tar-get. You never knew when you would be under attack and if you would be alive tomorrow. It was like living on a bull's-eye."[23]

Unlike the prevalent belief among the *Laffey* crew that kamikaze pilots were unintelligent robots mutely following orders, most came from highly educated families. Duty and honor fueled their sacrifice, and they hoped their deaths would directly help their nation to avoid defeat.

"This is, perhaps, hard to understand, for no man welcomes death," Cap-tain Rikihei Inoguchi, senior staff officer to Admiral Onishi, wrote after the war. "But it is more understandable if one bears in mind that, considering the heavy odds that our fliers faced in 1944, their chance of coming back alive from any sortie against enemy carriers was very slim, regardless of the attack method employed. If one is bound to die, what is more natural than the desire to die effectively, at maximum cost to the enemy?"[24]

The code of *Bushido*, observed by the ancient samurai warriors and re-vered for centuries in Japan, emphasized honor, courage, the ability to with-stand pain and hardship, and loyalty to the emperor. According to the code, voluntary death was preferable to living in shame. People revered warriors from the past, and school children could quote the words of the legendary hero, Masahige Kusunoki, who in 1336, as he was about to commit *hara kiri*, regretted that he did not have seven lives to give to the emperor. The highest honor, granted to most kamikaze pilots, was to be enshrined at Yasukuni, a special shrine visited twice a year by the emperor.

"If your hands are broken, fight with your feet," General Tokutaro Sakurai, commander of the 55th Infantry Division, exhorted his troops on the Arakan front in 1944. "If your hands and feet are broken, use your teeth. If there is no breath left in your body, fight with your ghost! We must have the determination to defend our positions to the death, and even after death."[25] The Special Attack Corps gave the pilots a chance for an honorable death rather than surrendering to the better-equipped, numerically superior American military.

Sub-lieutenant Saburo Sakai later contended that the pilots did not believe they were needlessly throwing away their lives. "This was not suicide! These men, young and old, were not dying in vain. Every plane that thundered into an enemy warship was a blow struck for our land. Every bomb carried by a *Kamikaze* into the fuel tanks of a giant carrier meant that many more of the enemy killed, that many more planes which would never bomb and strafe over our soil."[26]

Joseph Grew, who spent years in Japan as the American ambassador, continuously warned that Japanese society and the military would gladly sacrifice their lives for the emperor. In a popular 1944 book, *Until They Eat Stones*, author Russell Brines argued that the Japanese possessed a suicide complex developed by devotion to the emperor and by their belief that defeat is shameful, "a national humiliation so great that many Japanese would rather die than live under it." He claimed that the Japanese would never surrender, that they would fight for one hundred years if necessary, and that in any attack on Home Islands, the American military "would have to cut its way through men, women and children, who would line the shore with any available weapons." As proof Brines cited a popular Japanese quote, "we will fight until we eat stones!"[27]

Loyalty to family and emperor provided huge motivators for kamikaze pilots. Before taking off, each pilot wrote a farewell letter to his parents and placed fingernail clippings and a lock of hair in a sealed envelope to be sent home after his death. "I have been given a splendid opportunity to die. This is my last day," wrote Flying Petty Officer First Class Isao Matsuo of the 701st Air Group to his parents on October 28, 1944. "I shall be a shield for His Majesty and die cleanly along with my squadron leader and other friends.

I wish that I could be born seven times, each time to smite the enemy. How I appreciate this chance to die like a man!" After these expressions, Matsuo included a message for his parents. "Thank you, my parents, for the 23 years during which you have cared for me and inspired me. I hope that my present deed will in some small way repay what you have done for me. Think well of me and know that your Isao died for our country. This is my last wish, and there is nothing else that I desire."

Ensign Teruo Yamaguchi, of the 12th Air Flotilla, wrote his father, "During my final plunge, though you will not hear it, you may be sure I will be saying '*chichiue*' [revered father] to you and thinking of all you have done for me."[28]

"The Latest and Most Threatening Problem"

Becton studied kamikaze tactics to determine the best defense. The intruders invariably approached from either very high or extremely low altitudes, complicating matters for radar, which had no view directly above or close to the water. A plane coming in from twenty to thirty thousand feet forced the CAP to climb and reduced the effectiveness of American antiaircraft fire, giving kamikazes more time to reach their targets. This approach also gave the pilot a panoramic view of conditions below and made it easier to select which ship to target.

On the other hand, hugging the water's surface often enabled the plane to sneak in under the radar. However, when the pilot neared his target, he had to climb to sixteen hundred feet before diving so that the aircraft plunged downward into the ship and caused the greatest damage.

Kamikazes attacking in large numbers employed both high and low altitude approaches to complicate matters for CAP and for gun crews. The pilots tried to crash either into the ship's bridge and the center of the vessel, the most vulnerable portion as well as where the vital control and communication facilities were housed, or close to the waterline.

By the end of January 1945, ship commanders related harrowing tales of destruction and near misses, and in their action reports pled for tactics to neutralize the enemy pilots. Defensive moves to that time consisted of three steps: bringing to bear every antiaircraft gun possible, hoping for accuracy from gun crews, and rapidly altering course to make it more difficult for the pilot to hit the ship.

The Navy's Air Intelligence Group in Washington, DC, called kamikazes "the latest and most threatening problem that has yet confronted the U.S. Navy."[29] Before their appearance, American antiaircraft gun crews and CAP assessed as successful the shooting down of eighty to ninety percent of enemy attackers. With the dawn of kamikazes, they had to destroy every single aircraft to avoid serious damage.

Strategists, especially Rear Admiral Wilder D. Baker and Captain James Thach on Admiral John S. McCain's staff, devised countermeasures. They urged fleet commanders to arrange additional antiaircraft training, especially for the 20mm and 40mm crews, who constituted the last line of defense against the attackers. They reduced the number of dive bombers and torpedo bombers aboard aircraft carriers so that the vessels could almost double their complement of fighters. Rather than sticking close to the carriers and waiting for the kamikazes to arrive, CAPs began intercepting enemy planes as far from ships as possible. They established patrols at both higher and lower altitudes and at the four cardinal points around each task group. Carrier aircraft hit enemy airfields day and night to prevent kamikazes from taking off. Finally, destroyers manned picket stations sixty miles from task forces as early warning systems.

Becton and the other commanders received instructions on how to defend against kamikazes. In case of an attack, he should first increase speed and utilize tight turns in zigzag fashion, and as a kamikaze drew closer, cease zigzagging and turn the ship so that every available gun could fire on the target. Becton should present a stern target rather than a bow target, both because the damage sustained in the stern would be less than in the bow and because the bow housed some of the ship's control systems and the operations of many key personnel. Although radar handed commanders an advantage, they were told to post as many lookouts topside as possible to detect aircraft that radar missed.

Finally, instructions emphasized that a skipper's demeanor had a powerful impact on the crew. Men gain faith if their commander is calm and confident, and lose effectiveness if their skipper is indecisive and distant. "In destroyers and smaller ships," wrote Freseman, "the action of each commanding officer in handling the situation will, in large measure, determine the final effectiveness of the suicide plane attack. The development of the ship's fighting ability and morale to the highest peak is essential."[30]

With Becton at the helm, *Laffey* crew felt no need to worry on this point.

"Taking the War to the Enemy's Homeland"

Laffey's respite at Ulithi ended February 10 when she set to sea along with the hundreds of fast carriers, battleships, cruisers, and destroyers of Task Force 58 for a welcome mission. "Task Force 58 underway for Tokyo,"[31] Gauding mentioned in his diary.

The crew enjoyed the thought of hitting the enemy's homeland, which was both a form of gaining revenge for earlier defeats and a sign that the war progressed in their favor. Even before most had joined the Navy, many who eventually comprised the *Laffey* crew followed newspaper and radio accounts detailing Japanese barbarism in China and recoiled from the December 1937 Japanese air attack against the American gunboat USS *Panay* (PR-5) in the Yangtze River in China. Their repugnance toward the Japanese compounded with the sudden December 7 attack against American forces in Hawaii and the Japanese march to transform the western half of the Pacific Ocean into a vast empire. The opportunity to now turn the tables on the Japanese and strike directly against the Home Islands, as the enemy had done in December 1941, was one prospect that everyone welcomed. "We were all kind of excited by it," said Seaman Martinis of operating off the enemy's shores. "We were taking the war to the enemy's homeland."[32]

The ships had been operating off the Philippines and in the South China Sea as Task Force 38 under Admiral Halsey, while Admiral Raymond A. Spruance, the victor of Midway, planned the Iwo Jima assault. The two now switched places, positioning Spruance at the helm while Halsey remained at headquarters for rest and to plan subsequent attacks against the Japanese. *Laffey* crew could now boast that they had served in both theaters of war, had participated in both MacArthur's South Pacific route to Japan and Nimitz's Central Pacific route, and had chased the enemy with Halsey's Third Fleet, Spruance's Fifth Fleet, and Kinkaid's Seventh Fleet. Few crews could lay the same claim.

While *Laffey* had operated with one task group in the Philippines, they now steamed to war with multiple task groups, an awesome example of the productivity of America's factories. Vice Admiral Marc A. Mitscher, who oversaw five task groups, 58.1 to 58.5, commanded Spruance's fast carriers. *Laffey* operated with Rear Admiral Arthur W. Radford's TG 58.4, consisting of the fast carriers USS *Yorktown* (CV-10) and USS *Randolph* (CV-15), the light carriers USS *Langley* (CVL-27) and USS *Cabot* (CVL-28), two fast battleships, three light cruisers, and seventeen destroyers, including *Barton* and *O'Brien*. To the crew's delight, the force would close to within one hundred miles of the Japanese coast, from where aircraft would neutralize airfields on Japan's main island of Honshu before kamikazes could strike the ships approaching Iwo Jima for the February 19 landings. After blasting the enemy's airfields, the first such strike against the Japanese Home Islands since Jimmy Doolittle's heralded April 1942 bombing of Tokyo, the force would turn south to Iwo Jima and provide support for the troops fighting on the island.

Concerns tempered the exhilaration at hitting the heart of the Japanese Empire, which would be defended by greater numbers of kamikazes than the crew experienced off the Philippines. Hanson Baldwin wrote in the days before the air strikes that they would provide a stern test for the fleet, "for our ships must be prepared to meet surface, subsurface and air attack, day and night." He stated that casualties, "already very high for the Navy since the start of the Philippine campaign," could worsen, "for the closer we get to Tokyo the harder the Japanese—like cornered rats—will fight."[33]

Instead of adopting a direct course to Honshu, the force steamed northeast for several days in hopes of deceiving the Japanese and allowing the carriers to draw closer to the coast. This would shorten the distance from flight deck to target and permit aircraft to spend more time bombing and strafing factories and shipyards before they had to return to their carriers.

Even though they had just completed three grueling Philippine campaigns, Becton conducted drills to keep his men sharp. The war diary for February 14, for instance, recorded that Becton scheduled drills for "suicide plane hit on the bridge, fire in Ward Room, burning gasoline from plane sprayed over bridge and adjacent 40mm mounts, bridge control personnel and equipment knocked out."[34]

The next day the force upped the speed to twenty knots for the run in to the launch point, 125 miles southeast of Tokyo and 60 miles off the Honshu coast. The weather worsened as the ships neared Japan, with squalls drenching cold rain on the crew and reducing visibility to two hundred yards. Ships lifted and plunged in the swells, dousing the men stationed on *Laffey*'s fore sections in sleet and snow. Eyelashes clotted from the wintry conditions, and icy winds bit into exposed flesh, making the men on watch long for the chance to escape below to a waiting mug of hot coffee. Phoutrides in his bridge station and Lieutenant Hull in CIC were sheltered from the weather and kept comparatively warm at their posts, but they sympathized with their friends who stood watch at outside posts where the elements dominated.

According to the War Diary, on February 16 *Laffey* was "approaching main Japanese island of Honshu from the southeast. Sweeps and strikes were launched throughout the day at targets in the Tokyo area."[35] The first strike lifted off shortly after dawn, sending *Laffey*'s crew to battle stations for the next ten hours while the carriers launched and recovered aircraft. Becton, certain that the enemy would organize retaliatory raids to protect their heartland, had his radarmen and lookouts scouring every sector of the sky, while he stood in his customary spot on the open starboard wing of the bridge and kept his own watch on the skies for intruders. Japanese aircraft threatened the force five separate times over the next six hours, but each time CAP splashed the intruders before they drew within range of *Laffey*'s guns.

Becton moved closer to the carriers as they launched and recovered planes, a prime time for aviators in faulty aircraft to splash in the waters nearby. If that were to occur, Becton rushed to rescue the pilot. Lieutenant Al Henke's engines provided added power to answer Becton's call for increased speed, and men dashed to posts where they stood ready to retrieve the carriers' pilots as needed.

If they were not called to rescue an aviator, Becton kept *Laffey* on station anywhere from four hundred to five hundred yards out, steaming the outskirts as radar and sonar kept watch for the enemy. Screening for carriers proved to be exciting duty, more enthralling than escorting cargo tankers or landing craft, but lacked the impact an offensive engagement provided.

In air battles across Tokyo Bay, from the city of Tokyo in the north to the vital port of Yokohama and the Yokosuka Naval Base in the south, US fighters blasted aircraft engine and frame plants near Tokyo and engaged in dogfights with Japanese planes that rose to meet them. The final aircraft returned to the carriers by 5:30 p.m., at which time the force retired to the east for the night before turning back toward Honshu to be in position to launch a second round of air strikes in the morning.

Aircraft launched the next morning, but in deteriorating weather had difficulty locating their targets. A few planes hit plants and shipping near Tokyo, but Admiral Mitscher cancelled the remaining strikes and set a course south for Iwo Jima. The two-day raid succeeded in damaging plants, destroying aircraft at their bases, and sinking a few ships, including the 10,600-ton *Yamashiro Maru*, at the cost of 80 US aircraft lost.

"What a Year for an Eighteen-Year-Old!"

On February 18 the ships barreled south to be in position to support the next day's landings on Iwo Jima, an island 1,600 miles northeast of Lingayen

Gulf and 660 miles south of Tokyo. Admiral Nimitz wanted to seize the island to provide an emergency landing field for B-29 Superfortress bombers on their way back to Saipan from hitting Japan, a place to house fighters that could escort those bombers, and a base from which to strike at the next target, Okinawa.

As dawn broke on February 19, battleship and cruiser batteries blasted beaches, airfields, and other Japanese emplacements in the heaviest pre-invasion bombardment of the war. Two hours later landing craft dropped off the first of many waves that would, by nightfall, place thirty thousand Marines ashore. "I turned nineteen the day we landed on Iwo Jima," said Seaman Johnson. "What a year for an eighteen-year-old! I was forced to mature fast."[36] In one year the teenager had experienced combat at Normandy, in three Philippine invasions, and during the air strike mission against the Japanese homeland, but the main act was yet to come.

Over the next four days *Laffey* operated sixty-five miles offshore, screening for the carriers as they launched strikes, and from closer distances, providing fire support to the Marines trying to eliminate the hundreds of machine gun and mortar positions that dotted the island. Although Zack and Dockery were blocked from observing events on the island, Johnson on his starboard 40mm and Fern on his port gun watched the island erupt as Japanese and American forces closed on each other. Exploding mortar shells kicked up clouds of the black coral sand so common on Iwo Jima. US aircraft dropped bombs on Japanese pillboxes whose machine guns mauled American Marines as they charged into withering fire, and American Sherman tanks equipped with the Navy Mark I flame thrower responded with sheets of flame incinerating troops and armament. Fern and Johnson had once been eager to experience combat, but they could not then conjure what war was like. Iwo Jima offered glimpses of what their Marine cohorts, as well as the Japanese, faced. Being enveloped in flames or attacked by suicidal troops executing a banzai charge was something every man aboard preferred to avoid.

The Japanese air arm was surprisingly absent off Iwo Jima. A handful of kamikaze aircraft damaged two ships and sank one escort carrier, but the earlier air strikes against Honshu helped reduce the number of suicide attackers.

On February 24 *Laffey* and the task force turned northward for "more strikes against the Empire," according to the War Diary.[37] With the invasion of Okinawa looming, Mitscher wanted another crack at the thousands of enemy aircraft before they could be a factor off Okinawa. Wind, rain, and freezing temperatures shielded the force as it steamed close to Japan, but made life miserable for Becton and the others on the bridge. Becton's teeth chattered and he smacked his hands together to provide warmth to his fingers, but he remained on the bridge for hours at a time, trying to gain a visual on what the ship faced.

Cruising 190 miles southeast of Tokyo on February 25, the carriers launched daylight strikes against targets in the Tokyo and Yokohama area. Mitscher intended to send a second air strike later in the morning, but poor weather conditions canceled that operation. After retiring eastward for the night, the force returned for a second day of air attacks, but again rain and wind forced Mitscher to drop the strikes.

While Mitscher took the rest of his ships south for Ulithi, he ordered Becton to rush photographs and mail to Nimitz's headquarters at Guam. Steaming alone to the island, a thousand miles away, *Laffey* reached her destination without mishap. On March 1 Becton steered the ship into Guam's harbor, delivered the material to headquarters, and within three hours had departed for Ulithi, this time accompanied by a second destroyer.

Laffey neither fired a gun at the enemy nor received any fire in return during the air strikes against the Japanese homeland, but the air strikes directly into the mainland affected Japanese civilian and military morale and gained praise back home. Correspondent Warren Moscow wrote in the *New York Times* that the Navy, in "the most daring operation of the Pacific war to date," and striking "so close to the heart of the Japanese Empire and so close to their main land-based aircraft," had taken the war to Tokyo inhabitants in way they had never seen. Instead of Doolittle's high-flying bombers, "there are swarms of planes striking at tree-top level, hitting airfields, aircraft and other military targets around the city in strafing attacks."[38]

An editorial in the same newspaper claimed that with these strikes "the penultimate phase of the Battle for Japan has begun," and that by its actions the United States had let the Japanese know that an invasion could be expected. More important, Japanese propagandists could no longer fool their people and claim they possessed the military hardware and forces to withstand the United States. "Not when Tokyo's seven millions have seen hundreds of white-starred planes ranging over their capital city for two days, heard the explosion of American bombs, seen the 7,000-foot high columns of smoke blotting out the vista to Fujiyama, realized that almost within sight of their coast is arrayed the world's mightiest fleet, a fleet their propagandists many times had told them was destroyed."[39]

The crew could feel good about their recent operations. Not only had they assisted in placing land troops on Iwo Jima, the latest in a series of invasions leading to the doorsteps of Japan, but they had also participated in hitting the enemy where it would do the heaviest psychological damage—in their homes and work places. Almost three long years of hard fighting had occurred since April 1942, when Jimmy Doolittle and his bombers alerted people and industries in the Japanese heartland that they, too, could become casualties of war. Japanese civilians had since then grown accustomed to hearing war news, but whether good or bad, it unfolded at some distant place, far from home and family. That was now no longer the case, and the war had suddenly appeared off their shores. The *Laffey* crew did not pilot the planes that bombed those enemy factories and shipyards, but they could at least take pleasure in knowing they were a part of it.

Noticing the relative absence of kamikaze attacks in the recent operations, some of the crew harbored hopes that they had passed through the worst of their travails in the Philippine operations. Phoutrides and Johnson considered their actions off Iwo Jima and in the two raids against the Japanese homeland something of a lull, as so little opposition had appeared. The concern had been that as the American forces drew closer to Japan, the enemy would mount a more spirited, and bloody, defense, but that had not been the case.

If the Japanese failed to send swarms of kamikazes when Mitscher's ships had pulled so close to their coast, maybe that threat had ended.

Maybe the next place, Okinawa, would not be so bad after all.

PART III

HELL FROM
THE HEAVENS

CHAPTER 6

FIRST DAYS AT OKINAWA

After striking Nippon's home
Off Iwo Jima she did roam.
Then Okinawa to be eyes
And guns to clear the hostile skies.
　　—"Invicta," Lieutenant Matthew Darnell

In late morning on March 2, *Laffey* entered Mugai Channel of Ulithi Atoll. The men had never seen anything like the vast anchorage, filled with ships of every sort. A part of the vast Caroline Islands chain located 850 miles east of the Philippines, Ulithi, a volcanic atoll with coral islands, sand, and palm trees, encircled an anchorage fifteen miles across. "It was huge," said Sonarman Zack. "The entire task force could fit inside it."[1] Seabees constructed an airstrip on Falalop Island in the northeast, headquarters on Asor to its west, an advanced base hospital and ship repair facilities on Sorlen to the north, and—the reason most sailors looked forward to a stay at Ulithi— recreational facilities and beer on Mog Mog.

To sailors accustomed to weeks and months at sea, where death was a constant, Mog Mog was paradise. Though a minority, like Massachusetts native Tom Fern, wished for a little snow to break the sultry monotony, most men joked that it offered their four favorite "Bs"—bathing, baseball, boxing, and beer. Golden beaches and their luscious sand replaced the unforgiving decks of destroyers and cruisers, deep blue waters offered the chance for a refreshing swim, and cooks handed out ice cream, pies, and cake. Mog Mog's beer bars—little more than wooden stands set up to handle the eighteen to twenty thousand men who packed the island, dispensed two bottles of warm beer to each enlisted. Officers enjoyed their own facility where they could purchase a shot of Scotch for twenty cents and enjoy the company of Navy female nurses. Basketball courts, baseball diamonds, and a football field offered recreation for the athletically inclined, while a movie theater and a small chapel enticed those who sought more passive endeavors. Even former heavyweight boxing champion, Gene Tunney, who had twice defeated Jack Dempsey in compiling a sixty-five-win career, was there to arrange recreation events for the thousands of sailors. Until late that afternoon, when everyone had to return to his ship, Mog Mog provided a safe haven from the war. For the next seventeen days Fern, Johnson, and their shipmates could take their minds off kamikazes and bloodshed and be youngsters again.

To provide stability to a novice crew and to give the men time to gel into an efficient team, for the first year of a new ship's existence, Navy policy dictated that no officers would be transferred. As a year had now passed since *Laffey's* February 1944 commissioning, Becton lost his executive officer, Lieutenant Charles Holovak, who received command of his own ship, and his gunnery officer, Lieutenant Harry Burns, who became an executive officer elsewhere. Although Becton would miss the capable officers their replacements, Lieutenant Challen McCune Jr. as his new second in command and Lieutenant Paul B. Smith as gunnery officer, ably slipped into their new duties. Tougher to replace was the group of senior petty officers and other experienced men the Navy shifted to man the vessels coming out of shipyards.

During their stay at Ulithi the crew selected an emblem for *Laffey*: a black tiger with glaring yellow eyes and menacing fangs chewing on a twisted Japanese plane. The symbol was a natural outgrowth of Becton's wish to operate an aggressive ship that took the fight to the enemy, similar to a tiger attacking its prey, and recognition of the obvious role that Japanese aircraft had in Pacific combat. "It means we're bad luck, or death, to Jap planes," Seaman 1/c Ernest E. Belk later explained. "We didn't know how appropriate it was going to be, though."[2]

Although kamikazes had been largely absent from the air strikes against Tokyo and their operations off Iwo Jima, they could not be discounted, even at Ulithi, distant from the combat zone. On March 11, while the crew watched a movie on the forecastle, general quarters sounded. Men rushed to battle stations as Lieutenant Iroshi Murakawa and eleven enemy aircraft from the Mitate Unit No. 2 dived on the carrier USS *Randolph* (CV-15). One barreled through heavy antiaircraft fire and smashed into the carrier's starboard side just below the flight deck, killing 27 and wounding 105.

The next day Becton called Lieutenant Manson and Lieutenant Henke to his cabin. With only one more weekend in Ulithi before the planned Easter Sunday attack on Okinawa, Becton wanted a religious service for his crew before they left for what could be their toughest operation to date. "Look at that attack yesterday," he remarked to the pair. "If eight hundred miles of ocean won't stop them from trying, we are going to need help."

He asked Manson and Henke to organize an Easter service on the final Sunday, March 18. They turned to Seaman Belk for assistance, and together the three assembled a moving ceremony held three days before the ship left Ulithi. Lieutenant Henke read prayers, and Radioman 3/c Lawrence F. Kelley, whose heart-wrenching tenor voice had often entertained the crew in late afternoon sessions on the fantail, sang several religious pieces before turning to the popular "I'll Be Seeing You." The powerful song about a person who, although far from his loved one, sees her image wherever he turns, moved those who attended and had men thinking of family and loved ones. Lieutenant Youngquist, who attended every service held aboard *Laffey*, noticed an increased attentiveness in the men who would soon be entering combat. "I suppose there have been many grander and more impressive religious services held to celebrate Easter and to invoke the Almighty's blessing," wrote Becton. "But I doubt if any has ever been more sincerely touching than the one we had aboard the *Laffey* about two weeks before we sailed into hell."[3]

As Ulithi and its pleasures slipped from view, the crew's thoughts turned to the upcoming Okinawa operation. Facing another lengthy operation at sea, Seaman Fern had already dispatched a letter imploring his parents, "don't be mad when you don't get any letters for a while."[4] Men held mixed opinions as to what they might encounter. Kamikazes had been active while *Laffey* covered three Philippine landings, but had been conspicuously absent during their raids against Japan and off Iwo Jima. Most assumed the weapon was certain to appear, but hopefully the numbers would not compare to what they had witnessed off the Philippines.

Some argued that luck had so far sheltered the ship and crew. During stretches of time when kamikazes dived on battleships and smashed into cruisers, *Laffey* emerged unscathed, first off the Philippines and then again off Japan and Iwo Jima, apparently being one of those vessels good fortune favored. "At that time of our lives," said Seaman Martinis, "we considered ourselves indestructible. Kamikazes wouldn't happen to us."[5]

"It May Be a While Before You Hear From Me"

The United States gathered an immense force to seize Okinawa. More than twelve hundred ships, including eighteen battleships, two hundred destroyers, and over forty aircraft carriers escorted and transported the assault troops to the island. So great was the armada that forces had to assemble at almost every major US port in the Pacific, including locations in the Marianas, the Philippines, the Solomons, Hawaii, and the West Coast. Under the command of Admiral Spruance, the hero of Midway, and Vice Admiral Richmond Kelly Turner, the naval units rivaled those employed in the massive European D-Day operation staged at Normandy.

The campaign for Okinawa was the most recent in a long string of operations that shoved the Japanese out of the island bastions they proudly held in early 1942. Beginning in the Solomons, United States land and sea forces gradually leapt westward and northward in a simultaneous advance along two Pacific paths, gobbling up the Gilberts, the Marshalls, the Marianas, New Guinea, the Philippines, and Iwo Jima in the process. Now, they were poised to grab Okinawa, practically on the doorstep of Japan. Once successful, the Americans intended to use Okinawan airfields to house bombers to attack Japan, and Okinawa itself as a major staging area for the massive numbers of men, ships, and supplies required for the landmark invasion of Japan.

The Japanese considered Okinawa to be a part of Japan proper. American planners accordingly assembled a powerful landing force to counter the thousands of enemy soldiers defending the island. Three Marine and four Army divisions would land on Okinawa's western coast before splitting, with the Marines clearing out the northern part of Okinawa while the Army secured the south.

The Navy's role varied little from earlier assaults. Admiral Mitscher's carrier aircraft would conduct preliminary strikes against Formosa, Okinawa, and Tokyo and other strategic points in the Home Islands before turning south to support the April 1 landings. In the meantime *Laffey*, no longer with Mitscher's fast carriers, would join other ships to provide supporting gunfire to the landing force.

Suicide aircraft were on the minds of every American naval commander assigned to be a part of the operation. During a March 10 meeting, while *Laffey*'s crew rested at Ulithi, Admirals Nimitz, Spruance, and Mitscher expressed their concerns over the expanding toll of the Pacific War. Marines had suffered hideous casualties at Saipan, Iwo Jima, and other locations. Due to kamikaze attacks an increasing number of naval vessels had either limped back to port for repairs or wound up on the ocean's bottom. Mitscher warned the group to expect hundreds, if not thousands, of kamikaze aircraft during the Okinawa operation.

Three days later Mitscher guided Task Force 58 out of Ulithi on its pre-invasion mission of hitting Kyushu airfields, but suffered severe losses when Japanese bombers hit the carriers USS *Wasp* (CV-18) and *Franklin* on March 19. One bomb forced *Wasp* to return to the States for repairs, while two bombs ripped through the *Franklin*'s hangar deck, igniting gasoline-laden aircraft and demolishing the CIC. The Japanese pilots succeeded in killing more than seven hundred crew and knocking two vessels out of the war. The event showed how prepared the enemy was two weeks before the invasion, portending difficult times for *Laffey* and fellow vessels when they prowled the waters off Okinawa.

As much as the United States wanted Okinawa, the Japanese intended to prevent its loss. To them, retaining the island was a matter of honor and pride. Standing merely 350 miles south of Kyushu, Okinawa was considered one of Japan's forty-seven prefectures. Assaulting it would be akin to attacking Tokyo. The Japanese boasted that in their long history the Home Islands had never been invaded, but should Okinawa fall, little remained to stop the Americans from doing exactly that. The Japanese military would turn to any measure, any last resort, to prevent the unthinkable from occurring. On March 20, one day before *Laffey* left Ulithi for Okinawa, Imperial General Headquarters labeled the island "the focal point of the decisive battle for the defense of the Homeland"[6] and marshaled every weapon at their command to repel the invaders.

Desperate times called for desperate measures. Imperial General Head-quarters realized the enemy would come for Okinawa, but they lacked the necessary resources to stop them. Serious shortages existed in ships, oil, bombs, and bullets. Japanese factories, once humming with activity, now labored under devastating American bombing raids to produce a fraction of what they had previously manufactured. Placed in a precarious situation, the Japanese hoarded their remaining aircraft and turned to the one commodity they possessed in abundance—volunteers willing to die for their country and their Emperor by piloting aircraft into enemy ships. One aircraft, one ship—a simple equation that, if successful, might reverse fortune for the reeling Japanese.

In a March 29 meeting, Emperor Hirohito admonished his military commanders to adopt every possible measure to halt the United States. They informed him that because of the disastrous naval clashes in the Philippines, few surface forces were available, but that more than three thousand kamikaze aircraft stood ready to meet the Americans at Okinawa.

As Imperial General Headquarters stated in outlining the new plans, "there was no longer any alternative to general use of special attacks, in which even inexperienced pilots could score a hit."[7] The plan, named *Ten Go* ("Heavenly Operation"), earmarked a series of colossal air raids, called *kikusui* ("floating chrysanthemums"), to assault enemy ships off Okinawa. The newest aircraft and most experienced pilots would be retained in the homeland to defend Japan's shores, but otherwise every available aircraft, including seaplanes, outdated fighters, training planes, and scout planes, was sent to Vice Admiral Matome Ugaki's Fifth Air Fleet in Kyushu for use off Okinawa. Despite being given little training in flying, men willing to gain honor by yielding their lives quickly filled the kamikaze corps.

"As the air raids on the Japanese archipelago intensified, we noticed a definite change in the morale of the *kamikaze* volunteers," said Captain Rikihei Inoguchi, the senior staff officer to Admiral Onishi. "They became more desperate than ever. They became more agitated emotionally by the conviction that only by their deaths could the fatherland be saved from imminent destruction."[8]

Japanese soldiers fighting on Okinawa planned to slow the American advance on land with a series of defense lines anchored along Okinawa's numerous ridges and throughout the island's elaborate network of caves. In stalling the American drive on land, they would force American ships to remain offshore to lend air support, thereby turning them into tempting targets for kamikaze attacks. Lieutenant General Mitsuru Ushijima, commander of the Japanese defenders on Okinawa, exhorted his men to a spirited defense by heralding the feats of their brethren in the skies. "The brave, ruddy faced warriors with white silken scarves tied about their heads, at peace in their favorite planes, would dash spiritedly out to the attack."[9] Ushijima counted on the kamikazes to so seriously impede US naval support for the forces ashore that he would be able to defeat the Marines and Army infantry.

American ships and sailors would pay a heavy price as a result. "In the Ryukyus," remarked Vice Admiral Seiichi Ito on April 2, "we can best break the enemy's leg."[10] Ito would soon command Japan's final surface foray at sea.

One of the subjects of Ito's scorn, Tom Fern, only knew that he was again venturing into combat. He wrote his mother on March 21, "it may be a while before you hear from me after this—haven't got time to write you a regular letter so this will have to do."[11] Fern planned to send a longer letter as soon as he returned from the assignment, but for now his mother would have to be satisfied with the few words he could provide. Seaman Fern wished he could impart more, but the Navy clamped a tight lid on information. Outside of Becton, no one in the crew knew much about operations anyway. His mother would need to endure the coming weeks without knowing whether her boy was safe, a burden shared by other mothers and fathers throughout the United States.

"Lone Ranger Duty"

Laffey left Ulithi as part of Task Force 54, the largest bombardment group yet assembled in the Pacific, commanded by their old friend from Normandy days, Rear Admiral M. L. Deyo. Eighty-three ships, including ten battleships and ten cruisers screened by *Laffey* and twenty-three destroyers, exited the anchorage on March 21 to begin the three-day journey to Okinawa. The long line of warships impressed observers on shore, who watched the latest conglomeration of American military might—further proof of American industrial capacity—sweep into Pacific waters.

From other ports and anchorages troop transports, crowded with Army infantry or Marine units, bore the invasion forces toward Okinawa. Knots formed in stomachs and thoughts turned to family and home as the ships moved closer to the island, for whether Marine or Army, all had heard of the carnage that marked the most recent operation against Iwo Jima. This assault was likely to bring more of the same.

The *Laffey* crew held a different perspective as they took their ship to sea. Although they could not forget what had happened to the landing forces at Iwo Jima, at least the air opposition, the part with which they were most concerned, had slackened. Compared to what they had encountered off the Philippines, the enemy's air response during their raids against the Tokyo area and during the Iwo Jima operation had been surprisingly light. As far as the men were concerned, they would most likely encounter the same lack of air attack at Okinawa. Sonarman Zack expected some aerial fireworks to occur, only because they were moving closer to Japan and the enemy had already proven willing to resort to desperate measures, but few thought that squadrons of kamikazes would descend on them as they operated off the island.

Late in the afternoon Becton proceeded to his assigned station twelve miles ahead of the task force, forming the vanguard of Deyo's assemblage as it churned toward the island. The next day Becton conducted drills simulating a bomb hit near his forward five-inch gun mount and a suicide crash into the base of the number one stack. Most of the crew read nothing into the exercises—Becton had, after all, kept them busy with drills since the ship's commissioning—but the skipper's choices that day proved prophetic.

Largely due to Mitscher's carrier aircraft and Army B-29 bombers, Task Force 54 arrived in Okinawa waters late on March 24 without being attacked. Intelligence estimated that airfields on Okinawa, Formosa, and Kyushu housed as many as three thousand Japanese planes. To neutralize that weapon, on March 23 Army and Navy aircraft opened a series of air strikes to destroy those kamikazes before they lifted from the runways.

As American aircraft pounded enemy airfields, on March 25 five ships, including two cruisers screened by *Laffey* and two other destroyers, detached from Deyo's main force and proceeded toward Kerama Retto, a cluster of ten rocky islands fifteen miles off Okinawa's southwest coast. The islands, which fashioned a sheltered harbor large enough to anchor seventy-five ships, would serve as an advanced fueling and resupply base as well as a repair center for any ships damaged during the operation.

The March 26–29 seizure of these islands by the Army's 77th Division, backed by *Laffey* and the detached force, proved to be a sideshow to the main landings at Okinawa a few days later, but it reaped welcome dividends at minimal cost. The crews of numerous destroyers, including *Laffey*'s, would frequent the anchorage's repair facilities in the weeks to come. In addition, the infantry stumbled upon a surprise when they unearthed 350 suicide boats, camouflaged and hidden in caves. The plywood craft, eighteen feet long and five feet wide, each carried two 250-pound depth charges. Had the boats remained undiscovered, the Japanese planned to steer the craft toward the numerous troop-laden American transports floating in the waters near Okinawa. Those craft would now pose no threat to the landing force as it neared Okinawa.

Laffey again executed a variety of assignments during three weeks off Okinawa. Patrolling for enemy submarines occupied some days, while shore bombardments, night harassing fire, and screening filled the rest. As dusk approached, they joined with other ships in a circular cruising disposition designed for enhanced antiaircraft defense, and retired seaward for the night.

They started March 26, when they joined one battleship, two cruisers, and two destroyers to patrol the area southwest of Kerama Retto. While the *Laffey* crew enjoyed a quiet day, a kamikaze crashed into the aft gun mount of the USS *Kimberly* (DD-521), a destroyer screening with a different unit, killing four and wounding fifty-seven. This initial attack on a picket ship off Okinawa spared Becton and his crew, but he remarked that it "was a nasty hint of what was to come."[12]

Any lingering hopes among the crew that the kamikaze threat had dissipated ended early the next morning when seven Japanese aircraft damaged five ships, including the venerable battleship USS *Nevada* (BB-36), which lost eleven men killed and forty-nine wounded. Most wrenching, as far as *Laffey* crew were concerned, was the loss of their sister ship, *O'Brien*. After being constructed at the Bath Shipyard, the two had operated together in both the European and the Pacific theaters. Men from both ships had mixed with each other during shore liberties, and at sea delivered mail and exchanged personnel. The crews had already lost two ships from DesDiv 119—German mines and bombs sank *Meredith* off the coast of France, while kamikazes badly damaged *Walke* at Lingayen Gulf—and the third was now removed on March 27 when a sole kamikaze bore through thick antiaircraft fire and crashed forward of amidships on *O'Brien*'s port side. Fifty men were killed or missing and another seventy-six were wounded. Thirty-six minutes later a second kamikaze dived at *Laffey*, but gunfire from adjoining ships splashed the intruder two miles short of its target.

Action intensified March 28–29 when *Laffey* joined two battleships, one cruiser, and two destroyers and proceeded to another screening position ten miles west of Naha on Okinawa's western side. While the larger warships conducted a seven-hour bombardment of the Naha area, *Laffey* scoured the sea and sky for enemy patrol boats, submarines, and aircraft. All guns were manned and ready to fire, but no threat appeared until late that night. As the unit retired seaward for the night, *Laffey*'s radar picked up an enemy plane at twenty-five miles. Four minutes later, Becton ordered his forward five-inch guns to commence firing, and for the first time in the Okinawa campaign, *Laffey*'s forward gun mount crews jumped to action. The powerful guns trained on the incoming plane and boomed a line of shells toward the enemy, turning away the plane after firing more than one hundred rounds in four minutes. Shortly after midnight on March 29, Becton investigated a sonar contact that appeared at thirteen hundred yards, and two hours later a bogey closed to within seven miles before ship antiaircraft fire brought it down.

The next day *Laffey* left the formation to refuel at Kerama Retto. Ships of all sorts darted about the busy anchorage, filled mostly with vessels in need of repair from kamikaze damage or requiring more ammunition and supplies. Most men aboard *Laffey* took only a cursory glance at the hobbled ships, as they were preoccupied with replenishing their vessel. After refueling, the ship steamed to that day's patrolling station five miles northwest of Kerama Retto.

On March 31 *Laffey* patrolled off southern Okinawa when a kamikaze struck Admiral Spruance's flagship, USS *Indianapolis* (CA-35), forcing the cruiser out of action for repair. Spruance switched his flag to *New Mexico* (BB-40), but the incident illustrated that in the waters off Okinawa, no one was safe, from the lowest rank up through the commanding officer.

As evening approached, *Laffey* left to conduct night harassing fire on Japanese positions ashore, a potentially dangerous mission that often required the ship to operate alone. "We called it Lone Ranger duty,"[13] recalled Gunner's Mate Lawrence Delewski, the gun captain of Mount 53, because it reminded men of the famous Wild West cowboy riding alone into hostile lands. Becton carried out his mission without mishap, however, and all attention switched to the following day.

"Every Skipper Dreaded the Assignment"

Landing day, April Fool's Day, offered a cruel irony of its own by kicking off what would become one of the bloodiest land and sea operations of the war on one of its holiest of religious days—Easter Sunday. The day began with a 1:24 a.m. report of an enemy submarine prowling in the area, a report lent credence when a torpedo crossed the bow of the USS *Longshaw* (DD-559), a ship operating in conjunction with *Laffey*. The pair moved closer to shore to conduct harassing fire against enemy positions, with one ship screening seaward while the other fired her guns, then switching positions.

Shortly after dawn Becton took *Laffey* from the main landing site on Okinawa's west coast and headed to their decoy station in the southwest portion of the island. Although the main landings would occur in Hagushi Bay to the northwest, *Laffey* and other ships were designated to conduct a feint in hopes of tricking the Japanese into thinking the landings would happen in the south. Two minutes after turning southwest, *Laffey* radar spotted a bogey twenty miles out. Becton ordered his two forward five-inch guns to prepare to fire, and two minutes later, with the bogey now only seven miles out, the gun crews commenced fire. After firing forty-six shells in one minute the guns fell silent when the bogey turned away.

One hour later Becton placed his ship in position off the decoy beaches, where his gun crews began a busy day of firing toward shore targets. "We were deployed south," said Seaman Martinis, who became a renowned heart surgeon after the war, "and bombarded the south end of the island for several days. Our group was a decoy to get the Japanese to think we were hitting there."[14] Quartermaster Phoutrides and others on the deck watched landing craft approach the line of departure as if infantry was to land, then turn away at the last minute instead of continuing toward shore.

As *Laffey* engaged in her feint, the main landings unfolded smoothly. Japanese General Mitsuru Ushijima had left a token force at the beach so he could concentrate his forces at well-entrenched defensive positions inland, where he hoped to delay the assault as long as possible by making the Americans pay dearly for every yard they seized. In retarding the American land advance, as planned Ushijima would force his enemy to hold its fleet offshore, making the ships vulnerable to the kamikaze aircraft gathered at Kyushu airfields.

That morning the first American wave hit the beaches, rushed inland, and within ninety minutes seized Yontan and Kadena airfields. Kamikazes smashed into a battleship and an LST killing sixteen, but the rain of kamikazes many feared would strike the fleet had not materialized.

In fact the first five days of the Okinawa operation, from the April 1 landing through April 5, hinted that their stay might not be difficult. No kamikaze threatened the ship, and one might have thought *Laffey* maneuvered off the coast of France, where despite the carnage occurring ashore, the destroyer faced minor opposition.

On April 3 Becton moved *Laffey* to the island's western side, where for the next three days she continued to bombard land targets and conduct nighttime harassing fire. On April 3, her five-inch guns expended 413 shells in two separate bombardments, while her 40mm and 20mm guns exploded a floating mine.

Radar operators aboard the destroyer enjoyed a breather, as no enemy plane approached *Laffey*, but the same did not hold true elsewhere. On

April 3 gunners aboard the USS *Prichett* (DD-561), stationed far to the north at Picket Station No. 1, the location closest to Hyushu and thus the most exposed to kamikaze attacks, splashed two aircraft, but not before sustaining damage from a bomb. Later in the day the USS *Mannert L. Abele* (DD-733), in Picket Station No. 4 off Okinawa's northeast coast, shot down two aircraft.

Becton kept his crew sharp, for no matter where the ship operated off Okinawa, kamikazes remained a constant threat. Everyone admitted, though, that the stations to the north, particularly Picket Station No. 1, justifiably bore the reputation as being the most dangerous assignments near Okinawa. Destroyers screening at the northernmost post almost begged kamikazes to take a crack at them.

Though Picket Station No. 1 offered its perils, any of the sixteen radar picket stations that ringed Okinawa along the most likely air routes leading to the island offered challenges to the destroyers posted there. Part of the Navy's plan to defend troop transports, landing craft, and other ships operating closer to shore, the destroyers on picket stations, placed at distances between fifteen and seventy-five miles off the island's coast, provided an early warning system against incoming Japanese aircraft. Once their radar screens picked up enemy planes, they alerted other ships off Okinawa and vectored the CAP toward the intruders.

Unlike earlier assaults, where American air power and carrier aircraft helped neutralize Japanese air opposition, Okinawa's proximity to the Home Islands placed it within easy striking range of Japanese aircraft based in Japan and Formosa. Crafty camouflage and widespread dispersal of kamikaze aircraft made it difficult to spot them from the air, and Japan housed aircraft at so many airstrips that American fighters and bombers could not possibly eliminate them all. Placed in such a quandary, the US Navy had no alternative but to remain off Okinawa to provide air support for the troops ashore, a distasteful prospect to Admiral Chester W. Nimitz and Admiral Spruance, who knew their ships, tied so closely to land operations, would be sitting ducks for enemy aerial assaults. They trusted that the invasion forces would speedily seize Japanese airfields already on Okinawa, thus freeing the Navy to depart.

Beginning March 26, a destroyer or a destroyer minesweeper manned each station. After the April 1 landings, as soon as they could be spared one or two LCI gunboats, LSMs (Land Ship Medium), or LCS (Littoral Combat Ship) craft joined the destroyers to provide added antiaircraft firepower.

The ships lacked the punch offered by *Laffey* and other destroyers, however, causing the destroyer crews to label them the "Pallbearers," a grisly reference to the lethal toll exacted at the picket stations and the lack of offensive power added by the landing craft.

No one aboard *Laffey* wanted to compare an exposed picket station to a Marine unit charging into enemy machine gun fire, but they and other naval personnel understood the risks. By being the first ships that the kamikazes encountered, they occupied the most treacherous sea posts near Okinawa, similar to a solitary cavalry scout sent into Indian territory so he could provide an early warning to the main unit miles behind. Men aboard destroyers grimly joked that they were the bait to entice the kamikazes, and that it was only a matter of time before they were hit. As one sailor aboard a picket destroyer said, "the waiting was scary too, knowing what was coming when those pilots' one wish in the world was to kill you."[15]

Inexperienced Japanese pilots traveling one of those sixteen routes to Okinawa often attacked the first vessel they spotted, instead of searching for a carrier or battleship. They also had read the words of Admiral Ugaki, who urged his pilots to take out the picket ships and their radar so that subsequent kamikaze pilots could go after larger prey. Picket destroyers thus absorbed a disproportionate amount of damage.

Becton, a veteran of Pacific action, wrote of picket duty that "every skipper at Okinawa dreaded the assignment," not because of the dangers that came with it, "because danger was part of a destroyer's job. But all destroyer men are imbued with a tradition of aggressive offense, and waiting for an enemy to come to them was not much to their liking."[16] He preferred to put the enemy on the defensive rather than granting them the initiative.

"That One Chilled Our Blood"

Destroyers on picket stations drew kamikazes toward them like a magnet attracts iron filings. Although most operations consisted of twenty or fewer aircraft, the Japanese mounted ten major offensives, the *kikusui*, in which anywhere from fifty to three hundred aircraft pounced on American ships. Some broke through the destroyer picket line and attacked the larger ships, but the American destroyer pickets bore the brunt of the assaults.

The first *kikusui* hit the American fleet on April 6. "Red Alert. Many enemy aircraft reported closing from the north,"[17] blared *Laffey*'s public address system. None of the aircraft came within firing range of *Laffey*, then screening off Okinawa's western coast, but Becton kept the crew at general quarters throughout the day in light of the numerous reports of bogies in the area.

In the afternoon fifty kamikazes swarmed Picket Station No. 1 and the adjoining Station No. 2. Although the CAP splashed the majority, some battled through to hit the USS *Bush* (DD-529) at Station No. 1 and the USS *Colhoun* (DD-801) at Station No. 2. Both ships sank later in the day. Kamikazes dived into targets off southern Okinawa, off the east coast, and even inside Kerama Retto, sinking three destroyers, one LST, and two ammunition ships, while damaging ten others and killing 367 men.

The attacks emphasized the dangers of operating near Okinawa. *Laffey*'s crew had witnessed kamikaze attacks off the Philippines, but as Becton wrote, "none of us had ever experienced attacks of such magnitude and intensity"[18] as the ones that occurred on April 16. The longer they remained in Okinawa waters, the greater the likelihood that sooner or later, one or more kamikaze would target them.

Within twenty-four hours a threat from the sea grabbed their attention. Quartermaster Phoutrides was enjoying a few quiet moments belowdecks when the ship suddenly lurched forward and gained speed. Seconds later a call to general quarters sent him scrambling back to the bridge, where he observed a cluster of battleships and cruisers moving into the familiar circular cruising formation.

Reports had arrived that the world's largest battleship, Japan's mighty *Yamato*, and her escorting ships had left Japan's Inland Sea with the probable intent of attacking American surface forces off Okinawa. *Laffey* had been ordered to take station on the right flank of a unit hastily formed to race north to meet the enemy force.

Phoutrides believed that they had enough firepower in the task force—six battleships, seven cruisers, and twenty-one destroyers—to crush *Yamato* and her nine deadly eighteen-inch guns, but others were not as optimistic. Screening off Okinawa seemed more alluring than going up against those heavy guns. "Now, that one chilled our blood,"[19] wrote Lieutenant Manson of the expected fight against the most potent warship then afloat.

One hour after leaving, the task force changed from circular disposition to the rectangular battle formation, with *Laffey*'s division standing at the apex. "Our division was to go in first, and we were excited about that because we were finally on the offensive. Until now we had screened,"[20] said Phoutrides.

Within hours Admiral Mitscher's carrier aircraft intercepted the Japanese force and sent *Yamato* to the ocean's bottom, ending the need for the

American surface unit. At 10:00 p.m. *Laffey* and the other ships turned back to Okinawa to resume their stations.

"It was great to hear that the carrier aircraft had destroyed *Yamato*,"[21] said Sonarman Zack, who believed the odds favored the Japanese should his ship go head-to-head with the enemy battleship. The charmed life of the USS *Laffey* continued.

"At That Point, It Was Pretty Routine"

A variety of activities occupied *Laffey* April 7–12, some mundane and others fraught with peril. "We have been shelling the beach for the past few nights," Fireman Gauding wrote in his diary. "Using mostly star shells to aid our troops on the beach."[22] The crew became accustomed to the sound of general quarters, but unlike at Normandy, Phoutrides and his shipmates now hastened to their posts as veterans of war. The Normandy training ground had prepared them for Pacific duty.

Over the next four days they needed every bit of composure they could muster, as additional kamikazes buzzed the American fleet like angry wasps. They came singly or in pairs, rather than in the gigantic *kikusui* of April 6, but they exacted a disturbing toll, smashing into six warships in four days. Sailors kept close watch at dawn and dusk, when suicide pilots liked to attack from the rising or setting sun, and learned to be wary on moonlit nights when, as one sailor described it, kamikaze aircraft swooped down "like a giant bat gliding in." Admiral Spruance, normally a man of few words, labeled the nighttime kamikaze pilots "witches on broomsticks."[23]

While always cognizant of the kamikaze threat, Becton focused on other tasks during April's first week and a half. The ship patrolled offshore, keeping watch seaward for suicide boats, which had already smashed into three ships, or swimmers with hand grenades attempting to sneak up on vessels. They engaged in shore bombardment, exploded mines off Okinawa's east coast, and searched for possible launching sites for enemy suicide boats. On April 9 their supporting fire helped American ground forces in the Nago Wan area blunt an enemy counterattack backed by Japanese tanks, artillery, and mortars. They conducted nighttime harassing fire on the enemy in hopes of disrupting their rest.

Whenever an SFCP called in coordinates, *Laffey*'s five-inch gun crews blasted enemy troop concentrations and defenses, but they learned to be careful lest the Japanese trick them into firing on American units. "We were told the Japanese tried to cut in on our frequency and a soldier who spoke perfect English would act like a spotter and try to direct fire onto our own men," said Phoutrides. "We'd have to verify that they were American by asking questions, such as his name and ship. You did this every time."[24]

One morning the 40mm and 20mm crews joined the ship's five-inch guns when a kamikaze approached on the formation's port side with an American F4F Wildcat fighter in pursuit. They received credit for an assist when the plane crashed near the USS *Idaho*, (BB-42), but not before the plane had drawn uncomfortably close to the *Laffey*.

"The only time I got nervous was when we were tracking incoming bogies," said Phoutrides "I'd listen to the reports and notice the range closing. Becton would say, 'Commence firing,' and there would be four to five seconds between his order and the first shot, and I was really nervous. I'd think, 'What are you delaying for? That plane is getting closer!'"[25]

To some, those early April days off Okinawa proved less dangerous than prior Pacific operations. On April 8 Admiral Turner wrote Nimitz that it seemed the Japanese had slowed their operations off Okinawa. Others claimed the enemy had expended most of their kamikazes at Lingayen Gulf, and boasted that the seizure of airfields on Okinawa that could house Marine F4U Corsair fighters would prevent the Japanese from mounting a large-scale kamikaze attack. The kamikaze assaults that filled their days and kept them awake at nights in the Philippines were becoming distant memories.

"It seemed to be easier than before, easier than Iwo Jima," said Lieutenant Youngquist. "At that point, I felt good about things. It was pretty routine before April 13."[26]

Any hopes for continuing a quiet routine dissipated on April 12 with the second *kikusui* raid. Almost two hundred kamikazes, escorted by an equal number of fighters, fell on the fleet, with enough smashing through the CAP to damage the aircraft carriers, *Enterprise* (CV-6) and USS *Essex* (CV-9), four battleships, and more than twenty other ships. At Picket Station No. 1, kamikazes forced the destroyer USS *Cassin Young* (DD-793) to retire to Kerama Retto for repairs, smacked into the USS *Purdy* (DD-734), killing thirteen and wounding twenty-seven, damaged one landing craft, and sank a second. In one day at one station, the Japanese had eliminated four American warships from battle, and temporarily removed the ships that had to leave the line to escort the damaged vessels to repair facilities.

The *Laffey* crew counted their blessings. They had little about which to complain, other than the normal sailors' gripes about food or overbearing chiefs. If they wanted to moan about their duty, they only had to look to the north, where Picket Station No. 1 had been turned into an oceanic bull's-eye for kamikazes. The tasks might be boring where they were off Okinawa's coast, but at least they were not posted to Picket Station No. 1. Those poor guys got it every day.

"This Is One I'd Rather Not Give You"

On Picket Duty No. One
We took up our spot
To report the movement of the Rising Sun
   —"An Ode to the USS *Laffey* (DD-724),"
   Gunner's Mate Owen Radder

Lieutenant Theodore Runk realized that as the ship's communications officer he rarely enjoyed more than brief moments of solitude. He spent most of his hours in the coding room, overseeing the men who sent coded messages to Admiral Nimitz and other superior officers, and receiving similar items in return. Commander Becton, who believed that knowledge was a key component of being a good skipper, wanted to read every message sent to or from his squadron, even those relayed from one destroyer to another. This kept Runk and his men busy, but Runk never minded. The added workload made the hours pass more quickly. If a message arrived when he was away from his post, Lieutenant Youngquist or one of the enlisted men working in the coding room alerted Runk.

Laffey was screening for a battleship south of Naha the night of April 12–13 when near midnight a dispatch broke the monotony of routine ship messages. Runk read the note, but rather than handing it to an enlisted, he decided he should be the one to deliver this news to Becton. He climbed the ladder to the bridge and found Becton in his sea cabin.

"Captain, this is one I'd rather not give you," said Runk. Becton, slightly surprised to see Runk standing before him, figured something important was up. He displayed no emotion as he read the message Runk handed over, and then replied, "Yes, Ted, I see what you mean."

The order was the one each skipper commanding a destroyer off Okinawa preferred to avoid. After steaming to Kerama Retto to pick up a Fighter

Director Officer (FIDO) team, *Laffey* was to turn north and travel to the most exposed spot of the sixteen picket stations that ringed Okinawa: Picket Station No. 1. "That meant only one thing," wrote Becton. "*Laffey* was being assigned to a station on the radar picket line. The gates of hell awaited us."[27]

Word of their new destination, which destroyer crews had labeled "Purple Heart Corner" and "Bogie Boulevard," quickly spread about the ship that April 13. One of the men working near Phoutrides pointed out that it was now Friday the 13th, a fact that was certain to gain notice among sailors. When a second man urged those near him to add the three digits of the ship's number, 7-2-4, Phoutrides mentally calculated the answer: 13. "Sailors are a superstitious lot," said Phoutrides, "and we thought something was going to happen to us. It went through the ship like wildfire."[28] An assault that had begun on April Fool's Day now included orders to *Laffey* to operate at Picket Station No. 1, arguably the most dangerous location then in the Pacific, on Friday the 13th.

Lieutenant Manson's first thoughts were that the destroyer would stand directly in the flight path between Japan's southernmost airfields in Kyushu and Okinawa, and that most of the destroyers sent to Picket Station No. 1 had either been sunk or damaged by kamikazes. He said that, "it wasn't a question of whether it [*Laffey*] would get hit or not, it was just a question of when and with how many."[29]

Torpedoman's Mate 2/c John F. Schneider and his buddies discussed the possibility that they might not return alive from the station, and found that each man tried to convince the others that everyone would be fine. They assured one another that they would emerge unharmed, just as they had escaped unharmed off the Normandy beachhead, Cherbourg, the Philippines, and Iwo Jima. Luck had so far favored them, "and we thought that we might be able to break the jinx [of destroyers getting hit at Picket Station No. 1]. But we knew that just about everything that was sent out did get hit sooner or later."[30]

Gunner's Mate Delewski, who had done so much to prepare his gun crew for battle, understood the risks, but was confident his men would answer the challenge. "We were not blind and we were not stupid," he said. "We knew where we were headed and what could happen. We knew we had to be at our best."[31]

"That was the number one spot," said Seaman Johnson. "We knew we'd eventually go up there. We'd seen those ships that came back, so we knew

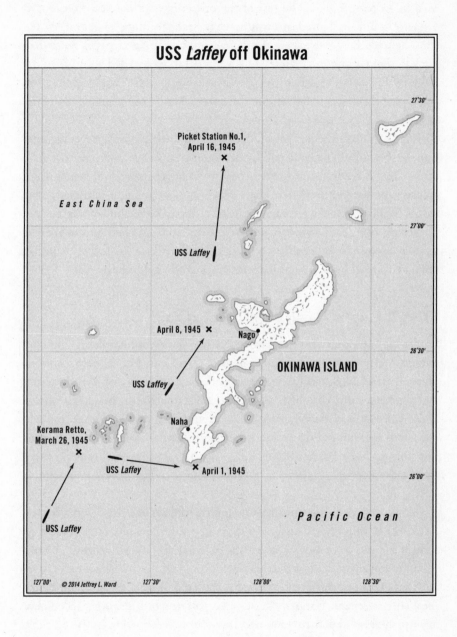

USS *Laffey* off Okinawa

27°30'

27°00'

East China Sea

Picket Station No.1,
April 16, 1945
×

USS *Laffey*

April 8, 1945 ×

USS *Laffey*

Nago

OKINAWA ISLAND

26°30'

Naha

Kerama Retto,
March 26, 1945
×

USS *Laffey*

× April 1, 1945

26°00'

USS *Laffey*

Pacific Ocean

127°00' © 2014 Jeffrey L. Ward   127°30'   128°00'   128°30'

we'd be in real trouble. The rest of the operations we were on were not as dangerous, but we figured this was it, we're probably going to get hit."[32]

Whereas others dwelt upon the damage inflicted on destroyers, Sonarman Zack thought about the reason why *Laffey* had so far avoided harm. "Off the Philippines, Japan, and Iwo Jima we were always with a battle group, and you figure the bigger ships will be the target. But if you're alone, you're the target."[33]

Kamikazes had selected the choicest vessels, the biggest ships, for destruction. In the Philippines some of the deck crew witnessed enemy aircraft drop into a dive directly toward them, only to change course and veer toward a cruiser or battleship. Where the *Laffey* was now going, Zack knew, they would be alone. They would be the biggest ship and the choicest target.

Becton overheard a steward's mate boast, "nothing's going to happen to us. Maybe to those other ships, but not to *Laffey*. We're too lucky!"[34] Becton remained silent, but doubted that their luck could hold out forever.

"They'll Keep on Coming 'Til They Get You"

Under cloudy predawn skies, *Laffey* left her station off southern Okinawa and turned west toward Kerama Retto. Crew had heard the nickname, "Busted Bay," which sailors bestowed on the anchorage for the numerous damaged warships that had limped into Kerama Retto, but until now it had meant little as the ship had avoided harm. They had observed some of the kamikaze-induced devastation during an April 6 visit to the anchorage, but no one—not Becton, Phoutrides, Gauding, or anyone—was prepared for the Dante-esque sights that greeted them as *Laffey* pulled into Kerama Retto.

"It was depressing as the devil and a little frightening, too," wrote Becton as damaged ship after damaged ship came into view. "It went on and on until it felt you were moving down the aisle in the middle of a hospital ward full of mangled and crippled casualties."[35]

Men on deck stared at the spectacle. "What a sight! What an awful sight!" recalled Lieutenant Manson. "Grotesque patterns of superstructures etched against the blue sky; mattresses and loaves of bread floating in the oil slicks oozing from torn hulls. All over the harbor colors were at half-mast, as damaged ships buried their dead." Small boats hastened from one damaged ship to another, bringing physicians for injured men and repair crews for bent propellers and torn masts. Streams of wounded, many hideously burned, poured from battle-scarred warships to hospital ships as "*Laffey's* sober-faced crew just looked, sadly shaking their heads."[36]

"Going into Kerama Retto was awful," said Sonarman Zack. "One cruiser had her bow blown off, and many destroyers were there that had been flattened by kamikazes. You [could] sure see the damage that one plane can do to a ship if it hit in the right spot."[37]

The veterans aboard *Laffey* spotted destroyers on which they had earlier served, or ships bearing buddies from old times. The bow of one destroyer minelayer had been wrenched back across her bridge, and the muzzle of a five-inch gun was twisted into a right angle. Ships sported scorched decks, ruptured fuel tanks, and collapsed sides. The signal bridge of the battleship USS *Tennessee* (BB-43) had vanished from suicide crashes, and Japanese bullets and bomb fragments had punctured hundreds of holes in superstructures.

Crew manning *Laffey's* 40mm or 20mm guns scrutinized similar locations aboard their damaged compatriots, now charred from bomb explosions and fires, grim foreshadows of what could happen to them. Lieutenant Matthew Darnell, the ship's surgeon, stared at the demolished wardroom of one destroyer and muttered, "that's my battle station."[38] On a destroyer that had once delivered mail to *Laffey*, a burial crew prepared bodies for the trip to the cemetery.

When *Laffey* pulled alongside *Cassin Young* to pick up a FIDO team consisting of Lieutenant E. L. Molpus, Lieutenant J. Vance Porlier, and three enlisted men, her skipper, Commander J. W. "Red" Ailes, whose ship had barely avoided sinking from kamikaze attacks at Picket Station No. 1, *Laffey's* destination, said simply, "duck as fast as you can, make as much speed as you can, and shoot as fast as you can." Members of *Cassin Young's* crew shouted their own warnings to *Laffey* sailors. "You guys have a fighting chance, but they'll keep on coming 'til they get you."[39]

The *Laffey* crew had gained valuable experience since the ship's commissioning, but the perils of Picket Station No. 1 presented a different scenario. They had never been ordered to occupy a static position and wait for the enemy to come to them. Becton and the crew hated being the bait, but they had their orders.

"You know what you are facing but you had no choice. It was our duty," said Seaman Johnson. "You were part of the ship and the ship was ordered to go, so you went." Quartermaster Phoutrides understood that the threat of a kamikaze attack always existed, "but it wasn't until we got to Kerama Retto that I thought much about it. It was hard to believe when you saw those ships." For the first time since he went to war he thought, "something might happen to us." Gunner's Mate Robert Karr said that "we all felt that our time of testing was at hand," and Gunner's Mate Delewski, added, "no one had to draw any pictures for us. No one had to say a word. We all knew we were in for the fight of our lives."[40]

After filling *Laffey*'s magazines with three hundred rounds of five-inch ammunition, Becton took the destroyer to the command ship USS *Eldorado* (AGC-11) for final orders from Admiral Turner. Radio and radar technicians boarded to check the equipment, reminding Lieutenant Manson of a physician who inspected a boxer moments before he was to step into the ring.

Coxswain George Falotico had long wanted to leave his station inside Mount 52 for a more open post. Now, directly before leaving for the most dangerous sea station at Okinawa, he and Gunner's Mate 3/c Stanley H. Ketron agreed to switch places. Ketron moved inside the mount and Falotico took his place on a 20mm gun. Falotico understood that he was now more exposed, but in his opinion that was a small price to pay for fresh air and an enhanced view of events.

"Our Turn Is Coming Up Tomorrow"

The bad news continued that Friday the 13th when an announcement over the public address system informed the crew that their president of the past twelve years, and their commander in chief, President Franklin D. Roosevelt, had succumbed to a cerebral hemorrhage. The death of their leader, who loved to sail and had long held a special place in his heart for the Navy, hit hard because Roosevelt had been the only president many of them had known. After assuming office in 1933, he had guided the nation through the depths of the Depression, stood as a principal opponent to Adolf Hitler, proclaimed the country the "Arsenal of Democracy," and oversaw the massive military build-up used to wage war in the European and Pacific theaters. Now, instead of the constant, ever optimistic Roosevelt at the helm, an unknown commodity would be in charge. Every ship and shore station was to conduct a memorial service on April 15.

Phoutrides had heard many of Roosevelt's famous radio chats, and was saddened that the president would not be around to see the defeat of Japan and Germany, objectives that had dominated the last years of his presidency. Others, like Lieutenant Youngquist and Seaman Dockery, nudged the news aside. Something that occurred thousands of miles distant had little impact on their immediate futures, and besides, they had more important matters on their minds.

Tokyo took advantage to drop propaganda leaflets behind American lines on Okinawa, claiming that Roosevelt died because the strain of huge losses on the island was too much for him to bear. The leaflets promised more of the same, and warned, "the dreadful loss that led your late leader to death will make you orphans on the island. The Japanese special attack corps will sink your vessels to the last destroyer. You will witness it realized in the near future."[41]

Better news followed with the unexpected delivery of bags of mail. Because they had been at sea for much of the past month, letters from loved ones had become a premium. With Picket Station No. 1 looming, Becton pulled every trick in his impressive bag to arrange a delivery before they left Kerama Retto for their post to the north.

Becton flashed a message to a nearby LST asking if they had any mail aboard. The LST replied that they did, but *Laffey* would have to wait her turn as the LST had been besieged with similar requests from other ships. Becton, about to take the crew to a post from which some might not return, and knowing how important even a few lines from mothers or wives might mean to his men, told a signalman to send the message, "Five gallons of ice cream for immediate delivery of any mail for the *Laffey*."

Within moments came the reply, "Send boat!"[42] *Laffey's* boat crossed to the LST and returned with seven bags of mail. Sons grabbed letters from parents and husbands clutched photos of children they had not seen in months. The crew forgot, if only for a few hours, the specter of the coming days, and morale soared for men about to head to Picket Station No. 1. Becton devoured a letter from Imogen Carpenter, but it took every bit of wisdom he possessed to console the man who received a Dear John letter from his wife, who informed the sailor that she had sold their store back home and moved away with another man.

Becton's thoughtfulness in arranging for the delivery, coming on the eve of their departure for the hottest naval spot around Okinawa, impressed everyone. "He got mail for us, which was a big deal for the crew," said Quartermaster Phoutrides. He wrote his brother in June 1945, "we had been underway for about 7 weeks without getting any mail and the crew was pretty much in the dumps about it. On top of that, many of us had a premonition we were going to be hit, and when you feel that way, a measly letter sure helps out." As he added almost seventy years later, "It shows how much he cared for the men."[43]

Mail provided a welcome break from the chilling sights that dominated recent days. "Have just seen the graveyard for our ships that have been hit while on picket duty," Fireman Gauding wrote on April 13. "Our turn is coming up tomorrow for picket duty. It sure looks like our turn is next. Every ship so far has gotten hit with a suicide plane. We have all got our fingers cross [sic] & hope for the best."[44]

Commander F. Julian Becton's spirit and superb leadership helped bring the ship and most of her crew home. NATIONAL ARCHIVES PHOTO #333787.

A young Ari Phoutrides, shown here during boot camp, wondered if he might ever find a man he would respect as much as his father. He found one in his skipper.
FROM THE ARI PHOUTRIDES COLLECTION.

The supply officer for the ship, Joel C. Youngquist was a young lieutenant at the time of the attack. He supervised a group of 40mm and 20mm guns located aft, and barely evaded serious injury or death when kamikazes smashed into his section.

From the Ari Phoutrides Collection and the USS *Laffey* (DD-724) Association.

Seaman 1/c Thomas B. Fern loved the ship he defended from twenty-two kamikazes. He spent his remaining years helping to arrange a permanent home for his destroyer, and participated in numerous work parties to scrape away rust and apply fresh paint to gun mounts and other portions of the vessel.

From the Thomas B. and Marguerite Fern Collection.

Sonarman 3/c Daniel Zack (second from left) enjoys a beer with shipmates at a Seattle bar after the ship returned to the United States. The crew enjoyed a warm reception from Seattle residents. The other men pictured are from (left to right) Seaman 1/c Richard W. Hyson, Zack, Yeoman 3/c Earl R. Kennedy, Seaman 1/c Alfred J. Dorris, and Yeoman 2/c Herbert J. Rick. PHOTOGRAPH COURTESY OF DANIEL ZACK.

Seaman 2/c Robert C. Johnson wrote a series of letters to his parents that his mother saved. He survived his service while operating one of the ship's 40mm guns and continues to reside in Richmond, Virginia.
FROM THE ROBERT JOHNSON COLLECTION.

Although it was against regulations, Fireman 1/c Wilbert C. Gauding kept a diary of his World War II experiences aboard the *Laffey*.
FROM THE WILBERT GAUDING COLLECTION.

During the kamikaze attack, Ensign James G. Townsley grabbed a headset and a microphone hooked to the ship's PA system, rushed atop the pilothouse, and from an exposed position calmly issued instructions to gun positions on where to fire.
FROM THE ARI PHOUTRIDES COLLECTION AND THE USS *LAFFEY* (DD-724) ASSOCIATION.

Seaman 1/c Herbert B. Remsen escaped a close call with the fires that engulfed the aft portion of the ship. After the war he enjoyed a successful acting career in Hollywood.
FROM THE ARI PHOUTRIDES COLLECTION AND THE USS *LAFFEY* (DD-724) ASSOCIATION.

This photograph of the USS *Laffey* was taken in August 1944 off the coast of Massachusetts, after the destroyer completed her Normandy operations and shortly before the ship headed to the Pacific. NATIONAL ARCHIVES PHOTO #244860.

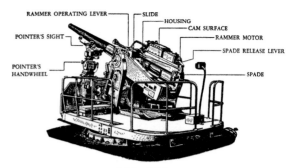

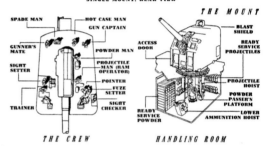

Gunner's Mate 2/c Lawrence H. Delewski's aft five-inch gun was one of three on the *Laffey*. Seaman 1/c Lee C. Hunt's station was inside the mount, while Sonarman 3/c Daniel Zack operated in the handling room below Mount 52, a forward five-inch gun.

REPRINTED BY PERMISSION, FROM THEODORE ROSCOE, *UNITED STATES DESTROYER OPERATIONS IN WORLD WAR II* (ANNAPOLIS, MD: NAVAL INSTITUTE PRESS, © 1953).

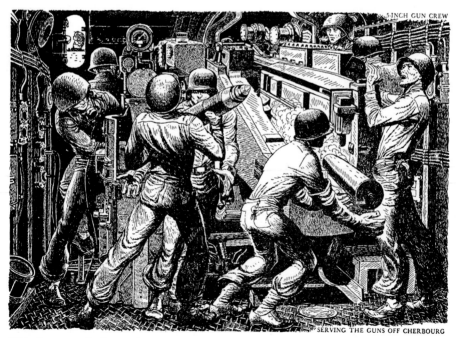

This drawing of a five-inch gun crew shows the teamwork that enabled the men to successfully execute their duties in the confined space.

REPRINTED BY PERMISSION, FROM THEODORE ROSCOE, *UNITED STATES DESTROYER OPERATIONS IN WORLD WAR II* (ANNAPOLIS, MD: NAVAL INSTITUTE PRESS, © 1953).

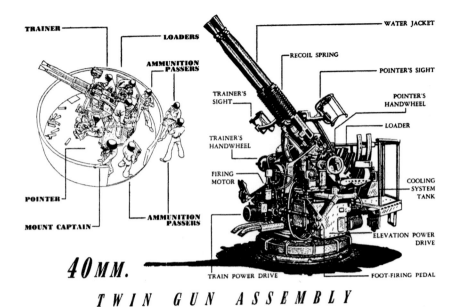

40MM.
TWIN GUN ASSEMBLY

Seaman 1/c Thomas B. Fern's aft 40mm gun was one of twelve on the ship. Seaman 2/c Robert C. Johnson operated on a similar gun forward.

REPRINTED BY PERMISSION, FROM THEODORE ROSCOE, *UNITED STATES DESTROYER OPERATIONS IN WORLD WAR II* (ANNAPOLIS, MD: NAVAL INSTITUTE PRESS, © 1953).

Eleven 20mm antiaircraft guns protected the ship. Torpedoman 3/c Jack H. Ondracek jumped into the straps of one of these guns in his attempt to deflect the bomb that spiraled toward him.

REPRINTED BY PERMISSION, FROM THEODORE ROSCOE, *UNITED STATES DESTROYER OPERATIONS IN WORLD WAR II* (ANNAPOLIS, MD: NAVAL INSTITUTE PRESS, © 1953).

20 MM. GUN

The surviving crew is proud that their efforts to save the ship have her harbored at Patriots Point Naval and Maritime Museum in Charleston, South Carolina. Here she floats alongside another proud World War II warship, the USS *Yorktown* (CV-10), with which the *Laffey* conducted wartime operations. FROM THE AUTHOR'S COLLECTION.

The *Laffey* participated in the Philippine landings. Here she is off Mindoro in December 1944 beneath a sky filled with antiaircraft shell bursts as kamikazes attack the unit. All three of *Laffey's* five-inch gun mounts are elevated and firing at the intruders. The puff of smoke near the water in the lower left indicates a kamikaze that had been splashed. Closer to land, cruisers and battleships bombard the beach area. NATIONAL ARCHIVES PHOTO #47470.

Laffey and other ships encountered more kamikazes during the January 1945 landings in Lingayen Gulf. Here on January 6 a kamikaze approaches the cruiser USS *Louisville* (CA-28) on her way to smashing into the ship. Another kamikaze charged toward *Laffey*, one-half mile from *Louisville*, before turning to the larger target and crashing into the cruiser. NATIONAL ARCHIVES PHOTO #342368.

The battered *Laffey* arrives at the Okinawa anchorage after the attack. To the right Sonarman 3/c Daniel Zack's five-inch gun is elevated, while Seaman 1/c Robert C. Johnson's 40mm gun, complete with a clip of ammunition, stands near the mast. FROM THE ARI PHOUTRIDES COLLECTION.

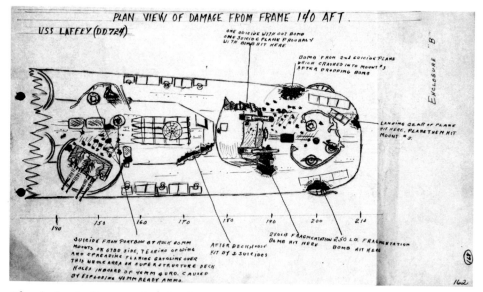

After the battle, Becton included in his action report this drawing of the damage his ship suffered aft. Shown (right to left) is the fantail section, where Radioman 3/c Lawrence F. Kelley and others died; Gunner's Mate 2/c Lawrence H. Delewski's Mount 53; and Lieutenant (jg) Joel C. Youngquist's 40mm and 20mm guns, where Seaman 1/c Thomas B. Fern's actions earned him the Silver Star. FROM BECTON ACTION REPORT, APRIL 29, 1945.

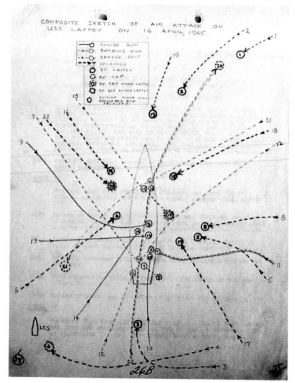

Becton also included in his action report this drawing of the twenty-two kamikazes that attacked his ship.
FROM BECTON ACTION REPORT, APRIL 29, 1945.

The starboard 20mm guns, as evidenced by this photograph, sustained heavy damage from explosions and shrapnel. Notice the numerous holes that surround the guns, each indicating shrapnel or bullets that smacked into the area. FROM THE ARI PHOUTRIDES COLLECTION.

Following the battle, little but empty space exists where guns should have rested in the ravaged fantail section, where Radioman 3/c Lawrence F. Kelley and others died. FROM THE ARI PHOUTRIDES COLLECTION.

The *Laffey* steams away after her action against the kamikazes. The aft section gun barrels look like broken matchsticks. FROM THE ARI PHOUTRIDES COLLECTION.

Still bearing signs of the attack, *Laffey* approaches Seattle, where the ship would be opened for visitation to the public. FROM THE ARI PHOUTRIDES COLLECTION.

Visitors eager to obtain a look at the heavily damaged destroyer waited in lines that stretched for blocks along the dock. Once aboard, they often viewed the devastation in silence.
NATIONAL ARCHIVES PHOTO #333797.

Gunner's Mate 3/c Francis M. Gebhart sits on what was left of Gunner's Mate 2/c Lawrence H. Delewski's five-inch gun. The sign, explaining the action at that gun, was placed there for the benefit of the civilians who visited the ship in Seattle after the *Laffey* returned to the United States.
NATIONAL ARCHIVES PHOTO #333792.

People who visited *Laffey* in Seattle were able to see where Motor Machinist's Mate 1/c George S. Logan and Machinist's Mate 1/c Stephen J. Waite were trapped belowdecks. Here Logan climbs out the hole he and Waite used to escape death during the attack.
NATIONAL ARCHIVES PHOTO #333793.

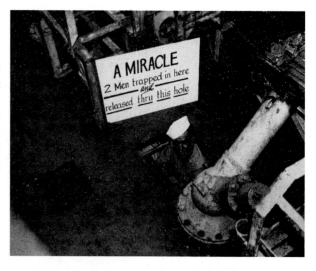

In Hawaii on Navy Day in October 1945, Seaman 1/c Thomas B. Fern receives a Silver Star for his actions of April 16. Also awaiting awards are Lieutenant Theodore W. Runk (second from right), Lieutenant (jg) G.A.G. Parolini (to Fern's left), and Ensign James G. Townsley (to Fern's right).
FROM THE THOMAS B. AND MARGUERITE FERN COLLECTION.

In her Massachusetts home, Marguerite Fern watches her husband, Tom, during a 1982 episode of *Real People*. The program focused on the efforts by the crew to keep *Laffey* in decent condition so that visitors could walk her decks and learn about the destroyer and crew.
FROM THE AUTHOR'S COLLECTION.

Seaman 2/c Robert C. Johnson and Seaman 1/c Robert W. Dockery, whose station in Mount 52 with Sonarman 3/c Daniel Zack was not far from Johnson's 40mm gun, remain lifelong friends. Here they are shown together at Johnson's Virginia home.
FROM THE ROBERT JOHNSON COLLECTION.

In 1945, Ari Phoutrides sits next to the fire control tower, where the crew mounted a scoreboard of the aircraft splashed and landings in which they participated.
FROM THE ARI PHOUTRIDES COLLECTION.

In 2014, during one of his many visits to his ship, Ari Phoutrides stands in front of the decals that now adorn the bridge area. Although the decals have been slightly rearranged, they represent the same actions as the decals that existed in 1945.
FROM THE AUTHOR'S COLLECTION.

On April 16, 2014, the sixty-ninth anniversary of his encounter with twenty-two kamikazes, Ari Phoutrides sits on *Laffey*'s aft deck and explains the events of that day to visitors who had traveled to Patriots Point, South Carolina, to see *Laffey*. A member of one generation shares with other generations the deeds of his shipmates and ship. FROM THE AUTHOR'S COLLECTION.

Ari Phoutrides wrote of this photograph, "upon my request, Admiral Becton gave me this photograph of himself. It has a position of honor next to my father's picture."
FROM THE ARI PHOUTRIDES COLLECTION.

CHAPTER 7

THE TRIUMPH OF
LAFFEY'S GUNNERS

> *On April 16 they threatened our position*
> *They got there early*
> *To make a clean sweep*
> *But they found out*
> *The Laffey wasn't asleep.*
> —"An Ode to the USS *Laffey* (DD-724),"
> Gunner's Mate Owen Radder

"We Knew We Were Going to Be Attacked in the Morning"

Under clear skies and with temperatures in the 60s, at 1:15 p.m. on April 14 *Laffey* left Kerama Retto for Picket Station No. 1, where she would relieve the destroyer minelayer, USS *J. William Ditter* (DM-31). The USS *Purdy*, damaged by a kamikaze on April 12 while on Picket Station No. 1, had been moored next to *Laffey*. Shortly before *Laffey* left harbor, a sailor from *Purdy* cautioned his comrades about the kamikazes they would surely encounter at the same station. "You'll knock a lot of them down, and you'll think you're doing fine. But in the end there'll be this one bastard with your name on his ticket."[1]

Everyone wondered if his name had been stamped on that ticket. They knew what happened to other destroyers at the same picket station, a posting that Quartermaster Phoutrides labeled "the hottest station of them all" in his letter to his brother. During off-duty bull sessions men exchanged stories of the hazards of Picket Station No.1, where ships arrived with a full crew only to depart within days a battered vessel bearing a lengthy casualty list. "As we were heading out to picket duty I was thinking about the destroyers that were coming back from their picket duty," recalled Seaman 1/c Lonnie H. Eastham. "I knew it was now our turn and that we were going to die. I remember seeing ships limping back from battle blown up. This gave me an even stronger feeling that we were all going to die."[2]

Some among the crew asked why a destroyer, with her vulnerable plating, was even sent to such a hazardous post. Wouldn't the thicker steel and more damaging guns of a battleship or cruiser better handle the risks? they asked one another. Others questioned why Marine and Army aircraft could not provide adequate air cover; why the Navy wasn't more speedily unloading the transports supplying the forces ashore, which in turn would enable the Navy pickets to leave their posts; or why a destroyer, meant to operate on the go, now worked in such a limited radius, like a tethered goat.

They had a right to be concerned. At Picket Station No. 1, *Laffey* would be the first target sighted by kamikazes eager to avenge the deaths of their countrymen and anxious to die for families and emperor. Becton, who vowed after the *Ward*'s loss in 1943 that he would be the best combat skipper he could be, would have to employ every one of his considerable talents to make good on his pledge.

Becton believed that action at Picket Station No. 1 was so imminent and critical that its gravity equaled the impact his young sailors felt when they faced their initial combat along the French coast ten months earlier. As he had done with the memo to his crew that he issued shortly before entering action off Normandy, Becton now addressed the crew's concerns by speaking over the public address system. He emphasized that although kamikazes had instilled fear with their suicidal tactics, the men piloting those aircraft were human beings, and reminded them that they had already emerged unharmed from similar aerial assaults in the Philippines. "You have tangled with this kind before and come out on top," he said. Exhibiting confidence in his gun crews and in himself, he stressed two key skills that would turn any encounter in their favor. "We're going to outmaneuver and outshoot them," he said. "They are going to go down, but we aren't."[3] He ended by promising that the enemy would rue the day they met *Laffey*.

Becton's brief statement steadied a crew that with each moment drew closer to Picket Station No. 1. The men appreciated the trust he expressed in them, which they returned triple-fold. "His confidence in his crew," wrote Lieutenant Manson, "was exceeded only by their confidence in him."[4]

Laffey arrived at Picket Station No. 1 on April 14 at 4:12 p.m. Accompanied by two landing craft operating a few hundred yards away, *LCS-51* and *LCS-116*, the ship steamed back and forth over a two-mile sector, with lookouts and radar scouring the sky. They had performed similar functions to the south, where they had the added comfort of knowing that radar picket destroyers to the north would send advance warning, but now they themselves would be the advance warning.

Becton ordered his gun crews to follow every aircraft spotted, even if they were friendly, because he wanted his men focused and crisp. Boredom could be an enemy, allowing weary men to relax their vigilance and thereby weaken the ship's defense. Besides, Japanese aircraft sometimes attached themselves to the rear portion of US aircraft formations in hopes of sneaking up on targets, making attention to detail vital to *Laffey*'s survival.

They did not have to wait long for the Japanese to show up. Although the commanding officer of the *J. William Ditter* confessed they had not spotted a Japanese aircraft while at the station, the Japanese wasted little time feeling out the *Laffey*. At 4:30 p.m. *Laffey*'s radar tracked eight aircraft closing fast from fifty-eight miles to the north. A destroyer at Picket Station No. 2 thirty miles east diverted CAP toward the incoming aircraft, and in a brief fight the American fighters splashed all eight enemy aircraft before *Laffey*'s gun crews had a chance to fire. "No damage done thanks to our fighter planes that shot them down before they got near us,"[5] wrote a grateful Fireman Gauding.

Within half an hour *Laffey* radar picked up another group of three Japanese aircraft twenty-eight miles to the north. The FIDO team aboard *Laffey* directed fighters toward the area, where they again splashed the enemy before they threatened *Laffey*.

At 6:58 p.m. CAP detached for the night, leaving *Laffey* and her crew on their own at the picket station. They had survived the first day, but would their luck hold on the second?

"Preacher" Belk, the ship's unofficial chaplain, opened April 15 with a dawn service on the fantail for those of the crew able to attend. The normally sparse crowd had, not surprisingly, multiplied. Afterward, a gunner from a 20mm mount confided to Belk his fears that he would not be up to the task of facing a kamikaze attack. Belk did his best to reassure the young man, telling him that everybody aboard was scared, and that he would react appropriately when the time arrived.

The young man had company, as no one could forget how exposed they were. "We felt way out there all alone," said Quartermaster Phoutrides. He and the crew could see the LCSs operating nearby, but the lightly armed craft provided small comfort. If *Laffey*'s guns could not splash an incoming kamikaze, the chances were slight that an LCS could do much better. "I also figured that the Japanese weren't going to dive on them anyway!"[6] added Phoutrides. *Laffey* would be their target, not two smaller landing craft.

That realization made for long days and nights at their new post. The crew enjoyed few breaks, as Becton kept them at battle stations for much of the time, and the tension far exceeded that of the previous few weeks. In addition to the frequent call to stations, men had their normal duty stations about the ship that required them to swab the decks, bake in the galley, or complete the hundreds of chores tossed at them by demanding chiefs.

For many, the waiting proved to be the worst part. Because it was only a matter of time at Picket Station No. 1 before kamikazes showed up, an edgy crew manned stations and broke for chow. If the enemy was almost certain to come, most preferred that it occur quickly so they could begin fighting. At least in that way their trials would end sooner.

After receiving reports of objects floating in the water, in the early afternoon Becton took *Laffey* ten miles north to investigate. When the ship arrived shortly after 2:00 p.m., crew found the bodies of three enemy pilots, one almost completely devoured by sharks, floating among the debris of their aircraft. They retrieved codebooks, logs, notes, and recognition books from the Japanese and then tossed the bodies back into the sea. Becton notified his superior officer, who asked that the items be delivered to him as soon as possible.

The remainder of April 15 proved routine as the destroyer steamed back and forth on her two-mile circuit, but crew took no comfort in the lull. Five separate sightings of enemy aircraft after dusk heightened the tension, with some men wondering if the quintet foreshadowed worse things to come.

After the cooks finished their chores for the day, Seaman Johnson and the other bakers reported to their duty stations in the galley to begin baking fresh bread and peach cobblers for April 16. Some of his friends remarked that it would be difficult for them to work throughout the night, and then have to sleep during the day, but Johnson did not mind. He enjoyed the enticing aroma that filled the galley each time they baked bread, but he had to admit he looked forward to collapsing into his bunk with daybreak.

Few could sleep the night of April 15–16. As if purposely trying to interrupt their slumber, Japanese aircraft flew barely outside the range of the ship's five-inch guns, requiring Becton to sound general quarters. Instead of attacking, the enemy pilots turned back, only to reappear later. "During the night, we were constantly harassed by observation planes whose sole purpose was to keep us awake all night," wrote Quartermaster Phoutrides to his brother. "They came within the maximum gun range of our ship and just circled us knowing we wouldn't fire at them. Nevertheless, we were forced to go to general quarters each time they approached the ship."

After the final alert sounded at 3:00 a.m., Phoutrides shuffled to his quarters for a few hours of sleep, but he could not shake an apprehension that upset his stomach. "When we finally hit our racks, we knew we were going to be attacked in the morning."[7]

Admiral Ugaki made certain of that. The commander had been placed in charge of the 6th Air Army for the third *kikusui*, scheduled for April 16. The optimistic admiral thought that the kamikaze raids might yet turn the fortunes of war in Japan's favor. He relished the opportunity to toss his three attack groups, waiting and ready at airfields spread throughout Kyushu, at the Americans. Captain Toshio Kimura's 1st Attack Group, consisting of the 59th Sentai (Air Group) and five suicide units, collected at Ashiya in northern Kyushu, while the 2nd Attack Group grouped Captain Masao Suenaga's 101st Sentai and Captain Iwao Hayaski's 102nd Sentai and their three kamikaze units at Miyakonojo in southern Kyushu. Major Michiaki Tojo's 103rd Sentai commanded another two suicide units at Chiran in the southwestern tip of Kyushu.

Ugaki nearly had to postpone the April 16 attack when US aircraft pounded his headquarters in southern Kyushu on April 15, destroying fifty-one planes on the ground and another twenty-nine in the air. Ugaki was shaken by the strike, but ordered the *kikusui* attack to proceed as scheduled.

Early the next morning the admiral watched as fifty-eight aircraft lifted from the airfield and turned south for the planned mid-morning strikes against US forces off Okinawa. Another one hundred army fighters and special attack planes rose from their Kyushu airfields, the drones of their engines drowning out all other sounds as the pilots ascended to keep the enemy away from their homeland. If all went as expected, by day's end American ships would be on the ocean's bottom and crews would be swimming for their lives.

The men aboard *Laffey* had no inkling that such an immense air con-glomeration headed their way.

"They Caught Us Without Any Fighter Coverage"

The early morning hours of April 16 reminded men of their favorite days back home, when clear blue skies and comfortable temperatures offered idyl-lic settings for grabbing a pole and sauntering to their favorite fishing hole. Calm seas, good visibility, light breezes, and sixty-degree temperatures greeted the crew as they started their third day at Picket Station No. 1. They had al-ready logged two days at the exposed post without mishap, but few thought they could let their guard down. Hatches had been battened down for days, and near constant sojourns at battle stations kept men on edge, as if, accord-ing to Lieutenant Manson, "the entire ship was just holding her breath."[8]

Becton kept close watch on the skies when on the bridge, which was al-ways, it seemed, and eight feet from the skipper the astute teenage observer, Quartermaster Phoutrides, expected an attack after the previous night's interruptions. Facing possible combat, Becton needed the ability to reach maximum speed at a moment's notice. Consequently the black gang oper-ating the belowdecks machinery had to keep the superheaters cut in, which elevated temperatures in the boiler and engineering spaces to well above a hundred degrees. Becton hated to ask this of his black gang, but he had no choice if he were to operate at maximum efficiency in the event a kamikaze attack occurred.

The two-plane CAP posted at low altitudes near the ship offered some comfort, as did the duo four-plane CAPs operating farther out and at higher altitudes. Just as *Laffey* provided an early warning system for the ships and forces closer to Okinawa, so, too, did these aircraft provide the same for *Laf-fey*. They were Becton's tentacles reaching northward, a tripwire that would alert him to potential danger while the aircraft attempted to intercept and eliminate the threat before they drew close to *Laffey*.

Three divisions of Corsairs from the "Fighting I," the aircraft carrier USS *Intrepid*, had lifted off that morning and proceeded to Picket Station No. 1, where they were to be the CAP for *Laffey* and other ships in the area. Nick-named the "Grim Reapers," the unit arrived near dawn, but was quickly directed to the north to meet Ugaki's attack groups racing down from Ky-ushu. Grim Reaper skipper Lieutenant Commander Wally Clarke and other pilots engaged the enemy, sending at least four Japanese aircraft in flames to the water below before receiving a call indicating that kamikazes had broken through the protective air screen to attack *Laffey* behind them. Clarke hoped that the destroyer could hold out until he and the others arrived.

Becton sounded general quarters at 4:52 a.m. when several bogies appeared on their radar screen. "Everyone knowing what we were up against," Gauding wrote in his diary, "being alone we were the enemy's only target. Everyone was on their battle stations in no time at all."[9] No longer did some men react sluggishly, as Becton had pointed out before Normandy. The urgency of their situation made his reminders moot.

One plane flew within twenty miles of the destroyer, but remained cautiously out of range of Delewski's five-inch guns. Although the plane turned away after a few minutes, Becton kept everyone at battle stations as sunrise, the time when everyone had to be at his post anyway, would soon occur. He decided that once the cooks had prepared breakfast, he would rotate a few men from each station while holding the rest at their posts until everyone was fed. A famished crew was no good to him.

An irritating glitch occurred at 7:30 when Becton's FIDO team lost communications with the inner two-plane CAP. That morning, American aircraft mounted air strikes on the island of Ie Shima off Okinawa's northwest coast, further burdening the overtaxed channels with their messages and making it impossible for *Laffey* to relay intercept orders to the two-plane CAP. A frustrated Becton hoped the confusion could be remedied before the Japanese staged a raid against his ship, or else he would have to engage suicide planes without having the ability to vector those fighters toward intercept points.

His concerns compounded five minutes later when *Laffey* radar spotted an Aichi D3A "Val" dive bomber at sixteen miles. When it had closed to within six miles, the ship's five-inch guns opened fire. The crew's apprehension increased as the Val approached the range of *Laffey*'s shorter-range 40mm and 20mm guns, but the bomber drew within thirty-five hundred yards, at which point the pilot dropped a bomb that exploded harmlessly in the ocean. He then retired to the north, almost as if he were taunting Becton and his gun crews. The aircraft would have been easy pickings for Becton's two-plane CAP, which flew at the same altitude as the bomber, but he could not relay intercept coordinates over the crowded channel.

An eight-minute respite ended at 7:55 when four aircraft approached at higher altitude from seventeen miles out. The outer eight-fighter CAP pursued the intruders, a tactic that diverted the bogeys from *Laffey* but at the same time denuded Becton of air cover, as he was still unable to contact his two-plane CAP. His air defenses were down for an indefinite time, leaving an opening through which the enemy could attack. If that happened, Becton would have to rely on his gun crews' accuracy and his own maneuvering skills to defend the ship.

Becton concluded that the four Japanese aircraft "were probably used to decoy our C.A.P. because they did just that," drawing the American fighters to higher altitude while kamikaze pilots swept in at lower altitudes. "The Japanese pulled a pretty fast one on us," Phoutrides wrote his brother shortly after the battle. While attention was focused toward the higher altitudes, "the 22 suicide planes which attacked us came in flying relatively low. They caught us without any fighter coverage."[10]

"Then the Fireworks Started"

At 8:20 a.m. Becton stood on the bridge, his eyes cemented on the sky. Other men, including Quartermaster Phoutrides, had gone below to enjoy their breakfast while their shipmates remained at their posts and waited their turn to relax with a cup of strong coffee. Most conducted their business as normal, but the appearance of those Japanese aircraft created a tension that most mornings lacked.

Radarman 2/c Philip E. Nulf on the radar in the CIC interrupted Becton's concentration by reporting that a large formation of aircraft was closing fast on the ship from the north. Becton immediately ordered the alarm calling his crew back to battle stations.

Men grabbed life belts and helmets, snubbed out cigarettes, and hurried to their posts. Sixteen-year-old Seaman 1/c Joe W. Edmonds recalled Becton's Normandy admonition to rush to stations and barreled out to his post in his undershorts, clutching the pants he would don when he arrived. Many, in the midst of breakfast, left half-consumed meals on their plates. A group of sharks swimming alongside the ship momentarily caught Fireman 1/c Oliver "Jim" Spriggs's attention as he left the long chow line. The thought of being "in the water with that bunch" unnerved Spriggs, "not realizing that in a very short time, it was probably the safest place to be."[11]

Quartermaster Phoutrides, disappointed that he had not finished breakfast, figured he would eat after general quarters ended, little knowing that he would not be able to go below for a meal for two days. The alarm interrupted Seaman Johnson, deep in slumber after a long night baking bread and peach cobblers in the galley. He shrugged off his concerns and made his way among the bustle to his station at Mount 41, the forward 40mm guns on the ship's starboard side.

"Here we go again!" Lieutenant Youngquist thought when he first heard the alarm. He had grown weary of the harassment from enemy aircraft, which pretended to attack the ship only to veer away. He was not alone, as most of the men with him at Mount 44, the aft 40mm gun on the port side, felt the same. "We'll wait it out here at the gun," they agreed, "and see what happens."

"Then," said Youngquist, "the planes came in and things changed."[12]

Lieutenant Molpus and Lieutenant Porlier of FIDO contacted the command ship *Eldorado* to inform Admiral Turner of the incoming Japanese, and asked that he send whatever fighters could be spared. "Between it [the Japanese formation] and our fighters flying to intercept," wrote Becton, "that screen had so many dots on it that it looked at times like an advanced case of chicken pox." At least fifty aircraft converged toward *Laffey*, leading Gauding later to write, "things really started to happen."[13]

"Give us all you got,"[14] Becton ordered Lieutenant Henke, the chief engineer stationed in the engine room. The ship, which had been cruising at fifteen knots, lurched forward as her engines groaned to reach flank speed. Gun directors began gathering the information, such as the ship's pitch and roll and the wind speed, needed to calculate the range from the five-inch guns to the aircraft, while Seaman Johnson in the 40mm Mount 41 stood ready to lift to his gunners the clips of four shells that would soon be on their way to their targets.

Inside Mount 52, one of the forward five-inch guns, sight setter Seaman Dockery took his post on the starboard side and checked the dials monitoring the gun's movements. In the handling room below Dockery, Sonarman Zack waited at the powder hoist and Gunner's Mate Glen Radder stood by on the ammunition hoist, both ready to start the rhythmic pattern that would send a steady flow of powder and shells to the gunners above. Neither Zack nor Radder dwelt on the fact that they worked inside a tiny room jammed with powder and shells, ready to ignite with even the tiniest of sparks. The pair listened as the guns turned and elevated in response to the information supplied by the gun director, much as they heard during exercises in Hawaiian waters. Zack prayed that the gun crew would execute as well today as it had during those calmer days.

Becton's main weapons, besides the guns, were his crew and *Laffey*'s speed and maneuverability. As the men rushed to their stations, Becton had little doubt that they would perform capably. He had conducted the many hours of drills and exercises with this moment in mind. He had trained the crew as best as he could, and he could now do nothing but rely on their skill and on his.

After ordering flank speed, Becton told Quartermaster Jack Doran that when the action started and the pace quickened, he would call out orders to him over the voice tube above his head to ensure Doran heard him. Out of touch with CAP, Becton would now have to rely on his skills in maneuvering and his gunners' accuracy. If he were talented with the first, he would hand his gunners the best chance to be accurate with the second. "I knew we'd have to maneuver like we had never done before and fast," he later wrote. "The only way to fight off those fanatics was to keep them broad on the beam where the maximum numbers of our guns could bear."[15]

On the bridge, Sonarman Charles Bell called the range as the planes narrowed the distance. When they had reached the nine-mile mark, Becton ordered, "stand by for main battery," at which the three five-inch mounts prepared to open fire. Crew on deck could now hear a faint hum coming from yet unseen objects in the distance. As the noise intensified, men with binoculars, according to Lieutenant Manson, spotted "gnat-like specks in the sky. That was the enemy, that was death, circling, tantalizing, far out of range."[16]

Laffey was the initial target of the *kikusui*, the third of the ten major kamikaze assaults launched against US ships off Okinawa. At that moment, 165 aircraft raced toward the island. While many veered away to attack other ships, twenty-two kamikazes selected *Laffey*, the first vessel spotted on their way south from Japan. As dots filled the sky, each one indicating a Japanese plane, Lieutenant Challen McCune, the new executive officer, was certain he would never see his family again. On the deck near his 20mm gun, Seaman 1/c Ramon Pressburger concluded he and his shipmates "had about four or five minutes to live." The thought of impending death frightened him, but "then I simply got mad. All I can remember saying was, 'I'm just not going alone.'"[17]

On the fantail, the ship's hindmost position, Seaman "Doc" Brown waited at his post with the aft torpedo tubes, mere feet from Youngquist's guns. As Brown gazed skyward the kamikazes, mere specks when first spotted, morphed into aircraft. "Then all hell broke loose."[18]

Starting at 8:27 and lasting until 9:47, *Laffey* came under unrelenting attack as twenty-two kamikaze aircraft dropped from above or attempted to sneak in from barely above the water's surface to destroy the ship. Twenty-two planes in eighty minutes, an average of one every three and a half minutes, charged the vessel on every side, keeping her gun crews busy and presenting challenges that taxed every maneuvering talent that Becton possessed.

"Then the fireworks started," wrote Becton. "Planes approached from all directions and all elevations."[19]

The attack had begun.

8:27 to 8:30 a.m.—Kamikazes Numbers 1 and 2

"Here They Come!"

"Sight 'em and shoot 'em" could have been the unofficial motto for the next eighty minutes. If Becton were to extricate his ship and crew from harm's way, he could ill afford to waste time pondering his moves, for every second he delayed brought an enemy aircraft closer to hitting the ship. The Val dive bomber traveled one mile every fifteen seconds, while her faster compatriot, the Asahi D4Y, nicknamed "Judy," covered one and a half miles in the same time.

It is easy to forget the manner and speed with which the kamikaze attacks occurred. The twenty-two kamikazes charging *Laffey* were more than the ship's gun crews had battled in a month of skirmishes off the Philippines. Seven breaks of five or more minutes handed Fern, Johnson, and the rest of the crew on deck momentary breathers, but throughout the eighty-minute attack they also faced periods when clusters of kamikazes dived simultaneously from multiple directions, including five kamikazes that came in at 8:30. For much of the battle, Becton and the gun crews had to select the most immediate of several threats speeding toward the *Laffey* and hope the port and starboard guns could quickly splash the kamikaze so they could turn their attention on the next invader. Crew on the 40mm and 20mm guns became embroiled in a real-life shooting gallery, with kamikazes instead of ducks popping up on all sides. Though it was an eternity for Zack and Phoutrides, the engagement lasted shorter than most Hollywood films. Yet in that period more heroism and fear, gallantry and sacrifice emerged than the most talented movie director could have packed into a box-office smash.

Instinct, honed from months of drills and hours of study, guided the crew. Measured calculation and thought were acceptable during training and in the classroom, but they were out of place in the fast-paced action at sea.

152

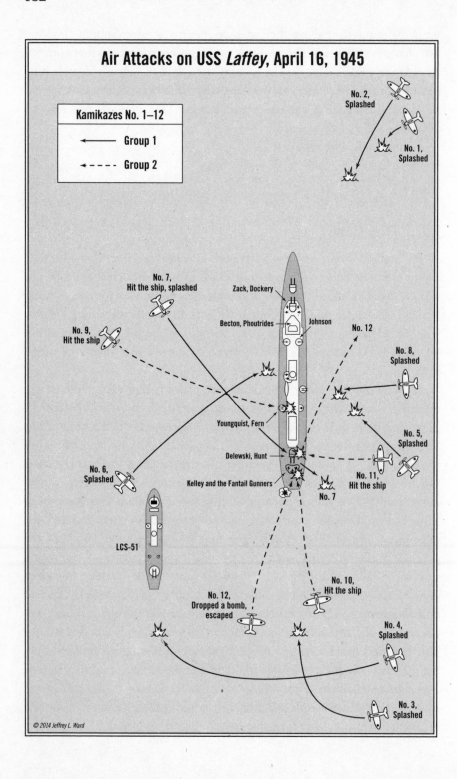

Air Attacks on USS *Laffey*, April 16, 1945

Kamikazes No. 1–12

⟵ Group 1

◄- - - Group 2

No. 2, Splashed

No. 1, Splashed

No. 7, Hit the ship, splashed

Zack, Dockery

Becton, Phoutrides

Johnson

No. 9, Hit the ship

No. 12

No. 8, Splashed

Youngquist, Fern

No. 5, Splashed

No. 6, Splashed

Delewski, Hunt

No. 11, Hit the ship

Kelley and the Fantail Gunners

No. 7

LCS-51

No. 10, Hit the ship

No. 12, Dropped a bomb, escaped

No. 4, Splashed

No. 3, Splashed

© 2014 Jeffrey L. Ward

At first men rushed to their battle stations wondering if this was yet another exercise, but they were soon disabused of that notion. Becton, who knew what they were likely in for, secured each item on his desk, including the photo of Imogen Carpenter. He then stepped to the bridge for what he expected would be an intense morning.

Quartermaster Phoutrides took his place on the bridge, glanced at Becton a few feet away, and wished he could emulate the same calm demeanor that his skipper always maintained. Sonarman Zack joined Gunner's Mate Radder in the handling room below Gun 52. Lieutenant Youngquist, in command of Mount 44, the aft quad 40mm guns on the ship's port side, as well as the two 20mm guns adjoining him to starboard, checked that Seaman Fern and the rest of the crew were in place and ready to fire. Mount Captain Delewski oversaw operations at Gun 53 on the ship's aft portion, expecting Seaman 1/c Lee C. Hunt and other members of his crew, including sixteen-year-old Seaman Joe Edmonds, to perform as capably as they had in Hawaii training when they captured awards for their gunnery skills. Those awards meant nothing, though, if his men failed to deliver during the heat of battle.

Manning one of Youngquist's 40mm guns, Seaman Fern scanned the sky for traces of the enemy. He almost unconsciously touched the medallion of the Sacred Heart of Jesus that his aunt, Sister Margaret Claire, a Catholic nun, had earlier mailed to keep him safe. Seaman Johnson disappeared into the ammunition room below Mount 41, the forward 40mm gun on the starboard side, and mentally prepared for what could be an intense period of handing clips of four shells to the men above.

Belowdecks the black gang, including Fireman Gauding and Seaman "Jim" Spriggs, hurried to their stations in the engine and firerooms that would be so crucial in executing Becton's commands and in keeping the ship afloat. Blocked from observing what occurred above, they would have to rely on sounds to form an image of the battle raging outside. Five-inch guns would announce the beginning of battle with their ship-rattling booms. Gauding and Spriggs had little to fear if the smaller guns remained silent, for that meant the five-inch guns had done their job, but if the staccato rhythm of Youngquist's 40mm guns and the faster, sharper retort of Falotico's 20mm machine guns joined in, the likelihood of a kamikaze crashing into their position rose precipitously. In that case, they and every other man in the engine and firerooms would have to force the dangers to the farthest recesses of their minds and execute the rapid course and speed changes called down from the bridge as Becton maneuvered the ship to give the kamikazes a poorer angle of attack on the ship.

Radioman Lawrence Kelley, whose melodic singing voice had so frequently made the men think of home and girlfriends, hastened to the 20mm guns on the ship's fantail, where the men had responsibility for knocking down any planes that attacked aft. Seaman "Doc" Brown on the aft torpedo tubes and Torpedoman's Mate Fred Gemmell on the starboard depth-charge launching K-guns, manned stations that were unlikely to play roles in the battle, for torpedoes and depth charges are poor remedies for targets that attack from the sky. They prepared, though, to rush to the aid of their shipmates on the 40mm and 20mm guns or help a wounded shipmate.

Their waiting ended at 8:27 a.m. when lookouts with binoculars spotted multiple aircraft eight miles ahead of the ship. The fixed landing gear identified many of the intruders as Val dive bombers, which gave Becton fewer than two minutes before the aircraft struck his ship.

Men on deck strained to catch a glimpse of their foes, still tiny specks peppering the blue sky. As the fifty aircraft, a mixture of bombers and kamikazes, approached, some peeled away toward other objectives, but the bulk selected *Laffey* as their target. "Just look at those bastards!" shouted Fern's buddy, Seaman Pressburger, a loader on Mount 43, the aft 40mm guns on the starboard side. In the battle's opening moments, eight kamikazes raced toward the destroyer in a coordinated multiple-angled attack that demanded action fore and aft, port and starboard. "Here they come! Here they come!"[20]

A quartet of Vals split from the other four to pose the opening challenge. They approached from dead ahead until they had drawn within four thousand yards, when two veered left toward *Laffey*'s starboard side while the other two swerved aft to charge in on Kelley's fantail group. In doing so, they made it more difficult for Becton to bring his broadside to bear on all four—if he turned the destroyer to port so that the majority of his guns faced the first duo, the two closing rapidly aft would have an easier path. Becton had no alternative but to trust his five-inch gun crews and hope that other kamikazes did not sweep down on other quadrants.

Becton moved outside to the flying bridge so he could gain a more comprehensive view of the action. To avoid a hit against the most vulnerable part of the destroyer, the mid-section containing not only the bridge and communications area, but also the engine and firerooms below, he ordered hard left rudder to bring his starboard guns broadsides and to present the narrowest portion of the ship to the enemy. He then ordered Lieutenant Smith, his gunnery officer, to open fire at his discretion, without waiting for Becton's command. He also made preparations to place every battery in local control if necessary, meaning that each gun captain would defend his quadrant of the ship and fire at anything that ventured into view.

Phoutrides looked for the CAP, but the aircraft were conspicuously absent. Becton was still unable to contact the lower-flying two-plane CAP, and the two four-plane CAPs had raced away in pursuit of other kamikazes. Stripped of that crucial first line of defense, Becton now had to rely on his gun crews, the final line of defense preventing the enemy from sinking the ship.

Twenty seconds after the initial sighting the two forward five-inch mounts—Gunner's Mate 2/c Edward Zebro's Mount 51 and Chief Gunner's Mate Warren Walker's Mount 52—signaled the opening of the conflict with a resounding BOOM! The ship shuddered, slightly jarring each man on deck, while the force shattered light bulbs in their sockets and tossed about unsecured items below.

After receiving the order to fire from Mount 52 Gun Captain Walker, Sonarman Zack concentrated on his one task—to supply Mount 52 with powder cans until he was ordered to stop, no matter what unfolded outside. "I had one focus during everything," said Zack, "to keep filling the hoist." For the next eighty minutes he repeated the same actions every three seconds—he took a twenty-five-pound powder can from a mess attendant and placed it on the automatic hoist that lifted it to the mount above. Like an assembly line in an automotive factory, the hoist moved steadily on, maintaining the same speed as it passed by Zack to deliver its contents to the powder man above. Zack's task was to keep every slot in the hoist full until the action halted, thereby ensuring that his mount buddies fired a shell every three seconds. Zack acted without thought, an automaton melding with the hundreds of other parts of the mount mechanism to produce one response: to keep shells racing toward enemy aircraft intent on killing them. "We had our rhythm. I kept loading the hoists until the target was gone, and then there was a pause until we fixed on another target and got orders to fire again. The rhythm was continuous."

Up above, where Seaman Robert Dockery stood, the powder man took the cans off the hoist and handed them to the projectile man, who inserted them into the barrel and turned back for another powder can as the gun sent the shells hurtling toward the enemy. Zack heard the boom and felt the gun's recoil—"more of a jar,"[21] in his words—but was too busy lifting the next can to reflect on what was happening. Working as he did in a stationary room, Zack could not feel the turning of the gun above him, but he knew when the guns quieted that the mount was swerving toward other targets. On the other side of the room, a few feet away, Radder mirrored Zack's actions, only with shells instead of powder cans.

Depending on how quickly the men worked, either both guns of each mount fired at the same time, emitting a single deafening BOOM! or they fired one after another—BOOM! BOOM!—creating a series of rattles and explosions that reminded some of earthquakes. Seaman Dockery thought it unique that while the mount itself never shook much, he could actually feel the shell leave the barrel and the gun recoil.

Black puffs from the shells of the forward mount dotted the sky near the first two kamikazes, which approached on the starboard bow. While employing maximum speed of thirty-two knots, Becton maneuvered to keep the enemy planes on his beam so that they attacked at right angles to *Laffey*, thereby bringing his broadsides to bear and enabling every gun on either port or starboard to fire at the intruder. This also presented a smaller portion of *Laffey* for the enemy to target. The last thing Becton wanted was to allow a kamikaze to attack from ahead or astern, where the pilot faced the entire length of the destroyer and could select his impact spot.

"Left twenty-five degrees rudder" ordered Becton as the pair came on, then "hard left rudder"[22] when the Val veered to the right in an effort to keep *Laffey's* bow in line. Zebro and Walker kept their guns trained, no mean feat when both ship and plane kept altering courses, but the initial Val doggedly closed the distance. With the crew on deck intently following each shell, trying with their thoughts to nudge it toward the plane, for thirty seconds the two mounts fired forty rounds at the Val. Suddenly, a half minute after the mounts commenced firing, a shell smacked squarely into the first kamikaze when it was still five miles away. The Val exploded in a fireball and disintegrated, throwing pieces of aircraft about as the plane splashed into the ocean.

The men on the two forward five-inch guns had no time to cheer as the second kamikaze raced in from the same direction. They had less time to splash this invader, however, as this plane had already drawn within six miles.

From the bridge Gunnery Officer Paul Smith shifted Mounts 51 and 52 to the second aircraft ten seconds after the plane was spotted at 8:30. Gun captains Ed Zebro and Warren Walker watched from the hatches of their mounts, ignoring the fact that they exposed the upper third of their bodies to enemy bullets and shrapnel, while inside Dockery and his mates maintained the rhythm Zebro and Walker had hoped to create during their drills and exercises.

As the men in Zebro's Mount 51 moved shell and powder, unburned powder in one of the two gun barrels singed the eyebrows of a loader. The startled young sailor flailed at his eyes and screamed in fear. Zebro, who could not allow havoc among men working in such a confined location, grabbed a rawhide maul, shook it in front of the young man, and ordered him to settle down or he would smack him with the instrument. The sailor stifled his fears and returned to his post.

Mounts 51 and 52 fired sixty rounds in forty-five seconds at the second kamikaze which, like its compatriot, exploded and disintegrated in a ball of flame, this time only three thousand yards from *Laffey*. Men on deck cheered, but Zack and the others below had little notion of what happened. "We were down below the water level and could hear things falling into the water," said Zack, "but we didn't know what they were. We heard a muffled boom. I couldn't hear any planes coming in." He continued to execute his tasks and placed his faith in the gunners above. "You bet I was pulling for the gunners to get those planes. You depend on them, and they depend on you."[23]

While Zebro's and Walker's crews had dispatched the first two attackers, another pair of kamikazes challenged *Laffey* from the rear. It was time for Delewski's men at Ole Betsy, the aft five-inch mount, to take over.

8:30—Kamikazes Numbers 3 and 4

"A Great Cheer Went Up"

Seaman 1/c Felipe Salcido, the bridge lookout standing next to Becton on the flying bridge, alerted his skipper to the two Val dive bombers attacking astern. Becton, whose view aft was blocked by the ship's stacks, counted on Delewski to deal with that threat.

At 8:30 their first target came in from the stern slightly to starboard. The mount's equipment, early forms of computers, determined the *Laffey*'s speed and direction, the target's speed and direction, and translated the information into a proximity fuse setting that would detonate the projectile when it neared the plane. The pointer, Boatswain's Mate Calvin Wesley Cloer, elevated the guns until they were on target, while his buddy and gun trainer,

Coxswain James La Pointe, swung the guns from side to side until they were also locked on target.

Once the guns boomed their first salvo, "a rhythm had to be developed to load the guns at the last split second to take advantage of the latest fuse setting," said Delewski. Every man at the mount, in the handling room and in the ammunition magazines below deck, had to work as a team to keep the guns firing, or else men would die. "Yes, my gun crew was experienced and well-practiced," said Delewski. "We had no trouble firing both guns of the mount every three seconds to take advantage of the latest fuse setting."[24]

Delewski's crew fired twenty rounds, ten from each gun barrel, at the aircraft for thirty seconds. They sighted their guns so low that the 20mm gun crew on the ship's fantail, yards behind the mount and barely below the firing angle of the five-inch barrels, felt they were the targets instead of the aircraft. Each blast made Kelley and the 20mm gunners flinch, duck, and hold their ears.

While Becton continued maneuvering, Fern on the 40mm and Falotico on the 20mm, who could not fire until the planes had drawn within their shorter ranges, watched the huge five-inch shells flutter toward their target. Sky bursts from exploding shells fore and aft reminded some of a massive July 4 fireworks display. Men with parched throats and heightened heartbeats silently followed the kamikazes as they shortened the distance to their destroyer. For them, and everyone aboard *Laffey*, life at that moment factored to a simple equation—either the ship's guns killed the kamikazes or the kamikazes would kill them.

Nineteen rounds from Delewski's mount produced airbursts all about the oncoming kamikaze before the twentieth ended its run. With the aircraft barely twenty seconds from smashing into *Laffey*, chunks of the wings and fuselage ripped away, causing the plane to dip lower to the water, where its landing gear caught the surface. "The third enemy cartwheeled flaming into the sea,"[25] recalled Lieutenant Manson.

Delewski, observing the action from the open hatch at the top of his mount, instantly switched his guns to the fourth target, which was farther from the ship than its predecessor because the pilot had swung around on a wider path. Delewski dismissed the risks he faced by standing in the exposed position and instead concentrated on bringing down the fourth plane.

Joined by antiaircraft fire from *LCS-51*, then one-half mile to *Laffey*'s port, Delewski's crew fired thirty-five rounds at the fourth kamikaze. Tracers from *LCS-51* and Delewski's shells ripped through the plane, which like the third cartwheeled across the water's surface before settling and sinking fifty-five hundred yards on the destroyer's port quarter.

"After the fourth one went down," said Gunner's Mate 3/c Francis M. Gebhart, the gun captain on the port side quad 40mm mount, "there was a great cheer that went up from all over the ship."[26] They had a right to be pleased, as few destroyer crews could boast that they had successfully defended their ship from four kamikazes.

Quartermaster Phoutrides, who had been annoyed that the CAP had been lured away, leaving *Laffey* to her own defenses, joined in celebrating the performance of the five-inch guns. For how long could those five-inch guns, even when backed by the ship's 40mm and 20mm guns, be able to tackle multiple kamikaze attacks?

Jubilation or concerns had to be quickly cast aside, however, as four more kamikazes, two to port and two to starboard, took advantage of *Laffey*'s preoccupation with the first four planes to sneak in from the sides.

The 40mm and 20mm gun crews were about to join in the action.

8:30—Kamikazes Numbers 5 and 6

"All Hell Broke Loose"

Johnson and Fern had no time to revel over downing the first four kamikazes as within seconds a fifth and sixth kamikaze appeared, one attacking on Fern's port side and the other on Johnson's starboard quarter, as if trying to sneak in while *Laffey*'s guns focused on the earlier kamikazes. Sighted at 8:30 along with the previous trio, the pair enjoyed a smooth run in until they came within range of Johnson's and Fern's smaller guns, whose tracers quickly sliced through the sky as bullets and shells sought their targets.

The fifth plane, a Judy, came in low and straight on the ship's starboard beam, making him an easy target for Johnson's 40mm gun near the bridge, Seaman Pressburger's 40mm guns just behind the aft stack, and Lieutenant Youngquist's 20mm guns toward the starboard side. The smaller guns, which had been silent while the five-inch mounts dispatched the first four kamikazes, now broke loose. For the next two minutes the longer-range 40mm crew fired one four-shell clip at the enemy every two seconds, while the smaller 20mm machine guns spat fifteen bullets in the same interval. Red and white tracers converged on the kamikaze as the pilot maintained a straight course toward the ship's mid-section.

"It was like all hell broke loose," said Torpedoman's Mate Gemmell as he watched the plane come in from his station at the starboard side K-guns aft of Youngquist's 20mm guns. "Everywhere you turned, you could see them coming in. All our guns were blazing as fast as they could do."[27]

Shells and tracers sped toward their target, the numerous antiaircraft bursts painting an image of grim combat across the sky. Men at other stations urged their shipmates manning the guns to down the kamikaze, which somehow eluded the arsenal that raced toward it. The steady thump!-thump!-thump! of the 40mm guns joined the louder booms of the five-inch guns as the plane drew closer. The men working belowdecks or in one of the enclosed mounts could not see the battle, but when the din of combat was joined by the rapid clatter of the 20mm machine guns, the added noise alerted them that a collision was imminently possible.

"The firing would get more intense as the planes got closer," said Seaman Dockery, who worked with Sonarman Zack in Mount 52, the second five-inch gun forward. "I knew if the 40s and 20s fired, that they were close and coming at me! It got tense. Fingers crossed until the 20s stopped firing. If they didn't stop firing, then you figured we'd be hit."

As did many of his shipmates, Dockery personalized the action. The kamikaze was out to kill him, not just the ship. At least, thought Dockery, he was "surrounded by steel and felt a bit safer than the guys on the 20s and 40s who were looking at the plane coming right at them." He knew that at any instant a kamikaze could smash into his gun and turn Mount 52 into his tomb, "but you put it out of your mind as much as you can. There wasn't anything I could do about it but hope for the best,"[28] so he focused on his tasks, figuring he could most affect the outcome by continuing to do his job.

At his station in the handling room below Mount 41, the forward starboard side 40mm gun, Seaman Johnson "didn't need the visual of planes diving right at me."[29] He knew from the sounds of firing whether an attack was coming aft, port, or starboard and how close a kamikaze might have drawn to the ship. Jolts rattled the destroyer, but blocked from observing the action aft, Johnson did not know whether the reverberations were from the firing of the five-inch guns or the impact of a kamikaze. He felt safer than his compatriots on deck, who were exposed to flying shrapnel and enemy bullets, but worried that flames could easily engulf him before he could escape the enclosed handling room, where explosives surrounded him. Like Dockery, he concentrated on passing the clips of four shells to the men above and blocked out everything else.

On deck Seaman Martinis watched incredulously as the kamikaze churned through the 40mm and 20mm shells that peppered the air space around him. Finally, with the kamikaze only one-half mile from the *Laffey*, tracers ripped into the aircraft, shredding the plane and sending it to the ocean. The kamikaze "was coming apart like a mess of burning confetti,"[30] wrote Lieutenant Manson of the spectacle.

While Youngquist and the other men on the starboard side dispatched their kamikaze, crews on the port side, including Fern's 40mm gun, took aim at the sixth attacker. At 8:30 a Judy dive bomber only three miles from the ship raced in on the port quarter at a forty-five-degree angle from the southwest. Quartermaster Phoutrides, acting as an additional lookout this busy day, saw him approach as most of the guns focused their attention on the fifth kamikaze speeding in to starboard. He tried to alert Lieutenant Runk, standing next to him, but the officer failed to hear his shouts in the pandemonium of the moment. Phoutrides did what many men aboard had longed to do to the stern lieutenant and smacked him on his kapok life jacket. "That's the only time I hit an officer," said Phoutrides, "but Runk was O.K. with it."[31]

Thankful that he was not fighting in the more narrow confines about the Philippines, which restricted his ability to maneuver, Becton ordered a hard right rudder to evade the sixth kamikaze and to make him a more attractive target for his port side guns. Delewski's five-inch barrels joined Youngquist's port 40mm and 20mm guns, and for the next minute all batteries fired more than eleven hundred rounds at the oncoming dive bomber, which had now begun strafing the ship's deck and superstructure as he neared. With his heart pounding wildly, Phoutrides witnessed a spectacle drawn from the Wild West era, when gunslingers faced each other in dusty cowboy towns and, one-on-one, determined who would live and who would die. This time, however, explosive-laden planes and antiaircraft shells replaced Colt .45 bullets.

Youngquist observed puffs of black smoke two miles out, indicating that Delewski's gunners had bracketed the target. A few seconds later his 40mm guns closed in, shortly before the 20mm crews locked onto the target.

Youngquist had one minute to down this plane before it reached the ship, and from his vantage it seemed that the kamikaze was barreling directly toward him. "Mostly," said Lieutenant Youngquist, "you think, 'Let's stop him before he gets us!'"[32]

Enemy bullets clanged against the waist-high steel barrier that shielded Youngquist's 40mm gun crew, but the 20mm gunners, under their petty officer, Gunner's Mate 2/c Stanley Wismer, co-captain of his high school football team, stood amidst the bullets without even that inadequate protection. The pilot strafed the superstructure as he steadily narrowed the distance, wounding some of the men posted at gun stations. Signalmen, radiomen, and anybody else whose duties were now irrelevant to the battle rushed in for those who fell and helped maintain a constant fire from the 40mm and 20mm guns.

The tracers and shells converging on the kamikaze cast a fiery web connecting ship and plane. The port side guns fired more than a thousand rounds at the kamikaze in one minute, erecting a thick curtain of shell bursts and tracers that seemed impossible to penetrate. While most rounds flew errantly by the target, others pierced the fuselage and ripped pieces of metal from the wings.

Eyes widened and voices rose as the kamikaze charged relentlessly toward the ship. At the last moment Becton ordered hard right to swing the destroyer out of the plane's path, giving Youngquist's batteries an open avenue to the kamikaze. With the enemy pilot fifty yards away, the portside guns ended the suicidal run with a startling explosion that scattered pieces of plane and pilot into the sea off Youngquist's position.

The plane impacted the water with such force that it ignited the bomb attached to its underbelly and hurled deadly shrapnel against the port side and the superstructure. The metallic shards wounded additional men and knocked out the ship's vital SG radar, which helped locate surface targets and low-flying enemy aircraft. "The Judy had blinded one of *Laffey*'s eyes,"[33] Becton later wrote.

With the sixth kamikaze accounted for, Youngquist checked on his men. The officer rushed to one 20mm gunner, still in his straps, and saw shrapnel protruding from the man's back. Youngquist administered morphine, and then asked another man to help the wounded to the wardroom for treatment. Another of Youngquist's gunners lost an eye to the shrapnel.

Becton, who like most commanders had doubted the ability of the small 20mm machine guns to bring down enemy aircraft, changed his tune. Youngquist's battery, including his 20mm guns, splashed this sixth invader, which was good news for the skipper. He needed every weapon at his disposal if he were to free his ship from the kamikazes circling above.

8:39 to 8:45—Kamikazes Numbers 7 and 8

"Oh, the Hell with It"

A seven-minute interval gave Becton's crew time to remove the seriously wounded and prepare for the next round of attacks. So far the ship had suffered no serious damage, but despite disposing of six kamikazes, the heavens seemed to add two more to every one splashed. Men gulped water and checked on their mates before again turning their attention to the skies.

The break ended at 8:39 a.m. when a Val dive bomber approached broad on the port bow from two miles out. As the plane hugged the water, Becton turned the ship to starboard at top speed to keep the plane on his broadsides and, like before, to protect the ship's vital bridge and communications area by forcing the pilot to choose *Laffey*'s aft portion.

The pilot altered course in an effort to keep pace with Becton, but the airman could not match Becton's skills. Phoutrides watched the plane skid farther aft, meaning that the likely target would no longer be the bridge, but the latter third of the ship. Phoutrides was safe for the time being, but he feared that Kelley and others on the fantail would bear the brunt of the impact if the kamikaze broke through.

Again Youngquist's gunners, including Tom Fern, joined by Mount 25, Kelley's 20mm on the fantail, must have felt as if they were being unfairly singled out by the Japanese as yet another kamikaze zeroed in aft. The guns fired nine hundred more rounds in forty seconds, with some hitting the mark and causing the kamikaze to lose altitude. Becton continued to turn the ship to the right but the Val, now only twenty feet above the water's surface, stubbornly kept pace in a three-way contest pitting Becton's maneuvering talents and the port side gunners' abilities against the determination of the kamikaze.

With the kamikaze less than one hundred yards out, the pilot stabilized his course and charged straight at the ship. Having lost to Becton's maneuvering skills, the pilot, according to one observer, "must have said, 'Oh, the hell with it,'"[34] and adopted a direct route to the destroyer rather than continue the cat-and-mouse game. Opting to hit any portion of the ship he could, the pilot charged through a hailstorm of bullets and shells from Youngquist's battery and every other portside gun.

Becton momentarily worried that the attacker's angle might mean the plane would hit *Laffey*'s engine room, but his maneuvering and the port guns deflected the kamikaze farther aft toward Delewski's Mount 53. Gun Captain Delewski would normally have been watching events from the oval hatch located atop and to the rear of the mount, with the upper half of his body exposed, but while Boatswain's Mate Cloer, Coxswain La Pointe, and the rest of the crew began moving shells and powder into position, one of the two gun barrels ceased operating. With the seconds ticking away, Delewski jumped from the hatch, grabbed a hammer, and gave the balky gun a potent whack. The weapon whirred to life at the instant the kamikaze pilot grazed the top of the gun mount and exploded in the water off the ship's starboard side. Had Delewski been at the hatch instead of dealing with the balky gun, he would have been sliced in half.

The plane demolished Delewski's hatch cover and sprayed burning gasoline and shrapnel into his mount. The crew quickly extinguished the flames, but fragments wounded Cloer and La Pointe. The slightly wounded La Pointe remained at his post, but Delewski sent the more severely injured Cloer to the wardroom to see Lieutenant Darnell, the shop's doctor. The immediate danger to the gun had ended, but it could not afford to take another hit if it were to maintain fire. Through a combination of skill, luck, and good fortune, *Laffey* had avoided her first direct kamikaze hit by yards.

Before the fires had been extinguished in Mount 53, at 8:45 lookouts spotted Kamikaze No. 8 three miles out, a Judy approaching on the starboard beam. In another exhibit of a coordinated attack, this plane made its run on *Laffey*'s starboard side while the seventh had conducted its charge against the port side. Becton, who had been swerving to the right to bring most of his guns to bear on the seventh kamikaze, now sent hurried orders to the engine room for a hard left turn to deal with the eighth.

The starboard side 40mm and 20mm gun crews, including Mount 43, where Fern's buddy, Ramon Pressburger, was stationed, unleashed streams of fire at the plane, now less than one hundred feet above the water. With the five-inch guns busy handling other threats, the starboard gun crews had to deal with this latest menace.

The plane drew close enough that Pressburger could see the pilot at his controls. Men depressed the 40mm guns until they were level with the surface and pumped nine hundred rounds in seventy seconds at the aircraft with such accuracy that the plane disintegrated in midair less than two hundred yards away. Pressburger and his mates let out a raucous cheer to celebrate their triumph.

Eight planes had attacked *Laffey*; eight planes had been dispatched, with only minor damage sustained from the kamikaze that had grazed Mount 53. Though Becton felt as if he had been fighting for hours, he and his crew had battled the octet in fewer than twenty minutes. While most destroyers subject to kamikaze attacks contended with one or two aircraft—and usually limped back to port with severe damage, if they survived at all—*Laffey* gunners handled four times that amount.

Becton praised his gun crews for erecting such a thick antiaircraft curtain that the enemy had failed to reach their objective. That could only have been achieved with the teamwork developed through hours of drills in the Atlantic, off Normandy, and in the Philippines. He was so impressed with the performance of his 20mm guns, which he had previously doubted, that he made a point of mentioning in his action report, "don't sell the twenty millimeter short!"[35] On the other hand, crew attributed much of the success to Becton's 1942–1943 encounters in Pacific waters, where he gained valuable experience and knowledge that paid dividends on April 16.

The officers and men had performed well to keep the ship safe from eight kamikazes. However, one glimpse above revealed the threats that remained. The heavens, filled with enemy aircraft circling like vultures, convinced them that their day was far from over. Gunner's Mate Robert Karr had only moments before joined Pressburger and his mates on Mount 43 in a loud cheer.

Their cheer was short lived; their ordeal had not even begun.

CHAPTER 8

AGONY ON THE AFTERDECK

Heroes' blood her decks bespattered.
Twenties, forties, five-inch clattered.
She kept firing e'en though battered.
　　—"Invicta," Lieutenant Matthew Darnell

The battle's opening quarter hour had gone well for *Laffey*. Becton's skillful maneuvering and the gunners' accuracy had dispatched the first eight kamikazes, but the agony of the afterdeck, twenty-five minutes of unadulterated hell, left survivors stunned with the ferocity of the attack.

8:45—Kamikaze Number 9

"*Laffey* Was Vulnerable to Death and Destruction"

In three harrowing minutes four separate enemy aircraft converged on the destroyer from four angles—two from port and two from starboard. Like a boxer absorbing a series of blows, *Laffey* took four punches in a remarkably brief, and deadly, stretch. "They came in thick and fast after that, beginning with the ninth plane"[1] said Becton of the kamikazes that attacked after the first eight had been shot down.

Fire Controlman 3/c George R. Burnett tried to describe for his parents what next occurred, and wrote that, "all hell broke lose." He added, "they all started to dive on us at once and poor little us all by ourselves out there so you can see we didn't have much of a chance because they were coming from all directions and you just can't shoot every way at once."[2]

At the bridge Phoutrides noticed that after the first eight kamikazes, "they came in groups of ones and twos. It almost appeared that they waited their turn. At one time we had 7 Vals circling overhead that didn't attack us until a few others went in. They used all the tricks they could—flying low, coming in fast, and diving from the sun. In fact, many of them made bombing runs on us before attempting a suicide dive. All of them," he added somberly, "strafed as they came in."[3]

In the CIC below the bridge Lieutenant Lloyd Hull, a product of the University of Pennsylvania's NROTC, supervised the men who operated the ship's communications system, including the recently added FIDO team. Leaving control of events outside the CIC to Becton and the men on the guns, he focused on his main responsibility—to collect and relay to Becton the information he needed, such as targets spotted and the numbers of friendly aircraft in the area, if any, to arrive at the decisions he had to make with lightning speed. As the battle swirled above, radarmen plotted surface and air targets, while radiomen and others manned the communications apparatus that linked the ship to the flagship, to other vessels, and to the outside world. Crew called "talkers" reported to Hull any updates they received over their circuits from the overtaxed lookouts on deck, and relayed information given them by Hull to Becton and other recipients.

Like Zack in Mount 52, Hull and the others in CIC labored in a closed world, blocked from witnessing the battle raging outside. Unlike Zack, Hull and his crew could at least follow the progress from the radar screens and any communications that arrived. Hull wished he could have observed more, and knew that a kamikaze could at any moment ravage his CIC and end his run as an officer, but he concentrated on his tasks and tried to be as helpful as he could to Becton and, ultimately, to his shipmates. Maintaining a flow of information to the bridge was the prime manner in which he could best contribute to the action, for without it, Becton would be blindly skippering his ship.

As he moved from radarmen to talkers, Hull wondered how his friends on deck fared. He knew he was fortunate to work in CIC, where the bulkheads protected him and his men from the bullets and shrapnel that would undoubtedly sweep the decks with each crash, but in some ways he longed to be above, sharing the hazards with those he had commanded and those with whom he had grown close.

Long-range radar, able to discern targets up to sixty miles away, has difficulty locating low-flying planes. With his CAP still missing and his SG surface-monitoring radar already disabled, Becton leaned on the young eyes of the ship's lookouts, most of them recent high school graduates. Until CAP arrived and imposed themselves between the kamikazes and *Laffey*, Becton would have to rely on his own resources.

At 8:45 a.m. one of his sharp-eyed lookouts spotted a Judy coming in low on the port side. As he drew closer, the pilot banked slightly, and then aimed at the ship's mid-section, hoping to destroy the bridge area. Even though the kamikaze raced in at more than three hundred miles per hour, men on the port side guns were surprised that the aircraft created the illusion of moving toward them in slow motion.

Lieutenant Youngquist checked the men on his 40mm and 20mm gun crews, one level above Delewski's five-inch gun on the main deck, but Tom Fern and the other men had opened fire almost as soon as the kamikaze was spotted. Fern and his companions stood their ground, exposed to the bullets pinging around them, and battled the instinct to crouch below the waist-high shield as the plane bore in.

While Becton executed frequent course changes to keep the plane away from the ship's vital mid-section, Lieutenant Frank Manson watched the kamikaze, uncertain whether it would veer toward the bridge and him or plunge directly into Youngquist's gun. Survival at this moment relied on those port-side 40mm and 20mm guns, the ship's last line of defense, to knock down the plane. "You know he's [the kamikaze pilot] going to die—you pray he won't take you with him," Manson said. "You're up against a desperation and fanaticism that leaves you cold all over." Manson had witnessed other suicide attacks in the Philippines, but this was "blood-chilling. They [kamikazes] have a kind of insanity that makes war more horrible than it's ever been before."[4]

Seaman Fern handed four-shell clips to his gunners, who fired them as rapidly as the loader placed them in the guns. Spent casings clanged into bins on the deck, adding their noise to the pow-pow of the 40mm guns and the rapid tat-tat-tat-tat of the 20mm guns. In return, bullets from the aircraft pinged off shields and mounts, igniting sparks and cutting into human flesh and bones.

Bullets from *Laffey* gunners kicked up hundreds of splashes in the water as they attempted to down the low-flying plane, making it appear as if crew could traverse from ship to plane by hopping along the splashes. Tracers nicked the aircraft, and the plane shuddered as 20mm slugs pierced the fuselage and wings, but on it came, astounding gun crews who had the target directly in their sights. If they could not hit the plane in the next few seconds, Fern and everyone else would become part of a fiery eruption that would turn the aft section into their funeral pyre.

Despite the 430 rounds fired in half a minute by the 40mm and 20mm guns, the kamikaze pilot barreled through. Men near Fern instinctively put their arms up to shield their faces as the moment of impact approached. The plane passed just behind the motor whale boat resting in its cradle, and rose slightly above Mount 44, barely missing Fern and the gun crew at that station. As its landing gear and part of one wing struck the two 20mm guns of Group 23 near Fern, burning gasoline spurted from the mangled wing and ignited a raging fire. The remainder of the plane tumbled over the starboard side and exploded close to the ship.

Men tried to process what they had just witnessed. "The shock, the flash of flame, the split second of awful silence, suddenly torn by the cries of injured men and the impassive voice of a bos'n on the bull horn, 'Fire, after deck house,'" wrote Lieutenant Manson after the battle. "The realization that it had actually happened. The pain of realization that *Laffey*, with all her power and security, like all other ships, was vulnerable to death and destruction."[5]

A resounding jolt from the plane's impact and the explosive force of the bomb attached to its fuselage shook everyone in and near Youngquist's guns and resonated throughout the ship. Seaman 1/c Robert Powell, who was tossing depth charges over the starboard side to prevent fires from igniting them, thought that a freight train had just smacked head-on into *Laffey*. The force of the blast hurled Seaman 1/c William L. "Lake" Donald out of a 20mm gun mount and under a torpedo tube. Shaken but unharmed, the sailor regrouped and rejoined his crew. Intense heat and flames enveloped the deck and mounts, trapping men in a lethal inferno. Shrapnel ripped through metal fixtures and human flesh, decapitating one man, wounding or temporarily blinding many others, and severing power cables connecting nearby stations to the bridge.

As happened with each kamikaze that rammed into *Laffey*, the impact spread gasoline over the adjoining area. The flammable material flooded Youngquist's gun mounts on the superstructure deck, eight feet above the main deck, and quickly ignited, engulfing men and equipment in a conflagration. Youngquist's Mount 44 and his 20mm guns were knocked out of commission, and Pressburger's Mount 43 directly across on the starboard side was badly damaged by the flames. The flames cooked off ammunition resting near the 40mm and 20mm guns, creating a fireworks display that punctured hundreds of holes in the superstructure deck. Gasoline and flames quickly poured through those holes into the handling room below Mount 44, threatening to ignite the store of explosives earmarked for Youngquist's gunners. The conflagration spread into men's quarters and a washroom belowdeck, burned or severed electrical cables, and created noxious gases that raced through the venting system into the engine room.

Youngquist administered first aid to a man severely wounded by shrapnel from the explosion, then gathered four men to counter an immediate threat—the collection of four-shell clips of 40mm ammunition standing near the guns. Should most of the unused ammunition detonate, the result would be the maiming or deaths of most men around Youngquist's position, seriously reducing the chances that the ship and crew would survive.

Younquist, Fern, Seaman 1/c Charles W. Hutchins, Machinist's Mate 3/c Donald J. Hintzman, and others ran to the shells and began tossing the clips over the side. Disregarding their personal safety, they hurled the ammunition into the ocean, despite pain from blistered and badly burned hands. "We used bare hands at first," said Lieutenant Youngquist. "We then wrapped cloth around the hands. What we did came from natural instinct. We were not trained for this."[6]

The men worked as fast as they could to reduce the stockpile, but there were too many gun emplacements and too many shells for them to dispose of them all. With raging fires drawing closer, ammunition started to explode. Razor-sharp shrapnel sliced through men and materials and punctured additional holes in the deck, through which more gasoline and flames gushed down to areas below.

Ignoring the aerial attacks from additional kamikazes, Youngquist organized efforts to contain the fires that ravaged the aft part of the ship and prevent additional damage to the destroyer. Men grabbed hoses from the main deck amidships and raced to Youngquist's superstructure, where the officer directed them in spraying cooling waters onto burning plane wreckage, unspent 40mm shells, and the fires that had spread from his deck to areas below his gun position.

Tom Fern administered first aid to a wounded man before ignoring the exploding shells and raging fires to direct streams of water onto the worst part of the conflagration. "I was just trying to keep busy," he said. "I was trying to keep my mind from what was happening." Fern did not fear the bombs on the enemy aircraft as much as he did the gasoline the planes carried, which upon impact with the *Laffey* created "an enormous fireball. If that fireball caught you within sixty feet you were dead."[7] There was no sense seeking shelter anyway, for where on the small ship could he find refuge?

Meanwhile, the force of one explosion blew Ship's Serviceman 2/c Jim D. Matthews into the ocean as he battled the fires. The cooling waters quickly extinguished the flames that covered part of his body, but he barely avoided being chopped up by the ship's propellers as Becton executed another turn. Matthews drifted in the waters, fearing he might be hit by falling bits of aircraft, shrapnel, or strafing, and became a spectator to the battle around him. When Metalsmith 3/c Rex A. Vest was also blown overboard, Matthews swam over and helped Vest with his jacket. The pair remained in the waters until a rescue craft picked them up after the battle.

After hitting Youngquist's mounts, the kamikaze had cartwheeled over the top of Mount 43, the starboard 40mm gun directly across from Youngquist, spewing gasoline over the mount and setting men afire. Most of the gun crew scrambled over the mount's side and tumbled to the deck below, but Gunner's Mate Robert Karr, the gun captain, and Seaman 1/c K. D. Jones Jr., his pointer, had trouble getting out. As exploding ammunition screamed by, the pair crawled on their stomachs around the gun tub toward the aft stack, hugging the deck to keep out of the way of the flames and ammunition. Karr and Pointer reached the gunner shack beneath Mount 41, the forward 40mm gun closer to the bridge, where Karr paused to regroup and to say a prayer. Gaining solace and strength from the moment, Karr continued to the main deck, where he helped treat wounded men.

The heroic efforts of Youngquist, Fern, and their mates had, for the time being, contained the fires and prevented *Laffey* from exploding into an uncontrolled inferno. However, Becton could not ignore the obvious—that more kamikazes would soon be rushing at the mauled ship to administer the coup de grâce.

"They like to find cripples," he said after the battle. "They'll go after one that's smoking." He could not hide the flames or the black smoke that curled upwards from the damaged destroyer and made *Laffey* an attractive target, "for the smoke towering above us marked us a crippled ship." Becton glanced skyward and said later that "everywhere you looked you saw dive-bombers or fighters converging on you. All you could do was hope your gunners would get them."[8]

Becton remembered his vow when he had faced dire situations in the Solomons and watched Japanese aircraft knock out two ships. The Japanese might be licking their chops over attacking a hamstrung vessel, but "they found out we were far from knocked out" and would soon learn that "we'd give them a fight."[9]

8:47—Kamikazes Numbers 10 and 11

"Plane Coming In!"

While Lieutenant Youngquist and his men battled the fires from Kamikaze No. 9, which had engulfed much of his gun position, the next two attackers converged to Youngquist's rear, targeting the fantail gun crews and Delewski's five-inch mount.

Kamikaze No. 10, a Val dive bomber, drew within one half mile of the ship before being spotted. The pilot flew so low to the surface that some of the crew thought the waves might slap the plane down, and arrived so suddenly that Delewski's men had no time to turn and fire the mount. That left the defense to the three 20mm gun crews on the fantail, who fired only a few rounds before the plane was on them. They remained at their posts in the gun mount and fired gamely as the kamikaze zoomed toward them, with the pilot answering their machine gun bullets with those of his own. Japanese slugs clanged against mount shields and deck, while American 20mm shells tore off pieces of the Val, but the suicide-bent pilot barged through the hail of bullets and the smoke from the preceding kamikaze to smack directly into Kelley and the others.

"You know, some of those kids have more damned guts," said the ship's executive officer, Lieutenant McCune. "They stayed right in that gun mount and kept firing." Like everyone else aboard *Laffey*, McCune hoped *Laffey* could avoid further harm, "But it doesn't make any difference how good they are. You just can't get them all."[10]

Kamikaze No. 10's landing gear ground into the fantail just inboard of the starboard depth charge rack, gouging an indentation in the deck two feet deep and three feet wide. The plane smashed against the aft and forward gun shields around Kelley and his shipmates, sending parts of men and machine flying through the air and knocking out of commission the three 20mm guns of Group 25. The kamikaze then crashed into the starboard aft corner of Ole Betsy, Delewski's Mount 53, where the plane and its bomb exploded, disintegrating the pilot and whipping plane parts forward and aft. The collision created pits in Delewski's gun barrels up to one and a half inches deep, blew the gun mount shield upward several feet, punctured large holes in the mount and the surrounding deck, and started new fires that soon joined those already endangering Youngquist's men. Additional gasoline and flames gushed through the deck holes into the crew's quarters below, sparking widespread fires that destroyed personal items and severed hydraulic and electrical lines.

Kamikaze No. 11, another Val that had drawn within one-half mile of the ship's starboard side before being detected, dropped a bomb that exploded two feet inboard on the starboard side, piercing the deck plating and creating a hole six feet square in the starboard edge. The pilot and plane then disintegrated as they smashed into the metal mounts, pulverizing bodies and bursting into flames against the starboard side of Delewski's Mount 53, causing further devastation to a gun already badly damaged by the preceding kamikaze. Additional flames turned *Laffey's* aft section into a firestorm, and black smoke billowed to the heavens, where more kamikaze pilots waited their turn.

Delewski had just selected the next target for his gun and shouted to Coxswain "Frenchy" La Pointe to turn the gun 135 degrees when the kamikaze hit. The explosion tossed Delewski, who had been standing in the open door on the side of the mount, fifteen feet upward and away from the mount. Had La Pointe turned the gun one or two more degrees, Delewski would have been blown out in the direction of the flames; had La Pointe turned the gun a few degrees less, Delewski would have been propelled over the side into the ocean. Instead, he landed on the port K-gun depth-charge thrower. When he regained consciousness, still draped over the K-gun, the stunned gun captain was surprised to see that he had suffered only minor burns and scratches. Groggy from the explosion, he slowly rose as men tossed unexploded shells over the side, and stumbled back to the mount. As he neared his damaged gun Delewski heard a familiar voice moaning, "Ski, please help me."[11] The engine of the plane that smashed into the mount had pinned his closest friend, Coxswain Chester C. Flint, to a bulkhead. Delewski tried to free the stricken Flint, but his buddy died before Delewski could extricate him.

Delewski had no time to mourn as ten yards away flames engulfed another of his crew, Seaman 1/c Herbert B. Remsen. He rolled Remsen around to extinguish his burning clothes, saving the sailor's life. Even though the seaman suffered burns to his face, left arm, and hair, he returned to the action.

The same explosion threw Seaman 2/c Merle R. Johnson out of the mount and set him afire. "I woke up on the portside hatch to the head," said Johnson. "Someone was spraying me with salt water because I was on fire." Crew manning hoses directed streams of water on Johnson to douse the flames, then carried him to the wardroom, where Darnell and his assistants carefully removed Johnson's jacket because the apparel's zipper had melded with his skin. "Burnt all over," said Johnson, "I lay in front of a blower from the engine room. The warm air felt soothing on my burns."[12] The battle was over for Johnson.

Burned and nicked by shrapnel, Boatswain's Mate Calvin Wesley Cloer, the preacher with two religious names, shuffled to the wardroom for treatment. He took one look at the busy Darnell, inundated with disfigured wounded and dying men, and turned back to the mount. His shipmates needed treatment more than he did. He could handle a little pain, he concluded.

Across the deck, Fern battled the fires from Kamikaze No. 9 when he heard a man shout, "plane coming in!" As men scattered to get out of the way of the aircraft and abandoned fire hoses shot water in all directions, Fern turned to see Kamikaze No. 11 yards from the ship. Fern leaped over the side of the mount to the deck just as the plane impacted against Gun 53, emitting heat that immolated some crew and badly burned Fern. "Shoes, belts, flak jackets and helmets," Fern said later. "Everything else was completely burned away."[13] Lieutenant Jerome Sheets, the officer who had penned the paean to *Laffey* at her commissioning, perished in the explosion.

Although partially blinded from smoke and flash burns to his face, Fern returned to the gun mount, retrieved his hose, and sprayed water onto burning areas until, weakened from his injuries, he had to be helped away to receive treatment from Doctor Darnell. Fern had been so focused on his task that, combined with the effects of his injuries, he lost all recollection of events until after the battle. Later, as Fern was being treated for brain concussion on a hospital ship, his shipmates told him what he had done.

In the meantime a new peril arose. Baker 1/c William H. Welch reached the bridge to report that flames threatened to ignite the five-inch shells stored in the ship's handling rooms below Mount 53. When Becton gave him permission to flood the rooms with salt water, Welch raced back just in time to open the valves and let cooling seawater into three ammunition rooms before the potent shells ripped *Laffey* in half.

The three kamikazes inflicted heavy blows to aft section personnel and equipment. Most of the crew manning the fantail 20mm guns were killed, including Gunner's Mate 1/c Frank W. Lehtonen Jr., who had earlier refused treatment for a shrapnel wound and now perished at his post, and Radioman Lawrence Kelley, whose soothing Irish tenor voice had often entertained the crew. Delewski's mount had suffered extensive damage. Six men had perished in the mount's blazing interior, including Frenchy La Pointe and Chester Flint, and six more suffered burns and internal injuries. Fires and explosions put Youngquist's guns out of action. "The whole stern of the ship was under a coil of smoke,"[14] said Becton after Kamikaze No. 11 ploughed into *Laffey*.

8:48—Kamikaze Number 12

"We Felt Like a Sitting Duck"

Only one minute after the previous pair, Kamikaze No. 12 attacked. While *Laffey*'s guns focused starboard, at 8:48 another Val came out of the sun in a steep glide, approached from the stern, leveled off near the water's surface, and turned toward the ship. From his post at the starboard side K-guns, Torpedoman's Mate Fred Gemmell watched yet one more plane attack in what appeared to be a long line of kamikazes waiting to take their turn at his ship. "Guns firing and planes coming in," said Gemmell. "When you heard gunfire, you paid attention to where it came from and what was happening. I recall thinking I wanted to get the heck out of here, but there was no place to go."[15]

The ship's 20mm guns near the aft stack fired 120 rounds at the plane, but the pilot avoided the gunfire and dropped a bomb that landed on the port quarter above the propeller, punctured through the deck, and exploded in a 20mm ammunition room. The pilot, who had apparently decided to drop his bomb without smashing into the ship, evaded intense gunfire as he flew to starboard and disappeared beyond the horizon.

The solitary bomb caused astounding damage. The bomb punctured a seven-foot hole in the deck, three feet inboard from the ship's edge, twisting the main deck upward in the process. It ignited new fires and added fuel to those already ablaze, where damage control personnel battled "raging fires dangerously near the after magazine."[16] Every gun aft of the ship's No. 2 stack had now been knocked out of action.

The bomb burst through the opening in the main deck to explode in the 20mm magazine, where fires speedily engulfed crews' quarters and storage areas. The force of the explosion thrust pieces of bunks and bulkheads from the ship's interiors upward and out through hatches, raining deadly shrapnel onto the deck crew. Shrapnel belowdecks ruptured or pierced the bulkheads of seven adjoining compartments, including the steering gear motor room, the carpenter's room, and the steering gear room. The bomb's explosion ripped bulkheads from hinges, threatened the ammunition storage areas, and produced thick smoke that hampered damage control operations. Bomb fragments penetrated both the ship's deck and skin, allowing water to gush through and flood the aft end.

More alarming, in Becton's view, was that the bomb damaged the ship's steering ability and hampered his ability to maneuver. Flying fragments ruptured hydraulic leads in the steering gear room located beneath the fantail and jammed the ship's rudder while it was turned twenty-six degrees to port. With the rudder locked in position, the ship steamed in a perpetual circle, leaving Becton with only one evasion tactic at his disposal—confuse the enemy by rapidly increasing or decreasing his speed. "Evasive maneuvers were confined to rapid acceleration and deceleration, as the ship swung through tight circles with full engine power still available," explained Becton.[17]

Becton faced a grim situation. Four kamikazes had smashed into *Laffey*'s aft quarter on three sides. He had lost the ability to maneuver, guns no longer protected the ship's stern section, and flooding in the aft areas hindered his attempts to change speed. The rear one-third of *Laffey* was a smoking clutter of mangled steel and dying crew. Unless Becton's damage control parties contained the fires and flooding, it would only be a matter of time before the end approached.

"Now *Laffey* circled madly like a wounded fish," wrote Lieutenant Manson after the fight had ended, "black smoke coiling above her like trailing viscera." Becton agreed. "We weren't quite a sitting duck," said Becton, "but we felt like one."[18]

Unable to control the steering from the bridge, Becton tried to contact Seaman Andrew Martinis in the aft steering room directly below the fantail to determine if Martinis could steer from that post. Because the telephone lines connecting them had been severed in the attack, Becton was forced to send two men aft to check on the situation.

At the same time Lieutenant Theodore Runk, who had been organizing the fire-fighting efforts aft, left to see if he could free the jammed rudder.

He worked his way through debris and bodies, stopping to toss overboard an unexploded bomb. When he arrived, he and Martinis disappeared into the aft steering room, already filled with smoke from the burning 20mm ammunition handling room adjoining them. "It was hard for us to breathe," said Martinis. "Runk had a wet handkerchief and he would cover his face, breathe, and then hand it to me." Passing the wet handkerchief back and forth to shield their faces from the smoke and flames, Runk and Martinis found that the hydraulic lines leading into the emergency steering room had been cut during the attack. Martinis moved into the steering gear room behind the steering room to see if he could free the jammed rudders, but could not budge them. "The smoke was getting thicker for us,"[19] said Martinis. Unable to relieve the pressure on the rudder and give Becton full maneuverability, the pair exited before their air supply ran out.

"Well that jammed our rudder all the way over to port," George Burnett wrote his parents after the battle. "So we were doing 30 knots around in circles and we had no guns aft to shoot with."[20] Becton faced a terrifying quandary. He required top speed to avoid the kamikazes that were certain to approach, but top speed would further fan the flames that already threatened the destroyer. If he slowed the vessel to give his damage control teams time to combat the fires, he presented a more enticing target to the kamikazes. A handcuffed Becton slowed the ship during the infrequent lulls, and then called for maximum speed whenever lookouts announced the arrival of another attacker.

Phoutrides Goes Aft

"There Were Bits and Pieces of Them Is All"

Needing a clear picture of the damage aft, Becton asked Quartermaster Phoutrides to leave the bridge for a quick inspection of the area. Phoutrides exited the bridge to the port side main deck below and slowly wound aft through the plane wreckage, death, and debris that littered his path. Although suffering serious wounds to his back and head, Seaman 1/c Marvin G. Robertson carried bloody Seaman 2/c Walter Rorie to the wardroom for treatment. Phoutrides passed by the body of a shipmate who had been burned to a crisp. The man's arms and hands covered his face, and he was frozen in a charcoal rigidity that depicted his final act of unsuccessfully warding off the blazing gasoline. Without pausing, Phoutrides gingerly moved aft alongside Delewski's Mount 53, now more a smoking, dented hunk of metal than an instrument of war, and approached the fantail.

"Then I saw the damage to the 20mm guns on the fantail," said Phoutrides. "There was a man still in his straps with both legs gone, bleeding. He was still alive and was begging, 'please get me out of these straps.'"[21] Phoutrides sickened at seeing the man's legs lying on the deck not far from the mortally wounded sailor, but regrouped to aid others who rushed to the man's side. Before they could lift him from the straps, the man succumbed.

Only feet away, a cluster of bodies from the fantail, including Radioman Kelley, lay grotesquely among the debris, mute testimony to the carnage inflicted by the kamikazes. "I saw five of them, all in different positions, one was flat on his face," said Phoutrides. He made mental notes of everything he observed—the burned guns and mounts, the decks punctured with hundreds of holes, the fires and smoke, the cries of the wounded, and the silence of the dead. "They were all just lying there. It didn't hit me much, right then. I didn't get much reaction. Then I went back toward the bridge, and got to thinking about it. Suddenly I knew I didn't want to see it again"[22]

Phoutrides thought he had witnessed the worst until, on his way back to the bridge along the starboard side, he "came upon three men just forward of Gun 53. The group had been hit, and it was more gruesome than the 20mm fantail guns. The three had been on damage control and were together, at a post, waiting for orders or something. A plane smacked right into them. There was nothing but bits and pieces of them left."

Phoutrides nudged the gruesome sight out of his mind and continued to the bridge. Along the way he came across his friend, Torpedoman's Mate John Schneider. "As I passed him I asked, 'How's it going?' He said, 'Greek [Phoutrides's nickname], if I could find a piece of rust on this ship I'd crawl under it!'"[23] Phoutrides and Schneider shared a mild laugh at the remark before the quartermaster completed his inspection and reported to Becton.

He delivered a sobering summary. Both the main deck and the superstructure deck aft, upon which rested many of the ship's guns, were a mass of flame. Enemy planes, bombs, and shrapnel punctured holes in the decks ranging from inches to several feet in diameter. The fantail was "all the way down in the water and still going down farther,"[24] engines and aircraft pieces protruded from gun mounts and belowdecks compartments, and every gun aft had been destroyed or badly damaged. Smoke billowed skyward, while flames on deck and flooding belowdecks threatened to scuttle *Laffey* before additional kamikazes even had the chance.

Yet hope remained. "Sure, our radar was gone and the rudder was jammed and almost every compartment aft of the stacks and engine rooms was flooded," said Delewski, "but *Laffey* still made steam and continued moving in a circle. But we were moving."[25]

Al Henke had much to do with that.

8:46 to 9:11 a.m.

The Black Gang Belowdecks

Stepping belowdecks was like entering a different world. The men stationed in the ship's bowels worked in confined areas, shut off from daylight. They could hear and feel the battle, but could not see it. Despite the noises of battle above and the encroaching fires and flooding below, they had to continue their tasks and dismiss the thought that at any moment a kamikaze might crash into their area or that the ship could begin descending and take them to watery graves.

Even before the repair parties rushed to the aft sections belowdeck, the black gang—the men who worked the engine and firerooms—had been fueling and maintaining the ship's engines and boilers to keep *Laffey* afloat and to give Becton speed and maneuverability when he needed it. Engineering Officer Lieutenant E. A. Henke concluded after the first eight kamikazes had attacked that, with so many planes and bombs, severed communications lines were a probability. In that event he would have to operate the engines while out of contact with Becton in the bridge. Thus cut off from the skipper, and operating in a vacuum, he would have to guess at the speed and course his captain wanted. Henke came upon an ingenious solution. He told his assistant engineering officer stationed in the aft engine room, Lieutenant William Shaw, that should they lose contact with the bridge, they would adjust their speed and course according to the sounds of gunfire. Depending upon which guns fired, he would order a port or starboard course. He would add speed as soon as the five-inch guns fired, and increase it further if the 40mm and 20mm guns joined in. Whenever firing ceased, Henke would reduce the speed to allow damage control parties to battle fires.

Henke said that "as the five-inch units starting firing again, we would accelerate as rapidly as possible, knowing that with the sea calm and the rudder jammed at 26 degrees port, this would be the most appropriate action we could promote." With the battle raging over their heads and the ship rattling from kamikaze hits, "everyone was fearful of what might happen. We had all seen the kind of damage and even complete destruction that the kamikazes could inflict." Each action would end "with either all quiet or a sudden shudder of the ship as it took another hit."

When Kamikaze No. 12 jammed the rudder, Henke implemented his plan. For the remainder of the battle Becton and Henke fashioned a makeshift team that, even though cut off from one another, worked remarkably well. Henke asked God for wisdom in what he was about to do, and took comfort in the words of the 23rd Psalm: "Even though I walk through the valley of the shadow of death, I will fear no evil, for You are with me."[26]

Receiving crucial information from Fireman Oliver "Jim" Spriggs, who listened to what was occurring topside through a headset of powered telephones, Henke calculated each move. His men labored through intolerable conditions to keep *Laffey* moving and to give Becton what he needed. The smoke and fumes from topside fires, which rushed through air blowers directly to the engine rooms, became so thick that men could barely see the gauges on panels a few feet away. Sweat coursed from every pore as temperatures soared to one hundred thirty degrees. Men remained at their posts, but when a panic-stricken sailor froze, Spriggs applied a hefty kick to his backside. The sailor directed a torrent of swear words toward Spriggs, but was soon performing his task. In the aft engine room Machinist's Mate 1/c John W. Michel crawled through smoke so thick that he had to feel his way to the exhaust fans, which he put on maximum strength to draw out the smoke and lower the temperatures.

Henke, Spriggs, Michel, and the rest of the black gang might not have been aiming a 40mm gun at the enemy, but they were just as vital to *Laffey*'s survival.

Repair Control Parties

"A Bunch of Boys That Fought So Hard for Each Other"

So, too, were the damage control and repair parties crucial to *Laffey*'s existence. What happened on the deck mirrored the actions below, where men labored to salvage the ship before flame and flood snatched *Laffey* from them. The aft end below Youngquist's and Delewski's guns contained the crew's quarters, steering mechanisms, and the ammunition handling rooms packed with explosives. If the damage control teams were to save the ship, they had to prevent that ammunition from igniting.

The repair parties and the men who no longer had a gun to fire rushed to rescue the ship that had been their home since the February commissioning. While the deck guns waged their duel with the kamikazes, a second contest unfolded on and below the decks. Work parties battled explosions, fires, shrapnel, and flooding, and if they could not find a way to contain the damage, it mattered little what the gunners did. Fail in this endeavor and the ship would go down, taking most of the crew with her.

The four kamikazes that had hit in the last onslaught had meted out considerable damage to the ship. While Becton and Henke kept *Laffey* moving and men in the forward guns maintained fire, damage control and repair parties battled the conflagrations on deck, and then moved below to contain the fires and flooding in those areas. They risked their lives to direct foam and streams of cooling water onto blazing gun mounts and wardrooms, only to see another kamikaze crash into the ship, requiring them to begin anew. They received assistance from men like Lieutenant Youngquist and Seaman Fern who, after their stations had been knocked out of commission, rushed to their aid and who, according to Becton, "showed great initiative in pitching in on the most urgent tasks at hand after their primary battle stations were rendered useless." These men and the repair parties "carried on undaunted, although succeeding hits undid much of their previous efforts and destroyed more of their firefighting equipment. They were utterly fearless in combating fires, although continually imperiled by exploding ammunition."[27]

The crew came together to save their ship. They had been trained to fight, and now that their guns had been demolished, they battled to keep *Laffey* afloat. "There were men who had never had a hypodermic needle in their hands before who administered morphine to wounded mates," said Lieutenant Manson. "There were men who hadn't been trained in firefighting manning fire hoses. And there were men who weren't gunners manning guns. I never saw a bunch of boys that fought so hard for each other."[28]

The desperate fire control work began when the officer of the day, Lieutenant (jg) Ernest G. Saenz, calmly announced over the public address system, "Fire amidships! Fire amidships!" after kamikazes ripped into the latter half of the ship. Repair parties rushed aft, where Youngquist's guns, Delewski's mount, and Kelley's fantail area were already "a mass of flames and wreckage.

Choking smoke was billowing up into the clear air and being wafted aft as *Laffey* raced through the water. The heat was intense, searing."[29]

Men raced to ammunition storage areas to toss overboard the 40mm shells no longer needed because their guns had been destroyed. Like Lieutenant Youngquist, they ignored their personal safety, approaching fires to lift shells over the side, often wrapping their hands with rags to prevent burns. Ship's Cook 3/c Jerome D. Pinkoff charged out of the wardroom to release depth charges on the fantail before they exploded, and before tossing ammunition overboard, Gunner's Mate Karr gave a man with a severed spine artificial respiration and then morphine in a futile attempt to keep the teenager alive. Men halted their labors only when powder cans cooked off or fires threatened to overwhelm the area.

Because most aft hoses had been destroyed or cut to pieces by the four kamikazes, damage control parties rigged hoses from available main deck fireplugs as far forward as Zack's Mount 52 in front of the bridge. Meandering hoses snaked through the littered decks all the way to the fantail, where Seaman Martinis "could feel the heat from the fires" as he suffocated one fire with foam. "There were dead men there, and I was directing foam on them, too."[30] Tom Fern, who cooled plane wreckage and ammunition with high-pressure streams of water, continued until an explosion injured him, after which he made his way topside and collapsed.

Sonarman 1/c Cyril C. "Cy" Simonis shot streams of water onto the torpedo tubes along the ship's side when he saw Chief Torpedoman's Mate Wayne H. Haley, his clothes aflame, stumbling along the deck. He veered the hose onto his shipmate, knocking him down with the blast but saving his life. Haley later recovered from his severe burns.

Men on deck directed water onto the flames below through the hundreds of shrapnel holes that kamikazes had punctured into the main deck. That water, combined with the ocean water seeping through holes below the waterline, completely or partially flooded many aft compartments, including three separate crew's quarters, the steering gear rooms, and a 20mm magazine. While that flooding extinguished some of the fires, the ship began settling by the stern, further imperiling the destroyer. Men broke out pumps to combat the waters, creating a delicate rhythm in which crew above and below shot water into the compartments to douse fires while others pumped out the water to prevent the ship from sinking. Becton later admitted that his destroyer remained afloat, in part, because before the battle started, his men had properly secured the hatches leading into all compartments be-low. This kept the undamaged rooms dry and filled with air, which in turn helped keep her on the surface. "A few tight and dry compartments aft kept our stern buoyant,"[31] Becton later explained.

Ensign Robert C. Thomsen, the ship's navigator, worked in the radar room when the battle started. No longer needed there now that the fight had begun, Thomsen left when he heard that fires ravaged his ship. The popular, unassuming graduate of Annapolis took two men with him and disappeared into the smoke-filled compartments beneath Delewski's guns. Disregarding his safety, Thomsen dragged a fire hose into the smoke and flame that had crept dangerously close to the five-inch ammunition, but died along with his companions when the suicide planes crashed aft. Thomsen received a posthumous Navy Cross, the Navy's highest honor, and second only to the Medal of Honor, for his courageous exploits. "He fought fires voluntarily in the spaces below Mount 53," Quartermaster Phoutrides wrote his brother shortly after the battle, "and was sealed in the compartment when 2 kamika-zes hit above him."[32]

Carpenter's Mate 2/c Henry Thompson worked with the forward repair party, tightening pipes and valves shaken loose when the five-inch guns went off. When the first kamikazes hit, he made his way below, but had to duck to avoid enemy bullets that "were coming through the aluminum like flies." He safely reached the steering compartment, which sported a hole in the port side through which ocean water gushed. "The hole was at the water line," said Thompson, who hurried over to patch it. "Every time the shipped pitched, I went under water. I finally succeeded in stopping the leak with a patch we had made up for damage control."[33]

Motor Machinist's Mate 1/c George S. Logan and Machinist's Mate 1/c Stephen J. Waite worked with the repair party when they saw smoke rising through a hatch. The pair went below to check out the origin, and found a bed burning in one of the crew's quarters. They began unraveling a fire hose from an adjoining compartment when an airplane engine from one of the kamikazes that struck Delewski's Mount 53 smashed partly into a hatch and stuck there, only yards from the couple. With burning gasoline gushing down, Waite and Logan were trapped in the compartment below Delewski's mount.

"Some fire came in and ignited the beds," said Waite. "We could not get up the ladder. Trapped below, George and I got to the after diesel generator room. The smoke was pretty thick and got worse as the paint on the door started smoking."[34]

They slammed the door to keep the fires at bay, but were now trapped and had to find a way to escape before the flames or suffocation killed them. Waite grabbed a telephone to inform someone in the adjoining after engine room of their predicament.

Machinist's Mate Michel drilled a small hole in the bulkhead between the rooms as a passage for fresh air, but was surprised when smoke burst into his room. Knowing he had to work fast to save his shipmates, Michel inserted a piece of copper tubing through to Waite and Logan. As the pair choked and suffocated in the acrid smoke, Michel hooked the tubing to an air hose, which soon sent a welcome rush of fresh air to the nearly unconscious men. Logan bent over and filled his lungs with air, then stepped back so Waite could do the same.

The two had been momentarily saved, but their dilemma was far from over. Trapped in the small room, they were doomed to suffocate or burn to death from the encroaching fires, or plunge to the ocean's bottom with the ship if *Laffey* began sinking. The pair had little time, for already the paint on the bulkhead blistered, and additional smoke and fumes filled their tiny room.

Welcome sounds came from above. The amidships repair party had brought cutting torches to free the trapped men, but found their path to the hatch blocked. The only way to free Waite and Logan was to climb topside, cut through the deck, and lift the men out of the compartment.

Grabbing an acetylene cutting outfit, Machinist's Mate 1/c Arthur E. Hogan and Machinist's Mate 1/c Elton F. Peeler rushed topside, where other men had already begun clearing away plane wreckage and the other debris of battle. They ignored nearby fires and stores of explosives and cut a small hole in the deck. Unfortunately, though, the hole opened directly above a maze of pipes that blocked the pair's escape. Using the phone to give instructions, Waite directed the repair party to move two feet over, where they cut a second, larger hole. Logan climbed on top of Waite's shoulders, grabbed someone's hand from above, and lifted himself out. Now alone, Waite looked up to see two long arms reach down and pull him to the deck, where he gulped a much-appreciated burst of fresh air.

Now safely on deck, Logan turned to Peeler, often the subject of friendly jibes about his unattractive looks, and said, "Elt, you may not be very pretty, but you sure look good to me. Thanks!"[35] Logan and Waite arose from their tombs to live again.

The wounded might have said something similar to Doctor Darnell and his pharmacist's mates, who had their hands full in the wardroom. Operating under the worst conditions, with planes and bombs rattling the ship, Darnell's crew calmly tended men with horrific burns, shrapnel wounds, severed limbs, and shock. When the numbers overwhelmed the small group, crew came from other stations to lend a hand, including radarmen after the ship's radar had been knocked out and gun crews from guns that no longer worked. Darnell gave them a hurried course in administering blood plasma and other routine medical procedures so he and his pharmacist's mates could look after the more serious cases.

Grievously wounded men on stretchers or on the deck patiently waited their turn for treatment. Yeoman 3/c Fred Burgess's mauled leg dangled by a single piece of flesh. Doctor Darnell applied a tourniquet to stop the bleeding, but doubted he could save the sailor, who had only recently celebrated his eighteenth birthday. He tried to at least make Burgess's final hours comfortable.

Lieutenant J. V. Porlier, one of the members of the FIDO team that had joined the ship before *Laffey* steamed to Picket Station No. 1, helped amputate the leg of one man as Darnell, whose hand had been injured from bomb fragments that blistered the wardroom, calmly issued instructions. Porlier took comfort in the presence in his pocket of his Rosary beads and a tiny prayer book that he had carried for two decades.

Darnell's wardroom became so congested with dying and wounded men, including Lieutenant Jay Bahme and two others who had come to help, that he had to place some injured in the passageway. Men laid the badly wounded Fireman 1/c Jack A. Ballenger on a footlocker in the passageway next to Electrician's Mate 3/c Henry M. Benson, who was dying from an enemy bullet that passed through his neck. Though in pain, Ballenger reached an arm across to Benson, gasping for breath as blood gushed out, and gently massaged Benson's throat while he died.

Fortunately, Doctor Darnell had dispersed medical supplies to six areas scattered about the destroyer, where corpsmen and volunteers treated other wounded. Bombs and shrapnel destroyed two of the dressing stations and contaminated medical supplies, but the corpsmen continued to work, thereby relieving some of the burden Darnell would otherwise have faced.

The courageous Darnell and his team worked nonstop, even though planes and bombs inundated the ship. They shoved aside personal concerns and performed their tasks, for as long as the battle lasted, more wounded and dying men would be brought to the wardroom.

They hoped that the twelfth kamikaze might be the last, but at 9:20 a.m. Doctor Darnell and everyone else still alive aboard *Laffey* realized the Japanese were far from finished.

There would be one more horrible minute.

CHAPTER 9

DEFYING THE ODDS

Rudder stuck and badly listing,
Bombs and planes her bulkheads twisting,
Abandon? No! She'd die resisting.
  —"Invicta," Lieutenant Matthew Darnell

9:20—Kamikazes Numbers 13 and 14

"CAP, hell. They're Jap Vals"

By 9:15 twelve kamikazes had attacked *Laffey* in forty-four minutes. *Laffey's* crews had shot down the first eight, but the next four sneaked through heavy fire to deliver the initial blows to the destroyer. Men left twisted gun mounts and smoking aft areas to battle fires and exploding ammunition, while on the bridge Becton slowed *Laffey* to five knots to reduce the winds that swept across the destroyer's decks and fueled the fires that damage control parties battled to eliminate.

Phoutrides had just returned to his position on the bridge when lookout Felipe Salcido spotted several planes. "Thank God the CAP has returned," said Phoutrides, thinking that American air cover had finally returned to aid the ship.

"CAP, hell," said Salcido. "They're Jap Vals."

Phoutrides "aged another 10 years" as four kamikazes ravaged the ship from stern to bow. The quartet arrived so quickly that Phoutrides, whose task as Quartermaster of the Watch was to record everything that happened, could hardly keep up with events. "During much of this time, I couldn't even hold a pencil, let alone write" because of the tense situation.[1]

The first two dropped in on *Laffey*'s vulnerable aft section, now almost completely unprotected because of the extensive damage inflicted by prior kamikazes. Salcido saw the pair coming in against the port side and alerted Becton. "Flank speed!"[2] shouted Becton through the voice tube connecting him with the engine room below, while every gun that could turn far enough aft fired at the pair only one-half mile out. Bullets chopped the water below the kamikazes and airbursts exploded above, but, still, the planes bored in. "The guys aft were sitting ducks,"[3] said Phoutrides. The survivors there, including Lieutenant Youngquist and Seaman Fern, would have to endure more.

The first kamikaze pilot could not keep pace with Becton's speed changes. He abandoned plans to hit the ship's vital communications center, took aim for the aft half, and slammed into *Laffey*, creating an enormous explosion and fireball that ravaged the deckhouse, shook the ship, and knocked men off their feet. The second plane, which attacked on a forty-five-degree angle on the port quarter, hit seconds later at almost the same spot.

The crew below had made progress battling the fires near Delewski's Mount 53 and in the living quarters when the two kamikazes ploughed into the aft deckhouse between Delewski's mount and Youngquist's guns. One kamikaze disintegrated against the port bulkhead of the deck house, killing several men working in the compartments directly underneath, including Lieutenant James Fravel, Electrician's Mate 1/c Ralph "Ross" Peterson, and Shipfitter 1/c Madoc Irish, and wounding many others. A portion of the wing and landing gear lodged in a nearby depth charge rack, and its bomb bounced across the decks before it halted without exploding. Crew rushed through flames and smoke to lift the bomb and toss it over the side.

More gasoline and flames swept across the decks, reigniting fires only moments after they had been brought under control, starting new conflagrations and killing some of the men who rushed aft to contain the damage. Shrapnel sliced through hoses, damaged the ship's aft sprinkling system and vent fans, and dented bulkheads below. Engine parts and wing pieces were again embedded in the bulkheads, bunks, and hatches, and anyone caught within the blast's arc was fortunate if he escaped with minor injuries. Fires erupted in the shower room and in the ship's passageway, destroying electrical cables and one of the crew's heads. Parts of the planes were later found in the crew's quarters, in the crew's washroom, and under a urinal in one of the heads.

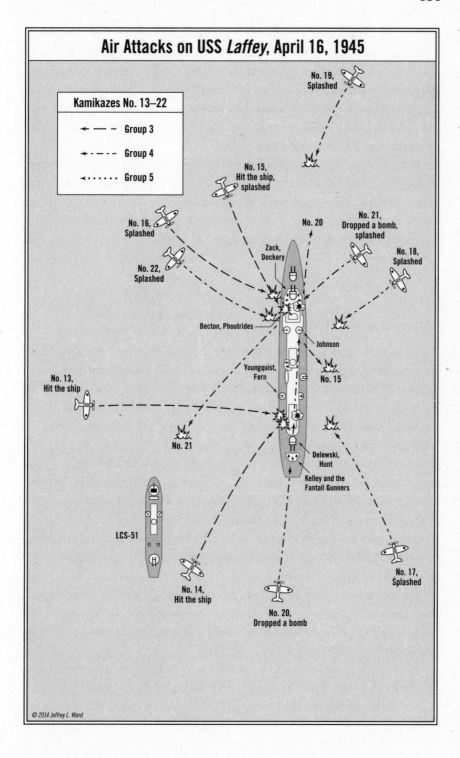

Air Attacks on USS *Laffey*, April 16, 1945

Kamikazes No. 13–22

- ← – – – Group 3
- ← – · – · Group 4
- ← · · · · · Group 5

No. 19, Splashed

No. 15, Hit the ship, splashed

No. 16, Splashed

No. 22, Splashed

No. 20

No. 21, Dropped a bomb, splashed

No. 18, Splashed

Zack, Dockery

Becton, Phoutrides

Johnson

Youngquist, Fern

No. 15

No. 13, Hit the ship

No. 21

Delewski, Hunt

Kelley and the Fantail Gunners

LCS-51

No. 14, Hit the ship

No. 20, Dropped a bomb

No. 17, Splashed

© 2014 Jeffrey L. Ward

Seaman Robert Powell, who left his station at the torpedoes to help fight fires, manned a hose with his buddy, Torpedoman 3/c Edward J. Brown. The pair doused one fire and began moving forward to attack a second when Brown remarked he had forgotten his binoculars at the previous spot. Powell told Brown to forget about them, but Brown insisted he needed the binoculars. Brown left Powell and went aft, where one of the two kamikazes that demolished the aft deck house killed him.

Damage control parties unwound more hoses, secured open hatches, and tossed overboard the shattered wing sections and other pieces of the kamikazes that had incinerated themselves on *Laffey*'s decks. They quickly contained the new fires in the passageway, but experienced difficulty checking the flames that gutted the crew's quarters and head.

9:20—Kamikaze Number 15

"Marines to the Rescue"

A glimmer of hope appeared amidst the carnage when the absent CAP arrived to defend the battered ship. Four FM-2 Wildcats from the aircraft carrier, USS *Shamrock Bay* (CVE-84), led by Lieutenant (jg) Carl J. Rieman, flew within range to find at least twenty Japanese planes hovering like vultures near *Laffey*. "All this time," said Rieman, "the destroyer *Laffey* was really taking a beating." He and the other three pilots charged into the group and began engaging the enemy to give Becton time to extricate his ship. They could not stop every aircraft from charging at the destroyer, but they could at least relieve some of the pressure on the ship below until more help, if any, joined them. As if a genie granted Rieman's wish, a group of Marine Corsairs suddenly raced over the horizon and hotly pursued the kamikazes. "Marines to the rescue," thought Lieutenant Manson watching from the bridge. "Just like Hollywood!"[4]

Rieman and his aviators splashed four planes within minutes. Rieman fired his machine guns until he ran out of ammunition, at which time the aviator, upset that he lacked bullets with so many targets around, made dry runs to deflect them from *Laffey*.

Intrepid's Corsairs returned from the north to add their firepower to that of Marine Corsairs based at Yontan and Kadena airfields on Okinawa and F6F-5 Hellcats from the light carrier, USS *San Jacinto* (CVL-30). Lieutenant

Commander Wally Clarke and his wingman, Ensign Jack Ehrhard, intercepted and splashed a trio of Vals approaching *Laffey*, while Ensign Alfred Lerch downed seven aircraft. By day's end the Grim Reapers had registered thirty-three kills in defending *Laffey*.

The *San Jacinto* Hellcats swept other enemy aircraft out of the skies, splashing suicide planes as they embarked on their runs toward the destroyer. Lieutenant (jg) H. N. Swinburne and Lieutenant (jg) L. Grossman orbited *Laffey* when they spotted a Betty barreling toward *Laffey*. The pair downed the plane before it could do any damage, and as Swinburne and Grossman flew over, one of the Japanese airmen floating in the water shook his fist in anger at the Americans.

While the previous two kamikazes raced toward *Laffey*'s port stern, the next two centered on the port bow. Kamikaze No. 15, a Nakajima KI-43 Oscar fighter, broke from a dogfight two miles out and turned toward *Laffey* with a Corsair on his tail. The Nakajima veered from side to side in an effort to shake the Corsair, but the Marine aviator followed, even though he waded straight into *Laffey*'s 40mm and 20mm gunfire as the ship's gunners tried to down the kamikaze.

The portside 40mm and 20mm crews pumped 280 rounds at the Nakajima as it neared the ship, but to avoid hitting the Corsair, fired most of their rounds too low to harm the kamikaze. The pair zoomed over the top of the five-inch gun director, barely missing Becton and Phoutrides on the bridge. They clipped the mast, toppling the bedspring-like radar equipment and sending it crashing to the deck, where it landed in a heap only six feet from Sonarman Cy Simonis and Signalman 3/c William M. Kelly. The planes then sliced off the port yardarm, sending the American flag curling to the deck, before the Japanese aircraft splashed into the water just off the starboard side. The Corsair aviator gained altitude, rolled his plane over, and bailed out before his plane also hit the water's surface, causing men aboard the *Laffey* to hope the brave man who risked his life to save them would be rescued.

The sight of their nation's flag spiraling to a deck splattered with debris and blood bothered those who saw it. "We've got to get that back up there," shouted Signalman 2/c Thomas B. McCarthy. McCarthy retrieved a new flag, ignored the bullets and shrapnel, climbed the mast, and attached it with ship's line from the deck. "We all felt much better seeing the ensign back in place,"[5] said Radar Technician 1/c August G. Englehardt.

"The Ship Was a Mess"

Kamikaze No. 16, another Judy, broke away from the aerial dogfight three miles out and, also pursued by a Corsair, came in on the port beam toward Zack's Mount 52, which had to this point escaped the attention of the kamikazes. The port side 20mm and 40mm guns still in operation, including Johnson's 40mm, splintered the sky as tracers sped toward the enemy plane. Hundreds of bullets ripped through the aircraft, which began disintegrating as it neared the ship, but the gunners maintained fire to obliterate the plane before momentum carried it into the ship. Black smoke poured from the plane's cockpit, wings, and fuselage until, in a grand finale, the plane dipped toward the water, exploded fifty yards from the port beam, and showered shrapnel and body parts across Mount 52, the nearby 20mm guns, and the decks.

Blinded to the action about him, and sealed below in his gun mount, Sonarman Zack could only guess what was occurring by sounds and feel. He experienced a jar whenever one of the kamikazes struck the destroyer or whenever the ship turned or changed speed. "The ship would shake and we knew a plane had hit," he said. He wished he could "have been able to see what was coming. I'd hear all this going on, and feel the ship getting hit, but had no idea how bad things were above. I'd think, 'This ship could go down, and I'd go down with her.'"

A distant rattle meant that a plane had collided somewhere behind his mount and he was not in any immediate danger, but a reverberating jolt, such as this one, indicated that the hit occurred closer to his mount. The explosion shot smoke and flame into the mount, some of which rushed into Zack's lower handling room, where Zack tried to ignore the fact that he held in his hands highly combustible cans of powder. "You just keep working and don't think about it," he said. "They needed the powder up above, so you keep going."[6]

The explosion dented the hull plating on the port side just above the waterline. A large chunk of metal from the kamikaze's bomb blew out the steel door to Mount 52 and shattered the mount's control panels, knocking out all power to the gun and severing communications with the bridge. The fragment sliced through Gunner's Mate 2/c Joseph E. Mele's back and exited from his stomach, leaving behind a six-inch gash in the badly wounded sailor before puncturing the door leading to Zack's handling room and destroying another control panel inside. One other man in the mount was killed and several wounded from plane and bomb pieces, which coated the mount's decks with blood and splattered it onto control panels, but Zack and Radder below were unharmed.

Zack's gun still functioned, but without power Zack and Radder had to load the powder and ammunition by hand and men above had to turn the gun manually, a laborious task. Fumes and smoke irritated their eyes and hampered their efforts, but despite the flames that threatened to engulf them, Zack and Radder kept placing powder and shells onto the hoists and turning by hand the cranks that lifted the material above.

"I worked it manually," said Zack, "and kept feeding whatever powder cans I could to the mount. We cranked up all the ammunition we could until they told us they had enough and couldn't handle any more."[7] The men above could not fire as many shells as before because they, too, had to operate the gun manually.

Seaman Martinis was helping a wounded man to sick bay as the kamikaze approached. He laid the shipmate behind the boat davit, shielded him with his body, and peeked over the side to see the kamikaze on a direct line with him. Living what he thought were his final moments, the teenager crouched low to the deck and prayed that gunners downed the plane before it annihilated him. His solicitations worked, as the plane exploded fifty yards shy of the pair. Martinis waited a few moments to regain his balance, and finally reached the wardroom with the wounded shipmate, where Dr. Darnell tended to the man's wounds.

The explosion, combined with earlier hits, severed most of the communications between the bridge and the ship's guns. To provide a temporary remedy, Ensign James G. Townsley grabbed a headset and a microphone hooked to the ship's public address system, rushed atop the pilot house directly above Phoutrides, and from an exposed position high above the deck, blared instructions to gun positions on where to fire. Glancing to port and starboard to pick up enemy planes, he issued orders to gun mounts that, without his courageous efforts, might have remained silent.

Townsley's calm voice could be heard above the bullets and explosions. "Mount 42 take plane coming in on port bow. Mount 43 take plane coming in on starboard beam. Start shooting, 43—start shooting, 22, port 20's, the plane is close. Take plane port bow. Mount 3 [53], take plane diving on fantail. Mount 3, Mount 3, dammit, Mount 3, open fire!"[8] From where he stood, Townsley could not see that Mount 53, Delewski's gun, had already been knocked out of commission.

"He was unprotected on top of the pilot house, the highest place to stand," said Phoutrides, marveling decades later that the officer had stood alone, amidst the planes, bullets, and shrapnel, to direct gunfire at the enemy. "He was a blessed man!"[9]

Townsley was awarded the Silver Star for his actions, which according to the citation helped cause the destruction of four enemy aircraft. In directing fire from his exposed spot atop the pilot house, Townsley "inspired his men to keep shooting to the last, although direct suicidal crashes looked inevitable on several occasions."[10]

The four kamikazes that attacked at 9:20 added to the damage *Laffey* had already sustained. Exhausted damage control parties continued to combat the fires and contain the flooding, but, their numbers pared by casualties, they had fewer men to battle more fires and help more wounded. Fires ravaged much of the aft sections and threatened to engulf the forward areas; gun mounts to port and starboard looked more like squashed spiders than weapons of war; body parts and blood splattered the fantail and other positions; airplane engines protruded from Delewski's Mount 53 and from the washroom in the after deckhouse; an aircraft wing and landing gear was lodged in the K-gun depth charges; and smashed hatches allowed smoke, fire, and flooding in compartments below. A twelve-inch incendiary shell lay in a urinal, "its cover peeled back like a banana, exposing the very flammable phosphorus."[11]

Seaman Martinis found the task daunting because of all the damage. "The aft part of the ship was a mess, with debris all over, almost like shipyard workers were still working on her. The deck there was pretty torn up, and body parts were scattered about. People were hanging in the guns. That was shocking for a nineteen-year-old." Martinis's training helped him suppress the images of death and damage that confronted him wherever he turned. "You focus so much that you don't realize what is happening. The training takes over. There was no place to hide anyway. Fires were burning and getting close to a 20mm magazine. It was a wall of fire. I was working near a magazine that could go off any second, but you don't think of it. You also had an attitude that you are indestructible and you don't think of the consequences."[12]

The ship was in such poor shape after the sixteenth kamikaze that *Laffey* reminded Lieutenant Manson of "a wounded fish, going in a big circle with a slight list." Despite the damage, Manson liked the spirit exhibited by a crew thoroughly trained by Becton, for the men were "spitting fire all the time."[13] As Manson looked around, he saw men battling not only for their own lives, but for their shipmates. Even the wounded, he noticed, seemed more concerned with how their buddies were faring than they were with their own wounds.

Even though sixteen kamikazes had charged the ship, with half either smashing into *Laffey*'s decks or inflicting bomb and shrapnel damage, their fight was far from over. Becton looked up from the destroyer, which he described as a "flaming inferno," and saw "more of those hawks of hell coming" toward him. "Put bluntly, *Laffey* was by then in one hell of a lot of trouble." But the skipper placed his faith in his men and their training. Those onrushing kamikazes "weren't going to get her," he said of the *Laffey*. "We could still steam in a circle and we could still shoot and we were fighting mad."[14]

9:30 to 9:35—Kamikazes Numbers 17 to 19

"Did You See That Bastard Explode?"

Most of the action from the previous eight kamikazes occurred aft as Becton and the pilots conducted their hide-and-seek maneuvering. Now, however, three kamikazes tested the forward gun crews by charging in on the starboard side. With practically every gun aft out of commission, the burden fell to the men at Zack's Mount 52, at Seaman Johnson's Mount 41, at Coxswain Falotico's 20mm Mount 21, and the other starboard gunners to defend the ship.

Quartermaster Phoutrides was surprised at the calmness with which he now reacted to the trio. He would have thought that with the wreckage and death he observed, fear would have frozen him to inaction. He attributed his unexpected serenity to one man—Becton. Fewer than eight feet from Phoutrides, Becton displayed the same calm leadership he had exhibited in every previous engagement.

"I was on the bridge for the rest of the battle, and Becton was calm throughout. You are influenced by your skipper. He's calm, so we're calm. We all took our cue from him. Even if you were not on the bridge and couldn't see him now, we had seen it at Normandy, the Philippines, the raid against Japan, and off Iwo Jima. Everybody knew what he was like in battle."[15]

Ensign Townsley's voice cut through the din at 9:30 to warn of a Judy approaching *Laffey*'s mid-section from two miles out. The men at the amidships gun stations turned toward the oncoming plane, and blasted 450 rounds at the plane in the next minute. Their bullets chopped through the waters around the low-flying kamikaze, kicking up sprays that splattered against the aircraft as the Judy narrowed the distance. Finally, at eight hundred yards the plane coughed, dipped to the surface, crashed, and bobbed in the waves before disappearing from sight.

That plane had barely hit the water when the eighteenth kamikaze raced in on the starboard beam toward Johnson's gun and the bridge area. Mount 52 gun captain, Chief Gunner's Mate Warren Walker, spotted it at almost the same moment Phoutrides saw it from the bridge. The crew manually cranked and loaded the lumbering five-inch gun as the aircraft remained steadfastly on its path, hugging the water's surface like its predecessor. The mount trainer, Coxswain Raymond H. Faginski, turned the gun to starboard where the mount pointer, Coxswain Kenneth J. Pitta, opened fire. Faginski, wounded by shrapnel earlier in the fight, made the sign of the cross and muttered, "this is it!"[16] as the zooming kamikaze threatened the coxswain's fiery demise at his station.

As Phoutrides watched the kamikaze fight through the American gunfire, the bomb attached to the plane's underbelly grew disproportionately larger for the quartermaster who, like most of the crew exposed on deck, believed the bomb was intended for him. For the next few seconds everything else faded into insignificance for the former MIT student while plane and bomb continued on a path that seemed to end at Phoutrides's feet. "I spotted it and fixated on it," said Phoutrides. "I thought, 'It's coming right at me! This is it!'"[17]

Despite the antiaircraft curtain erected by the starboard guns, the kamikaze maintained a direct course through the bursts. Finally, with the plane less than five hundred yards away, one of Mount 52's shells smacked into the nose of the kamikaze, which seemed momentarily to stand still before a monumental explosion incinerated plane and pilot. Working inside the damaged mount, Dockery heard a large BOOM!, and Chief Walker shouted, "we got the son of a bitch! What a beautiful sight!" Seaman Johnson, who had a clear view from his station at Mount 41, said to Steward's Mate 2/c Clyde A. Dunson, "Dunson, look at that!"[18]

Phoutrides welcomed the sight, for had the plane reached its destination, it would have crashed into the bridge area. One deck below Phoutrides, Seaman Johnson thought the same. That direct hit from a five-inch shell saved his life. Becton admired Mount 52's accuracy, for he knew Zack and the crew had to operate the gun manually, "and besides the great relief afforded, it was an added pleasure to see it [the kamikaze] poised in space a few feet above the water, then disintegrate into nothingness."[19]

As Mount 52 was dispatching its kamikaze, Seaman 1/c Andrew Stash in Mount 51 spotted a Val coming in on the starboard bow from one mile out. The mount turned and fired twenty rounds at Kamikaze No. 19, which spouted black smoke and plane parts in a death plunge to the surface five hundred yards away. "We got him!" shouted Stash to Gunner's Mate 3/c Welles A. Meier. "We got him! Good work, Welles! Did you see that bastard explode?"[20] In five minutes the forward guns had splashed three kamikazes, protecting the ship from worse damage, preserving her ability to fight, and earning Becton's praise for guns that had to be operated manually.

Because of wounds incurred, Walker and Faginski had to leave Mount 52 for treatment from Doctor Darnell. Combined with the damage from Kamikaze No. 16, the mount could now no longer operate. After splashing the eighteenth kamikaze, Zack and the rest of the gun mount crew received orders to secure the location, close the watertight hatches, and gather on deck.

Now topside and free of their mount duties, Zack and Radder asked the gunnery officer, Lieutenant Smith, for permission to assist the damage control parties, and after first denying the request in hopes that the gun mount could be placed back into action, Smith gave his assent. He told the pair to keep in touch in case Smith needed them back at the gun.

"The sights made us pause," said Zack as he surveyed the decks for the first time since disappearing into the mount. "Some 20mm and 40mm guns were wiped out. Ammunition was popping off from fires near the storage areas around gun mounts, and that was scary."

Radder headed forward while Zack turned aft, where he planned to retrieve whatever 40mm ammunition he could find and bring it to the forward guns that still operated. Zack stepped along the starboard side until he reached Mount 43, the starboard aft 40mm gun where Tom Fern's good friend, Ramon Pressburger, was stationed. "The gun was burned and browned, and there was no gun crew there," said Zack. "I had to be careful of the 20mm ammunition popping off."

Zack picked up some 40mm ammunition and brought it forward to Seaman Johnson's Mount 41, then returned for more. Along the way he carefully wound through debris and bodies, wary of the fires that burned amidships and aft. Like Martinis, Zack had to force the sights from his mind so he could do his job.

"At Gun 53 [Delewski's gun], I saw a Japanese plane smashed there, and I could see the pilot's chest and head on the engine and the rest of his body in the cockpit. You see this stuff, but you just keep doing what you need to do. It was there, but you didn't dwell on it. You're focused on what's going on."

While kamikazes continued to attack and guns maintained their fire Zack moved aft. He peered inside Delewski's mount and saw one man, a loader, with one foot on the deck and the other leg on the seat. "He was standing like that, but dead. He had flash burns all over, and his body was rigid. Whenever the ship moved, he didn't. His body never did move."

Zack passed by the blackened mount toward the fantail, where "20mm guns were a mess." At the tail end of the ship, now dipping lower, he found that water, not fires and bombs, formed the direst threat to ship and crew. "The water was breaking over the fantail, and I thought we might be in trouble of sinking. I wondered if we were going to be able to stay afloat because of the leaks. I had a brief thought that we might have to abandon ship."[21]

Zack continued carrying 40mm shells forward until the gun crews told him they no longer needed any more. Zack tossed those last shells over the side and looked around to see what else he could do.

In the meantime, Becton had returned to the pilot house from the open flying bridge. Lieutenant Manson, who had inspected many of the damaged areas and worried that the ship could no longer fend off additional attacks, climbed to the bridge to convey his thoughts.

"Captain, we're in pretty bad shape aft," the officer said to Becton. "Do you think we'll have to abandon ship?"

In the span of seconds Becton flashed back to the *Aaron Ward*, a ship he felt he should somehow have done more to save two years earlier. He thought of the gallant first *Laffey* that had performed so well off Guadalcanal before being sunk by Japanese, an experience forever etched in his mind. He thought of the men who had died within the past hour to protect this ship, and of those who were about to die from hideous wounds. He was moved by the performance of his gunners, who gamely defended the destroyer while kamikazes buzzed about the ship, and of Signalman McCarthy, who lifted a new flag to the mast. He would not now give up on a ship and crew that had fought so bravely. Becton, who never seriously considered the possibility of abandoning the ship, suppressed the anger he felt at Manson's query. "The ship might sink under us. We might not be able to sail her. But I wasn't going to abandon her,"[22] he thought.

Calmly, Becton turned to Manson. "Hell, *no* [emphasis Becton's], Frank," replied Becton, stifling his fury. "We still have guns that can shoot." In words that equal the utterances of naval greats from the past, from John Paul Jones to George Dewey, he added, "I'll never abandon ship as long as a gun will fire!"[23]

Emboldened by these words, and again taking their cue from the man on the bridge, the crew battled on. The Japanese would have to finish the job. Becton was not going to help them.

9:46—Kamikazes Numbers 20 to 22

"Some of Those Kids Have More Damned Guts"

While Zack carried ammunition forward, a trio of Japanese aircraft swooped in against the ship at 9:46 a.m. The first, a Val, materialized through the haze and the sun before lookouts spotted it and approached against the fantail through sparse gunfire from two 20mm machine guns. The pilot dropped a bomb that exploded behind Delewski's heavily damaged Mount 53, blew a hole in the deck ten feet wide and eight feet long, scattered deck equipment, pierced holes in the deck, and started additional fires below. The pilot dropped low and traversed almost the entire length of *Laffey*, knocking off the starboard yardarm with its landing gear and avoiding fire from Coxswain Falotico at Mount 21 before being splashed several hundred yards off the port bow by Marine Corsair pilots Second Lieutenant Marion I. Ryan and First Lieutenant Charles H. Coppedge of squadron VMF-441 out of Yontan airfield.

Ryan immediately turned to another Val but could not arrive in time to prevent the Japanese pilot from adding to the devastation that already marked the ship below. *Laffey* gunners on the starboard side forward, including Johnson's 40mm gun, zeroed in on the bomber as it approached in a shallow dive off the starboard bow, strafing the decks as she drew closer. "Down, Captain! Down!"[24] shouted Seaman Salcido to Becton when he noticed Kamikaze No. 21, another Val. As bullets splintered the bridge near Phoutrides and Becton, Salcido tackled Becton to the deck, preventing injury to both men, while the starboard 40mm and 20mm guns sprayed the area around the plane.

The pilot dropped a bomb from one hundred yards out. Carpenter's Mate Henry Thompson in the bow saw the bomb detach from the Val and dived head first down a hatch, landing hard on the deck below. Seaman Martinis jumped behind the nearest shelter and watched the bomb descend in an arc toward *Laffey*, not realizing until afterward that he had sought refuge behind the depth charge rack and its collection of explosives.

Sonarman Zack stood near Johnson's 40mm gun when someone shouted, "plane coming!" He and others rushed to the opposite side and huddled near his Mount 52. When Zack peered out to sea, he spotted three aircraft flying parallel to the ship, which he assumed were American fighters. As the third aircraft turned toward the ship and began his run in, Zack, still thinking the plane was friendly, concluded the pilot had to be crazy, "because our guns fired at anything that approached the ship. Then I saw the fixed landing gear and thought, 'Oh, shit!'"

He tried to move out of the way of the incoming Val but, reminiscent of the familiar nightmare where a person runs from a threat but cannot advance, his feet kept slipping. "The oil that shoots into the gun barrel was leaking onto the deck, and I wasn't moving."

Zack dropped to his hands and knees and slid closer to Mount 51, but the pilot maintained a steady course directly toward him. Zack "saw my life flash before me, in snapshot form, from being a young boy. I'm a skeptic about things like this, but it happened. The images were so beautiful and vivid."[25]

On the starboard side 20mm gun Coxswain Falotico, who had traded stations with Gunner's Mate Stanley Ketron so Falotico could leave the confines of Mount 51 and operate in the open, waved to his friend, Ramon Pressburger. Falotico had vowed to Pressburger before the action that despite the hazards, he would never leave his station, and he waved to let Pressburger know he was still at his 20mm gun. Bullets sparked against the deck and shields, wounding the gunner next to Falotico, as the Japanese pilot dropped his bomb. Nearby, Torpedoman Jack Ondracek leapt into the empty straps alongside Falotico and started what under normal circumstances might have been considered foolhardy—he tried with his bullets to explode the bomb as it spiraled toward the ship. If he were to succeed in this herculean task, Ondracek had to hit the weapon precisely in the proper spot, else the bullets would splinter off the bomb's metallic sides and produce harmless sparks along the projectile's path to the deck. Blocking out all other thoughts, Ondracek concentrated on his target as it continued, looming larger as the yards slipped away and it neared the destroyer. Standing less than fifty feet away, Torpedoman's Mate Fred Gemmell observed Ondracek's bullets nick the bomb and tracers zip by both sides, "but he couldn't hit the one spot to make it explode before it hit the ship."[26]

Knowing they had to ignite the bomb or die, Ondracek and Falotico remained at their guns, eyes widening as the target continued its arced descent. They fired until the final moment, when the bomb and guns and sailors conjoined in a mammoth explosion that vaporized the men, destroyed the gun mount, and wounded or killed other men scattered about the area. "You know," said Lieutenant McCune of Ondracek and Falotico, "some of those kids have more damned guts. They stayed right in that gun mount and kept firing."[27]

The bomb caused extensive damage to ship and crew. It destroyed Group 21, the forward 20mm gun emplacement, in the process killing Ondracek, Falotico, and others. Bomb fragments hit Lieutenant E. J. Samp in the head, severely wounding the officer in charge of *Laffey*'s forward 20mm guns as he walked from the bridge. Bullets splintered the bridge, deck, and gun shields, and riddled Becton's cabin. The bomb blew a large hole in the superstructure deck, and bomb fragments severed additional water lines and electrical cables, igniting electrical fires in the process. Other pieces killed Gunner's Mate Stanley Wismer and almost killed Sonarman Zack, who was knocked to the deck by the bomb's concussion. Zack flipped over on his back, still covered with the oil that had almost prevented him from seeking safety, and saw the Val zoom overhead and veer upward with Second Lieutenant Ryan's Corsair in pursuit. "The Corsair fired, and boy I could hear those machine guns because he was so close overhead! Bullets nipped the plane, which was still climbing, and it dropped fifty feet because he had been hit."[28] A final burst from Ryan ripped into the Val, which veered over, nosed into the drink, and exploded.

The bomb also ripped a hole five feet high and one foot wide in the bulkhead near Doctor Darnell's wardroom, instantly killing Pharmacist's Mate 3/c Earl E. Waters and further wounding several men being treated for prior injuries. Shrapnel sliced off the tips of two of Doctor Darnell's fingers, but the physician continued tending the wounded with his good hand after bandaging the other.

Seaman Martinis, one of the men assisting Doctor Darnell, lacked the skills to help the most severely wounded, but used words to console men in their final hours. He bent over one man who had been injured on the bridge and whispered, "God is with us." Through his pain, the man weakly joked, "Oh, is the captain here?"[29]

Boatswain's Mate Calvin Wesley Cloer, the preacher who had been carried to the wardroom earlier in the battle, was hit a second time by fragments from this latest bomb. Another man tried to reassure him by saying, "You'll be all right, Cloer," but Cloer knew he was dying. "You're not kidding me," answered the boatswain. "I know I'm going." The inspiring Cloer lasted until the next day when, during his final moments, he remarked to a buddy, "now I can go home to [wife] Peggy."[30]

On the deck, Sonarman Zack heard someone moaning for assistance. "Please help me,"[31] pleaded Yeoman Fred Burgess, who had fed shells into one of the portside 20mm guns. Zack, who had escaped injury from the same shrapnel that hit Burgess, saw blood gushing out of what was left of Burgess's leg, now nothing but mangled tendons dangling from a bloody knee. Gunner's Mate Karr grabbed an old shirt, held Burgess down on the deck, and applied a makeshift tourniquet to stem the blood flow before he and another man took Burgess to the wardroom for treatment.

The pair carried Burgess to the wardroom, now packed with wounded and dying men. Burgess spotted Signalman William Kelly across the room, holding the flag he had retrieved from the deck after a Japanese plane had clipped it from the mast, and asked Kelly to hand it to him. Kelly brought the flag to the mortally wounded Burgess, who tightly clutched it while Doctor Darnell tended to his wounds. Burgess died a few moments later, still holding on to the American flag he had so courageously defended.

As Burgess succumbed in the wardroom, Kamikaze No. 22, another Judy, dived in on the port bow with Corsairs in hot pursuit. "I've got to get out of here!"[32] thought Torpedoman's Mate Gemmell, who joined other men in diving to the deck for cover. The portside 40mm and 20mm guns engaged in a duel with the Judy, firing 205 rounds in twenty seconds while the Judy's slugs smacked off gun shields and ricocheted off bulkheads.

Quartermaster Phoutrides thought the plane might hit the bridge and leapt underneath the small navigating table just as two other men did the same. The trio huddled beneath the table, no larger than a child's school desk, and hoped its flimsy material would deflect any bullets. "If our lives depended on it," wrote Phoutrides later of three grown men squeezing into such a confined space, "I don't think we could duplicate this feat a second time."[33]

When a Corsair splashed the Judy off the port bow, the resultant explosion sprayed shrapnel across the fore sections, leaving Phoutrides and his mates unscathed, but peppering the 20mm guns a few feet below, slicing more hoses, and denting bulkheads. Seaman 1/c Donald Carter had taken shelter and thought he had avoided harm, but fainted after taking a few steps. Although he never felt a thing, thirty-seven pieces of shrapnel had pierced his body and knocked out a handful of teeth.

Phoutrides and others rose to their feet to prepare for yet one more kamikaze, but instead an eerie silence settled in. "Suddenly it was over," said Seaman Johnson, astonished at the unexpected calm. "After eighty minutes of noise, there was quiet."[34]

"We Were Cleaning Up and Licking Our Wounds"

> *When the last Jap was gone*
> *We were still looking for more*
> *To make sure those Rising Suns*
> *Would never wave over our shore.*
> —"An Ode to the USS *Laffey* (DD-724),"
>   Gunner's Mate Owen Radder

An incredulous Becton, learning that the ship's radar screen was clear of bogeys, was surprised that the enemy had not completed a job they had almost finished. "I couldn't believe it. Why just then, when they were so close, had they let up?"[35]

Sonarman Charles Bell, Becton's telephone talker, interrupted his skipper's thoughts by telling him to look above. Becton glanced skyward to see twenty-four Marine Corsairs and Navy Wildcat fighters circling above *Laffey*, ready to chase away any Japanese kamikaze that approached the hamstrung destroyer. "They knew we were badly damaged and I think all of us on board must have breathed a benediction on them as we looked up and saw twenty-four Corsairs and Wildcats hovering over us." For the first time since the fighting began, Phoutrides felt he might yet reach home and see his family. "The ship was surrounded in silence," he said, "and that was a weird feeling. I looked up and saw twenty-four aircraft protecting us. They were a beautiful sight! I felt totally safe."[36]

But no one discounted that another kamikaze could still sneak through. The destruction around them attested to that. A glass port directly behind Becton sported twelve bullet holes, showing how close Becton had come to death, and another bullet had pierced the ship's emblem painted on the bridge.

Men still tense from the battle gathered in groups about the ship to see who had made it through and to inspect the damage. Sonarman Zack saw Seaman Fern, his body covered with horrible burns, stumbling on the deck seeking help. Seaman Johnson wondered why he was not famished after the intense action, and then realized that it was only mid-morning. Everything he had just experienced, although it seemed a lifetime, had taken place in eighty action-filled minutes between breakfast and lunch.

Becton took advantage of the calm to inspect for the first time the damage that had all but ripped away the aft portion from the destroyer. "We were in bad shape aft with fires and flooding still not under control," he told the press later. "Our whole topside was strewn with plane wreckage from bow to stern—engines, landing gear, wings, the remains of Jap pilots. What a mess!"[37]

Becton used two pages in his action report to list the damage his ship absorbed. "For about twenty feet aft of Mount No. 3," he wrote, "the main deck is like a sieve with many small holes and 24 holes at least one foot in diameter. The same is true of the superstructure deck in the vicinity of the after 40mm mounts." Gun 53, Delewski's mount, was "completely demolished" and the forward 20mm group, starboard side had been "wiped out by bomb hit." Youngquist's 40mm gun mount had been destroyed and the other three sustained damage. Only four of the eleven 20mm guns could still shoot, and all those stood on the port side. The superstructure bulkheads to the wardroom and officers' rooms below the bridge on the starboard side were "riddled with bomb fragments,"[38] and bomb shrapnel had knocked out radars, radios, and the gyro compass. Large holes, ranging from two to ten feet in diameter, pierced the main deck, and shrapnel had riddled the decks, bulkheads, and compartments in hundreds of places.

The destruction below equaled the devastation above. All three aft living compartments for the crew were flooded, gutted by fires, riddled by hundreds of metal fragments, or suffered from a combination of the three. Kamikazes had destroyed the after head and washroom, knocked out the lighting and power aft, jammed the rudder, and flooded the steering gear room.

Crew examined similar incredulous sights. Phoutrides came upon the landing gear of a Japanese aircraft when he walked the deck below the bridge. Delewski thought about grabbing some food until he glanced downward to see near his feet a severed finger resting among the fire hoses and the debris. Gunner's Mate Radder stared at the charred body of a kamikaze pilot sitting up in the rear head belowdecks, resting on the motor to his plane, and Seaman Dockery paused before the line of dead shipmates stretching out along the port side.

Although his ship had been critically damaged, Becton intended to be ready to fight with the few guns at his disposal should the enemy reappear. The bridge and power plants had emerged largely unscathed, firefighting efforts were making headway, men were removing the dead and wounded, and the pumps seemed to be holding their own against the flooding that threatened the fantail. However, because he could not be certain that the holes existing below the waterline would not enlarge and allow more ocean water to gush through, he posted a man at each door belowdecks to keep watch and told them to immediately report any increase in the leakage.

Around the destroyer, every available man began removing the debris of battle. They lifted overboard engine parts, chunks of wings and fuselages, pieces of Japanese pilots, damaged antennae and radar screens, and hundreds of other items. "We were cleaning up and licking our wounds,"[39] said Seaman Martinis. Radder went to the aft steering compartment, where he kept the pump intakes clear of clothing or other matter so the outward flow of water could continue. Near Radder, Radarman 1/c Slavomir J. Vodenhal, one of the members of the FIDO team that had only recently boarded the ship, noticed a few photographs floating in the water. When he reached down to retrieve them, he found that they were pictures of his mother and father he had kept with his personal belongings.

Sonarman Zack volunteered for one of the most sensitive tasks—gathering the bodies of his deceased shipmates so they could be prepared for burial. He and other men gently placed the bodies on mattress covers laid out along the port side and tried not to dwell on what they saw. "You knew all the guys," said Zack, "but you don't think about what you are seeing, you just do your work. Some had parts missing, and most were burned, and the smell of burned flesh—you don't forget that."[40]

Reports of *Laffey's* ordeal reached Admiral Turner's flagship. He informed Becton that two tugs, USS *Pakana* (ATF-108) and USS *Tawakoni* (ATF-114), were on their way to help tow the destroyer back to Okinawa, but because of their slow sixteen-knot pace the tugs would not arrive before afternoon. After fending off the Japanese in the morning, Becton and crew now engaged in a race against time. Would the tugs arrive to save the ship, or would flooding or additional Japanese send her to the bottom first?

Becton later wrote that the time between the end of the battle and the time when the tugs arrived were "the longest three hours ever experienced by all hands on board." At any moment the flooding could worsen, or an explosion belowdecks could mortally damage the ship. "After the attack, we were dead in the water," said Phoutrides. "Waiting for assistance seemed like an eternity."[41] Becton and crew had to wait until the tugs arrived and hope no threat arose that might further impair the ship's ability to remain afloat.

Officers and enlisted admitted they were still in jeopardy, even though they had just survived an attack from twenty-two kamikazes. "There wasn't a moment when I thought it was over," said Lieutenant Youngquist, who had miraculously lived through the death and destruction inflicted on his aft guns. The crew agreed with Seaman Johnson, who stated, "We wondered how we ever stayed afloat. We came so close to losing the ship."[42]

In mid-morning help from other units began steaming toward the embattled destroyer. Rear Admiral Alexander Sharp, commander of TG 52.2, radioed Captain R. A. Larkin, commander of the Destroyer Minesweeper Group TG 52.3, to send the destroyer minesweeper USS *Macomb* (DMS-23) to Picket Station No. 1 to assist *Laffey*. Captain J. H. Wellings, commander of TG 53.6, the Northern Attack Force Screen, ordered the rescue craft, USS *PCE(R)-851* to remove the wounded and lend any other support she could to Becton. Both commanders understood that they could not afford to waste time if they were to save *Laffey*.

After having engaged in whirlwind, nonstop action for eighty minutes, Becton and his crew took comfort that CAP circled above, but those planes had not prevented the earlier attacks. Would more of the same occur as the day unfolded? "One very long hour went by, then two, then three, each minute dragging like a battleship anchor in deep mud," wrote Becton, who had lookouts scouring every section of the sky. "We were a sitting duck and we knew it."[43]

CHAPTER 10

A LASTING LEGACY

Homeward bound with Dashing Wave
List'ning to the media rave,
Coast war effort tried to save.
— "Invicta," Lieutenant Matthew Darnell

Few crews in naval history could boast of achievements that equaled the remarkable feats posted by *Laffey*'s officers and sailors from 8:27 until 9:47 a.m. The gun crews splashed nine kamikazes on their own and assisted CAP or *LCS-51* on another three, firing 7,090 shells and bullets in eighty minutes, an average of almost one and a half every second. Six planes battled through the antiaircraft fire and smashed into the ship, a seventh grazed Mount 53, while another five landed bomb hits or sprayed shrapnel across the decks.

The praiseworthy performance against what Becton called "this Val and Judy nightmare"[1] came with a high price tag. Thirty-two men died and another seventy-two were wounded, comprising one-third of the men Becton brought to the Pacific.

"Pieces of Jap Planes Were Still Visible"

Aid arrived within the hour. At 10:45 *LCS-51* pulled alongside *Laffey*'s starboard quarter to help quash the fires in the stern portion of the destroyer. When the crew of the landing craft observed the extent of the damage, they doubted they could do much to save the destroyer, yet strung hoses across to the smoking ship and manned pumps to try to keep *Laffey* afloat.

At 12:47 the minesweeper, USS *Macomb* relieved *LCS-51* and, though not as powerful as a tug, took *Laffey* in tow. The minesweeper's crew pitched in to combat the flooding, which was threatening to overwhelm *Laffey*'s pumps. The sight of dead bodies resting on *Laffey*'s deck unnerved men on the *Macomb*, causing one man to ignore the announcement that chow was ready and forgo lunch. "Coming up alongside the *Laffey*, preparing to take her in tow, the stricken ship presented a never-to-be-forgotten sight," wrote one of the *Macomb* crew. "An unbelievable mass of twisted steel and smoldering destruction—the grim picture of death lying about the decks, men a short while ago like ourselves—now, tossed about as if the devil himself reached up with a ball of fire. Pieces of the Jap planes were still visible about the decks."[2]

The *Macomb* remained alongside until 1:45, when the first of two powerful fleet tugs arrived to tow *Laffey* to Kerama Retto, the home of damaged vessels that had so affected the crew before *Laffey* departed for Picket Station No. 1. The USS *Pakana*'s more potent pumping capabilities could better contain the flooding and her powerful engines could pull the destroyer away from the area, but the jammed rudder hindered *Pakana*'s efforts. According to Gauding, by the time the tugs arrived, "the after part of the ship was pretty low in the water due to the flooded compartments. Men from the tugs came aboard & assisted us in pumping the spaces & keeping the *Laffey* afloat."[3]

Chief Machinist's Mate George R. Heffler of the *Pakana* watched the rescue efforts with added interest, as he had survived the sinking of the first *Laffey* earlier in the war. He now arrived to help save the second, organizing the salvage and firefighting crews who aided *Laffey*'s exhausted crew. By 2:30 p.m. *Pakana* had secured towlines with *Laffey* and prepared to leave for Kerama Retto.

Less than one hour later *PCE(R)-851*, stocked with medical equipment, pulled alongside *Laffey* and took aboard thirty-three of *Laffey*'s more seriously wounded men, including the badly burned Tom Fern and the mortally wounded Pharmacist's Mate Earl Waters, who feebly sang "Anchors Aweigh" as carrier stretchers took him from his ship. At 3:20 *PCE(R)-851* inched away from the destroyer and transferred the group to the hospital ship, USS *Hope* (AH-7).

While the relief efforts continued, Becton's crew cleared away as much of the devastation as possible. They removed one airplane engine from the inside of Delewski's gun. A second, containing the charred remains of a dismembered Japanese pilot, lay just outside the mount. Crew retrieved severed feet and fingers without knowing which of their deceased buddies they belonged to, and they peeled away the body of the young gunner who had shared his doubts about performing capably with Seaman "Preacher" Belk. The gunner's body was so badly charred that portions fell away when his shipmates tried to remove him.

Despite the combined efforts of the *Laffey* and *Pakana* crews, the seawater pouring in so overtaxed the pumping capabilities that Phoutrides feared the ship might go under. At 4:51 Becton requested help from a second tug, the *Tawakoni*, which pulled alongside *Laffey*'s port quarter at 6:17. The tug stretched suction hoses into *Laffey*'s flooded compartments, and contributed extra motor-driven pumps. With the *Tawakoni*'s added pumping facilities, water levels began dropping and the destroyer's stern slowly rose. Teams worked throughout the night, and by morning of April 17 every flooded compartment was dry.

As *Tawakani* helped with the pumping, *Pakani* towed *Laffey* at four knots first toward Kerama Retto, and then to Hagushi Beach, Okinawa, after receiving amended orders. During the seventy-five-mile trip Becton countered the ship's jammed rudder by backing the starboard engine and going ahead at five knots with the port engine. This corrected the veer caused by the rudder and enabled *Laffey* to keep pace with *Pakani*.

Fortunately, calm seas blessed their efforts. Had medium-sized swells slapped the ship or had a storm blown in, *Laffey* could easily have been swamped. With only a handful of guns operable and with the ship in such critical shape, though, their main concern was the appearance of additional kamikazes. There was not much the battered destroyer, able to make only four knots, could do to defend herself.

"We were sitting ducks if the Japanese appeared," said Seaman Dockery. "We still had guns that could fire, but not many. Most of the crew agreed that they would be finished if the Japanese came back for a second round of attacks." Despite the presence of twenty planes flying CAP—ten at high altitudes and ten at low—Phoutrides smoked non-stop to calm his nerves at this point. He said later that "we must have been in a semi-state of shock. We were nervous and anxious to get out of the area."[4]

Because Zack's sleeping compartment was under water, he and others slumped down wherever they could to get a little rest. Zack could have used a bunk in another compartment that had belonged to one of the dead, but declined the offer out of respect for his fallen shipmate. Instead, he stretched out in the more spacious sonar room, but discovered that whenever he turned, pain shot through his upper arm. Zack, who had no idea that he had been wounded, found a chunk of shrapnel the size of an eraser head in his right arm. When a corpsman later asked Zack about putting his name in for a Purple Heart, Zack declined. "I didn't want one. Not for that, after seeing all the guys missing arms, legs, and suffering serious wounds." For the same reason Lieutenant Youngquist, who suffered minor burns, left his name off the injured list. "I had seen guys before who were grievously wounded or killed, and mine wasn't the same."[5]

Night provided added security as the crew knew they were safe from ka-mikazes, which rarely attacked after dark. Becton released them from battle stations, allowing men time to share a mug of coffee with buddies or catch a quick nap. An alert at 2:42 a.m. April 17 sent everybody back to his post, but after nineteen minutes of antiaircraft fire from other ships in the area, the all clear sounded at 3:05 without *Laffey* gun crews having to take action.

At 6:14 a.m. on April 17, the tugs pulled *Laffey* to her anchorage off Ha-gushi Beach in southwest Okinawa. The destroyer had limped to port, but questions remained about whether she could be patched sufficiently to make the ocean trip to Saipan and its more extensive repair facilities.

"Our Ordeal Was Behind Us"

At 11:40 that morning Chaplain Curtis Junker from the USS *Eldorado*, with Becton and the crew standing at attention, conducted a funeral service for the thirty-two men who perished. Only seven of the bodies lay on the fore-castle, as some men had been blown out to sea in the fighting and were miss-ing, and crew had buried a few at sea while they were removing the debris of battle. Seaman Lonnie Eastham helped bury ten shipmates, including his close friend, Coxswain Bernard Edwards, gently wrapping them in fire-proof mattress covers to which they attached 40mm ammunition cans for sinking weight.

The simple ceremony moved the crew. Three officers, Fravel, Sheets, and Thomsen, and twenty-nine enlisted, including Ondracek, Burgess, Preacher Calvin Wesley Cloer, and crooner Kelley would no longer see family and home. "It was a serious moment," said Seaman Johnson. "Our shipmates had died. We had not experienced that yet. Until April 16, we had lived a comparatively charmed life."[6]

After the ceremony a landing craft transferred the bodies, accompanied by Lieutenant Manson, to the beach, where an Army truck transported them to the Sixth Marine Division cemetery that overlooked *Laffey*'s temporary anchorage off Hagushi. The driver remarked to Manson that he heard a ship had caught hell up north, and the cemetery chaplain, Lieutenant Commander Paul L. Redmond, a veteran of Guadalcanal, Saipan, Peleliu, and Iwo Jima, remarked that earlier in the war he buried mostly Marine bodies. Now, he was in charge of hundreds of Navy deceased as well.

At the cemetery, rows of shrouded bodies awaited burial, mute testimony to the savagery of the land battles. Redmond and Manson placed identification papers inside Coca-Cola bottles for later reburial, then lay the bodies side by side in a long row along with Marine dead.

Hagushi was heaven to the men aboard the battered destroyer. Becton said the crew believed Hagushi was "as beautiful as New York Harbor and her welcoming Statue of Liberty."[7]

The cook aboard a tug sent over breakfast as a way of recognizing a job well done, and men whose bodies had been tense since the fighting started now began to relax. Phoutrides talked with his friends and found that the one question most wanted answered was why so many kamikazes focused on *Laffey*? They never settled on a satisfactory answer, but agreed that if the Japanese had better coordinated their attacks, as Kamikazes Numbers 9–12 seemed to be, that they would now be dead.

The Japanese could not have provided a clear answer to the crew's question. Most of the inexperienced pilots simply pounced on whatever vessel they first spotted, and with *Laffey* operating at the post closest to Kyushu, she held that dubious distinction. In the heat of the moment, other pilots mistakenly identified the ship as a cruiser or battleship, the larger quarry they most yearned to land in their sites.

The ship remained in Hagushi for repair work from April 17 until April 21. Divers inspected the rudder and plugged shrapnel holes in the ship's plating, and welders attached plates over holes in the decks and the side of the ship. In the process, workers discovered a grim reminder of *Laffey*'s ordeal when they uncovered the body of a shipmate buried in the debris belowdecks.

Nightly enemy air raids over Hagushi indicated that while they may have escaped the enemy on April 16, they were far from safe. Phoutrides was more frightened at night off Okinawa's beaches than he had been during the battle, for ships in Hagushi had been given orders to withhold fire lest they give away their position. "Now I was petrified," said Phoutrides. "Hearing the planes come over and the bombs dropping, but being unable to fire, was absolutely terrifying."[8] At least they had been able to fight back on April 16, Phoutrides thought.

Becton took advantage of the time at Hagushi to write his official report of April 16 and to begin gathering the names of those who deserved notice. To make certain no man was overlooked, he asked Lieutenant McCune to speak to the officers and compile a list of those who had performed with distinction so that Becton could thank them for what they had done to help save *Laffey*. Becton also visited Admiral Richmond Kelly Turner to urge that his crew receive the Presidential Unit Citation, which the crew of the first *Laffey* had earlier received. Becton believed his men deserved the same honor.

While at Turner's flagship, Lieutenant Manson, whom Becton had asked to handle the reporters, met Commander Paul Smith, who in civilian life was the editor and general manager of the *San Francisco Chronicle*. "We heard you had a little excitement on the picket line," Smith said to Manson "We heard you guys on our voice radio. You put up quite a fight."

Within the hour Manson stood before a room packed with Admiral Turner and more than one hundred reporters eager to hear about a ship that had escaped twenty-two kamikazes. "I kept thinking of all the tragic and heroic scenes I had witnessed," Manson said, and he hoped he could convey the crew's heroism and Becton's leadership so that the nation had some idea of what unfolded that April 16 morning. "I knew this was my one moment," Manson said, to make the name *Laffey* familiar to readers in the United States.

Manson recounted April 16 with calm precision. "The wire services, the networks, many large city newspapers and the top flag officers at Okinawa, all listened, all at once. I had nothing to read from, no script, but I needed no notes."[9] He spoke of the planes diving on the ship, of the gun crews that splashed the first eight kamikazes and hindered the rest, of the Marine Corsair pilots who flew into friendly antiaircraft fire, of crew who battled fires and flooding, of McCarthy raising a new flag to the mast, and of a host of other actions.

Manson, knowing that his words would soon light up the communications wires connecting the reporters with their newspapers and magazines back home, saved the most dramatic comment for last. He recounted how, at one stage of the battle with the ship in jeopardy, he had asked Becton if he might have to abandon ship. Becton's promise that he would never abandon ship as long as a gun could fire so moved the reporters that they used the quote to anchor their stories written for home consumption.

While news of *Laffey*'s feats swept the nation, Tom Fern informed his family that he had survived. "Just a few lines to let you know I am still in one piece and no wounds," he wrote his mother on April 17 from the hospital ship, *Hope*. "Just a case of nerves from battle action & concussion. All I need is some rest & quiet for a while to get over it." Fern diplomatically avoided recounting the extent of his injuries, which included severe burns. Three days later he hinted at more in a letter to his aunt, the Catholic nun who had mailed him the religious medal Fern had clasped during the attack. "Just a few lines to let you know I'm still O.K.—after a terrible time." He added that he was on a hospital ship "getting over the effects of concussion from an explosion." He thanked her for the medal, and told her, "I had this in my pocket when death came my way the three times I can remember." Seaman Johnson was more succinct, informing his family on April 20, "There isn't anything to write only I wanted you to know that I am O.K."[10]

Repair crews quickly patched *Laffey* sufficiently that, within five days of arriving, Becton could depart for Saipan. With Mount 53's barrels twisted in multiple directions, gaping holes where Youngquist's guns had once stood, and with shattered masts, *Laffey* hobbled away from Okinawa and her picket stations.

"Finally," wrote Quartermaster Phoutrides, "on the 22nd of April, we got underway for Saipan, and our ordeal was behind us."[11]

"Most of Us Had Tears in Our Eyes"

On a cloudy, warm afternoon, Becton steered *Laffey*, with battle scars clearly visible fore and aft, from Hagushi to rendezvous with other ships bound for Saipan in the Mariana Islands. "Underway for Saipan along with about a dozen other ships," wrote Fireman Gauding. "Sure glad to get out of there."[12] Because of the damage, Becton operated without search radar, and he could not steer from the bridge. Instead, an officer took station in the cramped steering engine room aft, where he controlled the ship's movements according to the orders Becton relayed via headphones.

Aboard the USS *Gendreau*, (DD-639), Yeoman John P. Cosgrove watched his task unit depart, "including the famous *Laffey*, limping back to the States after becoming a casualty at Okinawa."[13] While Cosgrove initially feared an appearance by kamikazes, he relaxed more with each hour they steamed farther away from Hagushi, Becton was more concerned with the weather. Heavy seas could swamp his destroyer and finish what the Japanese had so brutally started. Fortunately, continued calm seas made the five-day passage easy, and on April 27 Becton anchored *Laffey* in the Inner Harbor, Saipan. By then the crew had time to shake enough of the effects of battle to marvel at the lumbering B-29 bombers that lifted from Saipan's runways and at the beautiful beaches.

Laffey remained in Saipan for repair work until May 1. Laborers fixed the steering so that the remainder of the trip could be handled from the bridge, and patched the radar so that Becton would enjoy functional surface radar.

The four days gave Becton and other men time to turn to other matters. Lieutenant William Shaw and other officers had the distasteful task of censoring the crew's letters, many of which had been written before the battle by sailors who had subsequently died in action. They read the notes with tears running down their cheeks, for they handled the final words from men to their loved ones. "They had been written just two days before when everybody was well and happy," said Lieutenant Shaw. "Most of the letters told of looking forward to coming back to the States. They brought tears to our eyes, and some of us officers had not cried in a long time."[14]

Becton and Darnell visited the wounded brought to Saipan by the hospital ship, including Tom Fern, who had started what became a six-week stay in the hospital for treatment of his burns and the effects of a concussion. Fern jumped at unexpected noises, and he remembered little of what he or anyone else had done during the battle. His friend, Ramon Pressburger, brought him up to date, but Fern laughed when Pressburger told Fern that ship scuttlebutt had Becton recommending Fern for a Silver Star for his actions at Mount 44 and for his firefighting efforts afterwards.

"Tom has hurt his hand and cannot write and say for you not to worry about him," Pressburger wrote Fern's mother on April 29, after visiting his friend. "He will write soon. While we are talking about Tom I want to tell you that you have a boy to be proud of. I can't tell you much, but like we say, he has a lot of guts."[15]

Fern learned enough information about the action from Pressburger, Becton, and others to enable him to relay it to family. In a May 1 letter he informed his aunt that the "concussion of the blast laid me low." He added, "we sure made a name for ourselves tho being credited for 17 planes. The skipper came around to see us—congratulated me for sticking to my guns so to speak." Although he needed time to recover, he wrote her that, "I'm O.K. now—they're keeping me here to give all the rest I need. Tho at times I get pretty nervous over trifles but I get over it in time." In a letter that same day to his father, Fern explained that Pressburger told him he was up for a citation, "and the old man himself congratulated me."[16]

In Saipan Becton also distributed to the crew a memo that contained the many laudatory messages the ship and crew had received for their actions. One destroyer commander conveyed that "your magnificent fight the other day was something we will never forget. We are proud to be destroyer sailors on the same team with you." Captain Frederick Moosbrugger, who had gained fame for his aggressive actions as a destroyer commander in the Solomons, wrote, "we are sorry to see your big blue team leave our midst but as long as you remain somewhere in the Pacific we will always know where to look for some punch in a pinch." To those and the other flattering dispatches, Becton remarked, "to the above I would like to add that I am extremely proud of all of you for I think that you and our shipmates who were struck down in this action have performed one of the most outstanding feats I have observed or heard of in this war."[17]

During the afternoon on May 1, Becton and *Laffey* departed Saipan for Eniwetok, leaving behind for treatment Fern and the other seriously wounded men. After a two-hour stop to repair a small hole below the water line, the ship continued her journey, arriving at Eniwetok on May 4.

The crew remained aboard the ship, however, as within less than twenty-four hours *Laffey* was underway for Pearl Harbor, acting as escort for the freighter SS *Dashing Wave* (XAP). Some saw the incongruity of the battle-ravaged *Laffey* and her few operable guns acting as protector for the freighter. "We were an escort ship in a convoy, but we couldn't do any escorting," said Torpedoman's Mate Gemmell. "We only had a few guns that could operate. It was comical to think we could escort anybody. They escorted us."[18]

Because the aft sections had been so badly damaged, the crew doubled up in sleeping compartments and men shared their extra dungarees. The fantail was so ravaged that "I wondered how the ship was going to hold together," said Sonarman Zack. "We were in the middle of the Pacific, and patched up all over." One time Zack swore that he saw the fantail slightly sway left and right in the comparatively calm seas. Though it might have been an optical illusion, the moment made him think, "Boy, I hope we don't have any bad weather!"[19]

Fortune proved kind, however, and *Laffey* entered Pearl Harbor on May 12. As *Dashing Wave* departed her companion, Captain Royal W. Abbott, Commander of Transport Division Fifty aboard the ship, radioed Becton, "it was an honor to be escorted by you." More impressively, as the destroyer slowly passed by moored cruisers and destroyers, the crews of each ship stood along the rails, saluting the game *Laffey* in a sign of respect. "The ships were along piers, and it was quite a sight to see ships dip their colors— lower the U.S. flag to half-mast and then back up," said Phoutrides. "Most of us had tears in our eyes."[20]

The Acting Commander, Cruisers and Destroyers, Pacific Fleet, Rear Admiral W. K. Phillips, invited the officers to a party at the Destroyer Officers' Club and treated the crew to a beach party, where they enjoyed all the beer, hamburgers, and hotdogs they desired. Admiral Nimitz sent over his congratulations, and headquarters asked Becton to draw a diagram outlining the twenty-two attacking kamikazes and to describe the battle in a series of presentations to headquarters personnel. Superiors subsequently relayed the drawing to the noted historian, Samuel Eliot Morison, who included it in his monumental history of naval operations in the war. Becton's family sent a telegram informing him that everyone back home in Hotsprings, Arkansas, was excited with the news and proud of his heroism.

"It was a good time to let down," explained Sonarman Zack. "I thought they'd fix us up at Pearl Harbor and send us back to the war, but I at least felt we would have a breather anyway."[21]

The ship had suffered such extensive damage, however, that, even though Pearl Harbor possessed the capabilities to repair most of it, officials did not want to tie up the facilities for one ship when so many other destroyers and cruisers could be patched up and returned to the war sooner. They decided to make temporary repairs and send *Laffey* back to the States, where West Coast shipyards could handle the remainder. "Good news," Gauding recorded in his diary. "*Laffey* to be repaired in States."[22]

"There was a lot of cheering and men shouting, 'We're going to the States!'" said Zack of the news that they would, at a minimum, be away from the war for a few months. "It didn't cross my mind that the war might end while we were home and that I was done with combat, though. I was always thinking that I would have to go back."[23] After eight months in the Pacific, capped by the incredible April 16 performance, most of the crew would see home and loved ones again.

"A Featherweight with a Joe Louis Wallop"

On May 14 the ship left for the United States. *Laffey* rendezvoused with the freighter SS *Wisconsin* (XAP), whom she would escort to San Francisco before turning north for the Seattle area. With time on their hands, sixty of the crew formed a betting pool centering on the minute the destroyer dropped anchor in San Francisco. Each man put in $20, making a tidy $1,200 to be split between the winner and the man who organized it, with $1,000 going to the winner.

As the ship neared the United States, the crew picked up music from home. Standards such as Glenn Miller's "(I've Got a Gal in) Kalamazoo" and Bing Crosby's smash "I'll Get By" made them think of times past, when high school girls and teen romances thrived. They soon shed the trappings of war. "When we saw land," said Sonarman Zack, "it was a wonderful sight! For the first time we could feel completely safe."[24]

On May 21 *Laffey*, with Seaman Johnson pocketing the betting pool winnings, left the *Wisconsin* behind at San Francisco and veered north to Seattle. Becton took advantage of two men with Seattle ties—Quartermaster Phoutrides and Seaman Martinis—by calling them to the bridge and asking them to point out navigational landmarks. Two days later, Becton moored *Laffey* in Seattle, according to Becton "thirty-nine days after the hell of radar-picket station 1."[25]

The ship arrived to a warm welcome from both the citizens of Seattle and the nation as well. The single sailors among the crew loved the greetings sent by female shipyard workers as the *Laffey* arrived. "As we pulled in, all these women working in the shipyards, driving forklifts, began waving and shouting, 'See you later, fellas!'" said Sonarman Zack. "It was a great feeling. It was strange to see females working these machines. Seattle was a good liberty town. People were very good to us."[26]

The Navy praised the ship that had seemingly evaded an inescapable trap, releasing photographs and stories about *Laffey* and her crew that appeared on page one of daily editions. "The destroyer USS *Laffey*, a featherweight with a Joe Louis wallop, came home today after taking the worst the Kamikaze could throw at her," announced the Navy in an official bulletin. After adding *Laffey* "lived through eighty minutes of hell," the Navy claimed her record off Okinawa "has placed her among the great Navy ships of all time."[27]

The nation's newspapers were as effusive. The *New York Times* called *Laffey* "a destroyer with a heart that couldn't be broken" and concluded that "her stand against a massed enemy fleet off Okinawa last April will go down in naval annals." The *Arizona Republic* said "a captain who 'would never abandon ship as long as a gun would fire' sailed into naval history with the gallant crew of the USS *Laffey* today."[28]

Seattle's media topped them all. "The newspapers here are sure giving us a big write up," Seaman Johnson wrote home on May 25. In the *Seattle Times* reporter Robert Mahaffay wrote, "under the eyes of Seattle in Elliott Bay today was the destroyer U.S.S. *Laffey*, heroine of one of Okinawa's most savage battles, still fire-blackened, still crippled and slashed from the death strikes of Japanese suicide planes." He said that kamikazes struck her so often that they ripped "her thin steel until it looked like torn confetti" and "her decks were a maze of wreckage. . . . She was reeling helplessly, out of control. Fires raged amid ships and along the stern." Mahaffay's rival at the *Seattle Post-Intelligencer*, R. B. Bermann, concluded that "if Francis Scott Key could have been aboard the destroyer *Laffey* when she was fighting off a horde of Japanese planes . . . he might have been inspired to write an even more moving national anthem than 'The Star-Spangled Banner.'"[29]

Becton freely handed out praise in his action report. He declared the work of the Combat Air Patrol excellent, but added that "more of the same would certainly have been appreciated during those warm 80 minutes." He praised his engineers for maintaining the speed necessary to fend off the swarms of kamikazes, and the men who left damaged stations to pick up fire hoses and contain the fires that threatened the ship. He called the damage control parties "fearless" for combating fires despite the proximity of exploding ammunition. He said the crew's performance was outstanding, both during the action and in the aftermath, when the survivors battled to save their ship and treat their wounded. "The courage, skill, and resourcefulness of the ship's officers and men during and following this action was inspiring and completely justified the commanding officer's faith in, and respect for, the personnel under his command. They fought their ship gallantly, they kept it afloat, and, with the help of the efficient tugs, they brought it back to safety."

He singled out the men on the 40mm and 20mm guns, including Seamen Johnson and Fern, who stood at their guns as multiple kamikazes charged straight toward them. "The courage of the machine gunners, in remaining at their unprotected stations and in keeping up their fire until put out of action was undoubtedly an important factor in saving the ship from more serious damage or complete loss. Especially deserving of mention were the 20mm gunners, of whom at least four were killed 'in the straps,' firing to the last. Too much credit cannot be given these fearless young men for their magnificent courage and devotion to duty."[30]

As any military unit under fire exhibits, the *Laffey* crew illustrated on April 16 that heroes come from the unlikeliest of places. The roster included college students and high school dropouts, a preacher and a playboy, a beloved officer and a detested one, yet on that April morning each nudged aside the dangers and nobly served their nation, their skipper, and their shipmates. Their combined efforts assured that the *Laffey* and her men would be recognized as one of those gallant ships that waged a triumphant fight despite the overwhelming forces that assailed her.

For their gallantry, Becton, his officers, and men were awarded the Presidential Unit Citation, an honor recognizing the efforts of a team in battle. What Becton began at the February 1944 Boston commissioning of the ice-covered ship and continued off Normandy and during the Philippine landings, matured on April 16, 1945. "Fighting her guns valiantly against waves of hostile suicide planes plunging toward her from all direction, the U.S.S. *Laffey* sent up relentless barrages of antiaircraft fire during an extremely heavy and concentrated air attack," proclaimed the award citation. The crew "withstood the devastating blows unflinchingly and, despite severe damage and heavy casualties, continued to fight effectively until the last plane had been driven off." The "courage, superb seamanship and indomitable determination of her officers and men enabled the *Laffey* to defeat the enemy against almost insurmountable odds."[31]

Becton came in for his own share of acclaim. Captain B. R. Harrison, the commander of Destroyer Squadron Sixty, praised "the outstanding ability displayed by the Commanding Officer in fighting his ship. His superb ship handling resulted in taking most of the damage aft and in many cases, avoiding the full effect of the crashes." Harrison claimed that the work of the gunnery, engineering, and damage control parties "show what an effectively organized ship under inspiring leadership can accomplish against almost hopeless odds."[32]

Becton received the Navy's highest honor, the Navy Cross, for his actions on April 16. The award mentioned that "Commander Becton skillfully countered the fanatical enemy tactics, employing every conceivable maneuver and directing all his guns in an intense and unrelenting barrage of fire to protect his ship against the terrific onslaught." The award said that Becton "emerged at the close of the action with his gallant warship afloat and still an effective fighting unit." Becton's leadership, according to the citation, was "inspiring to those who served with him."[33]

The men agreed that without Becton's abilities to mold an effective crew that could ably defend the ship, and without his talent in maneuvering the destroyer to avoid worse damage, *Laffey* would today rest at the bottom of the ocean, a silent tomb holding the remains of every officer and man. "His strategy saved the ship off Okinawa," Lieutenant Lloyd Hull asserted unhesitatingly. "Those of us who survived," said Seaman Lonnie Eastham, "are a direct result of Becton's leadership."[34]

"The Ship Was Cleaned Up, But It Still Looked Bad!"

Before *Laffey* left Pearl Harbor, the Navy Department had decided to turn a national spotlight on the ship and her crew. "There is a lot about the *Laffey* in the newsreels," Seaman Johnson wrote his mother. "I have seen quite a few."[35]

Now that they had reached Seattle, newspapers, magazines, and radio shows requested interviews with principal participants, and the Navy announced plans to take the extraordinary wartime step of opening the ship to public visitation in Seattle and Tacoma. With Hitler recently defeated in Europe, public apathy had set in. Workers, who considered Germany as the nation's main threat, began leaving defense plants and shipyards for more enticing jobs. The Navy Department estimated that in recent months, 16,000 workers had departed shipyards near Portland alone. Just as American forces neared Japan proper and the prospects of a bloody invasion of the Home Islands loomed, home front laborers exited their crucial work. Navy officials hoped that if the public viewed the mangled gun mounts and inspected the holes punched into *Laffey*'s decks—or read about what had happened to the *Laffey*—it would realize that the war was far from over.

From 1:00 p.m. to 9:00 p.m. each day, May 26 to May 30, the public was able to board the ship and walk the main decks. Lines of people stretched for two blocks along the dock, and 2,849 visitors boarded in the first two hours alone. Crew posted at various stations explained to men, women, and children what had happened at that spot. They told of Ondracek's courage in trying to detonate the enemy bomb with his bullets, of Waite and Logan being trapped belowdecks, of Youngquist and Fern on the 40mm gun, of McCarthy climbing the mast to raise a new battle flag, and of Delewski and his crew in the ravaged Mount 53. Mothers and fathers stared at the bullet holes punctured into bulkheads, including the one directly above the tiger in the ship's emblem painted on the bridge, all the while imagining what their own sons or acquaintances must then be enduring in the Pacific. "They seemed stunned," said Quartermaster Phoutrides. "It was quite a sight for anybody. The ship was cleaned up, but it still looked bad!"[36]

As the people moved from place to place, some asked questions of the crew. Their answers took on added meaning when relayed in the surroundings of the battered warship. "If shipyard workers could only see what men and ships have to go through, they'd stick to their jobs," said Phoutrides at the time to a reporter who asked why the Navy opened *Laffey* to visitation. "If the fellows who work could only see the men who died in their straps."[37]

The public relations move had the desired effect. The mangled barrels of Delewski's Mount 53 said more to the 65,000 people who visited the ship in the five days at Seattle than any flowery news article could convey. According to a reporter, "her scars revealed to a touched and misty-eyed crowd thronging across her decks" what happened when loved ones headed to war. "If you don't see things like this," said Al Hudson, one of the visitors, "you can't realize what has happened. Nobody else can tell you what things like that really mean. You have to see the results yourself."[38]

The number of men and women who applied for shipyard jobs skyrocketed following the destroyer's public inspection, and the stream of workers leaving for other occupations slowed. "Folks certainly got it, and it meant something, too," wrote reporter Robert Mahaffay in the *Seattle Times* on June 3 of the impact made on the public by the *Laffey*. "Ship repair workers and others who had begun to show signs of wanting to drift along home, decided the war wasn't as close to over as it had seemed, and took another hitch in their belts." He added, "We're still short of shipyard manpower, but more of it is beginning to show up as a result of *Laffey's* being here."[39]

Seattle citizens bestowed royal treatment on the crew. When she learned who they were, a waitress at one hotel restaurant set aside steaks—horribly difficult to find during the war—for Seaman Johnson and his buddies.

On Memorial Day, Captain J. P. Forsander, senior chaplain of the Thirteenth Naval District, officiated at a memorial ceremony aboard the *Laffey*. Guests included Ensign Thomsen's parents, Jack Ondracek's sister, and the families of other men who had been killed on April 16. On May 27 Becton appeared as a guest on the national radio show, *We the People*. In hopes of enticing civilians to open their wallets, a magazine and newspaper ad promoting war bonds prominently featured a photograph of the damaged *Laffey*, accompanied by oversized letters cautioning readers, "There's Still A Big Job To Do!" Becton spoke to the midshipmen at the Naval Academy about the methods he employed to extricate his ship from harm, and he and other officers addressed civic groups to spread the story of April 16 and to warn listeners the war was not over. "I'd like to have some of the people who think it's all over out there with me for just a few days," said Becton to one crowd on May 25. *True Comics* even featured the *Laffey* story in its Winter 1945 issue, concluding that "*Laffey*'s two hours of heroism and agony is one of the greatest sea epics of the war."[40]

The Navy Department followed the successful five-day exhibit in Seattle with a two-day stint in nearby Tacoma. From then until the end of August, the ship rested in Seattle's shipyards, where work forces mended battle damage so extensive that shipyard engineers at first concluded it was impossible to repair.

On June 26 the only skipper the destroyer had known stepped down when Commander Odale D. Waters Jr. assumed command so that Becton could take a new post in Washington, DC. In Becton's final remarks to his crew during the ceremony, he told his men how proud he was of their efforts, that he was fortunate to call them his shipmates, and that the ship's success was due to "the indomitable spirit of her men." Quartermaster Phoutrides, who respected Becton almost as much as he did his father, and the others choked back tears, and Sonarman Zack and the rest of the crew knew that they had witnessed the last of a revered commander. After handing command to Waters, Becton tried to leave before his men noticed the tears forming in his eyes, but an enlisted man stopped him. "Captain, sir," said the sailor Becton had retained despite a court-martial's recommendation to discharge him, "I just wanted to say goodbye and thanks."[41] With tears coursing down their cheeks, the two shook hands and Becton hurried along the pier, sad that he would never again command such brave men.

While the ship was being repaired, the crew enjoyed its first extensive leave since the previous summer. Becton wrote notes to the families of each man who perished in the April attack, an emotionally exhausting endeavor in which Becton individualized each letter to relate something personal about the man for his family. He ended most notes by writing, "in your hours of grief and sorrow the officers and men of the *Laffey* give you our heartfelt sympathy. The memory of your brave son will live forever in the hearts of all of us who had the honor and privilege of having him for a shipmate."[42]

Becton hoped a reunion with Imogen Carpenter might improve his spirits, but the relationship failed to blossom. He enjoyed dinner and attended parties with Carpenter, who had moved to Los Angeles to further her career, and met Robert Montgomery and Jimmy Cagney, but Becton could see that Imogen preferred an entertainment career to that of being a Navy wife. To her credit, she declined to send Becton a Dear John note during the war, instead mailing upbeat letters to boost his morale, but the romance had ended before Becton returned. Becton appreciated her loyalty in waiting until he was home to inform him of her feelings, writing that with her cheerful letters, "Imogen, in her own way, like all my men, had helped me save the *Laffey*."[43]

Lieutenant Youngquist experienced the opposite when on June 11 he married his college sweetheart. After Ari Phoutrides gave away his sister in marriage on July 22, he took a few days to visit the family of Ensign Thomsen in Portland. When Thomsen's mother asked Phoutrides if her son had suffered, instead of telling her that her son burned to death fighting fires, Phoutrides said he had died from a bomb concussion that left no visible wounds on his body.

After surviving kamikazes and bombs on April 16, Sonarman Zack almost died traveling to see family in Pittsfield, Massachusetts. As the train sped across the country, the blazing gasoline tank of a gravel truck hit by the train bounced off Zack's window and onto the terrain along the tracks. Although one man was killed, an unharmed Zack could not help but think of the irony of surviving a fiery battle, only to come close to dying by fire in a train rushing back home.

Tom Fern finally rejoined the crew on June 8 after a long sojourn in hospitals. He wrote home that "it sure was nice to get back with the crew again. The fellows were surprized [sic] that my face wasn't scarred up. I must have been a sight when I left the ship (on a stretcher)." He added that he still had difficulty remaining in confined spaces because "it gets on my nerves so."[44]

Seaman Dockery best captured everyone's feelings about being home. "We all thought, 'We made it. We're safe.' We now had no worries about kamikazes."[45]

"Most of Us Have Seen Our Share of War"

While shipyard workers repaired *Laffey*, events in the Pacific wound toward a conclusion. The early August atomic obliterations of Hiroshima and Nagasaki forced the Japanese emperor, Hirohito, to seek peace. In an August 15 broadcast to his nation, Hirohito explained that they had no recourse but to bear the inevitable and accept surrender terms from the United States.

The announcement caused wild celebrations in the United States. "Boy, people here were sure having a big time last night when they heard about the war being over," wrote Seaman Johnson of Seattle's celebration. "I guess they tore up Seattle."[46]

The crew was more relieved than jubilant at the news. They had seen enough combat on April 16 and did not look forward to returning to the Pacific for more. Fireman Gauding entered only one word in his diary on August 14, "Peace!!" Phoutrides wrote to Becton that "there was the usual amount of whistle tooting, slapping each other on the back, and talk of immediate discharge." Phoutrides agreed that neither he nor anyone in the crew should complain, but "most of us have seen our share of the war and resent any little thing that reminds us of it. We don't want to hear of or see Pearl Harbor, Ulithi, Okinawa, or Lingayen."[47] For the first time since they had gathered as a crew in Boston, though, the men could at least begin planning for a life after war.

The same was not true for *Laffey*'s antagonist, Admiral Onishi. After creating the kamikaze corps, which inflicted vast destruction on the American fleet, Onishi saw his creation disbanded. The day after Hirohito's announcement, Onishi penned final messages to family and friends. "I wish to express my deep appreciation to the souls of the brave special attackers," he wrote. "They fought and died valiantly with faith in our ultimate victory. In death I wish to atone for my part in the failure to achieve that victory and I apologize to the souls of these dead fliers and their bereaved families."[48] Onishi then spread a white sheet on the floor and disemboweled himself with his sword.

Laffey returned to the fleet in September 1945. On September 11, while leaving San Diego to participate in sonar exercises, *Laffey* collided with *PC-815* in a thick fog. *Laffey*'s stem hit abaft the PC's bridge, causing fires that sank the smaller vessel within five minutes and killed one sailor.

Tom Fern was in the forecastle with shipmates "when crash-boompty-boom. On the deck we went," he wrote to his mother. He and the others rushed to man hoses, and then realized what had happened. "The cause of all this was a ship wrapped around our bow burning like all get out. She sank so badly torn up was she. Only took about 3 minutes." Seaman Johnson was catching a few winks when the collision occurred. "We were doing about 20m.p.h. when we hit them so you know it was a hard hit. It sank within 3 minutes. I was asleep, and boy did I get up fast."[49]

Although there were no casualties aboard *Laffey*, the inauspicious start for Waters resulted in a Court of Inquiry. After an investigation, the Court declined to remove Waters from command.

In October Waters took the ship to Pearl Harbor, where in an impressive October 27 ceremony the Navy awarded medals to twelve of the surviving crew for their actions on April 16. Counting the deceased, twenty-seven men received awards for the battle, including the Navy Cross awarded to Becton and Lieutenant Runk, Silver Stars for Seaman Fern and Ensign Townsley, and Bronze Stars to Lieutenant Youngquist, Gunner's Mate Delewski, and Seaman Martinis. The ceremony applied the finishing touches to the World War II exploits of *Laffey* and her crew.

Laffey's service continued after World War II. In July 1946 the ship participated in the Bikini Atoll nuclear weapons tests. Although many of the World War II crew had already returned to civilian life others, including Seaman Lee Hunt, were still aboard. After being subjected to the ghastly April 16 kamikaze attack, Hunt and his shipmates now witnessed the birth of the ultimate kamikaze—a nuclear weapon that could destroy the world.

The ship was decommissioned in 1947, but returned to the fleet four years later during the Korean conflict. The ship operated in the Mediterranean as part of the Sixth Fleet before again being decommissioned in 1975.

"That One I Treasure Most of All"

The crew went their different ways after the war. Becton married Elizabeth Reuss in 1949 and remained in the Navy until 1966, when he retired a rear admiral. No matter how busy he became, he always had time to take a phone call from or exchange correspondence with his shipmates, who frequently sought his advice. Becton's home featured numerous memorabilia and photographs from the war and his career, but the plaque bearing the names of his *Laffey* crew occupied the most prominent spot. "The one over there with all the names," he explained in 1992 to a reporter to whom he showed his collection, "they're my crew on the *Laffey*." He added, "that one I treasure most of all."[50]

They treasured him as well. "The crew had faith in your judgment and profound respect in your ability as commanding officer,"[51] Ari Phoutrides wrote to Becton. During the Korean conflict Phoutrides, who had never lost touch with Becton and was now an officer, asked for Becton's advice on how to be a good leader. Becton reminded him to treat everyone with respect, and not to take on work that subordinate officers could do. If so, those officers would expect Phoutrides to continue to perform functions they should be conducting.

Phoutrides, who missed the presence of his former skipper, remarked to Becton that he had benefited from his service aboard *Laffey*. "I've received an education of a sort that would never be found in textbooks." He added that "my part in this war was minute and insignificant. However, there is a certain satisfaction knowing that I was doing a little something for the war. I will live to enjoy the comforts of a hard earned peace for many years. It would be foolish to have any regrets in this light." Typically, Phoutrides saved his most personal comments for last. "I am grateful for knowing and serving under you, Captain. I am extremely proud of your part in this war and your ability to pull our ship through whatever were the odds against us. I will always have the deepest respect for this ship and its crew."[52]

Following surgery for a brain tumor, Becton died at his Wynnewood, Pennsylvania, home on Christmas Day, 1995, at the age of 87. In his eulogy for the admiral Phoutrides attempted to explain what the man meant to him and to the rest of the crew. "He has traversed his road with honor, with a deep and unselfish devotion to his country, and with compassion and understanding for those under his command." Trying to contain his emotions, Phoutrides spoke to his now deceased leader. "Thank you for bringing the crew of the USS *Laffey* home safely. Thank you for your devotion and service to our great country. Thank you for the inspiration you provided us not only during a period of conflict, but also during a period of peace. Thank you for the manner in which you touched our individual lives."[53]

In a 2014 interview with the author, Phoutrides explained that his admiration for Becton remains fervent today. Phoutrides became a better person for having served under Becton, whose decency and command abilities affected an untested teenager. "I was just a young kid in the war, but he inspired me. He taught me lessons on how to get along with people. It was an honor to serve with him."[54]

Two photographs rest side by side on a table in Phoutrides's Portland home. One is of his father, a man Phoutrides respected above all. The second is of Becton, the officer whose actions during the war him earned a respect similar to the one the quartermaster had previously reserved for only one man.

Tom Fern left the Navy in late 1945, not yet fully recovered from his wounds. The physical ailments diminished, but he struggled with the mental adjustments. According to his wife, Marguerite, whom Fern married in

1950, in the first year following the war Fern was a scared kid who jumped at unexpected noises. Her companionship calmed the young man, and Fern remained proud of his association with the *Laffey* until his death in 2010. The huge scrapbook he and his wife assembled through the years, bearing a page containing the bold letters, I SERVED IN THE UNITED STATES NAVY, was testament to the love he carried for his ship. Each time Fern and Marguerite opened the volume, Fern could rest assured that his courageous actions against the kamikazes that assailed his ship on April 16 gained the respect of his commander and his shipmates, and that he had matched the Civil War and World War I exploits of Patrick and Henry Fern.

Ari Phoutrides left the Navy in 1946, only to be recalled in 1950 for the Korean clash. He completed his college education in mechanical engineering at the University of Washington, is still married to Betty, with whom he exchanged vows in 1949, and as of 2014 was in excellent health in Portland, Oregon.

Robert Johnson also left the Navy in 1946. He used the GI Bill of Rights to attend business school, after which he worked for an accounting firm for forty years. He and his wife, Loreen, today still reside in Richmond, Virginia.

Daniel Zack returned to Pittsfield, Massachusetts, where he currently lives after a thirty-nine-year career working in the testing program at General Electric. He married his wife, Phyllis in 1948 who, after a long life together, passed away in 2014. "The war matured me," he says. "I was very immature when I went to war, but I learned a lot about people. In war, people act differently. Some do what they're supposed to do, and others back down. It's an experience no one knows until they get into that situation."[55]

After leaving the Navy in 1946, Pay Youngquist earned a master's in business administration from Harvard. After briefly working in the banking field, Youngquist entered real estate and taught college business courses for thirty-seven years. He resides in Glendale, California, where the ninety-two-year-old splits his time between his real estate office, area golf courses, and his wife, Shirley, two daughters, three grandchildren, and three great-grandchildren.

Robert Dockery returned to high school to earn a diploma. After a career in bookkeeping, he joined the Los Angeles fire department, where he worked for a quarter century. He remains close to shipmate Robert Johnson, and spends time with his sons and daughters, eighteen grandchildren, and eight great-grandchildren.

Lawrence Delewski made a promise to God that if he survived the war, he would try to do something different with his life. He played college football for two years, where he earned a teaching degree. After graduating in 1949, he kept his pledge by teaching special education high school students and coaching football in Pottstown, Pennsylvania. Delewski passed away in 2010.

Andrew Martinis earned a medical degree in 1954 and became a prominent heart surgeon in Seattle, participating in some of the earliest heart surgeries in the northwest. He currently enjoys his retirement in Edmonds, Washington, with his wife, Magna, two children, and three grandchildren.

J. V. Porlier, one of the members of the FIDO team that joined *Laffey* shortly before the battle, vowed to focus on his family after the war. For the rest of his life, he declined to work late hours and avoided weekend golf outings so he could be home with his wife and children.

Bert Remsen may have enjoyed the most unusual postwar career. The handsome seaman, saved when Gunner's Mate Delewski rolled him about the deck to douse the flames then engulfing him, became a Hollywood actor, appearing in 191 television shows and films and becoming an acquaintance with Carl Reiner, Robert Altman, Jill St. John, and others. He started in television, commencing with his role as a guard in the 1952 program, *Suspense*, and continued through appearances in *Perry Mason*, *The Andy Griffith Show*, *The Dick Van Dyke Show*, *Columbo*, and *Dallas*. His film credits include parts in *Nashville*, *McCabe & Mrs. Miller*, and *The Bodyguard*. He died in 1999.

"The Ship Is Like a Magnet"

Although the crew went their different ways, the ship kept drawing them back. At a 1973 reunion in Alexandria, Virginia, Becton and the others discussed their concerns about the eventual fate of the *Laffey*. They hated seeing her slowly rust or go to the scrapheap, so they decided to save her, just as she had saved them in April 1945. "We didn't want the breakers to do what the Japanese had never been able to do—finish her," wrote Becton. "We were not going to abandon *Laffey* as long as there was one if us left to fight for her. And we were going to win."[56]

The USS *Laffey* (DD-724) Association began searching for a city willing to adopt and maintain the ship. In 1981 the Patriots Point Naval and Maritime Museum in Charleston, South Carolina, accepted *Laffey* from the Navy and placed her as a floating museum alongside another renowned World War II vessel, the aircraft carrier USS *Yorktown* (CV-10), whom

Laffey escorted to the coast of Japan for the February 1945 air raids against the Tokyo area. Five years later the ship was designated a National Historic Landmark.

With falling budgets, the ship fell into disrepair and rust ate small holes into the decks. With little prospect of aid from government agencies, the men of *Laffey* banded together to organize work parties that once or twice a year gathered at the ship to scrape, paint, and clean a ship that had been their home in trying times. The bond these men have with their ship led to newspaper articles and an appearance on a November 10, 1982, episode of NBC's *Real People*. Because of the work parties, which continue as of this writing, "the ship is good for another eighty years," said Seaman Joseph Dixon. "That makes us feel good."[57]

The attachment between ship and crew is undeniable. "The ship is like a magnet which brings us back together once more," said Tom Fern. "It's a living legacy which we can pass down to our children. I don't ever want to give it up or forget what it involved." Lee Hunt adds that he "grew up on that ship. I went on it when I was 17 and spent my 18th birthday killing people in Germany in the invasion of France and right on into Okinawa and the Philippines and what have you. This means a lot. I spent a lot of time on that ship."[58]

They hope to pass those feelings to family and to succeeding generations. When asked why people should know the *Laffey* story, crew provided a wide range of answers. "It's a story of a ship that wouldn't die," answered Torpedoman's Mate Gemmell. "There aren't many of those like that." Lieutenant Youngquist said the ship and crew provide a valuable lesson for today's world. "It seems that today people are so fragmented. We showed that we were united, and that people could do the job that had to be done." Doctor Martinis pointed to "the bravery of the people aboard. People stayed at their posts and did their jobs, even in the face of death, doing what they were trained to do," while Ari Phoutrides emphasized that people today "should know that people sacrificed to help others, not only our ship, but every unit. Future generations need to keep that in mind." The answer seemed simple, but powerful, to Robert Johnson. "People should know because of the hardships that service people had to endure. There's so much bravery. People volunteered, like I did, and we did our duty to our country."[59]

H. G. Walker, the son of Chief Gunner's Mate Warren Walker, who received a Bronze Star for his actions in charge of Mount 52, attended the

1966 reunion with his father. The then-fifteen-year-old was struck with the love the men exhibited toward *Laffey*. "To them, she is a shrine. It is visible in their faces as they gaze upon the majestic grey vessel." He added, "Here they lost the innocence of youth, and the hard, cold, unsympathetic reality of war was realized."[60]

Becton hoped that by keeping the ship afloat at Patriots Point, people through the decades would enjoy a living reminder of all that is important. Although the destroyer never leaves her moorings and crew no longer rush to battle stations, each time a visitor climbs her gangway, it rekindles the memories of Becton and Phoutrides on the bridge, of Youngquist, Johnson, and Zack at their guns, of Burgess clutching the flag as he died, and of the self-sacrifice of Jack Ondracek.

The ship's active days may be over, but as Becton related, "she is alive with shades and memories of brave deeds and the brave Americans who did them. They are still with her and will be always. It is my hope that those who visit her, most especially the young, will come to know and perhaps be inspired by them. If that happens, then what *Laffey* did will not have been in vain."[61]

The years and ailments have taken a toll on the men of the *Laffey*. Fewer than thirty remain alive as of this writing, and only a handful are able to make the pilgrimage to South Carolina to see their ship. However, the memories remain strong; the bond with ship and crew fervent; the impact on their lives undeniable.

The survivors are proud that succeeding generations can walk their ship and gain a feel for what it must have been like for the crew to man guns and swab decks. Because of their efforts to keep *Laffey* alive, she will long float as an example of what a group of individuals can do when united by sound leadership and a deep sense of duty.

"*Laffey*, the ship that would not die, did not die,"[62] wrote Becton.

Neither time, rust, nor the Japanese could conquer her.

> *The gallant deeds and heroes' lore*
> *Of DD Seven Twenty Four*
> *Will be enshrined forevermore.*
> —"Invicta," Lieutenant Matthew Darnell

LIST OF THE CREW
ON APRIL 16, 1945

Adams, Machinist's Mate 3/c William
Addison, Lieutenant W. T.
Anderson, Seaman 1/c Mark G.
Andrews, Fireman 1/c Ralph R., Jr.
Annino, Seaman 1/c Calvin W.
Asadorian, Water Tender 3/c Zorob
Babcock, Fireman 1/c Myron W.
Bahme, Lieutenant (jg) J.
Ballenger, Fireman 1/c Jack A.
Barbeau, Chief Fire Controlman
    William A.
Barber, Seaman 1/c Harold W.
Barlow, Seaman 1/c Fred E.
Bassett, Radioman 3/c George E.
Baumhardt, Boatswain's Mate 2/c
    Arthur
Beall, Fireman 1/c George G.
Becton, Commander F. Julian
Belk, Seaman 1/c Ernest E.
Bell, Sonarman 2/c Charles W.
Bell, Seaman 1/c James P.
Bell, Machinist's Mate 3/c John E., Jr.
Benson, Electrician's Mate 3/c
    Henry M.
Bineau, Seaman 2/c Roland
Boothe, Seaman 1/c Roy C.
Borcich, Seaman 1/c Emil C.

Bracci, Seaman 1/c Vincent F.
Branka, Fireman 1/c John E.
Brennan, Fireman 1/c Raymond F.
Brinkley, Machinist's Mate 3/c
    Clarence E.
Britton, Fireman 1/c Robert E.
Brock, Steward's Mate 3/c Isaac
Broussard, Coxswain Charles A.
Brown, Seaman 1/c Donald E.
Brown, Torpedoman 3/c Edward J.
Brown, Seaman 1/c James L.
Brusoe, Water Tender 1/c Richard A.
Burgess, Yeoman 3/c Fred D., Jr.
Burnett, Fire Controlman 3/c
    George R.
Bussert, Seaman 1/c Karl E.
Cahill, Boiler Tender 3/c Thomas J.
Cain, Radioman 2/c Joseph F.
Calafato, Fireman 1/c Anthony F.
Calisti, Seaman 1/c Bruno J.
Call, Fireman 1/c Grady E.
Campbell, Water Tender 1/c
    Robert L.
Carlo, Seaman 1/c Michael A., Jr.
Carney, Fireman 1/c Robert R.
Carter, Seaman 1/c Donald
Carver, Seaman 2/c Douglas C.

Cerce, Seaman 1/c James

Cibulka, Motor Machinist's Mate 3/c
John, Jr.

Cloer, Boatswain's Mate 2/c
Calvin Wesley

Coffman, Boatswain's Mate 1/c
Kenneth D.

Cooper, Seaman 1/c Edwin

Cronin, Radarman 2/c John E.

Crump, Fireman 1/c Douglas C.

Curtin, Radarman 3/c David M.

Dannelly, Seaman 1/c Fitzugh B.

D'Aquila, Seaman 1/c Anthony

Darnell, Lieutenant (jg)
Matthew C., Jr.

Daugherty, Radarman 3/c Robert H.

Decker, Electrician's Mate 2/c
Norris H.

Delewski, Gunner's Mate 2/c
Lawrence H.

Dickey, Coxswain Andrew T.

Dickey, Machinist's Mate 2/c
Dennis J.

Dixon, Seaman 1/c Joseph E.

Dockery, Seaman 1/c Robert W.

Donald, Seaman 1/c William L.

Doran, Quartermaster 1/c John F.

Dorr, Fireman 2/c Robert L.

Dorris, Seaman 1/c Alfred J.

Doyle, Chief Yeoman Pierce V.

Dubbs, Chief Machinist's Mate
Carl H.

Dunn, Steward's Mate 1/c John H.

Dunson, Steward's Mate 2/c Clyde A.

Earnst, Torpedoman's Mate 1/c
Jack O.

Eastham, Seaman 1/c Lonnie H.

Edmonds, Seaman 1/c Joe W.

Edwards, Coxswain Bernard

Englehardt, Radar Technician 1/c
August G.

Essig, Ship's Cook 2/c Daniel M.

Evans, Seaman 1/c John B.

Faginski, Coxswain Raymond H.

Falotico, Coxswain George

Faulkner, Seaman 1/c William D.

Fern, Seaman 1/c Thomas B.

Flanders, Seaman 1/c William A.

Flint, Coxswain Chester C.

Foard, Seaman 1/c Raymond R.

Fowler, Fireman 1/c Conley E.

Fowler, Seaman 2/c James L.

Fravel, Lieutenant (jg) James W.

Freimer, Electrician's Mate 3/c
William D.

Frey, Seaman 1/c Lyman L.

Gaddis, Chief Signalman Herman S.

Galvin, Machinist's Mate 2/c
Joseph P.

Gauding, Fireman 1/c Wilbert C.

Gebhart, Gunner's Mate 3/c Francis
M.

Gemmell, Torpedoman's Mate 2/c
Fred M.

Giles, Seaman 1/c Louis F.

Glatthorn, Seaman 1/c John A.

Gray, Carpenter's Mate 3/c
Clarence L.

Griner, Fire Controlman 2/c
Harwell M.

Gudelunes, Ship Fitter 3/c Stanley

Gulsvig, Fireman 1/c Clayton A.

Haberkam, Electrician's Mate 3/c
John H.

Haley, Chief Torpedoman's Mate
Wayne H.

Hallas, Fireman 1/c Francis R.

Hansen, Torpedoman's Mate 2/c
Raymond A.

Hanzel, Ship's Cook 3/c Frank M.

Hardway, Seaman 1/c Carl J.

Harrelson, Seaman 1/c Doris

Harris, Seaman 1/c John W.
Hartnett, Radioman 3/c William J.
Hazen, Machinist's Mate 3/c La
Verne G.
Hearn, Seaman 1/c George L.
Henke, Lieutenant E. A.
Herold, Machinist's Mate 3/c
Ernest C.
Heyes, Seaman 1/c William E.
Hile, Water Tender 2/c Claude C.
Hilton, Seaman 1/c Charles E.
Hintzman, Machinist's Mate 3/c
Donald J.
Hoag, Seaman 1/c Francis G.
Hogan, Machinist's Mate 1/c
Arthur E.
Hoopman, Fireman 1/c Werner F.
Hudgens, Fireman 2/c James H.
Hudgins, Seaman 1/c James R.
Hughes, Storekeeper 2/c Thomas J.
Hull, Lieutenant (jg) Lloyd
Humphries, Lieutenant Samuel M.
Hungerpiller, Chief Machinist's Mate
Marcellous D.
Hunt, Seaman 1/c Lee C.
Hutchins, Seaman 1/c Charles W.
Hyson, Seaman 1/c Richard W.
Irish, Ship Fitter 1/c Madoc K.
Irving, Seaman 1/c George, Jr.
Jackson, Electrician's Mate 2/c
Ralph D.
Janoski, Seaman 1/c George
Johnson, Machinist's Mate 3/c
John A.
Johnson, Seaman 2/c Merle R.
Johnson, Fireman 1/c Paul B.
Johnson, Seaman 2/c Raymond T.
Johnson, Seaman 2/c Robert C.
Johnson, Seaman 2/c Robert E.
Johnson, Fireman 2/c Tyrus R.
Jones, Seaman 1/c K. D., Jr.

Jump, Seaman 1/c Morris H.
Kachigian, Machinist's Mate 3/c
William K.
Kaniewski, Seaman 2/c S. D.
Kapaldo, Ship's Serviceman 3/c
Waitman
Karr, Gunner's Mate 3/c Robert I.
Kelly, Signalman 3/c William M.
Kelley, Radioman 3/c Lawrence F.
Kennedy, Yeoman 3/c Earl R.
Kennedy, Fireman 1/c Robert E.
Ketron, Gunner's Mate 3/c
Stanley H.
Keyes, Chief Boatswain's Mate
William J.
Klein, Radioman 3/c Andrew
Klein, Seaman 1/c Gabriel B.
Klimkewicz, Seaman 2/c Ambrose J.
Klindworth, Seaman 1/c Joseph H.
Kmiecik, Seaman 2/c John J.
Kodman, Chief Pharmacist's Mate
Francis, Jr.
Kohler, Seaman 2/c William R.
Kycia, Seaman 2/c Edward A.
Langevin, Fireman 1/c Reginald
La Pointe, Coxswain James M.
Laskowski, Water Tender 3/c Frank
Latwis, Fireman 1/c Michael
Leary, Radioman 2/c Howard J.
Lebrecht, Seaman 1/c Earl L.
Lefevre, Seaman 1/c Walter
Lehtonen, Gunner's Mate 1/c
Frank W., Jr.
Lesinski, Electrician's Mate 3/c
Frank L.
Letourneau, Sonarman 3/c
Roland E.
Liller, Yeoman 3/c John F., Jr.
Logan, Motor Machinist's Mate 1/c
George S.
Luczkow, Seaman 1/c Benny

Mackin, Fire Controlman 3/c
William H.

Mallette, Seaman 1/c Emile J.

Malone, Seaman 1/c Edwin D.

Malone, Ship Fitter 3/c Harold J.

Manson, Lieutenant Frank A.

Marini, Radioman 3/c Olivion S.

Martin, Radioman 3/c Ralph W.

Martin, Seaman 1/c Ronald G.

Martinis, Seaman 1/c Andrew J.

Masker, Pharmacist's Mate 2/c
William E.

Matthews, Ship's Serviceman 2/c
Jim D.

Matthews, Gunner's Mate 2/c
Marvin S.

Maxwell, Torpedoman's Mate 1/c
Cornelius A.

McBryde, Seaman 1/c Luther B.

McCarthy, Signalman 2/c Thomas B.

McClafferty, Seaman 1/c William T.

McCune, Lieutenant Challen, Jr.

McDonald, Fireman 1/c James F.

McGinnis, Fire Controlman 3/c
Robert L.

McIntyre, Chief Commissary Steward
Clarence B.

Meier, Gunner's Mate 3/c Welles A.

Mele, Gunner's Mate 2/c Joseph E.

Michel, Machinist's Mate 1/c
John W.

Mickle, Baker 3/c Ross W.

Migues, Coxswain Joseph C.

Miller, Seaman 1/c James P.

Miller, Electrician's Mate 3/c
Leonard B.

Miller, Fireman 1/c Morris, Jr.

Molohan, Seaman 1/c Michael A.

Molpus, Lieutenant E. L.

Morris, Seaman 1/c William L.

Mosher, Seaman 1/c Albert R.

Muckerman, Seaman 1/c
Walter B., Jr.

Murray, Radarman 3/c Lawrence J.

Murray, Seaman 1/c Patrick J.

Muskivitch, Seaman 1/c William E.

Najork, Chief Radioman Jack

Neifah, Radarman 3/c Sidney

Newell, Coxswain Francis P.

Nikirk, Fireman 1/c John M.

Nordstrom, Sonarman 3/c Louis D.

Nulf, Radarman 2/c Philip E.

Nulty, Seaman 1/c Ward K., Jr.

Odom, Seaman 1/c Roland

Ondracek, Torpedoman 3/c Jack H.

O'Shaughnessy, Seaman 1/c
William J., Jr.

Osman, Radarman 2/c George G.

Oyer, Seaman 1/c Herbert M., Jr.

Pagano, Radarman 3/c Gilbert A.

Palfy, Chief Machinist's Mate
Alexander

Parino, Machinist's Mate 2/c Frank F.

Parks, Commissaryman 1/c
Maurice C.

Parolini, Lieutenant (jg) G. A. G.

Peeler, Machinist's Mate 1/c Elton F.

Pelosi, Seaman 2/c Gaston J.

Perry, Seaman 1/c Joseph C.

Peterson, Fire Controlman 1/c
Ralph C.

Peterson, Electrician's Mate 1/c
Ross E.

Pezzano, Seaman 2/c Rocca V.

Phoutrides, Quartermaster 2/c
Aristides

Pinkoff, Ship's Cook 3/c Jerome D.

Pitta, Coxswain Kenneth J.

Pollard, Seaman 1/c Leonce E.

Porlier, Lieutenant J. V.

Powell, Seaman 1/c Robert W.

Pressburger, Seaman 1/c Ramon

Purrick, Signalman 3/c Theodore F.

Radder, Gunner's Mate 3/c Owen G.

Ray, Seaman 1/c Robert E.

Redd, Steward's Mate 1/c James R.

Regin, Machinist's Mate 3/c
  Charles W.

Remsen, Seaman 1/c Herbert B.

Revels, Steward's Mate 1/c Leon M.

Rick, Yeoman 2/c Herbert J.

Ring, Quartermaster 2/c Edward
  L., Jr.

Robertson, Seaman 1/c Marvin G.

Robertson, Seaman 1/c Shirley D.

Robinson, Ship's Serviceman 3/c
  Kenneth A.

Rogowski, Coxswain Joseph

Rooker, Seaman 1/c Burnard L.

Rorie, Seaman 2/c Walter

Rosania, Seaman 2/c Paul

Ross, Seaman 2/c Frank M.

Rothgeb, Fireman 1/c James T.

Runk, Lieutenant Theodore

Rusk, Fireman 1/c George D.

Ryder, Chief Quartermaster
  William D.

Saenz, Lieutenant (jg) Ernest

Salcido, Seaman 1/c Felipe

Samp, Lieutenant E. J., Jr.

Samuelian, Fire Controlman 3/c
  Frank

Sattler, Storekeeper 3/c Clarence A.

Schenk, Seaman 2/c Robert L.

Schmidt, Machinist's Mate 3/c
  William S.

Schneider, Torpedoman's Mate 2/c
  John F.

Scott, Electrician's Mate 1/c
  Claude E.

Scott, Machinist's Mate 1/c
  David M.

Secrist, Fireman 1/c Dale L.

Setmire, Boatswain's Mate 2/c
  Glenn M.

Shaw, Lieutenant (jg) William H.

Sheets, Lieutenant (jg) Jerome B.

Shepard, Machinist's Mate 2/c
  James I.

Shepherd, Radioman 2/c Stanley M.

Siegrist, Radarman 2/c Joseph F.

Simonis, Sonarman 1/c Cyril C.

Skvarka, Machinist's Mate 2/c
  Cyril M.

Sloan, Seaman 1/c Paul V.

Smith, Fireman 1/c George H.

Smith, Lieutenant Paul B.

Snyder, Gunner's Mate 3/c
  Jacob L., Jr.

Spitler, Fire Controlman 2/c
  James W.

Spriggs, Fireman 1/c Oliver J.

Stacy, Gunner J. L.

Stash, Seaman 1/c Andrew

Stein, Torpedoman's Mate 3/c
  Derrill W.

Storm, Lieutenant (jg) R. T.

Strangeff, Seaman 1/c Joseph R.

Strine, Fireman 1/c Jonathan W.

Strozykowsky, Machinist's Mate 2/c
  S. J.

Stuer, Fireman 1/c Joseph J.

Sussman, Radar Technician 2/c Irving

Swank, Chief Water Tender James L.

Taylor, Seaman 1/c Lester

Thompson, Machinist's Mate 1/c
  Buford L.

Thompson, Carpenter's Mate 2/c
  Henry

Thompson, Torpedoman's Mate 3/c
  Jay V.

Thompson, Gunner's Mate 3/c
  Martin S.

Thomsen, Ensign Robert C.

Townsley, Ensign James G.

Vece, Boatswain's Mate 2/c Samuel

Vengelist, Seaman 1/c Anthony

Vest, Metalsmith 3/c Rex A.

Vianest, Water Tender 2/c August E.

Vodenhal, Radarman 1/c Slavomir J.

Wachsman, Seaman 2/c Russell H.

Wade, Machinist's Mate 2/c Cecil E.

Waite, Machinist's Mate 1/c
Stephen J.

Walker, Chief Gunner's Mate
Warren G.

Wallace, Seaman 1/c Quincie R.

Warner, Fireman 1/c David L.

Waters, Pharmacist's Mate 3/c Earl E.

Weiss, Seaman 1/c Daniel

Weissinger, Seaman 2/c George N.

Welch, Baker 1/c William H.

Weygandt, Seaman 1/c Charles A.

Williams, Storekeeper 1/c David H.

Williams, Fire Controlman 3/c
Edgar E. C.

Williams, Machinist's Mate 3/c
Jack E.

Williams, Machinist's Mate 3/c
Richard

Wilson, Water Tender 3/c Henry T.

Wilson, Seaman 1/c John G.

Wilson, Seaman 2/c Lon B., Jr.

Wilson, Steward's Mate 1/c
Roscoe S.

Wingrove, Water Tender 1/c
Samuel F.

Wismer, Gunner's Mate 2/c Stanley

Wix, Seaman 2/c Fred M., Jr.

Wood, Chief Water Tender Roy

Wright, Seaman 1/c Merle E.

Wright, Fireman 1/c Rosier B., Jr.

Yazdik, Radioman 3/c Emanuel J.

Yeagley, Sonarman 2/c Charles J.

Yuochunas, Water Tender 1/c
Thomas C.

Youngquist, Lieutenant (jg) Joel C.

Zack, Sonarman 3/c Daniel

Zebro, Gunner's Mate 2/c Edward V.

Zilempe, Water Tender 3/c Vito J.

Zupon, Gunner's Mate 1/c
Philip M.

LIST OF THE CREW KILLED ON APRIL 16, 1945

Benson, Electrician's Mate 3/c
  Henry M.
Broussard, Coxswain Charles A.
Brown, Torpedoman 3/c Edward J.
Burgess, Yeoman 3/c Fred D., Jr.
Cloer, Boatswain's Mate 2/c
  Calvin Wesley
Edwards, Coxswain Bernard
Falotico, Coxswain George
Flint, Coxswain Chester C.
Fowler, Fireman 1/c Conley E.
Fravel, Lieutenant (jg) James W.
Hallas, Fireman 1/c Francis R.
Hazen, Machinist's Mate 3/c
  La Verne G.
Heyes, Seaman 1/c William E.
Irish, Ship Fitter 1/c Madoc K.
Johnson, Machinist's Mate 3/c
  John A.

Johnson, Fireman 1/c Paul B.
Kelley, Radioman 3/c Lawrence F.
Klindworth, Seaman 1/c Joseph H.
La Pointe, Coxswain James M.
Lehtonen, Gunner's Mate 1/c
  Frank W., Jr.
Martin, Seaman 1/c Ronald G.
Mele, Gunner's Mate 2/c Joseph E.
Morris, Seaman 1/c William L.
Ondracek, Torpedoman 3/c Jack H.
Peterson, Electrician's Mate 1/c
  Ross E.
Rogowski, Coxswain Joseph
Rothgeb, Fireman 1/c James T.
Sheets, Lieutenant (jg) Jerome B.
Thomsen, Ensign Robert C.
Waters, Pharmacist's Mate 3/c Earl E.
Wismer, Gunner's Mate 2/c Stanley
Wright, Fireman 1/c Rosier B., Jr.

MEDAL RECIPIENTS FOR ACTIONS ON APRIL 16, 1945

NAVY CROSS

Becton, Commander F. Julian
Runk, Lieutenant Theodore

SILVER STAR

Coffman, Boatswain's Mate 1/c
   Kenneth D.
Fern, Seaman 1/c Thomas B.
Parolini, Lieutenant (jg) G. A. G.
Ryder, Chief Quartermaster
   William D.
Smith, Lieutenant Paul B.
Townsley, Ensign James G.

BRONZE STAR

Darnell, Lieutenant (jg)
   Matthew C., Jr.
Delewski, Gunner's Mate 2/c
   Lawrence H.
Henke, Lieutenant E. A.
Hintzman, Machinist's Mate 3/c
   Donald J.
Hogan, Machinist's Mate 1/c
   Arthur E.

Hungerpiller, Chief Machinist's Mate
   Marcellous D.
Hutchins, Seaman 1/c Charles W.
Logan, Motor Machinist's Mate 1/c
   George S.
Martinis, Seaman 1/c Andrew J.
Matthews, Ship's Serviceman 2/c
   Jim D.
Parino, Machinist's Mate 2/c
   Frank F.
Peeler, Machinist's Mate 1/c Elton F.
Saenz, Lieutenant (jg) Ernest
Shaw, Lieutenant (jg) William H.
Waite, Machinist's Mate 1/c
   Stephen J.
Walker, Chief Gunner's Mate
   Warren G.
Youngquist, Lieutenant (jg)
   Joel C.
Zebro, Gunner's Mate 2/c
   Edward V.

NAVY COMMMENDATION AWARD

Manson, Lieutenant Frank A.

NOTES

PROLOGUE

1. Sharon Spohn, "Keeping the Story Alive," *The Mercury*, September 20, 2007. Found at http://www.laffey.org/Sept%202007/ww_ii_veteran_keeps_the _story_al.htm. Accessed July 22, 2013.

2. Samuel Eliot Morison, *History of United States Naval Operations in World War II*, Volume XIV, *Victory in the Pacific 1945*, Boston: Little, Brown and Company, 1960, p. 239.

CHAPTER 1: THE FORMATION OF A CREW

1. Eulogy delivered by Ari Phoutrides, reprinted in the Becton Memorial Issue, *Laffey News*, Winter 1996.

2. Rear Admiral F. Julian Becton, USN, Ret. with Joseph Morschauser III, *The Ship That Would Not Die*, Englewood Cliffs, NJ: Prentice-Hall, Inc., 1980, p. 9.

3. Becton, *The Ship That Would Not Die*, p. 1.

4. Commanding Officer to Commander in Chief, U.S. Pacific Fleet, "Report of Enemy Action Resulting in Loss of *Aaron Ward*," 16 April, 1943, pp. 8, 11.

5. "Destroyer Bombed, Crew Stuffed Up Holes in Futile Effort to Save It," *St. Louis Globe-Democrat*, September 25, 1943. Found in E. Andrew Wilde Jr., editor, *The USS* Aaron Ward *(DD-483) in World War II: Documents and Photographs*. Needham, MA: Privately published by the editor, 2001.

6. Becton, *The Ship That Would Not Die*, pp. 14–15.

7. Becton, "Report of Enemy Action Resulting in Loss of *Aaron Ward*," p. 14.

8. Found at http://www.fold3.com/page/461704584_frederick_julian_becton /stories/. Accessed November 20, 2013.

9. Becton, *The Ship That Would Not Die*, p. 31.

10. Becton, *The Ship That Would Not Die*, pp. 14, 20.

11. Becton, *The Ship That Would Not Die*, pp. 18–19.

12. Douglas W. Bostick, *The USS* Laffey *(DD-724)*, Charleston: Charleston Postcard Company, 2010, p. 27.

13. Ralph Linwood Snow, *Bath Iron Works: The First Hundred Years*, Bath, ME: Maine Maritime Museum, 1987, p. 351.

14. Oral History, Chief Electrician's Mate Albert Csiszar. Found at http://www.laffey.org/Oral%20Histories/ohalcs.htm. Accessed August 6, 2013.

15. Author's interview with Ari Phoutrides, November 4, 2013.

16. Phoutrides interview, November 4, 2013; Ari Phoutrides Oral History. Found at http://www.laffey.org/Oral%20Histories/ohphou2.htm. Accessed August 9, 2013.

17. Lt. Jerome Butler Sheets, "Our Lady," 1945. Found at http://www.laffey .org/jerome_butler_sheets_his_pa.htm. Accessed August 8, 2013.

18. USS *Laffey* War Diary, February 8, 1944.

19. Thomas B. Fern letter to his mother, February 8, 1944, in the Thomas B. and Marguerite Fern Collection.

20. Sheets, "Our Lady."

21. Thomas B. Fern letter to his mother, February 8, 1944, in the Thomas B. and Marguerite Fern Collection.

22. Ari Phoutrides Oral History.

23. *Laffey News.* Becton Memorial Issue, Winter 1996.

24. Becton, *The Ship That Would Not Die*, p. 65.

25. Sheets, "Our Lady."

26. Sheets, "Our Lady."

27. Becton, *The Ship That Would Not Die*, p. 48.

28. Ari Phoutrides eulogy; Ari Phoutrides letter to Aspasia, April 12, 1944, in the Ari Phoutrides Collection.

29. Sheets, "Our Lady."

30. Author's interview with Ari Phoutrides, December 5, 2013.

31. Author's interview with Joel Youngquist, August 21, 2013.

32. Becton, *The Ship That Would Not Die*, pp. 37, 69.

33. Becton, *The Ship That Would Not Die*, p. 80.

34. Author's interview with J. Bahme, July 16, 2013; author's interview with Joseph Dixon, July 16, 2013.

35. Ari Phoutrides letter to his parents, March 14, 1944, in the Ari Phoutrides Collection.

36. Phoutrides letter to Aspasia, April 12, 1944.

37. Phoutrides interview, November 4, 2013.

CHAPTER 2: OFF NORMANDY'S SHORES

1. USS *Walke* War Diary, May 14, 1944.

2. Author's interview with Robert C. Johnson, August 19, 2013.

3. Thomas B. Fern letter to his mother, May 15, 1944, in the Thomas B. and Marguerite Fern Collection.

4. Thomas B. Fern letter to his mother, May 1944, in the Thomas B. and Marguerite Fern Collection.

5. Johnson interview, August 19, 2013.

6. Youngquist interview, August 21, 2013.

7. USS *Walke* War Diary, May 16, 1944.

8. Becton, *The Ship That Would Not Die*, p. 90.

9. USS *Laffey* War Diary, May 27, 1944.

10. Youngquist interview, August 21, 2013.

11. Phoutrides interview, November 4, 2013.

12. Becton, *The Ship That Would Not Die*, p. 94.

13. Phoutrides interview, November 4, 2013.

14. Commander Becton memo to the crew, undated, in the Ari Phoutrides Collection.

15. Author's interview with Robert W. Dockery, October 31, 2013; author's interview with Daniel Zack, February 8, 2014; author's interview with Robert C. Johnson, August 20, 2013.

16. USS *Barton* War Diary, June 4, 1944; author's interview with Daniel Zack, February 15, 2014.

17. Author's interview with Ari Phoutrides, November 20, 2013; author's interview with Robert W. Dockery, November 5, 2013.

18. USS *Laffey* War Diary, June 4, 1944.

19. Zack interview, February 15, 2014.

20. Naval Commander, Western Task Force to All Hands. "Coming Events," 27 May 1944. Found in *Walke* War Diary, June 1944.

21. Johnson interview, August 20, 2013.

22. Gunner's Mate 2/c Lawrence Delewski, Oral History. Found at http://www.laffey.org/ohdew1.htm. Accessed October 9, 2013.

23. Zack interview, February 15, 2014.

24. Dockery interview, October 31, 2013.

25. Phoutrides interview, November 20, 2013.

26. Hal Johnson. "Even A Church Was Fair Game, Grove City Man Recalls." Sharon (PA) *Herald*, undated article. Found at the USS *Laffey* website, http://www.laffey.org/donaldbrownnews.htm. Accessed September 9, 2013.

27. Commander Cruiser Division Seven War Diary, June 6, 1944.

28. Thomas B. Fern letter to his mother, June 1944, in the Thomas B. and Marguerite Fern Collection.

29. Hanson W. Baldwin. "Where Is German Navy?" *The New York Times*, July 7, 1944.

30. Phoutrides interview, November 20, 2013.

31. Gunner's Mate 2/c Lawrence Delewski, Oral History.

32. Zack interview, February 15, 2014.

33. Gunner's Mate 2/c Lawrence Delewski, Oral History.

34. Becton, *The Ship That Would Not Die*, p. 115; Commanding Officer to Commander in Chief, United States Fleet. "Operations in Assault Area 'Utah' Beach, off Coast of France, Baie de la Seine Area between June 6, 1944 and June 21, 1944—report of," 30 June 1944, p. 3 (hereafter cited as Becton Action Report, June 30, 1944).

35. Becton Action Report, June 30, 1944, p. 3.

36. Phoutrides interview, November 20, 2013.

37. USS *Laffey* War Diary, June 9, 1944.

38. Becton Action Report, June 30, 1944, p. 6.

39. Commanding Officer to Naval Commander Western Task Force (Commander Task Force 122). "Chronological Narrative Report of Operations, June 3–June 17, 1944," 27 June 1944, pp. 12–13.

40. Hanson W. Baldwin. "Mines Still A Problem," *The New York Times*, July 6, 1944.

41. Zack interview, February 15, 2014.

42. Thomas B. Fern letter to his mother, June 15, 1944, in the Thomas B. and Marguerite Fern Collection.

43. Dockery interview, November 5, 2013.

CHAPTER 3: TO THE PACIFIC

1. Becton Action Report, June 30, 1944, pp. 7, 16.

2. Becton Action Report, June 30, 1944, p. 13.

3. Thomas B. Fern letter to his parents, June 19, 1944, in the Thomas B. and Marguerite Fern Collection.

4. Author's interview with Daniel Zack, February 22, 2014.

5. Author's interview with Joel Youngquist, August 22, 2013.

6. Johnson interview, August 20, 2013.

7. Gunner's Mate 2/c Lawrence Delewski, Oral History.

8. Becton, *The Ship That Would Not Die*, p. 129.

9. Phoutrides interview, November 20, 2013.

10. Johnson, "Even A Church Was Fair Game, Grove City Man Recalls."

11. Rear Adm. C. F. Bryant message, June 25, 1944, in the Ari Phoutrides Collection.

12. Commander Destroyer Squadron Sixty Officer to Commander in Chief, United States Fleet. "Bombardment of Cherbourg Defenses on June 25, 1944—report of," 1 July 1944, pp. 1–2.

13. Albert Csiszar Oral History. Found at http://www.laffey.org/Oral%20 Histories/ohalcs.htm. Accessed October 10, 2013.

14. Charles A. Weygandt Oral History. Found at http://www.laffey.org/Oral %20Histories/ohweygandt2.htm. Accessed August 14, 2013.

15. Becton, *The Ship That Would Not Die*, p. 133.

16. Samuel Eliot Morison. *History of United States Naval Operations in World War II*, Volume XI, *The Invasion of France and Germany 1944–1945*. Boston: Little, Brown and Company, 1957, p. 211; Dwight D. Eisenhower. *Crusade in Europe*. Garden City, NY: Doubleday & Company, Inc., 1950, p. 260.

17. Hanson W. Baldwin. "Navy Still Stings Hitler," *The New York Times*, July 4, 1944; Hanson W. Baldwin. "Cherbourg Only Beginning of French Campaign," *The New York Times*, July 2, 1944.

18. Commander Battleship Division Five to Commander in Chief, United States Fleet. "Action Report for Operation Period 3–17 June 1944," 10 July 1944, p. 34.

19. Commanding Officer to Naval Commander Western Task Force (Commander Task Force 122). "Chronological Narrative Report of Operations, June 3–June 17, 1944," 27 June 1944, endorsements of Capt. William Freseman and Rear Adm. M. L. Deyo; Commanding Officer to Commander Task Force One Two Two. "Bombardment of Cherbourg Defenses, Report of," 27 June 1944, endorsement of Rear Adm. M. L. Deyo.

20. Commander Destroyer Squadron Sixty Officer to Commander in Chief, United States Fleet. "Bombardment of Cherbourg Defenses on June 25, 1944—Report of," 1 July 1944, p. 2.

21. Ari Phoutrides letter to his brother, June 9, 1945. Found at http://www .laffey.org/Oral%20Histories/ohphou3.htm. Accessed August 9, 2013.

22. Johnson interview, August 20, 2013.

23. Author's interview with Robert W. Dockery, February 5, 2014; author's interview with Robert C. Johnson, February 5, 2014.

24. Youngquist interview, August 22, 2013.

25. Zack interview, February 22, 2014.

26. Wilbert C. Gauding. *My Navy Career*, July 3, 1944. Unpublished diary kept during the war.

27. The story of this meeting is found in Saburo Sakai, with Martin Caidin and Fred Saito. *Samurai!* New York: Simon B. Schuster, Inc., 2001, pp. 303–309.

28. Denis Warner and Peggy Warner. *The Sacred Warriors*. New York: Van Nostrand Reinhold Company, 1982, p. 69.

29. Captain Rikihei Inoguchi, Commander Tadashi Nakajima, with Roger Pineau. *The Divine Wind*. New York: Bantam Books, 1958, p. 25.

30. Zack interview, February 22, 2014.

31. Thomas B. Fern letter to his mother, August 22, 1944, in the Thomas B. and Marguerite Fern Collection.

32. Thomas B. Fern letter to his mother, August 26, 1944, in the Thomas B. and Marguerite Fern Collection.

33. Phoutrides interview, December 5, 2013.

34. USS *Laffey* War Diary, September 12, 1944.

35. Author's interview with Robert C. Johnson, August 28, 2013.

36. Johnson interview, August 28, 2013; author's interview with Robert C. Johnson, February 5, 2013.

37. Author's interview with Daniel Zack, March 1, 2014.

38. Johnson interview, August 28, 2013.

39. Becton, *The Ship That Would Not Die*, p. 148.

40. Thomas B. Fern letters to his mother, September 19, October 9, and October 21, 1945, in the Thomas B. and Marguerite Fern Collection.

41. Warner and Warner, *The Sacred Warriors*, p. ix.

42. Inoguchi, Nakajima, and Pineau, *The Divine Wind*, p. 169.

43. Albert Axell and Hideaki Kase. *Kamikaze: Japan's Suicide Gods*. London: Longman, 2002, p. 39.

44. Inoguchi, Nakajima, and Pineau, *The Divine Wind*, p. 18.

45. The account of this meeting is found in Inoguchi, Nakajima, and Pineau, *The Divine Wind*, pp. 3–18.

CHAPTER 4: KAMIKAZES STAGE
A TERRIFYING INTRODUCTION

1. Youngquist interview, August 21, 2013.

2. Sakai, *Samurai!*, p. 346.

3. Admiral Matome Ugaki. *Fading Victory: The Diary of Admiral Matome Ugaki, 1941–1945*. Pittsburgh: The University of Pittsburgh Press, 1991, p. 485.

4. Warner and Warner, *The Sacred Warriors*, p. 113.

5. Commanding Officer USS *Enterprise* (CV-6) to Commander in Chief, United States Fleet. "Action Report—Fleet Action and Operations Against the Philippine Islands Area, from 22 to 31 October 1944," 3 November 1944, pp. 5–6.

6. Fleet Admiral William F. Halsey and Lieutenant Commander J. Bryan III. *Admiral Halsey's Story*. New York: McGraw-Hill Book Company, Inc., 1947, p. 229.

7. "Tokyo Tells of 'Suicide Plane,'" *The New York Times*, November 3, 1944.

8. Zack interview, March 1, 2014.

9. Gauding, *My Navy Career*, November 2, 1944.

10. Becton, *The Ship That Would Not Die*, pp. 152, 154.

11. Author's interview with Daniel Zack, March 8, 2014.

12. Becton, *The Ship That Would Not Die*, p. 155.

13. Author's interview with Ari Phoutrides, January 22, 2014.

14. Commanding Officer to Commander in Chief, United States Fleet. "Action Report for Operations November 10–20, 1944, Inclusive, with Task Force 38," 25 November 1944 (hereafter cited as Becton Action Report, November 25, 1944), p. 3.

15. Becton, *The Ship That Would Not Die*, p. 159.

16. Becton, *The Ship That Would Not Die*, p. 160.

17. Al Phoutrides, QM 1/c. Letter written from San Pedro Bay, Leyte. December 3, 1944. Found at http://www.laffey.org/Oral%20Histories/ohindex .htm. Accessed November 25, 2013.

18. Gauding, *My Naval Career*, December 6, 1944.

19. Gauding, *My Naval Career*, December 7, 1944.

20. Commanding Officer to Commander in Chief, United States Fleet. "Action Report in Connection with Landing of 77th Division, United States Army in Ormoc Bay Area, Leyte Island, Philippine Islands, on December 7, 1944," 11 December 1944, pp. 3, 11 (hereafter cited as Becton Action Report, 11 December 1944).

21. Spencer Davis. "Japanese Stunned by Ormoc Landing," *The New York Times*, December 9, 1944.

22. Becton, *The Ship That Would Not Die*, p. 167.

23. Becton, *The Ship That Would Not Die*, p. 169.

24. Frank L. Kluckhohn. "77th Infantry Hits," *The New York Times*, December 8, 1944, p. 1; Davis. "Japanese Stunned by Ormoc Landing."

25. Gauding, *My Naval Career*, December 7, 1944.

26. Author's interview with Joseph E. Dixon, October 29, 2013.

27. Author's interview with Robert C. Johnson, October 29, 2013.

28. Becton, *The Ship That Would Not Die*, p. 170.

29. Becton, *The Ship That Would Not Die*, p. 170.

30. "Port Important for Future," *The New York Times*, December 11, 1944.

31. Becton, *The Ship That Would Not Die*, p. 171.

32. Becton Action Report, 11 December 1944, p. 12.

33. Douglas MacArthur. *Reminiscences*. New York: McGraw-Hill Book Company, 1964, p. 233.

34. Kluckhohn, "77th Infantry Hits," p. 4; "Battle of the Pacific: End Run, Touchdown," *Time*, December 18, 1944. Found at: http://content.time.com /time/magazine/article/0,9171,778257,00.html.

35. Gauding, *My Naval Career*, December 10, 1944.

36. Zack interview, March 8, 2014.

37. Oral History, Lieutenant (jg) Frank A. Manson. Found at http://www .laffey.org/Oral%20Histories/ohfrank.htm. Accessed November 30, 2013.

38. Johnson interview, February 4, 2014; author's interview with Fred Gemmell, February 5, 2014.

39. Becton, *The Ship That Would Not Die*, p. 174.

40. Gunner's Mate 2/c Lawrence Delewski, Oral History.

41. Thomas B. Fern letter to his mother, December 13, 1944, in the Thomas B. and Marguerite Fern Collection.

42. Hanson W. Baldwin. "Blow at Luzon Indicated," *The New York Times*, December 16, 1944.

43. Commanding Officer to Commander in Chief, United States Fleet. "Action Report for Period December 12 to 17, 1944, Inclusive, Involving Occupation of Mindoro Island, Philippine Islands," 19 December 1944, p. 2.

44. Zack interview, March 8, 2014.

45. "Toward Manila," *The New York Times*, December 17, 1944; Frank L. Kluckhohn. "'Greatest Japanese Defeat' Ends Campaign on Leyte," *The New York Times*, December 26, 1944, p. 12.

46. "Hard-Hitting Bath Destroyer Knocking Down Jap Plane," *The Bulletin*, Bath Iron Works, February 9, 1945, p. 1, in the Robert Johnson Collection.

47. "Airfield on Mindoro," *The New York Times*, December 23, 1944.

48. USS *Laffey* War Diary, December 31, 1944.

49. CincPac Message to the Fleet, December 20, 1944, in the Ari Phoutrides Collection.

50. W. L. Freseman Message to Desron 60, December 31, 1944, in the Ari Phoutrides Collection.

51. Hanson W. Baldwin. "U.S. Outlook In War," *The New York Times*, December 8, 1944.

CHAPTER 5: NORTH FROM THE PHILIPPINES

1. Gerald E. Wheeler. *Kinkaid of the Seventh Fleet*. Annapolis, MD: Naval Institute Press, 1996, p. 418.

2. MacArthur, *Reminiscences*, p. 239.

3. "Luzon Thrust Seen," *The New York Times*, January 7, 1945, p. 19; "Landing Predicted," *The New York Times*, January 8, 1945, p. 3.

4. Commander Destroyer Squadron Sixty to Commander in Chief, United States Fleet. "Action Report—Lingayen Gulf, Luzon Landing Operation, 2–18 January 1945," 2 February 1945, p. 2. Found at http://www.dd-692.com /comdesron_60_action_report.htm. Accessed December 5, 2013.

5. Author's interview with Ari Phoutrides, December 12, 2013.

6. Becton, *The Ship That Would Not Die*, pp. 186–187.

7. Zack interview, March 8, 2014.

8. Commanding Officer to Commander in Chief, United States Fleet. "Action Report for Period January 2 to January 17, 1945, Inclusive, Incident to Invasion of Luzon, Philippine Islands," 27 January 1945, p. 11 (hereafter cited as Becton, Lingayen Action Report).

9. Becton, *The Ship That Would Not Die*, p. 188.

10. USS *Barton* War Diary, January 6, 1945.

11. Zack interview, March 8, 2014.

12. Becton, Lingayen Action Report, p. 14.

13. Samuel Eliot Morison. *History of United States Naval Operations in World War II*, Volume XIII, *The Liberation of the Philippines 1944–1945*. Boston: Little, Brown and Company, 1959, pp. 110–111; Gauding, *My Navy Career*, January 7, 1945.

14. Warner and Warner, *The Sacred Warriors*, pp. 157–158.

15. Thomas B. Fern letter to Eddie, January 14, 1945, in the Thomas B. and Marguerite Fern Collection.

16. Thomas B. Fern letter to his mother, January 18, 1945, and to his father, January 21, 1945, in the Thomas B. and Marguerite Fern Collection.

17. Gauding, *My Navy Career*, January 28, 1945.

18. Becton, Lingayen Action Report, p. 28.

19. Frank L. Kluckhohn. "Whole War Can Be Shortened," *The New York Times*, January 10, 1945, p. 10; Hanson W. Baldwin. "Luzon Campaign Opens with Odds in Our Favor," *The New York Times*, January 14, 1945.

20. Phoutrides interview, December 12, 2013.

21. Phoutrides interview, December 12, 2013.

22. Commander Destroyer Squadron Sixty to Commander in Chief, United States Fleet. "Action Report—Lingayen Gulf, Luzon Landing Operation, 2–18 January 1945," 2 February 1945, pp. 32–33 (hereafter cited as Freseman Lingayen Action Report). Found at http://www.dd-692.com/comdesron_60_action_report.htm. Accessed December 5, 2013.

23. Author's interview with William Rowe, June 12, 1988.

24. Inoguchi, Nakajima, and Pineau, *The Divine Wind*, p. 7.

25. Warner and Warner, *The Sacred Warriors*, p. 62.

26. Sakai, *Samurai!*, p. 347.

27. Russell Brines. *Until They Eat Stones*. New York: J. B. Lippincott Company, 1944, pp. 9, 290–291.

28. The two letters are from Inoguchi, Nakajima, and Pineau, *The Divine Wind*, pp. 188–189.

29. Warner and Warner, *The Sacred Warriors*, p. 150.

30. Freseman Lingayen Action Report, p. 33.

31. Gauding, *My Navy Career*, February 10, 1945.

32. Author's interview with Dr. Andrew J. Martinis, January 16, 2014.

33. Hanson W. Baldwin. "Allies Take War to Foes," *The New York Times*, February 16, 1945.

34. USS *Laffey* War Diary, February 14, 1945.

35. USS *Laffey* War Diary, February 16, 1945.

36. Author's interview with Robert C. Johnson, February 20, 2014.

37. USS *Laffey* War Diary, February 24, 1945.

38. Warren Moscow. "First Great Blow," *The New York Times*, February 16, 1945, pp. 1, 4.

39. "The Target Is Tokyo," *The New York Times*, February 17, 1945.

CHAPTER 6: FIRST DAYS AT OKINAWA

1. Zack interview, March 8, 2014.

2. Hazel Millikin Tracy. "Sailor Risks His Life to Restore Flag," *Seattle Times*, May 25, 1945, p. 10.

3. Becton, *The Ship That Would Not Die*, pp. 217–218.

4. Thomas B. Fern letter to Eddie, March 9, 1945, in the Thomas B. and Marguerite Fern Collection.

5. Martinis interview, January 16, 2014.

6. Morison, *History of United States Naval Operations in World War II*, Volume XIV, *Victory in the Pacific 1945*, p. 93.

7. Inoguchi, Nakajima, and Pineau, *The Divine Wind*, p. 130.

8. Warner and Warner, *The Sacred Warriors*, p. 146.

9. John Costello, *The Pacific War, 1941–1945*. New York: Quill Books, 1982, p. 555.

10. Morison, *History of United States Naval Operations in World War II*, Volume XIV, *Victory in the Pacific 1945*, p. 129.

11. Thomas B. Fern letter to his mother, March 21, 1945, in the Thomas B. and Marguerite Fern Collection.

12. Becton, *The Ship That Would Not Die*, p. 220.

13. Gunner's Mate 2/c Lawrence Delewski, Oral History.

14. Author's interview with Dr. Andrew Martinis, January 23, 2014.

15. George Feifer. *Tennozan*. New York: Ticknor & Fields, 1992, p. 215.

16. Becton, *The Ship That Would Not Die*, p. 227.

17. Commanding Officer to Commander in Chief, United States Fleet. "Report of Operations in Support of Landings By U.S. Troops in Kerama Retto-Okinawa Area March 25 to April 22, 1945, Including Action Against Enemy Aircraft on April 16, 1945." 29 April 1945, p. 13 (hereafter cited as Becton Action Report, April 29, 1945).

18. Becton, *The Ship That Would Not Die*, p. 222.

19. Oral History, Lieutenant (jg) Frank A. Manson. Found at http://www
.laffey.org/Oral%20Histories/ohfrank.htm. Accessed August 6, 2013.

20. Phoutrides interview, January 22, 2014.

21. Author's interview with Daniel Zack, March 15, 2014.

22. Gauding, *My Navy Career*, April 7–11, 1945.

23. Alexander, Colonel Joseph H. "Hellish Prelude at Okinawa," *Naval History* Magazine, p. 4. Found at http://www.usni.org/print/3035. Accessed January 28, 2014.

24. Author's interview with Ari Phoutrides, January 27, 2014.

25. Phoutrides interview, January 27, 2014.

26. Author's interview with Joel Youngquist, February 5, 2014.

27. Becton, *The Ship That Would Not Die*, pp. 228–229.

28. Phoutrides interview, January 27, 2014.

29. Sgt. Harry J. Tomlinson. "Bogey Bait," *Yank*, no date. Found in Slavomir J. Vodehnal, *The Indestructible USS* Laffey. No date. Privately published, p. 96.

30. Tomlinson, "Bogey Bait," p. 96.

31. Gunner's Mate 2/c Lawrence Delewski, Oral History; Oral History, Lonnie Eastham, Seaman 1/c. Found at http://www.laffey.org/Oral%20Histories/oh eastham.htm. Accessed February 16, 2014.

32. Johnson interview, February 5, 2013.

33. Zack interview, March 15, 2014.

34. Press Release from Headquarters Thirteenth Naval District, Seattle, Washington, District Public Relations Office, 25 May 1945.

35. Becton, *The Ship That Would Not Die*, p. 229.

36. Lieutenant Commander Frank A. Manson. "Seventy-Nine Minutes on the Picket Line," *U.S. Naval Institute Proceedings*, September 1949, p. 999.

37. Zack interview, March 15, 2014.

38. Manson, "Seventy-Nine Minutes on the Picket Line," p. 999.

39. Manson, "Seventy-Nine Minutes on the Picket Line," p. 1000.

40. Gemmell interview, February 5, 2014; Johnson interviews, February 4–5, 2014; Phoutrides interviews, January 22 and 27, 2014; Oral History, Gunner's Mate Robert I. Karr. Found at http://www.laffey.org/Oral%20Histories/ohrkarr .htm. Accessed August 6, 2013; Gunner's Mate 2/c Lawrence Delewski, Oral History.

41. Commander Walter Karig, USNR, with Lieutenant Commander Russell L. Harris, USNR, and Lieutenant Commander Frank A. Manson, USN. *Battle Report: Victory in the Pacific*. New York: Farrar & Rinehart, Inc., 1949, p. 414.

42. Becton, *The Ship That Would Not Die*, pp. 231–232.

43. Phoutrides letter to his brother, June 9, 1945; Phoutrides interview, January 27, 2014.

44. Gauding, *My Navy Career*, April 13, 1945.

CHAPTER 7: THE TRIUMPH
OF *LAFFEY*'S GUNNERS

1. David Sears. *At War with the Wind*. New York: Citadel Press, 2008, p. 348.

2. Phoutrides letter to his brother, June 9, 1945; Seaman 1/c Lonnie H. Eastham, Oral History.

3. Becton, *The Ship That Would Not Die*, p. 234.

4. Manson, "Seventy-Nine Minutes on the Picket Line," p. 1000.

5. Gauding, *My Navy Career*, April 14, 1945.

6. Phoutrides interview, January 27, 2014.

7. Phoutrides letter to his brother, June 9, 1945.

8. Manson, "Seventy-Nine Minutes on the Picket Line," p. 1000.

9. Gauding, *My Navy Career*, April 16, 1945.

10. F. J. Becton, "Amplifying Report," 19 April 1945, p. 1; Phoutrides letter to his brother, June 9, 1945.

11. Oral History, Seaman 1/c Oliver "Jim" Spriggs. Found at http://www.laffey .org/Oral%20Histories/ohjimsp.htm. Accessed August 6, 2013.

12. Author's interview with Joel Youngquist, February 12, 2014.

13. Becton, *The Ship That Would Not Die*, p. 238; Gauding, *My Navy Career*, April 16, 1945.

14. Manson, "Seventy-Nine Minutes on the Picket Line," p. 1001.

15. Becton, *The Ship That Would Not Die*, p. 237.

16. Manson, "Seventy-Nine Minutes on the Picket Line," p. 1000.

17. Belinda Leslie. "U.S.S. *Laffey*: The Ship That Took A Licking and A Looking," College Essay for the University of Wisconsin-Whitewater, Whitewater, Wisconsin, November 1988, p. 7. Found at http://www.laffey.org/Belinda%20 Leslie%20Report/college_essay_by_belinda_leslie.htm.

18. Oral History, Seaman 1/c Donald E. "Doc" Brown. Found at http://www .laffey.org/Oral%20Histories/ohbrown.htm. Accessed August 6, 2013.

19. Becton, "Amplifying Report," p. 1.

20. Becton, *The Ship That Would Not Die*, p. 238.

21. Zack interview, March 15, 2014.

22. Becton, *The Ship That Would Not Die*, p. 238.

23. Zack interview, March 15, 2014.

24. Gunner's Mate 2/c Lawrence Delewski, Oral History. Found at http:// www.laffey.org/Oral%20Histories/ohlarde.htm. Accessed October 9, 2013 (hereafter cited as Delewski Oral History #2).

25. Manson, "Seventy-Nine Minutes on the Picket Line," p. 1002.

26. Leslie. "U.S.S. *Laffey*: The Ship That Took A Licking and A Looking," p. 7.

27. "*Laffey* Men Didn't Quit, Can't Understand Shipyard Quitters," *Seattle Times*, May 25, 1945, p. 10.

28. Author's interviews with Robert W. Dockery, February 12 and 19, 2014.

29. Johnson interview, February 20, 2014.

30. "Suicide Planes 'Chill Your Blood,'" *Washington Daily News*, July 19, 1945, p. 1. Found in Vodehnal, *The Indestructible USS* Laffey, p. 43.

31. Author's interview with Ari Phoutrides, February 3, 2014.

32. Youngquist interview, February 12, 2014.

33. Becton, *The Ship That Would Not Die*, p. 241.

34. Robert Mahaffay. "Destroyer, Hit by 8 Jap Planes, Limps Back Here," *Seattle Times*, May 25, 1945, p. 1.

35. Becton, "Amplifying Report," p. 4.

CHAPTER 8: AGONY ON THE AFTERDECK

1. Belinda Leslie. "U.S.S. *Laffey*: The Ship That Took A Licking and A Looking," University of Wisconsin-Whitewater, Whitewater, Wisconsin, November 1988, p. 8. Accessed February 19, 2014. Found at http://www.laffey.org/Belinda%20Leslie%20Report/college_essay_by_belinda_leslie.htm.

2. George Burnett letter to parents, Seattle, Washington. Undated, but written shortly after the attack. Found at http://www.laffey.org/george_burnett's_letter_home_page_1.htm.

3. Ari Phoutrides letter to his brother, June 9, 1945. Found at http://www.laffey.org/Oral%20Histories/ohphou3.htm.

4. "Suicide Planes 'Chill Your Blood,'" *Washington Daily News*, July 19, 1945, p. 1.

5. Manson, "Seventy-Nine Minutes on the Picket Line," p. 1002.

6. Author's interview with Joel Youngquist, February 19, 2014.

7. Jonathan Tilove. "He Resurrects Ship That Wouldn't Die," *Union*, p. 1, in the Thomas B. and Marguerite Fern Collection; "*Laffey* to Become a Shrine," *Charleston News and Courier*, March 21, 1982, in the Thomas B. and Marguerite Fern Collection.

8. Mahaffay, "Destroyer, Hit by 8 Jap Planes, Limps Back Here," p. 10; Press Release from Headquarters Thirteenth Naval District, Seattle, Washington, District Public Relations Office, 25 May 1945.

9. Press Release from Headquarters Thirteenth Naval District, Seattle, Washington, District Public Relations Office, 25 May 1945; Becton, *The Ship That Would Not Die*, p. 246.

10. Jack Illian. "On Heroic *Laffey*, Lt. McCune Rode Out 22 Suicide Attacks," *Cedar Rapids Gazette*, May 1945. Found at http://www.laffey.org/Laura%20McKagan/cedar_rapid_gazette.htm.

11. Becton, *The Ship That Would Not Die*, p. 247.

12. Oral History, Seaman 2/c Merle Johnson. Found at http://www.laffey.org
/Oral%20Histories/ohmjohn.htm. Accessed August 6, 2013.

13. Tilove, "He Resurrects Ship That Wouldn't Die."

14. Mahaffay, "Destroyer, Hit by 8 Jap Planes, Limps Back Here," p. 10.

15. Author's interview with Fred Gemmell, February 14, 2014.

16. Becton Action Report, April 29, 1945, p. 25.

17. Becton Action Report, April 29, 1945, p. 25.

18. Manson, "Seventy-Nine Minutes on the Picket Line," p. 1002; Press Release from Headquarters Thirteenth Naval District, Seattle, Washington, District Public Relations Office, 25 May 1945.

19. Author's interviews with Dr. Andrew J. Martinis, January 9, 2014; February 6, 2014; and February 20, 2014.

20. Burnett letter to parents.

21. Author's interview with Ari Phoutrides, February 24, 2014.

22. "*Laffey* Men Didn't Quit, Can't Understand Shipyard Quitters," *Seattle Times*, May 25, 1945, p. 10.

23. Phoutrides interview, February 24, 2014.

24. Burnett letter to parents.

25. Delewski Oral History #2.

26. Oral History, Lieutenant E. A. "Al" Henke. Found at http://www.laffey
.org/Oral%20Histories/ohhenke.htm. Accessed August 6, 2013.

27. Becton Action Report, April 29, 1945, p. 42A.

28. Leslie, "U.S.S. *Laffey*: The Ship That Took A Licking and A Looking," p. 11.

29. Becton, *The Ship That Would Not Die*, p. 243.

30. Author's interview with Dr. Andrew J. Martinis, February 27, 2014.

31. Becton Action Report, April 29, 1945, p. 44.

32. Ari Phoutrides letter to his brother, June 9, 1945.

33. Oral History, Henry "Hank" Thompson, CM2/c. Found at http://www
.laffey.org/Oral%20Histories/ohhankt.htm. Accessed August 6, 2013.

34. Oral History, Steve Waite, Machinist's Mate 1/c. Found at http://www
.laffey.org/Oral%20Histories/ohwaite.htm. Accessed August 6, 2013.

35. Becton, *The Ship That Would Not Die*, p. 251.

CHAPTER 9: DEFYING THE ODDS

1. Ari Phoutrides letter to his brother, June 9, 1945.

2. Becton, *The Ship That Would Not Die*, p. 249.

3. Phoutrides interview, February 3, 2014.

4. Manson, "Seventy-Nine Minutes on the Picket Line," p. 1003; "An Oral History by Carl Rieman." Found at http://www.laffey.org/VC%2094/rieman .htm. Accessed August 6, 2013.

5. Tracy, "Sailor Risks His Life to Restore Flag," p. 10.

6. Zack interview, March 15, 2014.

7. Zack interview, February 22, 2014.

8. Manson, "Seventy-Nine Minutes on the Picket Line," p. 1002.

9. Phoutrides interview, February 24, 2014.

10. Citation for Ensign James G. Townsley, Silver Star. Found at http:// projects.militarytimes.com/citations-medals-awards/recipient.php?recipientid =56563. Accessed April 2, 2014.

11. Becton, *The Ship That Would Not Die*, p. 249.

12. Martinis interviews, February 6 and February 20, 2014.

13. R. B. Bermann. "Gallantry of Crew Brings Warship Through Flaming Ordeal," *Seattle Post-Intelligencer*, May 26, 1945. Found in Vodehnal, *The Indestructible USS* Laffey, pp. 20–22.

14. Becton, *The Ship That Would Not Die*, p. 249.

15. Phoutrides interview, February 24, 2014.

16. Becton, *The Ship That Would Not Die*, p. 254.

17. Phoutrides interview, February 3, 2014.

18. Becton, *The Ship That Would Not Die*, p. 254; author's interview with Robert C. Johnson, February 7, 2014.

19. Press Release from Headquarters Thirteenth Naval District, Seattle, Washington, District Public Relations Office, 25 May 1945.

20. Becton, *The Ship That Would Not Die*, p. 255.

21. Zack interview, February 22, 2014.

22. Larry Fish. "*Inquirer* Recalls Becton's Life, Career," *Philadelphia Inquirer*, no date, found in *Laffey News*, Becton Memorial Issue, Winter 1996.

23. Becton, *The Ship That Would Not Die*, p. 255.

24. Becton, *The Ship That Would Not Die*, p. 256.

25. Zack interview, February 22, 2014.

26. "*Laffey* Men Didn't Quit, Can't Understand Shipyard Quitters," *Seattle Times*, May 25, 1945, p. 10.

27. Illian, "On Heroic *Laffey*, Lt. McCune Rode Out 22 Suicide Attacks."

28. Zack interview, February 22, 2014.

29. Martinis interview, February 20, 2014.

30. "*Laffey* Men Didn't Quit, Can't Understand Shipyard Quitters," p. 10; Brian Hicks. "The Love That Would Not Die," *The Post and Courier* (Charleston, SC), September 26, 2012, p. 2. Found at http://www.postandcourier.com /article/20120926/PC16/120929483/world-war-ii-widow-visits-laffey-where -her-husband-died. Accessed February 6, 2014.

31. Gunner's Mate Robert I. Karr, Oral History.

32. Gemmell interview, February 5, 2014.

33. Ari Phoutrides letter to his brother, June 9, 1945.

34. Johnson interview, February 20, 2014.

35. Becton, *The Ship That Would Not Die*, p. 258.

36. Press Release from Headquarters Thirteenth Naval District, Seattle, Washington, District Public Relations Office, 25 May 1945; Phoutrides interview, February 24, 2014.

37. Mahaffay, "Destroyer, Hit by 8 Jap Planes, Limps Back Here," p. 10.

38. Becton, "Amplifying Report," pp. 3–4.

39. Author's interview with Dr. Andrew J. Martinis, February 27, 2014.

40. Zack interview, February 22, 2014.

41. Becton Action Report, April 29, 1945, p. 26A; Ari Phoutrides letter to his brother, June 9, 1945.

42. Author's interview with Joel Youngquist, February 26, 2014; author's interview with Robert C. Johnson, February 25, 2014.

43. Becton, *The Ship That Would Not Die*, p. 260.

CHAPTER 10: A LASTING LEGACY

1. Becton Action Report, April 29, 1945, p. 26A.

2. Recollection found at http://ussjpkennedyjr.org/macomb458/maclaffey.html. Accessed March 27, 2014.

3. Gauding, *My Navy Career*, April 16, 1945.

4. Dockery interview, February 19, 2014; Ari Phoutrides letter to his brother, June 9, 1945.

5. Author's interview with Daniel Zack, March 29, 2014; Youngquist interview, February 19, 2014.

6. Johnson interview, February 25, 2014.

7. Press Release from Headquarters Thirteenth Naval District, Seattle, Washington, District Public Relations Office, 25 May 1945.

8. Author's interview with Ari Phoutrides, March 3, 2014.

9. Lieutenant (jg) Frank A. Manson, Oral History.

10. Thomas B. Fern letter to his mother, April 17, 1945, and to his aunt, April 20, 1945, in the Thomas B. and Marguerite Fern Collection; Robert Johnson letter to his mother and brother, April 20, 1945, in the Robert Johnson Collection.

11. Ari Phoutrides letter to his brother, June 9, 1945.

12. Gauding, *My Navy Career*, April 22, 1945.

13. Lewis M. Andrews Jr. *Tempest, Fire & Foe*. Charleston: Narwhal Press, 1999, p. 284.

14. Found in Vodehnal, *The Indestructible USS* Laffey, p. 61.

15. Ramon Pressburger letter to Mrs. Fern, April 29, 1945, in the Thomas B. and Marguerite Fern Collection.

16. Tom B. Fern letter to his aunt, May 1, 1945, and to his father, May 1, 1945, in the Thomas B. and Marguerite Fern Collection.

17. Memo from F. J. Becton to All Hands, found in Vodehnal, *The Indestructible USS* Laffey, p. 15.

18. Author's interview with Fred Gemmell, February 28, 2014.

19. Zack interview, March 29, 2014.

20. Ship's Dispatch, Comtransdiv 56 to *Laffey*, April 27, 1945, in the Ari Phoutrides Collection; Phoutrides interview, March 3, 2014.

21. Zack interview, March 29, 2014.

22. Gauding, *My Navy Career*, May 12, 1945.

23. Zack interview, March 29, 2014.

24. Zack interview, March 29, 2014.

25. Becton, *The Ship That Would Not Die*, p. 267.

26. Zack interview, March 29, 2014.

27. Press Release from Headquarters Thirteenth Naval District, Seattle, Washington, District Public Relations Office, 25 May 1945; US Pacific Fleet and Pacific Command Areas, Office of PUBINFOR. USS *Laffey* Ship's History, "Background Memorandum."

28. "6 Suicide Planes and 2 Bombs Hit Destroyer *Laffey*, She Gets Home," *The New York Times*, May 26, 1945, p. 1; John R. Henry. "Ship's Heroic Battle With Enemy Revealed," *Arizona Republic*, May 26, 1945, p. 5. Found in Vodehnal, *The Indestructible USS* Laffey, p. 25.

29. Robert Johnson letter to his mother and brother, May 25, 1945, in the Robert Johnson Collection; Mahaffay. "Destroyer, Hit by 8 Jap Planes, Limps Back Here," p. 1; Bermann. "Gallantry of Crew Brings Warship Through Flaming Ordeal." Found in Vodehnal, *The Indestructible USS* Laffey, pp. 20–22.

30. Becton Action Report, April 29, 1945, pp. 42A, 45.

31. Presidential Unit Citation, found in Vodehnal, *The Indestructible USS* Laffey, p. 7.

32. Commander Destroyer Squadron Sixty to Commander in Chief, United States Fleet. "Report of operations in support of landings by U.S. Troops in Kerama Retto-Okinawa area, March 25 to April 22, 1945, including action against enemy aircraft on April 16, 1945," 15 May 1945, p. 1.

33. Becton Navy Cross citation found at http://projects.militarytimes.com /citations-medals-awards/recipient.php?recipientid=20208.

34. Author's interview with Lloyd Hull, June 10, 2014; Seaman 1/c Lonnie H. Eastham, Oral History.

35. Robert Johnson letter to his mother and brother, June 11, 1945, in the Robert Johnson Collection.

36. Phoutrides interview, March 3, 2014.

37. "*Laffey* Men Didn't Quit, Can't Understand Shipyard Quitters," p. 10.

38. "Crowds Visit Heroic *Laffey*," *Seattle Times*, May 27, 1945, p. 8.

39. Robert Mahaffay. "Be It Ever So Humble, Etc., Joe," *Seattle Times*, June 3, 1945, p. 4.

40. Ad appeared in numerous publications, including *Seattle Times*, June 10, 1945, p. 7; Bermann. "Gallantry of Crew Brings Warship Through Flaming Ordeal." Found in Vodehnal, *The Indestructible USS* Laffey, pp. 20–22; "Name to Remember," *True Comics*, Winter Issue, No. 46, p. 5, in the Robert Johnson Collection.

41. Becton, *The Ship That Would Not Die*, pp. 269–270.

42. Found at http://www.laffey.org/ltrsifcondolence.htm. Accessed March 26, 2014.

43. Becton, *The Ship That Would Not Die*, p. 272.

44. Tom B. Fern letter to his father, June 12, 1945, and to his mother, August 10, 1945, in the Thomas B. and Marguerite Fern Collection.

45. Dockery interview, February 19, 2014.

46. Robert Johnson letter to his mother and brother, August 14, 1945, in the Robert Johnson Collection.

47. Gauding, *My Navy Career*, August 14, 1945; Ari Phoutrides letter to F. J. Becton, September 21, 1945, in the Ari Phoutrides Collection.

48. Inoguchi, Nakajima, and Pineau, *The Divine Wind*, p. 165.

49. Tom B. Fern letter to his mother, September 17, 1945, in the Thomas B. and Marguerite Fern Collection; Robert Johnson letter to his mother and brother, September 12, 1945, in the Robert Johnson Collection.

50. John Rooney, "Sailor," *Naval History*, 1992, reprinted in *Laffey News*, Spring 1996, p. 6.

51. Ari Phoutrides letter to F. J. Becton, May 27, 1946, in the Ari Phoutrides Collection.

52. Ari Phoutrides letter to F. J. Becton, September 21, 1945, in the Ari Phoutrides Collection.

53. Becton Memorial Issue, *Laffey News*, Winter 1996.

54. Phoutrides interview, February 3, 2014.

55. Zack interview, March 29, 2014.

56. Becton, *The Ship That Would Not Die*, pp. 277–278.

57. Dixon interview, July 16, 2013.

58. "'Real People' Targets Local Hero Tom Fern," *The Agawam Advertiser/ News*, November 16, 1982, in the Thomas B. and Marguerite Fern Collection; Bruce Smith. "Bath Iron Workers-Built 'Ship That Would Not Die' Returns to

S.C. Berth," *Portland Press Herald*, January 25, 2012. Found at http://www
.laffey.org/portland_press_herald_courtesy_o.htm. Accessed February 19, 2014.

59. Gemmell interview, February 28, 2014; Youngquist interview, February 26, 2014; Martinis interview, February 27, 2014; Phoutrides interview, March 3, 2014; Johnson interview, February 25, 2014.

60. *Laffey News*, Autumn 1993, p. 4.

61. Becton, *The Ship That Would Not Die*, p. 279.

62. Becton, *The Ship That Would Not Die*, p. 278.

BIBLIOGRAPHY

WAR DIARIES AND ACTION REPORTS

War Diaries

USS *Laffey* (DD-724) War Diary, February 1944–December 1945
USS *Arkansas* (BB-33) War Diary, June 1944
USS *Aucilla* (AO-56) War Diary, May 1944
USS *Barton* (DD-722) War Diary, May 1944–February 1945
USS *Davis* (DD-395) War Diary, May–June 1944
USS *Hobson* (DD-464) War Diary, June 1944
USS *Jouett* (DD-396) War Diary, May–June 1944
USS *Kimberly* (DD-521) War Diary, January 1945
USS *Meredith* (DD-726) War Diary, May 1944
USS *Monssen* (DD-798) War Diary, March 1944
USS *Nelson* (DD-623) War Diary, June 1944
USS *O'Brien* (DD-725) War Diary, May 1944–April 1945
USS *Osprey* (AM-56) War Diary, June 1944
USS *Plunkett* (DD-431) War Diary, June 1944
USS *Somers* (DD-381) War Diary, May–June 1944
USS *Walke* (DD-723) War Diary, March 1944–January 1945
Combatdiv 5 War Diary, June 1944
Comcrudiv 7 War Diary, June 1944
Comdesron 60 War Diary, June, October–December 1944
Commander Destroyer Squadron Sixty War Diary, May 1944

Action Reports: USS Laffey (DD-724)

Normandy and Cherbourg

Commanding Officer to Commander Task Force One Two Nine (F. J. Becton to Rear Admiral Morton L. Deyo). "Report of Bombardment of Cherbourg Defenses on June 25, 1944," 26 June 1944.

Commanding Officer to Commander Task Force One Two Two (F. J. Becton to Rear Admiral Alan G. Kirk). "Bombardment of Cherbourg Defenses, Report of," 27 June 1944.

Commanding Officer to Naval Commander Western Task Force (F. J. Becton to Rear Admiral Alan G. Kirk). "Chronological Narrative Report of Operations, June 3–June 17, 1944," 27 June 1944.

Commanding Officer to Commander in Chief, United States Fleet (F. J. Becton to Adm. Ernest J. King). "Bombardment of Cherbourg Defenses on June 25, 1944—Report of," 30 June 1944.

Executive Officer to Commanding Officer (C. Holovak to F. J. Becton). "Report of Action During the Night of 11–12 June between Enemy E or W Boats and the Day Shore Bombardment of the Cherbourg Defenses on the 7–8 June 1944," 30 June 1944.

Executive Officer to Commanding Officer (C. Holovak to F. J. Becton). "Report of Action During the Bombardment of the Cherbourg Defenses on June 25, 1944," 30 June 1944.

Commanding Officer to Commander in Chief, United States Fleet (F. J. Becton to Adm. Ernest J. King). "Operations in Assault Area 'Utah' Beach, off Coast of France, Baie de la Seine Area between June 6, 1944 and June 21, 1944—Report of," 30 June 1944.

Commanding Officer to Secretary of the Navy. "Ship's History, 8 February 1944 to 20 October 1945," 20 October 1945.

The Philippines

Commanding Officer to Commander in Chief, United States Fleet. "Action Report for Operations November 10–20, 1944, Inclusive, with Task Force 38," 25 November 1944.

Commanding Officer to Commander in Chief, United States Fleet. "Anti-Aircraft Action, Report on," 30 November 1944.

Commanding Officer to Commander in Chief, United States Fleet. "Action Report in Connection with Landing of 77th Division, United States Army in Ormoc Bay Area, Leyte Island, Philippine Islands, on December 7, 1944," 11 December 1944.

Commanding Officer to Commander in Chief, United States Fleet, "Anti-Aircraft Action, Report on," 18 December 1944.

Commanding Officer to Commander in Chief, United States Fleet. "Action Report for Period December 12 to 17, 1944, Inclusive, Involving Occupation of Mindoro Island, Philippine Islands," 19 December 1944.

Commanding Officer to Commander in Chief, United States Fleet. "Action Report for Period January 2 to January 17, 1945, Inclusive, Incident to Invasion of Luzon, Philippine Islands," 27 January 1945.

Air Strikes on Japan and Action off Iwo Jima

Commanding Officer to Commander in Chief, United States Fleet. "Operations with Fifth Fleet Between February 10 and March 2, 1945—Involving Strikes on Tokyo and Support of Landing on Iwo Jima," 3 March 1945.

Okinawa

F. J. Becton, "Amplifying Report," 19 April 1945.

Commanding Officer to Chief of the Bureau of Ships. "Report of Damage by Bombs and Suicide Planes during Air Action on April 16, 1945," 27 April 1945.

Commanding Officer to Commander in Chief, United States Fleet. "Report of Operations in Support of Landings By U.S. Troops in Kerama Retto-Okinawa Area March 25 to April 22, 1945, Including Action Against Enemy Aircraft on April 16, 1945," 29 April 1945.

Action Reports: Other Ships

Off Normandy

USS *Arkansas* (BB-33) Commanding Officer to Commander in Chief, United States Fleet. "Action Report—Operations June 25, 1944," 11 July 1944.

USS *Barton* (DD-722) Commander Destroyer Squadron Sixty to Commander in Chief, United States Fleet. "Bombardment of Cherbourg, France, 25 June, 1944, report of," 30 June 1944.

USS *Barton* (DD-722) Commanding Officer to Chief of the Bureau of Ships. "War Damage to USS *Barton* (DD-722)," 26 June 1944.

USS *Barton* (DD-722) Commanding Officer to Commander in Chief, United States Fleet. "Bombardment of Cherbourg, France, 25 June, 1944, report of," 28 June 1944.

USS *Barton* (DD-722) Commanding Officer to Commander in Chief, United States Fleet. "Bombardment of Enemy Positions, Baie De La Seine, June 6–10, 1944—report of," 28 June 1944.

USS *Barton* (DD-722) Commanding Officer to Commander Task Force One Twenty-Seven. "Narrative of the USS *Barton* (DD-722) for the period 3–17 June 1944 for the invasion of France," 28 June 1944.

USS *Davis* (DD-395) Commanding Officer to Commander in Chief, United States Fleet. "Action of the USS *Davis*—Report of," 29 June 1944.

USS *Hobson* (DD-464) Commanding Officer to Commander in Chief, United States Fleet. "Report of Action Against Shore Batteries in Cherbourg Area, 25 June, 1944," 26 June, 1944.

USS *Jouett* (DD-396) Commanding Officer to Naval Commander Western Task Force. "Report of Operations, June 5–17, 1944," 27 June 1944.

USS *Nelson* (DD-623) Commanding Officer to Commander in Chief, United States Fleet. "Enemy Surface Action, report of," 23 June 1944.

USS *O'Brien* (DD-725) Commanding Officer to Commander in Chief, United States Fleet. "Action Report, USS *O'Brien* (DD-725), Bombardment of Cherbourg, France, June 25, 1944," 29 June 1944.

USS *O'Brien* (DD-725) Commanding Officer to Commander in Chief, United States Fleet. "War Damage to the USS *O'Brien* (DD-725) during the Bombardment of Cherbourg, June 25, 1944, report of," 28 June 1944.

USS *O'Brien* (DD-725) Commanding Officer to Naval Commander Western Task Force. "Chronological Narrative, June 5–17 (inclusive), Operations USS *O'Brien*," 21 June 1944.

USS *Osprey* (AM-56) Commanding Officer, USS *Osprey* (AM-56) to Secretary of the Navy. "USS *Osprey* (AM-56)—Report of Loss of," 17 June 1944.

USS *Plunkett* (DD-431) Commanding Officer to Commander in Chief, United States Fleet. "Report of Action Between Ships and Shore Batteries near Cherbourg 25 June, 1944," June 26, 1944.

USS *Somers* (DD-381) Commanding Officer to Naval Commander Western Task Force. "Operations from time of departure for Assault Area to and including 17 June 1944, report of," 27 June 1944.

USS *Texas* (BB-35) Commanding Officer to Commander in Chief, United States Fleet. "Report of Action, USS *Texas*, 25 June 1944 off Cherbourg, France," 12 July 1944.

USS *Tuscaloosa* (CA-37) Commanding Officer, USS *Osprey* (AM-56) to Naval Commander Western Task Force. "Action Report from 3 June 1944 through 17 June 1944," 27 June 1944.

USS *Walke* (DD-723) Commanding Officer to Commander in Chief, United States Fleet. "Action Report for Period 22, 23, and 24 June 1944," 29 June 1944.

USS *Walke* (DD-723) Commanding Officer to Commander in Chief, United States Fleet. "Action Report for Period 3–21 June 1944," 2 July 1944.

USS *Walke* (DD-723) Commanding Officer to Naval Commander Western Task Force. "Report of Operations—3–17 June 1944," 26 June 1944.

Combatdiv 5 Commander Battleship Division Five to Commander in Chief, United States Fleet. "Action Report for Operation Period 3–17 June 1944," 10 July 1944.

Combatdiv 5 Commander Battleship Division Five to Commander in Chief, United States Fleet. "Report of Action off Cherbourg, France, 25 June 1944," 15 July 1944.

Comcrudiv 7 Commander Cruiser Division Seven to Commander-in-Chief, United States Fleet. "Bombardment of Cherbourg, 25 June 1944, Action Report on," 6 July 1944.

Comdesron 60 Commander Destroyer Squadron Sixty to Commander in Chief, United States Fleet (Capt. W. L. Freseman to Adm. Ernest J. King). "Bombardment of Cherbourg Defenses on June 25, 1944—Report of," 1 July 1944.

Comdesron 60 Commander Destroyer Squadron Sixty to Commander in Chief, United States Fleet. "Report of Action off Cherbourg, France, on 25 June 1944," 17 July 1944.

Comdesron 60 Commander Destroyer Squadron Sixty to Naval Commander Western Task Force. "Narrative and Report of Operations by Comdesron Sixty in Operation (3 June 1944 to 17 June 1944)," 24 June 1944.

Comdesron 60 Commander Destroyer Squadron Sixty to Naval Commander Western Task Force. "Report of Action off Cherbourg, France, on 25 June 1944," 27 June 1944.

Naval Commander Western Task Force to All Hands. "Coming Events," 27 May 1944.

The Philippines

USS *Allen M. Sumner* (DD-692) Commanding Officer to Commander in Chief, United States Fleet. "Action Report USS *Allen M. Sumner* (DD-692) for Luzon Attack Force Operation, 2–13 January 1945," 16 January 1945. Found at http://www.dd-692.com/action1.htm. Accessed December 5, 2013.

USS *Barton* (DD-722) Commanding Officer to Commander Destroyer Squadron Sixty. "Mindoro Landing 12–17 December 1944," 18 December 1944.

USS *Barton* (DD-722) Commanding Officer to Commander Destroyer Squadron Sixty. "Ormoc Bay Action Report 6–8 December 1944," 10 December 1944.

USS *Barton* (DD-722) Commanding Officer to Commander in Chief, United States Fleet. "Action East of Philippine Islands, 10–20 November 1944—report of," 24 November 1944.

USS *Enterprise* (CV-6) Commanding Officer USS *Enterprise* (CV-6) to Commander in Chief, United States Fleet. "Action Report—Fleet Action and

Operations Against the Philippine Islands Area, from 22 to 31 October 1944," 3 November 1944.

USS *Moale* (DD-693) Commanding Officer to Commander in Chief, United States Fleet. "USS *Moale* (DD-693), Action Report 2–44, Night of 2–3 Dec. 44," 5 December 1944.

USS *O'Brien* (DD-725) Commanding Officer to Commander in Chief, United States Fleet. "Action Report USS *O'Brien* (DD-725), 10–20 November 1944 (inclusive) Air Strikes against Philippine Islands by Task Groups 38.2, 38.3, 38.4, and 38.1," 25 November 1944.

USS *O'Brien* (DD-725) Commanding Officer to Commander in Chief, United States Fleet. "Action Report USS *O'Brien* (DD-725), 6–7 December 1944, Landing and Supporting 77th Division, U.S. Army, in Ormoc Bay Area, Leyte Island, P.I.," 12 December 1944.

USS *O'Brien* (DD-725) Commanding Officer to Commander in Chief, United States Fleet. "Action Report USS *O'Brien* (DD-725), 2–14 January 1945, Landing and Support of Assault Troops, U.S. Army, in Lingayen Gulf area, Luzon, P.I.," 25 January 1945.

USS *O'Brien* (DD-725) Commanding Officer to Commander in Chief, United States Fleet. "Action Report, USS *O'Brien* (DD-725), 10 February 1945 to 1 March 1945, inclusive; Air Strikes against Tokyo, Japan and the Bonin Islands in Support of the Occupation of Iwo Jima by Task Force 58," 1 March 1945.

USS *Walke* (DD-723) Commanding Officer to Commander in Chief, United States Fleet. "Action Report," 21 November 1944.

USS *Walke* (DD-723) Commanding Officer to Commander in Chief, United States Fleet. "Action Report for 6–8 December 1944," 9 December 1944.

USS *Walke* (DD-723) Commanding Officer to Commander in Chief, United States Fleet. "Action Report for 12–18 December 1944," 18 December 1944.

Comdesron 60 Commander Destroyer Squadron Sixty to Commander in Chief, United States Fleet. "Action Report—Support of the Mindoro Landing Operation, 12–18 December 1944," 31 December 1944.

Comdesron 60 Commander Destroyer Squadron Sixty to Commander in Chief, United States Fleet. "Action Report—Lingayen Gulf, Luzon Landing Operation, 2–18 January 1945," 2 February 1945. Found at http://www.dd-692. com/comdesron_60_action_report.htm. Accessed December 5, 2013.

Comdesron 120 Commander Destroyer Division One-Twenty to Commander in Chief, United States Fleet. "Comdesdiv 120 Action Report—Support of the Luzon landing operation, 2–13 January 1945," 15 January 1945. Found at http://www.dd-692.com/comdesdiv_120_action_report.htm. Accessed December 5, 2013.

Air Strikes on Japan and Action off Iwo Jima

USS *Barton* (DD-722) Commanding Officer to Commander Destroyer Squadron Sixty. "Fast Carrier Operations 10–19 February 1945," 1 March 1945.

Okinawa

USS *Barton* (DD-722) Commanding Officer, (USS *Barton* (DD-722) to Commander in Chief, United States Fleet. "Report of Capture of Okinawa Gunto 21 March to 17 May 1945," 12 April 1945.

USS *Clamp* (ARS-33) Commanding Officer, USS *Clamp* (ARS-33) to Commander in Chief, United States Fleet. "War Diary of for the month of April 1945."

USS *Macomb* (DMS-23) Commanding Officer, USS *Macomb* (DMS-23) to Commander in Chief, United States Fleet. "War Diary for the Month of April 1945."

USS *O'Brien* (DD-725) Commanding Officer to The Commander in Chief, United States Fleet. "Action Report, USS *O'Brien* (DD-725), 21 March–4 April 1945, Operating in Task Group 51.1 During Landing and Support of U.S. Army and Marine Corps Troops on the Island of Kerama Retto in the Nansei Shoto Group of the Ryukyu Islands," 12 April 1945.

USS *Pakana* (ATF-108) Commanding Officer, USS *Pakana* (ATF-108) to Commander in Chief, United States Fleet. "Action Reports, of the USS *Pakana*, covering period 20 March to 8 June 1945."

USS *Pakana* (ATF-108) Commanding Officer, USS *Pakana* (ATF-108) to Commander in Chief, United States Fleet. "War Diary of USS *Pakana* (ATF-108) for month of April 1945."

USS *PCE(R)-851* Commanding Officer, USS *PCE(R)-851* to Commander in Chief, United States Fleet. "Action Report—Okinawa Operation."

USS *PCE(R)-851* Commanding Officer, USS *PCE(R)-851* to Commander in Chief, United States Fleet. "War Diary Submission of," 20 May 1945.

USS *Tawakoni* (ATF-114) Commanding Officer, USS *Tawakoni* (ATF-114) to Commander in Chief, United States Fleet. "Action Report, USS *Tawakoni* (ATF-114), Okinawa Operation—forwarding of," 6 August 1945.

Squadron Ninety-Four Commanding Officer to Chief of Naval Operations. "History of Composite Squadron Ninety-Four, 29 February 1944 to 14 June 1945," 18 June 1945.

Miscellaneous

USS *Aaron Ward* (DD-483) Commanding Officer to Commander South Pacific Force. "Report of Action, Night of November 12–13, 1942," 20 November 1942.

USS *Aaron Ward* (DD-483) Commanding Officer to Commander in Chief, United States Pacific Fleet. "Report of Enemy Action Resulting in Loss of *Aaron Ward*," 16 April 1943.

Desron 2 Commander Destroyer Squadron Two to Commander Task Group 51.15. "Defense Against Suicide Plane Attacks," 10 May 1945.

COLLECTIONS

Thomas B. and Marguerite Fern Collection
Wilbert Gauding Collection
Robert Johnson Collection
Ari Phoutrides Collection

INTERVIEWS

USS Laffey *Crew*

Bahme, J., Lieutenant
Telephone interviews, June 10, 2013; July 16, 2013; August 21, 2013.

Becton, F. Julian, Commander
"Oral History: Battle for Okinawa, 24 March–30 June 1945," Operational Archives Branch, Naval Historical Center.

Dixon, Joseph E., Seaman 1/c
Telephone interviews, June 12, 2013; July 16, 2013; October 29, 2013; January 21, 2014; January 23, 2014.

Dockery, Robert W., Seaman 1/c
Telephone interviews, October 31, 2013; November 5, 2013; November 12, 2013; February 5, 2014; February 12, 2014; February 19, 2014; March 5, 2014.

Gemmell, Fred M., Torpedoman's Mate 2/c
Telephone interviews, January 20, 2014; January 23, 2014; February 5, 2014; February 14, 2014; February 28, 2014.

Hull, Lloyd N., Lieutenant (jg)
Telephone interviews, June 10, 2014; June 17, 2014.

Hunt, Lee C., Seaman 1/c
Telephone interview, July 17, 2013.

Johnson, Robert C., Seaman 2/c
Telephone interviews, August 19, 2013; August 20, 2013; August 27, 2013; August 28, 2013; October 29, 2013; February 4, 2014; February 5, 2014; February 7, 2014; February 20, 2014; February 25, 2014.
Personal interview, April 22, 2014.

Martinis, Dr. Andrew J., Seaman 1/c
Telephone interviews, January 9, 2014; January 16, 2014; January 23, 2014; February 6, 2014; February 20, 2014; February 27, 2014.

Phoutrides, Aristides S., Quartermaster 2/c
Telephone interviews, November 4, 2013; November 20, 2013; December 5, 2013; December 12, 2013; January 22, 2014; January 27, 2014; February 3, 2014; February 24, 2014; March 3, 2014.
Personal interview, April 17, 2014.

Youngquist, Joel C., Lieutenant (jg)
Telephone interviews, August 21, 2013; August 22, 2013; January 24, 2014; January 29, 2014; February 5, 2014; February 12, 2014; February 19, 2014; February 26, 2014.

Zack, Daniel, Sonarman 3/c
Telephone interviews, February 8, 2014; February 15, 2014; February 22, 2014; March 1, 2014; March 8, 2014; March 15, 2014; March 22, 2014; March 29, 2014.

Others

Becton, Julie (daughter)
Telephone interview, July 26, 2013.

Fern, Marguerite (wife)
Telephone interview, June 7, 2013.
Personal interview, June 25, 2013.

Gebhardt, Jack, Sonarman 1st Class (USS *Pringle* [DD-477])
"Oral History, 1943–1945," Operational Archives Branch, Naval Historical Center.

Healy, John and Renee (daughter of Lieutenant J. V. Porlier)
Telephone interview, October 30, 2013.

Ondracek, Ray (brother)
Telephone interviews, November 13, 2013; November 19, 2013.

Rowe, William, Seaman 2/c (USS *Bunker Hill* [CV-17])
Personal interview, June 12, 1988.

ORAL HISTORIES FROM SHIP'S WEBSITE

http://www.laffey.org/Oral%20Histories/ohindex.htm
Brown, Seaman 1/c Donald E.
Csiszar, Chief Electrician's Mate Albert
Delewski, Gunner's Mate 2/c Lawrence H.
Eastham, Seaman 1/c Lonnie H.
Gauding, Fireman 1/c Wilbert C.
Gebhart, Gunner's Mate 3/c Francis M.
Henke, Lieutenant E. A.
Johnson, Seaman 2/c Merle R.
Karr, Gunner's Mate 3/c Robert I.
Langevin, Fireman 1/c Reginald
Manson, Lieutenant Frank A.
Phoutrides, Quartermaster 2/c Aristides
Radder, Gunner's Mate 3/c Owen G.
Rieman, Lieutenant (jg) Carl J. (USS *Shamrock Bay* [CVE-84])
Remsen, Seaman 1/c Herbert B.
Simonis, Sonarman 1/c Cyril C.
Spriggs, Fireman 1/c Oliver J.
Stuer, Fireman 1/c Joseph J.
Thompson, Carpenter's Mate 2/c Henry
Waite, Machinist's Mate 1/c Stephen J.
Weygandt, Seaman 1/c Charles A.

BOOKS

Andrews, Lewis M., Jr. *Tempest, Fire & Foe*. North Charleston, SC: Narwhal Press, 1999.
Axell, Albert and Hideaki Kase. *Kamikaze: Japan's Suicide Gods*. London: Longman, 2002.
Barbey, Vice Admiral Daniel E. *MacArthur's Amphibious Navy*. Annapolis, MD: Naval Institute Press, 1969.
Becton, Rear Admiral F. Julian, USN, Ret. with Joseph Morschauser III. *The Ship That Would Not Die*. Englewood Cliffs, NJ: Prentice-Hall, Inc., 1980.
Bostick, Douglas W. *The USS* Laffey *(DD-724)*. Charleston, SC: Charleston Postcard Company, 2010.

Brines, Russell. *Until They Eat Stones*. New York: J. B. Lippincott Company, 1944.

Cannon, M. Hamlin. *United States Army in World War II: The War in the Pacific. Leyte: The Return to the Philippines*. Washington, DC: Center of Military History, 1987.

Costello, John. *The Pacific War, 1941–1945*. New York: Quill Books, 1982.

Dorr, Robert F. *Marine Air: The History of the Flying Leathernecks in Words and Photos*. New York: Berkley Caliber Books, 2005.

Eisenhower, Dwight D. *Crusade in Europe*. Garden City, NY: Doubleday & Company, Inc., 1950.

Feifer, George. *Tennozan*. New York: Ticknor & Fields, 1992.

Friedman, Norman. *U.S. Destroyers: An Illustrated Design History*. Annapolis, MD: Naval Institute Press, 1982.

Gandt, Robert. *The Twilight Warriors*. New York: Broadway Books, 2010.

Gauding, Wilbert C. *My Navy Career*. Unpublished diary kept during the war.

Goldstein, Donald M., and Katherine V. Dillon. *Fading Victory: The Diary of Admiral Matome Ugaki 1941–1945*. Pittsburgh, PA: University of Pittsburgh Press, 1991.

Gow, Ian. *Okinawa, 1945: Gateway to Japan*. Garden City, NY: Doubleday & Company, Inc., 1985.

Griggs, William L. *Preludes to Victory: The Battle of Ormoc Bay in World War II*. Hillsborough, NJ: Atlantic Press, 1997.

Halsey, Fleet Admiral William F., and Lieutenant Commander J. Bryan III. *Admiral Halsey's Story*. New York: McGraw-Hill Book Company, Inc., 1947.

Hata, Ikuhiko, Yasuho Izawa, and Christopher Shores. *Japanese Army Fighter Aces, 1931–1945*. Mechanicsburg, PA: Stackpole Books, 2002.

Inoguchi, Captain Rikihei, Commander Tadashi Nakajima, with Roger Pineau. *The Divine Wind*. New York: Bantam Books, 1958.

James, D. Clayton. *The Years of MacArthur*, Volume II, *1941–1945*. Boston: Houghton Mifflin Company, 1975.

Karig, Commander Walter, USNR, with Lieutenant Earl Burton, USNR, and Lieutenant Stephen L. Freeland, USNR. *Battle Report: The Atlantic War*. New York: Farrar & Rinehart, Inc., 1946.

Karig, Commander Walter, USNR, with Lieutenant Commander Russell L. Harris, USNR, and Lieutenant Commander Frank A. Manson, USN. *Battle Report: Victory in the Pacific*. New York: Farrar & Rinehart, Inc., 1949.

Krueger, General Walter. *From Down Under to Nippon*. Washington, DC: Combat Forces Press, 1953.

Laffey News. Autumn 1993.

———. Spring 1996.

———. Becton Memorial Issue, Winter 1996.

Leary, William M., editor. *We Shall Return!: MacArthur's Commanders and the Defeat of Japan, 1942–1945*. Lexington: The University Press of Kentucky, 1988.

MacArthur, Douglas. *Reminiscences*. New York: McGraw-Hill Book Company, 1964.

Manchester, William. *American Caesar: Douglas MacArthur 1880–1964*. Boston: Little, Brown and Company, 1978.

Miller, Nathan. *War at Sea: A Naval History of World War II*. New York: Oxford University Press, 1995.

Millot, Bernard. *Divine Thunder: The Life and Death of the Kamikazes*. New York: The McCall Publishing Company, 1970.

Morison, Samuel Eliot. *History of United States Naval Operations in World War II, Volume XI, The Invasion of France and Germany 1944–1945*. Boston: Little, Brown and Company, 1957.

————. *History of United States Naval Operations in World War II, Volume XII, Leyte June 1944–January 1945*. Boston: Little, Brown and Company, 1958.

————. *History of United States Naval Operations in World War II, Volume XIII, The Liberation of the Philippines 1944–1945*. Boston: Little, Brown and Company, 1959.

————. *History of United States Naval Operations in World War II, Volume XIV, Victory in the Pacific 1945*. Boston: Little, Brown and Company, 1960.

————. *The Two-Ocean War*. Boston: Little, Brown and Company, 1963.

Nagatsuka, Ryuji. *I Was A Kamikaze*. New York: Macmillan Publishing Company, Inc., 1972.

Ohnuki-Tierney, Emiko. *Kamikaze, Cheery Blossoms, and Nationalisms*. Chicago: The University of Chicago Press, 2002.

Okumiya, Masatake, Jiro Horikoshi, and Martin Caidin. *Zero*. New York: Simon B. Schuster, Inc., 2002.

Reilly, Robin L. *Kamikazes, Corsairs, and Picket Ships*. Philadelphia: Casemate Books, 2008.

Sakai, Saburo, with Martin Caidin and Fred Saito. *Samurai!* New York: Simon B. Schuster, Inc., 2001.

Sears, David. *At War with the Wind*. New York: Citadel Press, 2008.

Sheftall, M. G. *Blossoms in the Wind: Human Legacies of the Kamikaze*. New York: NAL Caliber, 2005.

Snow, Ralph Linwood. *Bath Iron Works: The First Hundred Years*. Bath, ME: Maine Maritime Museum, 1987.

Solberg, Carl. *Decision and Dissent: With Halsey at Leyte Gulf*. Annapolis, MD: Naval Institute Press, 1995.

Spector, Ronald H. *Eagle Against the Sun*. New York: The Free Press, 1985.

Ugaki, Admiral Matome. *Fading Victory: The Diary of Admiral Matome Ugaki, 1941–1945*. Pittsburgh: The University of Pittsburgh Press, 1991.

Vodehnal, Slavomir J. *The Indestructible USS* Laffey. No date. Privately published collection of newspaper articles and photographs.

Warner, Denis, and Peggy Warner. *The Sacred Warriors*. New York: Van Nostrand Reinhold Company, 1982.

Wheeler, Gerald E. *Kinkaid of the Seventh Fleet*. Annapolis, MD: Naval Institute Press, 1996.

Wheeler, Keith. *The Road to Tokyo*. Alexandria, VA: Time-Life Books, 1979.

Wilde, E. Andrew, Jr., editor. *The USS* Aaron Ward *(DD-483) in World War II: Documents and Photographs*. Needham, MA: Privately published by the editor, 2001.

ARTICLES

"Airfield on Mindoro," *The New York Times*, December 23, 1944.

"Air: First and Foremost," *Time*, January 1, 1945. Found at http://content.time .com/time/magazine/article/0,9171,791844,00.html. Accessed November 16, 2013.

Alexander, Colonel Joseph H. "Hellish Prelude at Okinawa," *Naval History* Magazine. Found at http://www.usni.org/print/3035. Accessed January 28, 2014.

Baldwin, Hanson W. "Allies Take War to Foes," *The New York Times*, February 16, 1945.

———. "Blow at Luzon Indicated," *The New York Times*, December 16, 1944.

———. "Cherbourg Only Beginning of French Campaign," *The New York Times*, July 2, 1944.

———. "Invasion's Start Good," *The New York Times*, January 11, 1945.

———. "Luzon a Major Military Venture," *The New York Times*, January 8, 1945.

———. "Luzon Campaign Opens with Odds in Our Favor," *The New York Times*, January 14, 1945.

———. "MacArthur's Next Step," *The New York Times*, January 1, 1945.

———. "Where Is German Navy?" *The New York Times*, July 7, 1944.

———. "Navy Still Stings Hitler," *The New York Times*, July 4, 1944.

———. "Our Stepping-Stones to Japan," *The New York Times*, December 28, 1944.

———. "Sights Raised for Luzon," *The New York Times*, December 22, 1944.

———. "Two War Surprises," *The New York Times*, December 20, 1944.

———. "U.S. Outlook In War," *The New York Times*, December 8, 1944.

———. "Mines Still A Problem," *The New York Times*, July 6, 1944.

"Battle of the Pacific: Bold Stroke," *Time*, December 25, 1944. Found at http://
content.time.com/time/magazine/article/0,9171,791722,00.html. Accessed
November 16, 2013.

"Battle of the Pacific: End Run, Touchdown," *Time*, December 18, 1944. Found
at http://content.time.com/time/magazine/article/0,9171,778257,00.html.
Accessed November 16, 2013.

"Becton's Word," *Time*, June 4, 1945. Found at http://content.time.com/time
/subscriber/article/0,33009,775738,00.html. Accessed March 1, 2014.

"Conquest of Leyte," *The New York Times*, December 27, 1944.

"Crowds Visit Heroic *Laffey*," *Seattle Times*, May 27, 1945.

Davis, Spencer. "Japanese Stunned by Ormoc Landing," *The New York Times*,
December 9, 1944.

"Destroyer Bombed, Crew Stuffed Up Holes in Futile Effort to Save It," *St. Louis
Globe-Democrat*, September 25, 1943. Found in E. Andrew Wilde, Jr., editor, *The USS Aaron Ward (DD-483) in World War II: Documents and Photographs*. Needham, MA: Privately published by the editor, 2001.

"Drift-Out in the Shipyards," *Time*, June 4, 1945. Found at http://content.time
.com/time/subscriber/article/0,33009,775720,00.html. Accessed March 1,
2014.

Ewing, Dr. Steve. "USS *Laffey* and a Place Called Okinawa," *Sea History*, Spring
1995, pp. 14–16. Found at http://www.laffey.org/ewing1.htm. Accessed
June 13, 2013.

Fish, Larry. "*Inquirer* Recalls Becton's Life, Career," *Philadelphia Inquirer*, no
date. Found in *Laffey News*, Becton Memorial Issue, Winter 1996.

"Going Home," *Time*, May 21, 1945. Found at http://content.time.com/time
/subscriber/article/0,33009,852265,00.html. Accessed March 1, 2014.

"Hard-Hitting Bath Destroyer Knocking Down Jap Plane," *The Bulletin*, Bath
Iron Works, February 9, 1945, p. 1, in the Robert Johnson Collection.

Hewlett, Frank. "Troops Land Fast on Mindoro Beach," *The New York Times*,
December 16, 1944, pp. 1, 3.

Hicks, Brian. "The Love That Would Not Die," *The Post and Courier* (Charleston, SC), September 26, 2012. Found at http://www.postandcourier.com
/article/20120926/PC16/120929483/world-war-ii-widow-visits-laffey
-where-her-husband-died. Accessed February 6, 2014.

Horne, George. "373 Planes, 17 Ships Smashed at Luzon," *The New York Times*,
December 17, 1944.

Illian, Jack. "On Heroic *Laffey*, Lt. McCune Rode Out 22 Suicide Attacks," *Cedar Rapids Gazette*, May 1945. Found at http://www.laffey.org/Laura%20
McKagan/cedar_rapid_gazette.htm. Accessed February 3, 2014.

"Invasion of Luzon Near, Says Enemy," *The New York Times*, January 1, 1945.

"Invasion Pictured," *The New York Times*, January 9, 1945, pp. 1, 3.

"Invasion Prelude," *The New York Times*, January 7, 1945.

"Japanese Swimmers Try To 'Torpedo' Transports," *The New York Times*, January 12, 1945, pp. 1, 3.

"Japanese Communique," *The New York Times*, December 11, 1944.

"Japanese Report on Mindoro," *The New York Times*, December 17, 1944.

"Japanese 'Suicide' Air War Fails in Mission, Says Admiral Nimitz," *The New York Times*, April 14, 1945.

Jones, George E. "Absence of Enemy Is Luzon Mystery," *The New York Times*, January 17, 1945.

———. "Yanks Land From 800 Ships; MacArthur Ashore With Men," *The New York Times*, January 10, 1945, pp. 1, 4.

Johnson, Hal. "Even A Church Was Fair Game, Grove City Man Recalls." Sharon (PA) *Herald*, undated article. Found at http://www.laffey.org/donald brownnews.htm. Accessed September 9, 2013.

"Ketron Cheated Death by Days When *Laffey* Was Hit," Kingsport *Times News*, June 19, 1945. Found at http://www.laffey.org/kingsporttimesnewslaffey .htm. Accessed February 2, 2014.

Kitchen, Rueben P. "The Destroyer That Refused to Die," *Sea Classics*, May 1983, pp. 45–48. Found at http://www.laffey.org/Articles/seaclassics1.htm. Accessed April 12, 2013.

Kluckhohn, Frank L. "Convoy Is Blasted," *The New York Times*, November 30, 1944, pp. 1, 12.

———. "Foe in Leyte Trap," *The New York Times*, December 20, 1944, pp. 1, 13.

———. "Foe Is Surprised," *The New York Times*, December 16, 1944, pp. 1, 2.

———. "Foe's Line Is Cut in Drive at Ormoc," *The New York Times*, December 7, 1944, pp. 1, 17.

———. "4 Ormoc-Bound Ships Sunk; 2 Damaged by Our Planes," *The New York Times*, December 3, 1944, pp. 1, 3.

———. "'Greatest Japanese Defeat' Ends Campaign on Leyte," *The New York Times*, December 26, 1944, pp. 1, 12.

———. "Japanese Tricked by MacArthur Coup," *The New York Times*, December 17, 1944.

———. "Lead Ship's Voyage to Luzon A Grim Saga Written in Fire," *The New York Times*, January 13, 1945, pp. 1, 3.

———. "MacArthur's Daring Move Adds A Valuable Base," *The New York Times*, December 17, 1944.

———. "Master of Amphibious Warfare," *The New York Times*, December 31, 1944, pp. 11, 32.

———. "77th Infantry Hits," *The New York Times*, December 8, 1944, pp. 1, 4.

———. "28 Ships Also Sunk," *The New York Times*, December 19, 1944, pp. 1, 11.

———. "2 MacArthur Gains," *The New York Times*, December 18, 1944, pp. 1, 10.

———. "U.S. Fliers Using Mindoro Airfield," *The New York Times*, December 17, 1944, pp. 1, 9.

———. "Whole War Can Be Shortened," *The New York Times*, January 10, 1945, p. 3.

"*Laffey* Men Didn't Quit, Can't Understand Shipyard Quitters," *Seattle Times*, May 25, 1945, p. 10.

"Landing on Mindoro," *The New York Times*, December 21, 1944.

"Landing Predicted," *The New York Times*, January 8, 1945, pp. 1, 3.

Leslie, Belinda. "U.S.S. *Laffey*: The Ship That Took A Licking and A Looking," University of Wisconsin-Whitewater, Whitewater, Wisconsin, November 1988. Found at http://www.laffey.org/Belinda%20Leslie%20Report/college _essay_by_belinda_leslie.htm. Accessed February 19, 2014.

Logan, Clint. "The Ship That Refused to Die," *Sea Combat*, April 1979. Found at http://www.laffey.org/seacombat. Accessed April 12, 2013.

"Luzon Thrust Seen," *The New York Times*, January 7, 1945, pp. 1, 19.

Mahaffay, Robert. "Be It Ever So Humble, Etc., Joe," *Seattle Times*, June 3, 1945.

———. "Destroyer, Hit by 8 Jap Planes, Limps Back Here," *Seattle Times*, May 25, 1945, pp. 1, 10.

Manson, Lieutenant Commander Frank A. "Seventy-Nine Minutes on the Picket Line," *U.S. Naval Institute Proceedings*, September 1949, pp. 997–1003.

"Marine Pilots Find Mindoro Foe Easy," *The New York Times*, December 19, 1944.

Moore, Mechlin. "Navy Officer Relives Battle for Son, 8," *Washington Post*, April 14, 1958, p. A8.

Moscow, Warren. "First Great Blow," *The New York Times*, February 16, 1945, pp. 1, 4.

"Name to Remember," *True Comics*, Winter Issue, No. 46, p. 5, in the Robert Johnson Collection.

"Nimitz Eyes Bases Closer to Japan," *The New York Times*, December 31, 1944.

"Opposition Slight," *The New York Times*, December 17, 1944, pp. 1, 13.

Parrott, Lindesay. "Units Drive Inland," *The New York Times*, January 10, 1945, pp. 1, 3.

"Port Important for Future," *The New York Times*, December 11, 1944.

"'Priorities of 1943' Will Open Tonight," *The New York Times*, September 15, 1942.

"Roosevelt Son Fights at Luzon," *The New York Times*, January 13, 1945.

Saxon, Wolfgang. "F. Julian Becton, 87, Admiral Whose Ship Repelled Kamikazes." *The New York Times*, December 30, 1995.

Shalett, Sidney. "Japan's Inner Citadel Brought Under Attack," *The New York Times*, February 18, 1945.

Sheets, Lieutenant Jerome Butler. "Our Lady." 1945. Found at http://www.laffey.org/jerome_butler_sheets_his_pa.htm. Accessed August 8, 2013.

"6 Suicide Planes and 2 Bombs Hit Destroyer Laffey, She Gets Home." *The New York Times*, May 26, 1945, pp. 1, 3.

Smith, Bruce. "Bath Iron Workers-Built 'Ship That Would Not Die' Returns to S.C. Berth," *Portland Press Herald*, January 25, 2012. Found at http://www.laffey.org/portland_press_herald_courtesy_o.htm. Accessed February 19, 2014.

"So Far, So Good—On Mindoro," *The New York Times*, December 19, 1944.

Spohn, Sharon. "Keeping the Story Alive," *The Mercury*, September 20, 2007. Found at http://www.laffey.org/Sept%202007/ww_ii_veteran_keeps_the_story_al.htm. Accessed February 19, 2014.

"Stalin Hails Cherbourg," *The New York Times*, July 1, 1944.

"Suicide Pilots Green, Say U.S.S. *Laffey* Men," *Los Angeles Times*, June 10, 1945, p. 6.

"The Target Is Tokyo," *The New York Times*, February 17, 1945.

Tilove, Jonathan. "Role Relived on Ship That Would Not Died," *The Morning Union* (Springfield, MA), November 10, 1982.

"Tokyo Papers See Perils on Mindoro," *The New York Times*, December 18, 1944.

"Tokyo Tells of 'Suicide Plane,'" *The New York Times*, November 3, 1944.

"Toward Manila," *The New York Times*, December 17, 1944.

Tracy, Hazel Millikin. "Sailor Risks His Life to Restore Flag," *Seattle Times*, May 25, 1945, p. 10.

Trumbull, Robert. "Navy Holds Key to Luzon Victory; Must Bar Reinforcements to Foe," *The New York Times*, January 10, 1945, pp. 1, 3.

"U.S. Warship Survives Six Jap 'Death Blows,'" *Los Angeles Times*, May 26, 1945, p. 1.

"War Bond Show Set for Stadium Tuesday," *The New York Times*, July 1, 1944.

"War Worker Exodus Hits Ship in Oregon," *The New York Times*, May 6, 1945.

"Wounded General Leads on Mindoro," *The New York Times*, December 18, 1944.

Wukovits, John F. "Life on a Bull's-Eye," *Military History*, December 1988, pp. 27–32.

NEWSPAPERS

Chicago Tribune
Los Angeles Times
New York Times
St. Louis Globe-Democrat

DVDS

"Dogfights—Kamikaze." *The History Channel*, 2007.
"Hero Ships—USS *Laffey*." *The History Channel*, 2008.
"*Laffey* Men." Written and Directed by Jessica Cribbs. Media City Productions, 2008.
"Pacific: The Lost Evidence: Okinawa." *The History Channel*, 2005.

WEBSITES

Kamikaze Images website, http://www.kamikazeimages.net/index.htm
Laffey website, http://www.laffey.org
Patriots Point website, http://www.patriotspoint.org/explore_museum/uss_laffey/

INDEX